AUSTRALIA

*Four Inspirational Love Stories
from the Land Down Under*

Mary Hawkins

BARBOUR
PUBLISHING, INC.
Uhrichsville, Ohio

ISBN 1-57748-641-2

Published by Barbour Publishing, Inc., P.O. Box 719, Uhrichsville, Ohio 44683
http://www.barbourbooks.com

Cover art by Dick Bobnick.

Member of the
Evangelical Christian
Publishers Association

Printed in the United States of America.

Mary Hawkins
A resident of New South Wales, Australia (outside Sydney), Mary and her husband have three grown children. Her first inspirational novel, *Search for Tomorrow*, was voted the second most favorite contemporary romance by **Heartsong Presents'** readers. Mary has written seven inspirational romances for **Heartsong Presents**.

SEARCH FOR TOMORROW

To Raymond. . .
my chief encourager, best friend,
perfect lover, wonderful husband—
God's perfect gift.

Chapter 1

"They're here, Gail!" Ann said.

Abigail Brandon raised her bowed head and looked at her friend as she burst into the bedroom.

Ann took one look at Gail's face and her own cheerful, freckled features crinkled with laughter. "Gail! You've got to be kidding! You've been crying!"

Gail sniffed and wiped her eyes again. She glared at Ann. "Sympathetic friend you are," she began. The smile vanished from Ann Green's face and an anxious look appeared.

Gail relented. She jumped up from the bed and flung an arm around Ann's shoulders. "Oh, don't mind me. There's nothing really wrong. It's just. . ."

Ann hugged her. "I know," she said briefly, "I felt like that yesterday at the graduation service." Her eyes began to twinkle again. "Only I didn't get around to shedding any tears over it."

Gail moved over to the bare dressing table and peered into the mirror. She brushed the honey-colored curls off her forehead and reached for her bag. "Well," she said defensively as she began to repair her makeup, "I was all right until I walked back into this room after breakfast. All my luggage was gone and it just looked so. . .so bare somehow." She turned and surveyed the small, sparsely furnished room. "I guess it all just hit me. Three years of my life, in rooms like this one, are suddenly gone."

"And then you realized that it was wonderful!" Ann laughed again. "I should be the one shedding tears because I don't have an impatient fiancé waiting downstairs to take me away and marry me and set up our own happy home. Come on, or he'll be storming up here to find you."

"Ann, I know it's stupid, but. . ." Gail swallowed on the lump rising in her throat again, "last night I was so thrilled and excited and now I'm really sorry the three years are over. I'm getting married next week and even when I come back here after our honeymoon as a fully fledged nursing sister, it's all going to be so different. You'll be gone, too, and so many of our friends, and—"

"And you'll be so happy with Wayne in your own home that you won't give us a second thought," Ann interrupted her abruptly. "If you don't stop being so soppy you'll have me in tears in a moment. Now, do get a move on."

She straightened the crumpled bedspread and waited impatiently near the door. Gail threw her makeup back in her bag and couldn't resist one last look around the room before following Ann out into the corridor.

The senior clinical nurse educator was talking to Wayne James near the front entrance of the Nurses' Home that had been converted into low cost accommodations for students and other staff members of the hospital. They turned and smiled as the two women hurried toward them.

"Well, Sister Brandon, you're ready at last." Sister Jean Drew chuckled at the startled look on Gail's face. "Oh, I know you are now Miss Brandon, State Registered Nurse, but I'm afraid you'll still be called 'Sister' by us older generation of nurses. And if I don't call you that now I'll never get another chance. It'll be Sister James the next time I see you. I do wish you God's richest blessings for your wedding, my dear."

Gail caught the sudden gleam in Wayne's eyes, and color flooded her cheeks. Somehow, she found herself murmuring the correct responses and farewells. Then, Wayne was holding her hand and hurrying her outside towards her father's green Holden Commodore sedan.

"Boy, Abbey! We've been waiting for ages. I thought you'd be waiting on the doorstep for us." Her brother Bill's excited face appeared at the back window. From the front seat, Mrs. Brandon smiled understandingly at her daughter as Wayne opened the back door.

He hesitated, and said to Gail's father, "Sure you wouldn't like me to drive, Mr. Brandon?"

"No, no. Not until we're over the mountains, Wayne. You can drive the last hundred or so kilometers." He grinned at Gail. "You sit in the back and keep that daughter of mine in order for a while."

Gail smiled back at him. Love for her family flooded through her. They had always been close, and Gail had hated leaving them and the large country town to do her nurse's training in Sydney. When Wayne appeared on the scene, she saw even less of them. But, they had welcomed him as her choice and lovingly helped her in every way to plan for their wedding that was now only two weeks away. She started to climb into the back seat when she thought of something. "Are you sure you packed that small red case in the boot, Dad?"

"Of course he has, silly," Wayne said from behind her. He caught at her arm and pulled her from the car. "Come on, I'll get in first and sit in the center. You can wave good-bye to the old place from the window. And, seeing that you get travel sick so often on those bends over the Blue Mountains. . ."

As the car moved off, they all waved to Ann. They continued to gently tease Gail as they traveled to join the stream of traffic on the Western Freeway.

The conversation gradually turned toward the graduation ceremony at the university and the special dinner that was held after it. Gail answered their comments and questions about the various people they had met and seen. Over the years, they had heard Gail speak of some of them, but they had found it very interesting to see them "in the flesh" as Bill put it.

"Old Sister Drew doesn't seem too bad," said Gail's mother. "I remember how scared you were of her three years ago during your first clinical experience in the wards and you expected to meet a real old dragon."

"Well, she's changed these last couple of years. They say she never misses going to church now. We think God must have tamed her."

Gail's flippant words created a little pool of silence instead of the expected, automatic rebuke that such a mention of God would have brought from Gail's mother or father.

"We haven't missed church for a while ourselves," Mrs. Brandon said so quietly that for a moment Gail thought she must have misunderstood her. She turned and cocked an eyebrow at Wayne, but he was looking at her a little anxiously.

Before she could speak, Bill leaned forward across Wayne and touched his mother's shoulder. "Don't you think we could tell Abbey now, Mum?"

Mrs. Brandon turned and exchanged a glance with Wayne.

"What on earth do you need to tell me now that you couldn't have told me last night?" Gail's laugh was a little uneasy. There was something in the atmosphere in the car that she couldn't quite put her finger on. "Have you some deep, dark secret, Bill?"

"No, it's not really a secret, darling." Mrs. Brandon looked reproachfully at her son. "Bill, you know we agreed to let Wayne tell her in his own good time."

"That's right, you young terror." Wayne's clasp on Gail's hand tightened and his smile seemed a little forced.

Suddenly, Gail knew that whatever he was going to tell her would be important. "Good grief! You all sound so mysterious," said Gail.

"Don't look so alarmed, Abbey." Wayne pretended to duck as he used the forbidden nickname only Bill was still allowed to use, mainly because Gail had given up trying to stop him. Although Gail tilted her chin at him in the way they played this game, she had the strangest feeling that he was thinking hard about something else, and she felt a hint of alarm that did not entirely disappear as Wayne slipped his arm around her for a quick hug.

"It's really something very wonderful that's happened," Wayne said. "I'll tell you when we get home. Now, what's so special about that small red case?"

Gail frowned at the decisive tone in his voice as he changed the subject. But the wedding dress in that small red case had been picked up from the dressmaker only a couple of days before, and her eyes lit up at the thought of it.

They were still discussing clothes and plans for the wedding some time later after the freeway was behind them and the Holden was swinging around the sharp curves in the mountain roads. Bill had gradually dropped out of the general conversation and was sitting forward, behind his father, watching the road and trying to anticipate when Mr. Brandon would have to change gears as the car climbed steadily upward. He was becoming more and more fascinated with the thought of learning to drive and was already allowed to drive the small tractor around the orchard.

Gail noticed his rapt attention and touched her mother, nodding silently towards Bill. Mrs. Brandon winked at her, and they grinned at each other.

"Gail, there are some goodies to chew in that bag on the floor near your feet," Mrs. Brandon said. "I'm sure a certain young man with hollow legs must be feeling a little hungry by now."

Gail felt around the floor near their feet, but the bag had somehow been kicked under the front seat. She unfastened her seat belt and leaned down. She heard Wayne start to protest when a startled cry came from Bill.

"Wow, Dad! That semi! It's coming—"

Gail heard his voice rise to a scream that suddenly mingled with and was lost in the tortured screech of brakes. She felt her body being thrown down onto the floor into a tangled heap. Almost simultaneously, the world exploded into screeching, grinding metal and violent movement. Searing pain reached out to clutch her and the noise, at last, faded into darkness.

Once, she felt rough hands pulling at her body. Someone was shouting again, over and over. A sudden roar cut off the frantic voice. A wave of heat hit her. Pain was swamping her, but the relentless hands wouldn't let her go. Someone was screaming again and then the pain engulfed her until she slid thankfully back into the welcome blackness.

Chapter 2

G ail walked quickly up the steps and into the old red brick building. Its neat sign still told the world it was the ROYAL HOSPITAL NURSES' HOME, although it had been several years since the switch from hospital to college training that meant that not only nurses now occupied the building. She was neatly dressed in matching amber slacks and jacket. A close observer would have noticed the slight favoring of her left leg as she swung down the corridor leading to Sister Jean Drew's office. It was the only outward sign of the weeks spent in the hospital and the long convalescence since the accident. Her mind was in a turmoil.

A few days ago, she had been so relieved to be told she could start work again that she had eagerly rung the hospital and made an appointment to see the director of nursing. Now, her cheeks were still flushed after that interview with Miss Fisher. Tears were not far from her brown eyes as she hesitated outside the nurse educator's office.

What on earth am I going to do now?

She fought down a rising tide of panic and lifted her hand to knock on the door, but it suddenly swung back and Sister Jean Drew briskly welcomed her.

"Oh, there you are, Sister Brandon. I was just beginning to wonder if Miss Fisher remembered to give you my message. Do come in for a few minutes. I haven't seen you since your discharge from the hospital."

Before she could voice a protest, Gail found herself ushered in and seated in the room's only comfortable chair. The last thing she felt like doing was to have a session with Sister Drew! But, when she saw the morning tea tray neatly arranged on the desk, she realized there was no escape. She had come only because Sister had been so kind to her all through those lonely, black days. She quickly tossed off that thought, as she had forced herself to do so many times since leaving the safety of the hospital ward. She couldn't dare let herself dwell on those nightmarish days.

Sister Jean Drew had been busy pouring boiling water into the teapot and, as she returned to her desk, she said, "Although it's nearly lunch time, I knew you'd feel like a cup of tea after seeing Miss Fisher."

So she knew, Gail thought grimly and waited silently.

Sister Drew was noted for not beating about the bush and, as she efficiently dealt with cups and saucers, she came straight to the point. "I understand that Miss Fisher finds herself unable to employ you for some months."

"Did she tell you why, Sister?" Gail couldn't keep the resentment from creeping into her low, attractive voice.

Sister Jean Drew glanced at her sharply. Then she frowned, as though Gail had confirmed a thought of hers. "Er, well, yes. She told me that she'd had to fill the original position she had intended to keep for you after graduation." As she poured their tea, she continued in a gentler voice. "Also, I believe your last doctor's report did not whole-heartedly recommend that you were fit enough for ward work yet."

"Well, Doctor Wentworth told me I could start work, but apparently told Miss Fisher that all bones were mended but not. . .not my mind, and my. . .my memory. . . ."

The attempt at flippancy failed miserably. Gail bit her lip, and stared down at her tightly clenched hands. No! She mustn't cry here!

"Both your body and mind have certainly taken a whipping these past few months," Sister Drew said crisply. "I know Miss Fisher did not decide hastily or lightly that you needed more time to adjust."

Adjust had not been the word the director of nursing had used, thought Gail grimly. Her fingernails were biting into the palms of her hands as the quiet, reluctant tones of Miss Fisher's voice echoed again in her ears.

"In one dreadful experience, you have lost the people you most loved—your parents, brother, fiancé." Miss Fisher had swallowed

13

quickly, and then looked away for a moment. "Too dreadful to think about!" she had murmured before continuing firmly, "Apparently you are still having a few nightmares. How can you be expected to be emotionally and mentally stable enough to be put in charge of a ward full of very sick, dependent people?"

Gail suddenly realized Sister Drew was waiting for her to take the proffered cup of steaming tea. Numbly, she unclasped her hands and reached out to take it. She made a conscious effort to control the trembling hand that shook so much that some of the tea spilled into the saucer.

"Milk and sugar, Sister Brandon?"

The voice was crisp and businesslike. When Gail shook her head silently, not at that moment trusting her voice, Sister Drew just politely handed her a plate of cake. "Sister Brandon, have you ever given any thought to the wisdom of getting right away from Sydney for a while?"

Gail felt as though food would choke her. She managed to politely refuse the cake and sipped a mouthful of the hot drink, hoping it might help to dislodge the hard lump in her throat. At last, she raised her head and managed to look directly at the woman standing near her. "Run away, you mean, Sister?"

Sister Drew frowned slightly at the hint of bitterness in Gail's voice. "You need to get away and start a new life. Here, you have too many painful memories." She paused. Gail felt she may as well have said, "and your mind can't cope with them yet." Instead, Sister Drew continued, "I don't think you can call that running away, just common sense."

"But where could I go? Jobs are so hard to get now, and I need to work. I must work." Gail saw concern flash into the older woman's faded blue eyes and added quickly, "Oh, I don't mean I'm short of money. In fact, when. . .when Dad's estate's finalized, I'll have more than enough. It's just that I've had nothing to do but think these last few ghastly months. I thought it would be easier when I came back. But now. . .I don't know what to do. I must find something to do. Somewhere to live!"

An edge of panic had crept into Gail's voice, and it did not escape the experienced ears of the older woman. "I believe you spent your convalescence with your mother's sister. Is there no chance of staying on there for a while?"

"No." Gail's answer was abrupt, final.

Sister Drew looked at her thoughtfully, hesitated for a moment, and then moved around her desk and sat down. Her back was very straight as she stared at Gail.

Gail suspected that Aunt Harriet must have rung Miss Fisher about the nightmares Gail had experienced during the week. As she wondered how she could explain Aunt Harriet to Sister Drew, Gail was tense and still. She knew that the hospital staff had been relieved when they had been told that Gail was going straight to her aunt's when she was discharged.

Aunt Harriet had been an unknown quantity to Gail. During the past few years, Mrs. Brandon had seen very little of her only sister. After Gail had been living in the cold, perfectly kept house for a few days, she knew why.

She was a childless widow to whom the impression that others had of her was the vital factor in her life. Very active in her local church, she was a woman "full of good works," but with a heart that Gail had discovered lacked any real warmth and affection. Gail had soon begun to realize that one of her aunt's main aims in life was to make sure people knew how religious she was by her ceaseless involvement in the activities of her local church and district social service organizations.

Gail shuddered as she remembered the final confrontation with her aunt last night. Since it was Gail's last night, Aunt Harriet had apparently decided it was her duty to "have a little chat" with her poor bereft niece before seeing her back off into the hard, cruel world. Many pious platitudes had flowed forth and Gail had at first endured them with a suitable demeanor.

The final straw had come when Aunt Harriet had put her carefully manicured, heavily ringed hand on Gail's arm and said, "And of course, my dear, you must try harder to accept what has happened. If you would only get involved in the church, I'm sure it would help.

God is love, and—"

Gail had rounded on her. "Accept what has happened! I don't want to have anything to do with your God or your church!" She had almost choked with fury. "You're nothing but an old humbug, and a hypocrite as well! I haven't seen one thing here, or elsewhere, to make me want to get involved in religion. And I won't listen to another word, Aunt Harriet!"

Sister Drew had been silently studying the girl who was lost in thought. Her weeks of convalescence had done little to restore color to the thin, drawn face. Gail heard a sigh and looked up. She shrugged as she saw the look directed at her.

"No," Gail said again. When Sister Drew raised an eyebrow inquiringly, she blurted out, "She's too religious for me," and then bit her lip in embarrassment as the suggestion of a twinkle appeared briefly in the kind eyes watching her intently. She remembered the gossip about the reason Sister Drew had changed from the cranky, fault finding disciplinarian they had all been scared of to this warm woman, who was always so concerned about her "girls."

Gail felt relieved when her remark was ignored as Sister Drew leaned forward in her chair and picked up a couple of sheets of paper from her desk. "Well, if that's the case, I may be able to help you and an old friend at the same time."

Gail tensed and looked intently at Sister Drew, who was fiddling with the papers in her hand.

"I received this letter a couple of days ago from the son of a very old and dear friend of mine, Marian Stevens, who suffers from periodic attacks of asthma," Sister Drew continued. "I knew she had been in and out of the hospital several times this year. Now Jim, her son, tells me she's just recovering from an attack of pneumonia as well. The family's had one misfortune after another. Some years ago, her husband and eldest son jointly bought the property where they now live. They had to take out a mortgage to help pay for it, and were still battling to pay it off when John, Marian's husband, was killed. Since then, things have been rather difficult for them financially."

Sister Drew paused. When she hesitantly continued, Gail felt she was choosing her words very carefully.

"Earlier this year, she wrote and told me her daughter's husband had walked out after a bitter quarrel and they didn't know where he was. Then, some. . .er. . .time ago, she wrote and said they had been informed that he had been seriously injured."

Gail was beginning to feel a little puzzled. Sister Drew had not once looked directly at her, was still fidgeting about, and altogether was not at all like her usual direct self. For some reason Gail began to feel more and more uneasy. She forced herself to remain silent as Sister Drew quickly continued.

"The daughter immediately left her two children with Marian and John and rushed off to be with her husband, hoping for a reconciliation. The husband's. . .er. . .injury is apparently going to mean a long period in the hospital. My friend ended up in the hospital herself with this pneumonia and, since then, Jim's had the sole responsibility of the children and, of course, his younger brother, Will. From what I gather, neighbors have rallied around and he has coped reasonably well. But, now it seems that Marian is fretting to come home. It'll be harvest time in a few weeks, and Jim's afraid she'll try to do too much and trigger off more asthma attacks. He's asked me if I know of a reliable woman I could recommend who'd be able to go and help them out at such short notice. He's warned me they can't afford a very large salary and he hasn't a clue how long he'll need help. He has to get someone as soon as possible, as Marian's doctor has agreed to let her out this weekend if suitable arrangements can be made." The words had gradually quickened to a virtual torrent. Sister Drew took a deep breath, and almost flung the next words at Gail. "Do you think you could possibly consider this position?"

Gail stared at her with increasing apprehension. "But. . .but. . . Sister Drew, I'm a trained nurse, not a housekeeper. I can't even cook! Surely, your friend doesn't need any nursing care."

Sister Drew relaxed slightly. "Well, Jim didn't say anything about that in his letter," she admitted reluctantly. "But I would certainly feel happier knowing there was someone in the house with some professional knowledge. Marian's also a victim of arthritis. But don't you think a complete change of lifestyle may help you, too?"

Gail studied her thoughtfully. "It mightn't be such a change as you think. We. . .we lived on a farm. Where do your friends live?"

"Oh, how silly of me! I should have told you that first of all. I'm afraid it's in Queensland."

"Queensland!"

"Yes. I believe it's about a thousand kilometers north of us, well over a hundred kilometers west of Brisbane. Have you ever heard of the Darling Downs?"

"Isn't Toowoomba on the Darling Downs?"

"Why, yes. It's called the 'Queen city of the Darling Downs' or 'The Garden City.' Their property's some distance west of there."

The Garden City. The Carnival of Flowers.

Gail stood up abruptly. Blindly, she moved across to the open window.

She could hear her mother's excited voice saying, "Harold, we must try and have a trip to Toowoomba. They say it's the most beautiful city. The whole place gets ready for a Carnival of Flowers every September. Apparently it's unbelievably beautiful. Do let's try and go!"

The trip had been planned for this year. Now, it was November. And her parents would never go anywhere. . . .

Sister Drew sat rigidly in her chair. There had been sheer agony in Gail's dark brown eyes. She had desperately wanted to go to her and had even started to stand, before sinking back helplessly onto her chair as Gail had moved away. She closed her eyes tightly, and her lips moved soundlessly in a desperate prayer. *Dear God. Please. Please help her. Only let her agree if You know it's the best way for her and the Stevenses!*

So much depended on the next few moments. For hours last night, Sister Drew had lain awake praying and planning. She looked down at her clenched fist. Deliberately, she relaxed her grip and straightened out the crumpled pages of the letter. She pushed back her chair and slowly stood up.

The noise penetrated Gail's memories. She turned and looked at

Sister Drew. Gail's eyes were burning and dry, but she had control of herself again.

Compassion made Sister Drew's voice very gentle. "My dear, I know you'd like time to think this over but, unfortunately, I need to know straight away. Jim followed this letter with a phone call last night. He's flying to Sydney today, but has to return tomorrow. If you decide you don't want to go, I will have to make other arrangements."

Gail put her fingers to each side of her pale cheeks. "I don't know that I have much choice."

At the desolation and pain in Gail's voice, Sister Drew walked quickly over to her.

"Do you think I could meet him first?" asked Gail. "He might not think I'd be suitable."

As she finished speaking, Gail felt Sister Drew's hand rest gently on her stooped shoulders and saw understanding and caring in her eyes.

"I'm afraid he sounded so desperate, anyone I can persuade to go would be 'suitable.' I'm not sure about meeting him. He's here on urgent family business and will be dreadfully rushed for time."

Gail interrupted her. "Have you said anything to him about me?"

"Why, no. As a matter of fact, he rang me just before Miss Fisher saw me last night and told me about you." Sister Drew smiled a little ruefully at the expression on Gail's face. "Yes, I'm afraid I did know all about it. Miss Fisher is very concerned about you."

Gail moved away and shrugged her shoulders lightly. "You're both probably right. It was just so. . .so disappointing. But what I'm wondering is, does he have to know about the accident?" A strange expression flashed across Sister Drew's face. For a moment, Gail wondered if she had imagined it. She hurried on, "You see, I find it so. . .so awful. It either embarrasses people, and they don't know what to say, or else they," she gulped, "they say too much. I would feel more at ease if they treated me just like anyone else."

Sister Drew was staring thoughtfully at Gail. "I wonder," she began very slowly. "Gail, do you think you would take it one step farther and even change your name slightly? You see," she hurriedly added as Gail's eyes widened, "they may have read, or heard about the accident and remembered your name. When you get to know them, I'm sure you'll want to tell them. But. . .but. . .at your own leisure," she finished rather weakly.

Gail stared. That the day would ever have come when upright, straight-from-the-shoulder Sister Drew would suggest such a thing!

A touch of color tinged Sister Drew's cheeks as she read the amazement in Gail's face. She avoided looking at Gail as she added, "He doesn't even need to know you're a trained nurse if you like. He may wonder why on earth a trained nurse wants to take on a job like this." Sister Drew stopped abruptly.

Gail began to feel more uneasy about the whole thing. "I don't know," she said hesitantly, "there could be all kinds of complications. My lawyers haven't finished sorting out all. . .all the business yet, and—"

"Oh, I could forward all your mail to you," Sister Drew said eagerly.

There was silence. They looked at each other. Gail's brown eyes were very dark. The older, pale blue eyes looking into hers were pleading. They even seemed to be asking for more than her words had expressed. Gail shook off the fanciful thought. She straightened. A reckless expression lightened her face. Her chin tilted. After all, what did it matter? What did anything matter any more?

"Okay, Sister Drew. From now on I'm Gail Brand, not Abigail Brandon as the news reports called me. Surely, after nearly four months, that will be enough."

Relieved, Sister Drew closed her eyes for a moment. "Oh, my dear! Yes, that should do it. They really are a delightful family and I'm sure it won't be long before you'll feel free to tell them your real name." Suddenly, she became her usual businesslike self and moved briskly back to the desk. "Look, let's sit down again and sort out some of the details. How soon do you think you could go?"

"As soon as it takes me to get my luggage from the cloakroom at Central Station," Gail said a little grimly. At Sister Drew's raised eyebrows, she added, "You see, the train was late, so I just left them there and caught a taxi straight here. I thought that once I was sure of being allocated a room here I could go back and pick them up then. Now, I can take them to a motel room. I couldn't very well leave them at the entrance to the Nursing Administration offices."

Sister Drew's lips twitched. "Not very well," she murmured. "I don't think there's a vacancy here at the moment. When I see Jim I'll ask him, but I wouldn't be surprised if he jumps at the chance to take you with him tomorrow. It would save an extra trip from their farm to Brisbane to pick you up." She paused, and said hesitantly, "There. . . there's no one you have to visit before you leave?"

"No. Ann—Sister Green—has gone, and I don't feel like coping with anyone else at the moment."

Sister Drew hesitated again. She picked up a pen and started to doodle with it before looking up intently at Gail. Gail stiffened. She suddenly suspected what Sister Drew was thinking.

"Gail, I wondered if you'd given any more thought about visiting that unfortunate young man I spoke to you about before you were discharged?"

Gail's lips tightened and remained stubbornly closed. She looked away.

"He's still paralyzed, my dear," Sister Drew said sadly. "Isn't that enough punishment?"

She waited silently and, when Gail eventually spoke, her voice was very low, but the bitterness and anger made Sister Drew wince.

"So he's paralyzed. Unfortunate man? He was drunk! Because of that, he wiped out a car full of people—my people! He had no right to be driving that truck. I'm not going to see him. I think I would probably try to kill him if I did." She stared defiantly at Sister Drew.

The color drained from the wrinkled cheeks of Sister Drew, who suddenly looked stricken as she jumped to her feet. Gail thought she muttered something like "what have I done?" as her pen clattered down on the desk.

"I know you vowed something similar before. But I hoped. . .I. . . you. . .I hoped you might be feeling a little differently now that the. . . the shock has had time to. . .to. . ." Sister Drew gulped and came to an abrupt halt. Then she added, almost to herself, "But I hadn't dreamed how deep the bitterness had gone."

Gail had refused to let anyone even mention Arthur Smith's name during those first black days after she had been told why the ones she longed for the most never visited her. Only Sister Drew, in her usual forthright way, had at last dared to insist on telling Gail about him.

There had been a severe injury to his spinal cord. Extensive tests had eventually shown that it was not completely severed, but he remained paralyzed from the waist down. He still had not shown any improvement after a couple of apparently successful operations.

Sister Drew had even told her how he had begged and pleaded with the doctors to let him die when he had first realized that he had been responsible for the death of four people. Later, he had pleaded to be taken to see Gail, but she had always refused. It had become an obsession with him and he begged and pleaded so much that, just before Gail's discharge, Sister Drew had confronted her again, telling her there was something he insisted she should know, something he would not tell anyone else.

Gail had looked her old nursing educator in the eye with a cold, uncompromising "No," and then turned away without another word.

"Oh, my poor dear. Please don't harbor such bitterness," Sister Drew now implored her. "An unforgiving spirit can twist and warp your soul, and—"

A loud rap on the door prevented Gail from blurting out hot, angry words. Sister Drew bit her lip and frowned. She moved toward the door, hesitated, and then turned as though to say something more. She looked at the compressed lips, the flushed cheeks, and furious eyes. With a sigh of defeat, Sister Drew opened the door.

A tall, dark-haired man in a dark brown suit stood in the doorway. His face lit up in a warm, affectionate grin. Two large hands reached out to give Sister Drew a huge hug that was followed by a light kiss.

"Hello, Aunt Jean."

"Jim!"

It hardly needed Sister Drew's muffled exclamation to warn Gail that this was her new employer.

"I'm sorry if I'm interrupting you," the deep tones began and then cut off as he looked over his Aunt's head and saw Gail. His eyes lit with a glint of appreciation for a beautiful woman. Then, his smile stilled for a moment as he studied with interest the flushed cheeks and the anger that still lingered in her attractive features.

His glance was suddenly piercing and it brought Gail to her feet. She felt added warmth leap to her face as he continued to stare at her while Sister Drew ushered him in and closed the door.

"I thought I'd just let you know I've arrived." He turned his attention back to his Aunt. "Beth's outside in a hired car, so I can't stay."

"Oh, Jim, it is good to see you. I've been so concerned for you all." Sister Drew broke off and gestured toward Gail, who was more than a little flushed. "Before you race off, I want you to meet a young friend of mine. Gail. . . ," she paused for a second as though a little undecided, and then said distinctly, "Gail Brand. This is the Jim Stevens we've just been talking about, Gail."

Gail extended her hand to meet the large one stretched out to her. It tingled as it was taken firmly by the strong, deeply tanned hand of the man still staring at her. She felt a little dazed and hardly realized her new name had been used for the first time.

He must be well over six feet! He should have dark brown eyes to match his brown face, brown hair, and brown suit, she thought ridiculously. Instead, clear, bright blue eyes twinkled down at her. Then, the twinkle faded and the eyes darkened. They seemed to be searching out her very soul. He wasn't merely seeing her well-shaped features and the short, honey brown curls that now bounced around her face in gay abandon. She knew by his suddenly serious expression that he had recognized the strain in her darkly ringed eyes and the tightly controlled smile that had briefly tilted her shapely mouth.

After a moment, he allowed the twinkle back and smiled gently at her. "Talking about me, was she, Gail? Well, don't believe everything she says, will you?"

"Jim!" Sister Drew's exclamation was so sharp they both turned quickly toward her. Red crept into Sister Drew's cheeks as they stared at her in surprise. Her eyes were filled with distress. The fingers of one hand were pressed to her lips.

Gail's uneasiness returned with a rush. Sister Drew was behaving completely out of character.

Jim whistled softly. "Wow! If ever anyone looked an absolute picture of guilt! What on earth have you been saying, Aunt Jean?"

"Well, I. . .er. . .we. . ." Sister Drew broke off, and Jim's teasing smile disappeared. He gave her his sudden piercing look. She took a deep breath and, with a touch of defiance said, "Why, about your problem with the children and your mother, of course. I've just managed to persuade Gail to go and help you out."

Jim looked taken aback and a little dismayed. He recovered swiftly and, with an embarrassed laugh, he said, "Well, that's great. But Aunt Jean, I was hoping. . .that is, well, you. . .Mum very much wants you to come."

Gail opened her mouth, but Sister Drew said rapidly, "No, I'm afraid that's out of the question this time. In fact," she continued crisply, "Gail has just told me that as her previous plans have unexpectedly fallen through, she is quite able and willing to return with you."

Jim looked doubtfully at Gail. "Did she tell you what little terrors the children can be, and that—"

"Don't worry," Sister Drew interrupted him. "Gail is very capable and can cope. I wouldn't have asked her otherwise. Didn't you say Beth was outside, Jim?"

"Good grief, yes." The slight drawl that had been in his deep tones before disappeared. He straightened abruptly. "In fact, she's driving round and round because we couldn't get a parking space within a kilometer of here. I told her I'd only be a few minutes. So, unfortunately, there's no more time to talk this out. We're going flat hunting before the next visiting hours." His brisk voice paused, and then continued a shade apologetically, "Aunt Jean, I actually called in to see if you could come as soon as possible, and to apologize for not coming to tea tonight, because I want to catch this evening's plane back."

Sister Drew gave an exclamation of protest and dismay that he ignored. He turned to Gail and shot at her, "I guess that rules out any idea of your coming back with me."

To her own surprise, Gail felt something within her rise to meet the challenge in his keen and brisk words.

"Not necessarily," she said coldly. She heard her voice match his for crispness. "My cases are still at Central Railway Station. It's just a matter of picking them up on the way to the airport."

A glint of something like admiration as well as curiosity touched the brilliant blue eyes intently studying her, but he didn't voice any of the obvious questions. He suddenly rubbed the palm of his hand over his face and then decisively picked up a pen from the desk and scribbled on a note pad.

"There. That's the flight number. Perhaps you could ring through and book Gail's seat for us, Aunt Jean. Must go. See you in the flight lounge, Gail." A quick hug for his aunt and he was gone.

As the door closed behind him, the two women looked at each other. Simultaneously, they smiled. Sister Drew suddenly realized it was the first real smile she had seen on Gail's face since that last day with Wayne.

"Phew! Is he always like that?"

"You mean, like a sudden squall blowing in and out? By no means. He must have a lot to do today with Beth." A shadow drove away the smile on Sister Drew's face and she abruptly continued as though she sensed the questions hovering on Gail's lips. "Well, I'm afraid I must get on, too. I'll ring the booking office and then I'd better do some of the work this hospital pays me to do."

Gail knew she was being gently dismissed, so she stood silently while the booking was being made. She longed to ask who Beth was. Jim had flown all that way apparently to help her.

I must be mad, she thought suddenly as Sister Drew put down the phone. *I can't possibly just fly off like this to people I know so very little about.*

Sister Drew seemed to sense her sudden panic and, without giving Gail a chance to speak, handed her the piece of paper with the flight number and departure time written on it as well as some money. Almost before she realized it, Gail found herself being ushered to the door. Sister Drew brought her brisk instructions to a close and unexpectedly kissed Gail on the cheek.

"Gail, dear, please write to me and let me know how you are getting on." Her voice revealed all her depth of compassion behind the professional front. She hesitated for a moment and, as Gail found herself too moved by the unexpected gesture to say a word, she heard Sister Drew say anxiously, "I know you'll find a true home and friends with the Stevenses. You might find it unexpectedly difficult to tell them who you are and, if so, do tell me and I'll help all I can. And, if by some chance it all doesn't work out, never forget that God loves you so very, very much, and there will be a home for you somewhere, someplace."

She smiled a little unsteadily at Gail and turned to reenter her office, leaving Gail even more apprehensive but with no option but to turn and walk away.

Chapter 3

The rest of the afternoon, Gail was a turmoil of indecision and trepidation as she wandered around Sydney's inner city shops until it was time to collect her luggage and head for the airport. A couple of times she was on the verge of ringing Sister Drew to say she had changed her mind. But what alternative did she have?

Reluctantly, she at last hailed a taxi but her eyes remained tightly closed for the whole trip as she sat tensely in the backseat. She ignored the driver's smirk as she paid him. It was none of his business that travel in any car still made her stomach churn and her legs tremble. Let him think it was his prowess in negotiating Sydney's horrible peak hour traffic.

She lingered in the airport terminal's coffee shop as long as possible. When she went to the departure lounge, Jim Stevens was nowhere to be seen.

"A home for you. . .somewhere, someplace." Sister Drew's words flowed unbidden into her mind as a wave of weariness swept through her.

A home. She had no home. . .no family, no loved ones, no one who really cared. No, perhaps that wasn't quite right. For some reason Sister Drew had seemed to care what happened to her. She was still puzzled about that ridiculous name change idea. Surely, who she was couldn't matter to these strangers. A deep, desperate longing swept through her to find a home somewhere, a future. Home had always been where people who loved each other lived together, teased each other, sometimes argued fiercely, but always knew they were loved and accepted. . .and were together.

Loneliness, with all its horror and fear, began to grip her tired mind and she jumped up to peer out of the window overlooking the tarmac. Reluctantly, she knew that Miss Fisher and Sister Drew were right about her mind not being healed. The nightmares and the fear of traveling in cars probably meant that some patient's injuries could impair her professional ability.

Gail deliberately switched her thoughts to her new employer. She tried to remember all that Sister Drew had said about him and his mother. Sister Drew had certainly been very keen for her to work for them. She stared with unseeing eyes out at the lights of the airport, remembering what Sister Drew had been trying to say when Jim had interrupted them.

Arthur Smith. She didn't want to think about him, nor those dreadful weeks in hospital, nor the accident.

As she had gradually surfaced from the fog of pain-killing drugs, the nursing staff had tried to keep any news of the accident from her. But it had been too late. They didn't know she had regained consciousness just long enough to have her brain seared by a repeat of one of the "on the spot" interviews. Another patient's radio had been left on and, at first, she had felt only mildly irritated at being disturbed until she had suddenly heard her own name mentioned.

And then, "They think the semi must have been drifting all over the road. The poor people in that car didn't have a chance. The driver of the semi was drunk, of course."

Later, she had refused to accept any other accounts of the accident. The police had told her the truck's brakes had failed. She had looked at them with cold, angry eyes and said nothing. A drunk had wiped out her family and future, and she wished that the person who had dragged her from the crushed and burning car just in time had left her to die, too. The police hadn't been able to establish just how she had escaped from the tangled wreckage, but had been certain her injuries would have made it impossible for her do so without help.

"Miss Brand? Gail!"

A hand touched her shoulder and she turned dazed agonized eyes to look straight into the penetrating blue of distant horizons.

"Afraid it's time to go," said Jim Stevens.

People were moving toward the exit. Jim Stevens put his hand under her elbow as she stumbled slightly. Their seat allocations were not together, and Jim smiled briefly at her as they separated.

Gail's limp was worse by the time Jim joined her again in Brisbane. With scarcely a word, he helped her collect her cases on a trolley before ushering her out of the brightly lit terminal. With a few muttered words of explanation, he left her with her things while he went for his car.

His car. He had left his car here all day. Tension mounted higher as she waited, watching others hurrying away into the darkness. An early model Holden Commodore slid into the curb. It was exactly the same color and model as. . .as. . .

She gasped and began to tremble as Jim climbed out of the driver's seat and walked around to open the boot. She closed her eyes for a moment, but when she opened them the green car was still there.

She didn't notice the sharp, concerned glance that Jim gave her as he picked up one of the cases.

"You must be very tired," he said quietly. "Why don't you sit in the car and relax while I stow these things away."

"No!"

The word was barely more than a whisper as she turned from staring at the car to look at him. Jim's forehead creased for a moment. He hesitated.

"I'm all right." She tried to clear her throat, fighting for control.

Even to her own ears she sounded a little panic stricken and hoped that perhaps this handsome guy would think she was only getting cold feet at the thought of trusting herself to a stranger.

"Why don't you stretch out on the back seat then and have a sleep for a while."

Gail drew a ragged breath. She opened her mouth then closed it again and shook her head vigorously.

"No, no," she managed to gasp after failing miserably to control her trembling. "Definitely not the back."

Jim stared silently at her for a moment and then, without further comment, slammed the door closed again and opened the front one. It was as though her limbs were frozen to the spot. Then she felt his warm hand on her arm and, with a feeling of helplessness, let him guide her into the car.

She sat bolt upright and didn't move an inch as the car pulled away from the curb.

"Afraid the trip will take nearly three hours," Jim said as they stopped at a set of traffic lights. He glanced at her, and when she still didn't move said very gently, "Look, I don't know what you're afraid of, but you'd better do your seat belt up before an irate policeman stops me."

A sudden thought jolted through Gail. Seat belt. There had been something about a seat belt. Wayne's voice. Why couldn't she remember those last precious moments before the smash?

Jerkily, she moved at last and, with stiff fingers, fumbled with the seat belt. She was vaguely aware that Jim was still watching her until the lights changed.

"We'll stop off somewhere and have a cup of coffee," he said in a soothing voice when she stiffened up again as the car moved forward. "When we get home I'll drop you off first before I go over to the neighbors to pick up the kids."

The words hardly registered. She sat as though frozen to the seat, scarcely aware of him or his growing concern. Jim concentrated on driving through a patch of heavy traffic for a while and, when she still hadn't moved, began to quietly point out places of interest. Not even the large bridge over the wide Brisbane River drew her gaze from the lights of the oncoming traffic.

Gail's stomach started heaving as the car's speed increased. She dreaded the open road. The only thing that made the nightmare bearable at all was that it was night time and she wouldn't be able to see the semitrailers bearing down on them until they roared past.

Suddenly, Jim flicked on his indicators and pulled into a brightly lit service station.

"I think this'll be a good spot for some petrol and that cup of coffee," Jim said as the car rolled to a stop.

Relief brought the taste of bile to Gail's mouth, and she wrenched open the door just in time.

Jim gave a sharp exclamation. A moment later Gail felt gentle hands helping her from the car, holding her head, as his distressed voice murmured, "You poor kid. Why didn't you say? You must have been feeling sick in the plane."

He waited until she had stopped heaving before he thrust a large handkerchief into her hand and then pulled her slight body to lean against his tall frame.

"Let's go and find a chair for you and something to settle your poor old stomach," he murmured softly when she at last stirred and moved back from him.

A sympathetic attendant managed to supply a glass of water and some antacid and, before long, Gail was feeling much better, although very much ashamed and embarrassed.

I guess Miss Fisher was definitely right after all. If I react like this to the car, what would happen if a severely burned patient were admitted to my ward?

Jim's voice stopped that dreadful line of thought.

"Feeling better?" He was smiling sympathetically at her.

"I'm so sorry," she faltered, "you've been very kind."

His eyes twinkled at her over his coffee cup as he took a sip. "The children have given me rather a lot of practice these past few months with people getting carsick. But you should have told me earlier, and I could have stopped."

Gail was quite happy for him to go on thinking that that's all it had been, and grasped at his first statement to change the subject.

"I'm afraid Sister Drew hadn't really finished telling me about any of you before you arrived and then there was no time afterwards." Gail wondered silently about that again as she added, "I don't really know any more than the fact that your mother's been in the hospital and you've been responsible for the children while your sister has been away."

He told her briefly about seven-year-old Jacky and her five-year-old brother, Robbie, and then added casually, "You must know Aunt Jean well to be prepared to trust her word enough to take us all on,

31

sight unseen."

Or desperate, she thought, but said sharply, "And you must trust her judgment to give me a job without knowing anything about me."

Unexpectedly, he grinned. "Quite a woman is our Aunt Jean. Have you known her long?"

"About four years. And you?"

"Oh, all my life. She was a bridesmaid at Mum and Dad's wedding. We've seen her off and on as long as I can remember, but lost touch not long after her fiancé was killed only a day before their wedd—are you going to be sick again?" She was staring wildly at him as he half rose to his feet. Her mouth opened, but no words would come. She shook her head and, with a shaking hand, raised her coffee cup to her suddenly dry lips.

"Are you sure?" Jim looked anxiously at her as he subsided again. "You went dreadfully pale again."

"I'm. . .I'll be fine soon," she gasped at last and was grateful when he waited silently for a while until she had sipped more of her hot drink. At last she managed to say huskily, "You said you've known Aunt—Sister Drew all your life?"

He hesitated for a moment and then rubbed his hand briefly over his face and sat back in his chair.

"Oh, yes. She's a marvelous person but was very bitter and unhappy for a long time, though. She really loved her student nurses, especially when she was the tutor sister when they had hospital training. Now she finds it harder, she says, when the students spend so much less time actually in the hospital with the patients and more time at the university. At the time we met up with her again, her whole life revolved around her work and Mum couldn't get over the change in her. But, that was just before she became a Christian and she's just so different now."

Jim was smiling at some fond memory and didn't appear to notice that Gail sat up a bit straighter and stared at him. She closely watched his reaction as she said, "I heard she'd become very religious during the past two years."

"Religious? I suppose you could call it that. Only I've found that religion and true Christianity are often two entirely different things. Are you a Christian, Gail?"

Jim was smiling gently but, to her annoyance, Gail found it hard to meet the penetrating blueness of his eyes. Before the accident and her stay with Aunt Harriet, she would have blithely said, "Why, yes, of course. Isn't this a Christian country?"

She decided to be blunt. If these people were religious, or whatever he called it, it might be just as well if they knew what she thought from the word go.

"I don't know what I think about God anymore. I certainly don't like what some people seem to be sure He is like. And what's more, I'm not at all interested in finding out either," she finished defiantly.

The blue eyes darkened, and Jim's smile disappeared.

"Are you religious?" As soon as the impulsive words were out, Gail regretted them.

Jim lowered his eyes and toyed with the handle of his cup, and then looked at her and spoke slowly as though he were choosing his words carefully. "No, I wouldn't say I was religious, but I have handed over complete control of my life to Jesus Christ." He ignored her slightly puzzled expression and glanced at his watch, before rising to his feet. "I'm afraid we'll have to get going. Perhaps we can talk about this some other time when we aren't quite so tired."

This time, somehow, getting into the car was all a little easier. After he closed her door, Gail quickly busied herself fastening the seat belt, and she forced herself to look around the interior. The inside was familiar, but the upholstery was a different color, and there was a cassette player in the dashboard as well as a radio.

Then, the car was in motion and Gail felt the waves of tension beginning to reach for her again.

Jim began to talk quickly about Will. He chattered on cheerfully about the fourteen-year-old who was still in high school and then, without waiting for her to respond, rambled on about his mother and life generally on the farm.

Later, Gail remembered very little of what he had said. She guessed that he was using the therapy he handed out to the carsick children. Take the mind off the car's motion and hopefully the stomach will stop churning.

It had been a long, sleepless night at Aunt Harriet's and an even longer and emotionally fraught day. His quiet voice was somehow soothing. It didn't demand any response. It just droned on and on, and gradually faded away.

Several times, Jim glanced at the sleeping woman. Once, her head slipped sideways and, as he steered with one hand and slowed the car, he reached over into the back for a pillow. As he tried to ease the pillow under her head, she opened her eyes for a moment. With her eyes still closed, she took it from him and tucked it under her head and leaned against his shoulder.

"Thank you, darling," she murmured softly, and then was asleep again.

Jim grinned to himself. He rather liked the way she snuggled against him, and wondered who "darling" could be.

Then his forehead creased with thought, as the smile disappeared.

"I think you've sent us a curly one here, Aunt Jean," he mused silently to himself.

At last he shrugged and glanced at the clock on the dashboard. He gripped the steering wheel a little more firmly and pressed his foot down on the accelerator.

Gail jolted awake as the car left the smooth highway. She was dazed and, for a moment, wondered where she was.

"We're nearly there, Gail," a quiet voice said. "Sorry about the rough road."

Gail jerked upright. "Ouch!"

"Stiff? I was afraid of that. You must have been exhausted to sleep so soundly. I've decided to drop you off first and then I'll go over to the Garretts' and pick up the children. What on earth!"

The tired voice sharpened at the same time the car slowed down next to a belt of dark trees. Through their branches Gail saw the outline of a house. Several lights were blazing.

"There shouldn't be anyone here," Jim muttered.

He hit the brakes and the car stopped with a jerk. With a brief

"Wait here!" he was out of the car and disappearing among the trees.

Gail stretched, moving her head gingerly. She had never slept like that before in a car. She hoped Jim wasn't too fed up with her. She opened the door and climbed out. A dog not very far away started barking furiously. After peering in its direction, she decided it must be tied up somewhere because it didn't appear, so she moved a few paces away from the car. Suddenly, the barking stopped and the stillness of the night settled around her.

It was a little cool, but not a breath of air stirred the drooping branches of the trees that Gail could now see were pepper trees. A path disappeared amongst them. She hesitated, and decided she had better do as he had told her and stay put. She glanced up. It had been a long time since she had seen stars sparkling so brightly in such a dark sky. City lights always dimmed the stars, she thought regretfully.

A door slammed and footsteps crunched on the path. Gail swung around as the dim figure of a girl came up to the car.

"Miss Brand? Jim sent me to get you." The voice was a little high-pitched and bossy. "He said to come on in and he'd unload the car in a few minutes."

The voice was also cold and unfriendly. Without waiting for Gail to move, the girl spun around and disappeared. Gail reached back into the car for her purse and then hurried after her.

Something must definitely be wrong. The path curved through the trees and then across a lawn badly in need of some attention. It finished at a brightly lit patio.

Gail paused and hesitantly pushed open a screen door that led into a wide, long corridor. A rattle of plates came from a room on her left, so she made her way toward it.

It was a large kitchen and the girl was putting cups and saucers onto the large table in the center. When Gail appeared in the doorway, she paused and carefully looked her up and down. Gail began to bristle at her rudeness until something like dismay flew across the girl's pretty face as she took in Gail's tousled curls, her attractive features, and neat figure.

"You're the woman Jim said had come to help out, but. . .but you're no older than I!" She spat the low words at Gail. "Why on earth did you have to come?"

The words were choked off as footsteps sounded in the corridor. She grabbed an electric kettle and turned to fill it as Jim walked into the room.

"Sorry to desert you, Gail. This is Hilda Garrett, a neighbor," he said briefly. Gone was the quiet relaxed face that had laughed across at her in the restaurant. His eyes were red-rimmed and his expression grim.

"How do you do, Gail? I'm so glad Jim managed to get you at such short notice. How fortunate that you were out of work."

The change in Hilda's face and voice was such a contrast that Gail had a sudden hysterical desire to laugh. The words had been accompanied by a sweet smile that did not light up the venomous, pale blue eyes.

"Hilda brought my mother and the children home." Jim's voice was abrupt and Gail was glad it was Hilda he was scowling at. He continued in a voice dripping with icicles. "What on earth possessed you to go into town with the children and let her persuade you to get the doctor to discharge her today? You know I wanted her in the hospital until I had someone to look after things. We'd have been in a fine mess tomorrow if I hadn't been able to bring Gail back with me."

Gail felt a little sorry for the girl who blushed scarlet and said miserably, "Well, I thought that. . .er. . .I could stay a few days, and—"

"Look, Hilda, I thought we'd already discussed that. Your own father needs your help at the moment." Jim bit his lip, as though choking back more words, and then continued in a softer voice, "Oh, well, I guess as it happens it's worked out okay. Let's have that cup of tea and plan to get around a bit in the morning before you go home."

He turned toward the door and missed the savage look that Hilda flung at Gail.

"But. . .but Jim," she protested angrily, "couldn't I just stay a few—"

"I'm afraid the answer's no, Hilda." Jim paused as another thought struck him. "I suppose you've got your things in Beth's room," he said ungraciously. When Hilda jerked her head speechlessly, he sighed and wiped his open hand over his face. "Sorry, Gail. Afraid you'll have to bunk down in the sleep-out for what's left of the night. I'll get our things out of the car."

There was a grim silence in the kitchen as the screen door slammed behind him. Hilda swung around, but not before Gail saw the tears in her eyes. With her back carefully to Gail, she busied herself with the teapot and then went to a large, built-in cupboard and whipped out a cake tin.

"Look, I'm sorry," began Gail in her pleasant voice, "perhaps we—"

"I don't need your sympathy!" snapped Hilda. "And don't expect any help from me in the morning, either."

"If you could just show me where the sleep-out is, perhaps I could make my bed," Gail tried again after a brief pause.

"You bet you'll make your own bed. But his lordship wants some supper first. I'll show you when I'm ready!"

Gail gave up. There was silence until Jim appeared, laden down with cases, and it was he who showed her to the sleep-out and helped her make up the bed.

When they finally made their way back to the kitchen, they found it deserted. Gail sensed that Jim shared her relief as he reboiled the kettle. They sat talking easily for a short while. Gail apologized for sleeping all the way. It didn't seem to matter anymore as Jim dismissed it lightly, teasing her gently. Then he chased her off to bed while he turned out the lights.

It had been an exhausting day, but the sleep in the car made it hard for Gail to settle down. She thought of their conversation in the restaurant and suddenly hoped that one day Jim might explain to her what he meant about handing over complete control of his life to Jesus Christ.

She had never heard anyone else talk like that before. In fact, she knew she had never met anyone like Jim before. . .or Hilda for that matter. She grinned into the darkness. She didn't realize until the morning that, as she at last drifted off to sleep, she hadn't once had to deliberately stop herself from thinking of Wayne and her family.

Chapter 4

D on't ya think she can wake up now, Jacky?" It was a very loud whisper that penetrated the haze of sleep.

Gail stayed very still as a much softer whisper said "Sssssh! Uncle Jim said we weren't to disturb her."

The very loud whisper dropped a fraction. "But the 'Orror's gone now, and she'll need'er breakf'st. She must be starved!"

Gail thought it was time to stretch and open her eyes.

"Now look what you've done!"

The soft whisper sounded worried and then there was the sound of small feet scurrying away. A few moments later, Gail heard a bustle out in the hallway.

"Hang on a minute, I'll push open that door a bit more." Jim's voice was a little anxious. "Watch that jug, Robbie."

A small procession marched into Gail's room.

A dainty, snowy-haired girl carried a breakfast tray up to Gail. An even smaller, fair boy clutched a china jug in two small hands.

"Oh, you darlings!" said Gail.

Jim's lips twitched. Warmth flooded Gail's face.

It had been a long time since Gail's mother had brought her a small tray on her first morning home on holidays and then sat on the bed and chattered away about all the things that interested them both.

Tears pricked at Gail's eyes. She sat up and leaned over the tray to hide them.

"We made it ourselves, didn't we Uncle Jim? Only I wanted to cook you an egg, but he thought you might just feel like toast on your first morning," said Jacky.

"An' I made that, too," Robbie piped up.

"Oh, you only buttered it—" began Jacky loftily.

"Now you two, what about we let Gail eat in peace before it gets cold," interrupted Jim as he began to usher them toward the door. He glanced back at her from the doorway and started to say, "You can say hello to—" and then stopped. He hesitated, and then gave her an uncertain smile before following the children, pulling the door firmly behind him.

Gail scrubbed furiously at the tears trickling down her cheeks. Idiot! And she hadn't even thanked them! What on earth must he think of her now? She had been sick, slept all the way home, and now he had seen her blubbering over a breakfast tray.

She swung her legs over the side of the bed and examined the tray. Everything was daintily arranged, including a perfect, pink rosebud.

A glance at her watch made her give a slight gasp. It was horribly late. She ate quickly, wondering about the rest of Robbie's whisper. Who was the 'Orror? Then she sat up a little straighter. Hilda! She jumped off the bed and rummaged for her bag. She swallowed the rest of her tea and toast as she rapidly dressed in a pair of slacks and a blouse.

When Gail walked into the kitchen a little later, Jim was washing up and had two small assistants waving tea towels. He turned and gave her a piercing glance that briefly reminded her of that moment in Sister Jean Drew's office. With a gulp, she remembered her deception and hurried into speech.

"Thank you so much for my lovely breakfast," Gail said quickly before anyone could speak. "It's been a long time since I've had such a nice breakfast in bed. . .er. . .like that." Her voice trailed away lamely as she thought of the weeks of hospital trays. She busied herself putting the tray on the table and stacking up the dirty dishes before carrying them over to the sink. "I'm sorry I slept so long. Hello. You must be Jacky and Robbie." She smiled at them, avoiding Jim's face.

They said hello a little shyly and returned to wiping the dishes.

"Well, I'm afraid I wasn't going to let you sleep much longer, as I have to go down to the sheds soon and Mum's still asleep."

"Grandma sleeps and sleeps," remarked Robbie as he dried a plastic cup.

"That's cause she's been sick, silly," said Jacky.

"But I wanna tell her about Bennie—"

The small boy stopped abruptly, and his mouth began to quiver as Jacky wailed, "Robbie!"

He glanced up guiltily at his uncle and then grabbed a spoon off the pile of shining wet cutlery just put on the drainer. Jim's hands stilled as Jacky also glanced quickly at him and then applied herself more industriously than ever to polishing the plate in her hand.

"What did you want to tell Grandma, Robbie?" Jim asked very quietly.

Poor Robbie opened his mouth and then snapped it shut. He looked at Jacky and then back up at Jim. Two big tears welled up.

"Perhaps I could finish clearing up in here for you, Jim," said Gail quickly. "And seeing the children made my breakfast, perhaps they could go and play outside for a while."

Jim hesitated. He was frowning and for a moment Gail was afraid he was going to pursue the matter. Then he grabbed a hand towel and wiped his hands dry. His smile at the two children was so unexpectedly gentle that Gail caught her breath.

"Off you go, you villains. But Jacky, don't forget Grandma will get tired very quickly and you mustn't bother her with anything I or Gail can help you with."

As the screen door slammed behind two flying figures, Jim looked at Gail. He sighed. "I don't suppose you know much about little boys and puppies?"

"Puppies?"

"Yes, puppies," he mimicked. "Or I should say, a puppy. If I remember correctly, Bennie was a name selected by Hilda for one of her collie's pups." Jim frowned again. "She offered to give the children one of the pups, but I asked her not to mention it to them for a while. Things have been hectic enough without an untrained puppy running riot."

Gail moved closer and picked up one of the discarded tea towels.

"Do you think Hilda might have promised Robbie the puppy?"

"That's more than likely," said Jim a little grimly. "Look, put down that tea towel and come and sit down for a minute. Mum will be awake soon, and I'd better put you in the picture a little."

He pulled out a chair for her, then looked at it in dismay before pushing it disgustedly under the table and pulling out another one. He looked ruefully at Gail as she sat down.

"I'm afraid the peanut butter smeared on that chair brings me to the first couple of things—my mother's health and the state of this house. Did Aunt Jean tell you Mum is an asthmatic?"

"Yes, she did." Gail thought for a moment, and then suddenly heard herself saying, "Look, before we go into that, I'd like to say that as it happens I've had a bit to do with a boy and his puppy. My. . .my brother had one," she finished abruptly and looked down at the tablecloth.

"Oh," he said blankly. "Oh, well then, perhaps you can talk that over with Mum. The poor little kids need something to take their minds off their last disappointment." He rubbed his hand over his face with the gesture that was becoming familiar and Gail saw how drawn and weary he still was. "They're disappointed that I didn't bring their mother home. I tried to keep their minds off that by helping them make the tea and toast." He stopped, a sheepish expression entering his face. "In fact, I. . .I'm sorry, but would you like more breakfast than that?"

She smiled and shook her head. "No, that was fine, thanks. I loved what you brought in."

She wondered about giving some explanation for the tears, but he grinned and said "That's okay, then. Look, about Mum." He rested his chin on both hands and looked at her consideringly. "I don't suppose you've ever seen anyone in an asthma attack, have you?"

Jim's eyebrows rose slightly as she felt her cheeks grow hot. "Well, yes, as a matter of fact, I have."

"Oh good, that's a relief. At least you mightn't panic as poor Hilda did once and be convinced that she is gasping her last." He looked a bit ashamed when he went on to say, "Sorry, that's a bit hard on her I

41

guess. But those sudden severe attacks were one of the reasons why I was hoping Aunt Jean would have been able to come. Mum's had occasional bouts of asthma the last few years, but since a. . .a family upset earlier this year, she's been getting worse. The doctor refused to discharge her this time unless she had more help at home. I'm doing all I can, but I'm getting more and more behind with my work."

"How was your mother last night?"

"She was exhausted," he said abruptly. "Hilda had no right to take the children in to see her. I was forced to accept her offer to look after them yesterday. I didn't dream she planned to bring Mum home so she would be entrenched here when I returned. She claimed this morning she knew Aunt Jean wouldn't be able to get away on such short notice at this time of the year and—" He stopped short, as though realizing how angry he was starting to sound, and finished in softer tones, "Anyway, she went home early this morning."

The large brown hand moved over his face again. He stared at Gail. She managed to look steadily back at him.

"So, that leaves you. Aunt Jean seemed to think you would be capable of being housekeeper, mother, and nurse, all in one."

"Nurse!"

"Don't tell me that disturbs you the most? I only meant you'll have to keep a close eye on Mum and somehow try to stop her from doing too much again."

"Oh. Oh, I see. What about the mother bit then?"

He looked anxious. "Those poor little scraps are pretty bewildered about the whole business. Did Aunt Jean also tell you about Beth?"

"Beth? The woman you were with in Sydney? No, she didn't mention her. Look, all she said was that your sister's husband had been injured in an accident and, because there had been marriage problems, she didn't want to leave him at all. Isn't that what you meant about not bringing their mother home?"

Jim looked puzzled for a moment, and then his face cleared. "Oh, it sounds like we never mentioned my sister's name. She's Beth," he said simply. "She's just had confirmation from the doctors that her husband's stay in a hospital in Sydney will be longer than they thought. We've been trying to get him transferred to a Brisbane hospital, but they're still too worried about the effect of the trip on him. She's been staying with church people, but we had to find a flat closer to the hospital."

"The poor dear. I didn't dream. . .of course, Beth's room." She saw the look of inquiry on Jim's face and added quickly, "I thought Beth must be your girlfriend—" Jim was grinning madly, and she stopped in confusion, then raised her chin again and spoke with what dignity she could muster. "Last night you said Hilda had her room. I thought you must have gone to Sydney to. . .to. . . Anyway, that's beside the point," she hastened to add as the grin became a smothered chuckle. "It's a shame Sister Drew didn't tell me your sister was in Sydney. I might have been able to meet her so she would know who was going to help care for her children."

All the amusement drained out of Jim's face. "I doubt we would've had time. It was pretty hectic. She's been under tremendous pressure for the last few weeks. She and her husband were separated. He had his accident some months ago, and she was dreadfully upset because he had refused to let anyone contact her until recently. He was involved in a dreadful accident in the Blue Mountains."

Jim paused as they heard a soft footstep in the hallway. He didn't notice the sudden drawn-in breath of his companion as he sprang to his feet.

"Hello, you must be Gail."

Gail stood up as Mrs. Stevens entered the kitchen. She put her hand in the soft, thin hand extended towards her. A faded version of Jim's clear, searching blue eyes studied her from a pale face framed by softly curling, graying hair. She looked thin and frail, as had many chronic asthmatics Gail had seen over the years, and was obviously glad to sink down onto the chair Jim had been using. She must have been awake for a while after all as she was dressed in an attractive cotton frock.

Jim scolded her gently. "Mum, you should have stayed in bed today."

"Not on your sweet life," she interrupted him cheerfully. "I've spent days and days in a wretched bed. I want to get to know Gail. Why don't you go and see how Will is getting on and leave us to start doing that very thing."

Jim hesitated, and then smiled a little ruefully at Gail. "I don't know how you're going to do it, but do try and stop her from starting the spring cleaning or something equally as strenuous. I guess Will does need help."

He bent and kissed his mother on her cheek. Her frail hand came up and touched his face. With a pang, Gail saw the look of affection that passed between them.

Well, at least he didn't let that screen door slam quite so hard, Gail thought as she and Mrs. Stevens looked at each other in silence.

"Yes, they do rather let that door slam," Mrs. Stevens said. She gave a low chuckle at the look on Gail's face. "I guessed the children had been banished when I heard that door before."

"Yes, they're outside somewhere. Perhaps I should check on them?"

"No, no, they'll be with Will down at the machinery shed. Perhaps you could put the kettle on though, and make us a pot of tea instead."

As Gail filled the electric kettle and switched it on, she decided it best to confess straight away.

"Look, Mrs. Stevens, I'm afraid I can't cook very well."

The older woman chuckled, and said in a relieved voice, "Well, that's a relief." She saw Gail's look of astonishment and laughed outright. "If you knew what I've had to put up with these past few weeks from someone trying to convince me she was a paragon of all the virtues, you'd know what a relief it is to have someone who will admit she can't cook!" She suddenly looked a little contrite and added quickly, "But that's not very kind. It's just that I'm so relieved Jean sent you."

Her voice and manner were so friendly and warm that Gail felt some deep inner coldness and reserve begin to dissolve. It didn't take long to make the tea and toast. Gail opted for a cup of coffee, and soon they were chattering away as though they had known each other much longer than just a few minutes.

As they talked, Gail began to realize what a strain Mrs. Stevens had been under. She was much younger than Gail had thought she would be, and, although she didn't say so outright, the task of looking after her own two sons as well as the two children had become just too much for her after her recurring asthma attacks. Jim had at first been able to help a great deal, but the harvest was only a few weeks off. He was too busy now on the property to spend much time in the house. Mrs. Stevens's face glowed as she talked about her eldest son.

"He's been absolutely marvelous. God's been so good to me, giving me such a son. Since his father died when Will was only eight, he's tried so hard to fill the gap that that loss meant to us all." Her face clouded and she sighed. "I suppose you know about Beth and Arthur? She changed so much after they were married, and even more after he left her. She'd been drifting along, and that really shook her up. And now—"

The screen door slammed, and a tall gangly boy with a mop of unruly dark auburn hair appeared in the doorway. "Hi, Mum! Sure good to have you home!"

"It's sure good to be home," Mrs. Stevens said fervently. "Will, have you said hello to Gail yet? Why Gail, what—"

Gail had sprung to her feet. She felt dizzy and disorientated.

He was the same height. His voice was the same—uneven, cracking a little. And that unruly auburn hair. . .the freckles. . .

"Will, did you say? But his name's Bill," she croaked in a dazed voice.

The boy gave a self-conscious laugh. "Well, it's really William, but Dad's name was Bill, so they've always called me. . ."

His voice wavered again on some of the same deep notes as that other fourteen-year-old had. Gail sank back into her chair and, with a low moan of anguish, covered her face with both hands.

Mrs. Stevens went into action. "Will, how many times have I told you to wash yourself in the laundry first before coming into the house after you've been in the shed."

She winked at him and jerked her head significantly towards the door. He disappeared fast. Then she went to Gail and laid her hand on the bowed shoulder.

"You mistook him for someone else, dear."

Gail knew she had made a fool of herself, but couldn't find her voice. She felt gentle fingers soothing her, and at last took her hands from her face and looked up.

Mrs. Stevens's kind face changed as she saw the ravaged features.

"I thought he was Bill. My. . .my young brother." Gail closed her eyes tightly for a moment and, for the first time, forced herself to put the dreadful knowledge into words.

"He. . .he. . .was. . .was killed. Car accident." She opened her eyes and again fought for control at the horrified expression on Mrs. Stevens's face. "Your son. He's uncannily like him. Especially his voice. I. . .I never gave a thought to how old your other son might be."

"I'm so very sorry, my dear. Will was a most unexpected gift from the Lord rather late in our marriage. He goes on the bus to high school during the week and that doesn't leave much time for him at home. He's a tremendous help to Jim on the weekends." The gentle voice went on quietly, allowing Gail time to recover, while at the same time busy hands started stacking their dirty cups and plates. "Look, I'd rather welcome the chance to putter around in here for a while if you think you could start on the bedrooms, Gail. And then I can help you get lunch."

Gail thankfully escaped. She worked swiftly, using the defense mechanism she had tried to perfect at Aunt Harriet's. Busy hands and feet forced her to concentrate on the task at hand and protected her emotions from utter chaos.

By the time she had transferred her things to the bedroom next to the kitchen, she was feeling calmer and began tidying the children's room. As she went to put away some clothes in a drawer of the dressing table, she noticed a small plastic container with some holes in the lid. Her tight lips relaxed when she lifted the lid. She hesitated for a moment, took one glance around the now tidy room, and carefully carried the container back to the kitchen.

"Mrs. Stevens, what do you think I should—" she paused as Will turned and looked uncertainly at her. A knife thrust shook her for a moment, but the distress on his face made her force a smile at him and hurriedly say, "The children weren't the only ones to occupy their room last night. Look."

With a relieved expression Will approached her and peered into the container. He chuckled. "Hey, Mum, Robbie's collecting snails again."

"Oh, he's a positive menace with his creepy crawlies. Do take the wretched things out to the back patio please, son. I suppose we should be thankful they aren't spiders!"

Gail shuddered as Will disappeared. "That's one thing I have a real thing about. Them and snakes."

"Well, I'm afraid at times we have both. Do be careful near any long grass, Gail. The children are pretty good now at watching out for them. Jim killed a large brown snake on the back patio a few weeks ago."

"They don't come into the house, do they?"

"Well, we've never had one in this house, but it isn't unknown on the Downs."

The rest of the morning passed quickly. Gail unpacked her cases as quickly as she could, only pausing to sit on the bed when she pulled out the bundle wrapped in an old towel at the very bottom of the last case. She hesitated and then lovingly cradled it in her hands. At last she reluctantly unwrapped the two photo frames with their precious contents. Pain ripped through every cell in her body as she looked down at the smiling faces.

It was still too soon. Time heals, people had told her. But how long does it take, her heart cried in anguish? With shaking hands, she placed them face down under a pile of winter jumpers.

Perhaps by next winter, she thought bitterly as she walked quickly from the room.

There was only one thing about the rooms in the lovely old house that struck the wrong chord with Gail. As she moved from room to room, she was disappointed as she realized that these people must be as religious as Aunt Harriet. The religious pictures and texts were not as ostentatiously displayed, but each room held at least one. On her own bedroom table a daintily framed painting told her that "Prayer changes things." The largest painting of all hung above the bed she figured must be Jim's.

Aunt Harriet had a painting of the head of Christ prominently displayed in her lounge room. It had portrayed Him as a gentle, Anglo-Saxon type. Gail stood for several moments before the one in Jim's room. This was a man's Man. The features were strong and rugged. The face was deeply tanned with dark hair blowing in the wind. There were beads of sweat on His forehead. And those eyes. . .

Gail turned from it with an impatient shrug and a frown. Her eye caught a small plaque on the dressing table. It pleaded, "Please be patient. God hasn't finished with me yet."

She glanced back up at the painting before thoughtfully making her way back to the kitchen. Well, at least these people may not think they had all the answers.

When she entered the kitchen, she saw with dismay that the table was set and lunch preparations were well underway. Mrs. Stevens was sitting down, talking to Jim as he sliced some cold meat. Abruptly, they stopped their quiet conversation when they saw her, and her head unconsciously went up.

"Oh, I'm sorry. It took me longer than I thought."

Jim grinned at her. "Not to worry. I've been doing this for quite some weeks now. I didn't intend for you to start today anyway. Perhaps you could call the children and supervise their hands."

Lunch was a cheerful affair. Afterward, the kitchen was tidied in record time so Gail could be taken on a tour of the farm. When this had been suggested during the meal, she had tentatively mentioned she should really start on the huge pile of washing. This had been greeted with disappointed cries from Jacky and Robbie. Mrs. Stevens stated she intended to have a sleep while they were all out. Jim had said decisively that after putting up with chaos so long, one more day was neither here nor there. So she gave in.

Gail was very relieved their transport was a rather battered utility and not in the Holden and, when their first stop was the huge machinery shed, she found herself enjoying Will as he took it upon himself to point out to Gail the various machines essential for operating a successful grain farm.

She heard in rapid succession about the monster harvesters, called "headers" on the Downs, the huge bulk bins that would be fitted onto the semitrailer truck, the large tractor, combines and rakes, the sundercuts or "disc ploughs" as some people apparently called them. As Jim at last steered them back to the utility, Will was still explaining carefully to a bemused Gail that the large cylinders, called "rollers," had to be used some years to press the soil down onto the planted grain. When they eventually scrambled back into the ute, Gail's head was whirling with a mass of farming lore.

Jim started to laugh a little as he let in the clutch. "Sorry about that, Gail. We don't expect you to remember all that in one sitting— or even three! Afraid when you live here all your life you take it a bit for granted. You'll get used to all the new words and ways gradually."

She nodded and smiled ruefully. "It did all come a bit fast and furious."

They had driven away from the sheds down a bumpy track that led around the fence of a paddock filled with golden, waving wheat. No hill or rise obstructed her view across miles and miles of plains.

"There are miles and miles of treeless, black soil plains here. There's only a few patches of scrub, mainly around the Condamine River and its branches farther west. The farmers never had to clear anything except prickly pear cactus."

"I think I remember my. . .my dad saying something about that once. Didn't some insect have to be imported to get rid of it?"

"Aussies are peculiar people," Jim mused. "Most of the pests we have, whether animal or vegetable, have been deliberately brought here. The prickly pear was brought in, and by 1925 had covered over thirty million acres. Then, the government had to bring in a moth from South America to let its larvae eat it out. The old-timers reckon they couldn't ride a horse across the plains once for the pear. Its sharp cactus points would rip a horse to pieces. It was all grazing land then of course, but wasn't even much good for cattle in large areas. Now, most farms only have house cows and concentrate on grain crops, although more and more are turning to cotton when they can get the underground water to irrigate."

Gail could see a faint smudge on the horizon toward the east, and an even fainter, lower one toward the west. She was too polite to say so, but she had always thought flat country looked monotonous. But she looked with new eyes at the waving wheat on each side of them. It was all rather beautiful. The only green patches followed the few fences, and even they were few and far between. It was vast, and perhaps a little intimidating for someone who had only known the rolling hills around the fruit-growing areas where she had been raised.

When they had traveled a couple of kilometers from the sheds, Jim pointed out a distant clump of trees around some buildings. "That's the Garretts' place. Hilda's dad is a fine man. Her mother died a few years ago and there's only the two of them now. His faith in God hasn't faltered at all. If you'd like to come to church with us on Sunday, you'll probably meet him. Look! There's a snake!"

Gail was just in time to see the flash of sun on the long shiny reptile as it whipped across the rough track into the wheat.

She shivered. "Your mother said you killed one on the patio. Do you have a lot of them?"

She was glad to have a chance to prevent him from saying more about religion. For a moment she wondered what she was going to do if they expected her to go along to church with them.

No way, she thought.

"Not really," Jim answered her and then commented, "If this hot weather holds, it should only be another couple of weeks and we can start harvesting. Grain's not hard enough yet," he explained in answer to Gail's questioning look. "I'm glad, too. We've got a lot of work to catch up on beforehand. You'll be extra busy then, Gail."

"I like being busy. But perhaps you'd better tell me what to expect."

This Jim did for the rest of the drive across the paddocks. He explained that he had to hire men to drive the trucks and they would need to be fed. She would have to do all the running to and from school with the children until the summer holidays started in a few weeks' time, shop for supplies, and do a variety of things that could come up.

There was no further opportunity to talk about religion. Gail had been wondering if she should tell him straight out about her aversion to going to church with them. As it happened, after tea that evening, she was glad nothing more was said. She would certainly have been more embarrassed than she was before.

Everyone had finished their meal and she began to gather the dirty plates. Robbie said reprovingly, "Aren't we 'avin' our readin'?"

Gail had briefly wondered why the two children had not raced off the moment they had finished eating. She had put it down to just good training, but now she paused and looked inquiringly at Jim.

He stood up and took a book down from the top of a cupboard. He hesitated for a moment and then said quietly to Gail, "We always try and have a brief Bible reading and prayer after tea every night. We'd love you to share it with us, but if you'd rather not—"

"Uncle Jim!" Jacky sounded scandalized. "Of course she's going to share! You made us to start with and now it's right up to an exciting bit she won't want to miss. We missed our reading last night at the Garretts'."

Gail looked down helplessly at Jacky's indignant face. She put down the pile of plates and meekly sat down in her place again. She was looking at the precariously piled plates and missed the glance Jim and his mother exchanged. At her barely perceptible nod, Jim sat down also and opened the Bible.

"Right," he said cheerfully, "what were we up to Robbie?"

The small face frowned in thought for a moment, and then lit up. "The boy was just loadin' 'is shanghai, and the giant was comin'."

"It's the story of David and Goliath, silly," Jacky said importantly.

It was a very long time since Gail had been told this story by an enthusiastic Sunday school teacher. It had been a long time since she had bowed her head and listened to such a simple, but sincere prayer. But never before had anyone included her by name in their prayer, as, with a start, she realized Jim was doing.

". . .and please be with Gail and help her as she gets to know us and we get to know her. Amen."

Later that night, Gail lay staring into the darkness thinking again of Jim's prayer. She felt confused. With these people, their religion seemed such a natural part of their everyday life. Mention of God or faith seemed to crop up very regularly in their conversations.

In comparison, her Aunt Harriet's religion was forced, kept for Sunday observances and special meetings. From Jim's attitude over the Bible reading, she knew she only needed to say she didn't want to go to church and nothing would be said. Perversely, she wondered if she should go and see how their church services compared.

She was still wondering about it all when she fell asleep.

Chapter 5

O n Sunday, Mrs. Stevens decided she still was not strong enough to venture out to church. Gail happily grasped the excuse to stay home with her. By the time they all returned, Gail and Marian, as she insisted Gail call her, had thoroughly enjoyed a cooking lesson and established an easy rapport.

The days sped by as Gail attacked the neglected household tasks. Most nights she fell exhausted into bed with the comfortable feeling of having worked well, and slept deeply.

Jim was very busy preparing the machinery for the quickly approaching harvest but, one afternoon, Gail heard him call out to her a moment after the screen door slammed behind him.

She answered him, but her smile faded as she looked up from her never ending ironing and saw the unusual look of determination on his face.

"Right, it's time for you to come with me to pick up the children," he said.

"But I've still got all this. . ." Gail faltered to a stop and felt a tremor pass through her as his eyes hardened.

"You've no choice, I'm afraid, Gail. I have to be sure you know where to go and that you can drive in any emergency. It's essential on a farm."

His tone was quite gentle, but she knew he would be inflexible on this as she knew with a sinking heart that he was right. Reluctantly, she switched off the iron.

He simply turned and headed toward the back door. Slowly, she followed him as he disappeared through the pepper trees. By the time she reached the driveway, he was waiting for her beside the old utility.

"I'm afraid we'll be a bit cramped for room as I don't let the children in the back when we're out on the road," he said carelessly as she felt the relief flow through her. "There's the bread, milk, and mail to fit in, too."

To Gail's horror, he opened the driver's door and gave a mock bow. "After you, madam."

"Oh!" she said blankly.

Blue and brown eyes locked.

"You do have a license, don't you?"

"Yes, of course. But I—"

"In you get, then. I'd rather you practiced with me as a passenger than with the kids."

The firm set of his mouth, and the equally firm hand under her elbow, gave her no option. Before she knew it, she was sitting behind the steering wheel staring at it. The door banged closed beside her and, a moment later, the passenger door also was closed decisively.

"Better do up your seat belt first," Jim said blandly.

Her eyes flew to meet his now expressionless ones. Somehow he knew that her sickness after leaving the airport had been more than simple motion sickness. She fumbled with the seat belt.

"Haven't you ever driven a utility before?"

"Yes. But I—"

"Was it so different from this old bomb?"

Gail took a deep breath. She turned her head to tell him she would not—could not—drive this or any other vehicle.

"Yes, of course you can drive this old ute," he said crisply before she could even open her mouth. "And the Holden, too!" he added for good measure.

Suddenly, a surge of anger swept through Gail. How dare he ignore her feelings about this! Both small, capable hands hit at the steering wheel.

"You do need keys, though."

There was a distinct drawl in the soft voice. Gail snatched the dangling bunch of keys from him and their fingers touched for a brief moment. Then one large, strong brown hand gently held hers while one finger touched one of the keys.

"Ignition key."

How dare he! Her hand was trembling so much that it took a moment to push the key into the ignition and turn it until the motor caught. They jolted forward a couple of paces and the motor died.

"It has a clutch," the soft drawl reminded her.

She gritted her teeth, shoved a foot firmly down on the clutch, and turned on the motor again. She worked the pedals and they jerked forward a little unevenly. But they were moving. Gail gripped the wheel tighter and tried to dodge the potholes, but seemed to succeed in hitting every one. By the time she had driven onto the main road, she was still tense, but had stopped trembling.

"Atta girl!" The soft drawl had a smile in it this time.

Gail glared at him after she had changed fairly smoothly up into top gear, and they were rattling along at a reasonable pace. There wasn't a flicker of a smile on his face as he gazed at the road ahead. She refused to speak to him. There wasn't even any need to give her directions, she fumed. The road was long and straight and led to another wider road that was also without a curve as it disappeared into the hazy distance.

When they arrived, the bus was already there. Jim jumped out, called greetings toward another couple of drivers of large sedan cars, and quickly bustled the three youngsters to the utility.

"Something wrong with the Holden, Jim?" she heard Will ask as he climbed into the back.

She didn't hear Jim's reply but, as she suddenly realized he had come in the utility for her sake, she felt her anger drain away. He could have insisted she drive the Holden.

With Jacky and Robbie squashed in between them on the return trip, chattering about their day, Gail was forced to break her silence. She made suitable comments in the right places, but never once glanced at Jim again. They stopped at the small shelter near the property's front entrance to collect the bread and milk delivered by the mailman and, by the time they reached the house, Gail was beginning to feel very foolish and embarrassed. How stupid Jim must think she is.

After the others had climbed eagerly out of the vehicle, she just sat anchored behind the steering wheel, staring blindly through the windscreen until her door was at last wrenched open.

"Are you all right?"

There was a wealth of concern now in his crisp tones. She didn't look at him, just nodded her head once.

"I'm sorry, Gail. I had to know you could drive. Some days I may not be here, and if ever anyone became sick and needed to be taken to the doctor. . ."

At last, she turned her head and looked at him. Jim smiled at her. It was a very beautiful smile. There was concern, even admiration for her courage in it. But what caught at some hidden part of Gail's heart was the wealth of gentleness lighting up his dark face.

"Good, Gail. You'll do," he said softly, and then leaned right into that dirty old utility and kissed her.

Jim had disappeared along the track to the house before Gail at last moved. She slowly climbed down from the cab of the utility and, for a moment, leaned against it for support. Her legs were a little shaky. Whether it was because of the fact that she had actually driven again or because of that soft, tender kiss, she wasn't quite sure. Her fingers rested on her lips. It had been the merest butterfly of a kiss, right on the mouth.

At last she straightened and started toward the house. Gradually, her steps became more buoyant. After all, Jim had bullied her in his own subtle way. It had only been a gesture to express his apology. And she had actually driven again!

Why then did she go crimson when she reached the kitchen and Jim turned and smiled very gently at her?

In the days that followed, Gail was only too thankful to be able to drive again. Jim was so busy she took over the grocery shopping as well as the school run.

And then the three children came down with chicken pox. Poor Jacky had a sudden, raging fever and had to be fetched all the way from school. The boys were not as sick initially, but all three needed a lot of time and patience until they were allowed back at school. Beth called often and Gail's heart went out to this mother so far away.

And not only Beth rang. The friendly farming community inundated them with offers of help, including one of the young male schoolteachers Gail met the day she had picked up Jacky. One day, while she was finishing off the kitchen curtains, he even asked her for a date, which she politely refused. Will had answered the phone, but when she turned after hanging up, Jim was standing behind her. Her chin lifted a little as she realized he must have heard part of the conversation. She didn't have a clue why he was frowning at her.

"That was Tony," she said, and added quickly as his eyebrow tilted, "Tony Blair, Jacky's schoolteacher."

"Oh, that Tony," said Jim blandly, and then added a little nastily, "A nice enough young fellow, I've found. Asking after his pupil, I suppose?"

Gail was annoyed with herself as she felt her cheeks getting hot for no apparent reason. She nodded rather abruptly and moved past him into the kitchen. Jim followed her. He looked around at the clean walls and cupboard doors. The vinyl chairs no longer dared to have peanut butter or vegemite sticking on them.

"Very nice," he observed.

Gail was still feeling annoyed. She wasn't quite sure if it was with herself, with Tony, or with him. A couple of curtains were still waiting to be threaded back on the rods and, without answering, she walked over and picked them up.

"Gail, I hope you feel free to accept any invitations you might receive," Jim drawled softly.

She swung around just in time to see him rub his hand over his face. Before she could speak, he spoke again.

"You haven't had a day off, in fact, since you arrived." The drawl in the deep tones was even more pronounced and there was a very thoughtful look on his face.

"Oh, it hasn't seemed like an ordinary job at all," she said impulsively. "It's been more like sharing the life and work of a family. I. . .I mean—"

She broke off, suddenly feeling very embarrassed. After all, she was not a member of the family. She was still just an employee and she had known them for only a very short time. He must think her very presumptuous.

Jim had not said a word. He was so still that at last she ventured a glance at him. She stared.

He was beaming from ear to ear. "Why, Gail," he said with a warmth that lit a glow in Gail's lonely heart. "That's the nicest compliment I've heard for a long, long time."

They were still smiling at each other when Will burst into the kitchen.

"Got a date, yet, Gail?" he said breezily.

Gail did not notice that the smile was wiped off Jim's face in a flash as she turned to Will.

"I just might have, young fellow me lad," she said lightly, still grinning widely.

"Don't ask personal questions, Will."

Jim's words were so stern, and the words said with such a snap, that Gail and poor Will gaped at him.

He scowled at them both, turned abruptly, and marched out of the kitchen.

The children had been back at school only a couple of days when Jim arrived home with the mail as usual and handed two bulky letters to Gail, several to his mother, and retired to read his own in peace. With a slight shock, Gail noted that both of the envelopes had Miss G. Brand typed neatly on the front as Sister Jean Drew had arranged.

The first envelope contained a letter from Ann Green. She was delighted, and eagerly tore it open. Ann wrote as she talked, and told all the latest news about her obstetric training, concluding her letter with an appeal to Gail to write to her and let her know why she had disappeared off into the blue the way she had.

Gail sighed as she put the letter down. Ann's hospital talk was like the echo of a past life in which, Gail suddenly realized, she had lost a lot of interest. It was a relief to be away from the wards full of sick and even dying people. She was enjoying home life so much with the Stevenses. They had so quickly accepted her as one of themselves and, as she thought of the noise and frantic life of the city of Sydney, she felt a great yearning to be able to stay on. No one had mentioned any time when they would no longer need her, but she guessed it would not be until well after the harvest had finished. Jim thought they should be able to start fairly soon. Then it would take about three weeks, if all went well, and finish just before Christmas, he had told her.

Gail picked up the other envelope. Two letters fell out, one looking official enough to be an account. Then she saw her lawyer's name printed on the back. She stared at it, and then slowly and reluctantly opened the envelope.

It contained information about the legal winding up of her father's estate and the sale of her old home. It also told her the date in the future for the coroner's inquest into the accident. As she read it through slowly, it brought with it the smell and the reminder of the small office she had visited a couple of times since her discharge from the hospital. Worse than ever, it reminded her afresh of all she had lost.

Her eyes were dry and burning, her throat aching. Why had this come today when for the first time she had begun to feel she might at last be able to find a new tomorrow? She threw it down, and grasped hold of the other letter.

This one was from Sister Jean Drew. She read it through quickly, and then stared blindly into space. So even this haven was threatened. What should she do? She slowly read several parts again. There was no doubt it had been written only after a great deal of careful thought. It seemed that Sister Drew's main concern was that she had persuaded Gail to change her name, but there was something else about the letter Gail couldn't quite put her finger on, and she began to feel more and more uneasy as she read.

"You see, my dear," Sister Drew had written, "I'm afraid I'm far too impulsive. I still have so much to learn about letting God control my life—and my lips. And so I have put you in what I realize is a position of deceit. I've become more and more convinced that God would never want one of his children to use deceit as we have, even with the best of motives. So I think you should talk to Marian at least.

"Have they told you about Beth's husband yet? I'm sure they

would have, and so I guess by this time you know the rest of my plan as well. I hope you can forgive me if I have caused you more hurt. I did so want you to live in a loving Christian home for a while.

"Do please let me know as soon as you can how you've been getting on. Perhaps Marian and Jim know already. I sincerely hope so."

She concluded her letter by urging Gail to let her know if ever there was anything at all she could do for her. And then she added, "My dear, I know you have lost all those who loved you deeply. I want to tell you that over these past few months, you have become very, very dear to me. You have been constantly in my prayers. Oh, how I long for you to have that close relationship with God through Jesus Christ. He alone can fill your life with meaning and purpose again."

As Gail read her final words over and over, the tears were at last released and streamed down her cheeks. The hard knot in her throat gradually eased.

Sister Drew had signed herself as "Your loving friend."

Once before she had mentioned to Gail that the only One Who could really help her was Jesus Christ. Lying in her hospital bed of pain and bitter loss, she had barely listened then. Now, although worried about the future, she felt warmed by the love that reached out to her from the pages of the letter. Gail supposed that the plan she mentioned might be something to do with this "becoming a Christian" business.

But what should she do?

She knew very well by now the high standards Jim and his mother lived by. They would probably despise her. She couldn't lose their respect and friendship now. Where would she go? Back to the once earnestly desired haven of a lonely room in the Nurses' Home?

She shuddered.

Here, she was part of a family again. Inevitably, the Stevenses would have to know.

But not just yet, her lonely heart cried. Not just yet.

The rest of that day she drove herself ceaselessly. She thought of all the reasons why it was best not to say anything for a while. She would probably have to leave once they knew. They needed her help too much, until at least the harvest, she tried to convince herself.

Gail went to her room early that night, telling Jim she had a headache, which was perfectly true by then. She missed the sharp, intense look he gave her as she dejectedly left. But several times during the evening, Gail had caught Marian staring at her with a strange expression on her face. she had also been very quiet for most of the day.

She must know something's upset me, thought Gail, and almost panicked at the possibility of facing awkward questions.

It was a relief to lie staring into the darkness, away from that searching glance. She so much dreaded the questions that would have to be answered when she told them her real name. She couldn't even allow herself to think about the accident, let alone talk about it. *Even to Jim*, she thought for no real reason before tossing and turning for what seemed hours.

There was something tight around her. Holding her down. She couldn't get away. She couldn't breathe.

And someone was screaming. . .over and over. . .

"No! No! No! Leave me alone! Let me go. They're burning. . . burning. . ."

It was dark. So dreadfully dark. She couldn't move.

Then hands were holding her firmly. Warm, comforting hands. Strong hands. There was a beam of light, a tender voice. She stopped struggling and felt herself lifted and held against something warm with a steady throb. Crooning, soothing words reached out to her.

"Hush now, Gail, dear. It's all right. Only a bad dream. Wake up now. . . ." Gradually, the dreadful moaning and shuddering eased. At last she stirred and reluctantly moved away from her secure haven.

"Jim?" she whispered hoarsely.

"Yes, it's only me. You were calling out, and I came," he murmured simply.

She felt the warmth of his arms leave her as she sank back on her pillow and stared up at him. He had switched on the bedside lamp. It's light shone on his pale, anxious face. As she looked at him, slow tears began to trickle down her cheeks. She threw up one hand and covered her eyes. She felt his warm fingers close gently around her other hand.

"I haven't had that nightmare for such a long time," she managed at last. "I can never remember what it's about. Only I'm so scared when I wake up."

Jim remained sitting silently on the side of her bed, just holding her hand until she stirred again with a deep, shuddering sigh.

"Would you like to talk about it?"

She froze.

"No," she replied at last in a frightened whisper, and pulled her hand away from his warmth.

"Would. . .would you like me to make you a hot drink, or just an aspirin—"

Gail abruptly interrupted his low, hesitant words. "Just an aspirin would be fine."

He brought her the medicine with some water to drink.

"I'll be okay, now. Thanks, Jim," she felt compelled to say to him while he stood silently beside her.

She slid down in the bed and turned her head away as though she couldn't bear to have him see her tear-stained face.

"Gail, you know you're going to have to talk to someone about what's troubling you." She didn't move, and she heard him sigh, and then felt the brush of his lips on her forehead. "Just call if you need anything," he said very softly, and then he was gone.

Gail lay in tense huddle until faint light crept through the window and at last she dozed off.

They all overslept. There was such a rush to take the children to catch their school bus that no comment was made about dark circles under two pairs of eyes.

Gail retreated into herself; Jim made no attempt to break through the barrier of averted eyes and compressed lips.

In the days that followed, he never referred to that night even though Gail drove herself mercilessly. She was vaguely aware that he and his mother anxiously watched over her. They both made a few attempts to get her to slow down. She tried to smile and even made a weak joke about employers usually urging their workers to do more work, while hers tried to stop her. Marian had looked hurt and Jim had just scowled and walked away.

After that, Gail made a determined effort to be bright. She knew by the look on Marian's face that she was fooling no one. The tension in the house increased until even the children began to eye her warily. Before, they had accepted her freely and easily into the pattern of their lives as only young children can.

It couldn't have lasted, Gail acknowledged much later. The day it all blew up had been a particularly hot one. Despite the heat, Gail had still insisted on doing some more baking to finish filling the freezer before the harvest commenced. Marian had stayed in the hot kitchen and helped her, despite all of Gail's arguments. They prepared a cool salad for the evening meal. By then, Marian's face was white and drawn.

Straight after tea, Jim packed his mother off to bed. Will raced off with some friends who picked him up each Friday to take him to the youth fellowship meeting at the church hall. The children were told to do their homework by such a stern Uncle Jim that they went into the lounge room without a single protest and watched a favorite movie on television.

Gail apprehensively glanced at Jim as he strode back into the kitchen and picked up a tea towel to help her with the dishes.

"You know, there was nothing I could do," said Gail anxiously. It was the first time she had ever seen him really angry. "Your mother just ignored me. She organized us both in the kitchen and insisted on racing around."

"Righto, righto! I get the message!" Controlled anger seethed in the deep voice. He remained silent until Gail reached down into the cupboard for something to scour the saucepans. Then he exploded.

"Oh no you don't!" Jim flung down his towel. He snatched the pan from Gail as she began to vigorously scrub it.

"That wretched thing is clean of food and can do without a polish tonight! Gail! You don't know when you've had enough. But I do!" he roared. "You're not going to do another thing now. You're going into the lounge room to put your feet up and relax. You can watch television, or read, or even talk to me—or go to bed for all I care! But you're not washing one more teaspoon tonight! Or mending another school shirt! Or sewing on another button! Or helping Jacky with her home-work! Or. . .or any other thing you can dream up!"

While he roared, brown hands whipped plates away into cup-boards at a furious rate. Doors slammed shut. Blue eyes flashed with fire. As he finished the tirade, he grabbed Gail's arm, and began to bundle her out of the kitchen.

They were almost to the door when, to Gail's absolute horror, she felt the tears of exhaustion and hurt at his anger well up and a small sob escaped.

Gail felt hot with embarrassment when she thought about it later. But then, it seemed the most natural thing in the world to rest her aching head on his shoulder when he sighed at her and drew her to himself.

Then, Jim put both of his strong arms right around her. It was the same comfort she had known the time of the nightmare. It was bliss. It was peace. She relaxed completely against his solid warmth. The tears trickled down her ashen cheeks. She felt his breath stir her hair. For a moment, he seemed to envelope her even closer into himself and then his arms relaxed. She felt a large handkerchief begin to mop up her wet cheeks, and only then did she fight for self-control and move away from him.

Jim pulled out a chair, and gently sat her down. He turned away to fetch a glass of water and, when he returned, placed it on the table near her before he, too, sat down. He frowned down at his clasped hands resting on the table and was very still as she picked up the glass and sipped from it.

He certainly knows the value of silence, Gail found herself think-ing as at last she raised her head and looked at him.

"I'm sorry, Gail. I shouldn't have spoken like that, especially when you're so tired."

He rubbed his hand over his face with the gesture that Gail sud-denly recognized, with a little shock, had become not only very famil-iar but very dear to her since that first time in Sister Drew's office.

"You're very tired, too," she said huskily after a pause.

"Yes," he said briefly. "All this work on the machinery should have been finished ages ago. It's nearly done now. Another few hours tomorrow should do it." He stopped, and after a moment said slowly, "Gail, you've been driving yourself too hard. Perhaps you don't realize it, but you're making it all even harder on Mum. And me."

Her lips opened to protest, and he added quickly, "No, don't say anything, but I know that her overdoing it today was her own way of trying to help you not do so much. She's very worried about you." His voice dropped, and he said very softly, "We both are, Gail."

Gail's head drooped down as she continued the battle to control herself. She gritted her teeth as the pressure mounted.

"I didn't bring you here to slave like this. Some of the house could have waited—"

"No, no!" Gail burst out. With a sense of helplessness she heard herself say, "You don't understand! I've got to keep busy. I can sleep at night then. I don't have to lie awake in bed. I don't have time to. . . to remember. . . ."

The last words were barely audible as her head went down on the table. Sobs—deep wrenching sobs—started to rip through her frail body.

At first Jim sat as though stunned—these were more than tired tears. They came from some deep hidden well and showed the depth of the pain that was tearing her to pieces.

"Dear God, help her," he choked, and was half out of his chair when she raised her head.

"I'm. . .I'm. . .sorry. . .I'm. . .so. . . ," she gasped between sobs.

As she rose, shaking violently, Jim was beside her. She shrank from his touch, shook her head, and blindly groped toward the doorway.

"The. . .the children. . .I'll be all right. . .I. . ." She moved out into the hallway and added softly, hopelessly, "Somehow. . .have to be. . ."

Jim let her go. As she stumbled to her room, she was vaguely grateful that he had not tried to stop her. Some grief was too poignant, too private, for any audience.

Once safely in her room, she fell across the bed. The sobs were moans of anguish. Tears that had been stifled so many times flowed like a fountain bursting out of an irrepressible spring.

Gradually, the storm subsided. The physical and mental strain of the past few days took their toll, and she fell into a deep, deep sleep.

The exhausted woman did not hear the hushed voices of Jacky and Robbie as Jim put them to bed. He answered their anxious questions as best he could, helping them to say their prayers for poor Gail who had been crying because of some very sad things that had happened to her.

Will came home late and found the screen door tied back so he wouldn't forget and let it slam. An exhausted Jim came out of the lounge room cautioning him to silence, briefly explaining.

Several times, Jim had crept to Gail's door and listened intently. Once or twice he nearly went in to her while she was still sobbing. Will had been in bed for some time when Jim went to listen once more. His knock was very soft before he opened the door and crept across the room. Light from the open doorway fell on the curled up Gail on the bed.

He stood there for a while, rigidly watching her even breathing, with only the very occasional catch of breath from the storm of tears. Then large, calloused, but tender hands finally moved to slip off her shoes and ease her beneath the blankets.

He yielded to the temptation to kiss her very gently on the lips he had so briefly touched once before. Her deep sigh made the tall figure straighten and freeze as she rolled onto her side. In the dim light, he saw her lips tilt in a smile. She murmured something he couldn't catch, and she snuggled deeper into her pillow as a child does when she knows she is secure and loved.

The man's heart was breaking as he stumbled into his own bedroom, onto his knees beside his bed, and cried out to the One Who had never failed him.

Chapter 6

The slam of the screen door woke Gail the next morning. She stirred and stretched luxuriously. Then she stilled as she remembered the previous night. Her eyes felt sticky and her throat dry. She frowned, trying to remember if she had removed her shoes, and was sure she had not. And someone must have pulled back the blankets and covered her. She glanced at her watch and sat bolt upright. As she began to scramble from the bed there was a brief knock on the door.

"It's only me," Jim's voice called.

The memory of his warmth and comforting arms brought a confused blush to her face. What a spectacle she had made of herself!

"Come on, Gail, you sleepyhead. It's late."

Gail tried to straighten her badly crumpled dress before calling reluctantly to him to come in.

Jim grinned at her as though it was the most natural thing in the world to sleep all night in daytime clothes. With a flourish, he placed a tray across her knees, stepped back, and gave a mock bow. "Your servant, madam!"

Gail looked anywhere but at his face. She felt the tide of red spreading wildly across her face.

"And I did cook you an egg this time, and I cooked the toast, and I buttered it, too. So make sure you eat every crumb. And hurry up. We're going on a picnic."

He shot the last words at her as he went out the door.

She looked at the daintily arranged tray. It was the same as her first morning except for the boiled egg. This time, the rosebud was red and even its thorns had been broken off.

When every crumb was gone, she quickly pulled out her clothes for the day and raced to the bathroom for a quick shower.

Marian was buttering several slices of bread when Gail carried her tray into the kitchen. Without giving her a chance to murmur the apology trembling on her lips, Marian said briskly, "Hello, my dear. I'm glad you've had a good rest. Now, if you'd like to rescue those boiling eggs on the stove and mash them, we'll finish making these sandwiches. I've packed some cake, fruit, and drinks. I thing that's all we need for our picnic."

Gail quickly did as she was asked, relieved that no explanation was apparently necessary, and said slowly, "I thought Jim still had some work to do on the header?"

"Jim laid down the law this morning. No more work today. We're going to the river for a swim and a picnic. About time, too. We've all been working far too hard without a break."

The older woman's voice was filled with gentle compassion, and Gail raised her head and looked at her miserably. Marian hesitated for a moment, and then put her hands on Gail's shoulders and looked into the dark brown eyes, bright with unshed tears.

"My dear, Jim told me about last night. He feels very ashamed at upsetting you. We've become very fond of you in the short time you've been here, Gail. We know that something tragic has happened to you in the past. Whenever you feel able to, we'd count it a privilege to share your suffering. Talking a little about it may help you, too."

Gail swallowed, managed a brief nod, and then reached out and gave Marian a quick hug, kissed her on the cheek, and moved back to the table, not trusting herself to speak.

"Now, if you've finished with those eggs, I'll slap them on this bread and you could go out to the laundry and bring in the cooler. Then, we might be ready when they come up from the sheds."

Marian's brisk words sounded very like her son at his bossiest and, when a slightly bemused Gail returned, Marian was cutting the sandwiches as though her life depended on it.

"Bathing suits," Marian said rapidly. "Just thought of them. I do hope Beth packed the children's, otherwise they'll have to wear an old pair of shorts. Do go through their drawers, Gail, and grab a few towels out of the linen cupboard. I hope you have a suit?"

"No. Sorry, afraid that's something I didn't buy."

As Gail raced out of the room, she thought of the shopping spree Aunt Harriet had taken her on to replace all her clothes destroyed by the fire that had raged through the wrecked car. Suddenly, she was amazed to realize it was the first time the unbidden memory had lost most of its jabbing pain.

It was a scramble to get ready and there was no time left for dwelling on other things. The children were excited and in everyone's way until Jim banished them to the back seat while the adults finished loading the car.

Gail had caught some of the children's excitement, and never gave a thought to the green Holden into which they were packing the picnic gear. At the last moment, she raced inside for some forgotten travel rugs and, when she returned, breathlessly accepted the seat in the front as Jim held the door open for her. She was busy passing the rugs over to Marian as the car went into motion. As she turned around and automatically grabbed for her seat belt, she stilled. Robbie was bouncing up and down in the center of the wide front seat. Across the top of his head her glance caught Jim's very serious expression.

"Okay?" he queried softly.

She took a deep breath, and suddenly it was all right. "I'm fine."

His answering smile reminded her vividly and unexpectedly of that soft kiss in the utility. Color flooded her cheeks and she quickly turned away. She missed the way Jim's smile changed to a broad grin of sheer amusement.

The car was eventually parked under some tall river gum trees on the bank of a gently flowing river. As they all scrambled from the car, a flock of pink and gray galahs rose with a screech. Only Jim's roar stopped the children from rushing down the grassy slope to the water.

"Jacky and Robbie! No one goes near the water until the car's unloaded, you're in your suits, and I'm ready, too! Come here you terrors and spread out this blanket for your grandmother."

Reluctantly, the children helped the adults set up the gear. Then,

Will took off his clothing under which were his swimming briefs, while Gail helped two wriggling young ones do the same thing.

"Come on, Uncle Jim," they chorused impatiently as he appeared in his swimming trunks. They cheered, poised for flight. Jim quirked one eyebrow at Gail.

"Sorry," she laughed, "no swimming suit."

"Well, you can jolly well come for a paddle. Roll up those trousers and let's put these three out of their misery."

Gail hesitated, and glanced at Marian.

"Go on, off you go, dear. I might wander down later."

As they raced off, Will took a hand of each child. Jim reached out and grabbed Gail's hand and pulled her after them. Neither saw Marian's rather startled look at her son.

"Come on. I've got to make sure there are no unexpected hazards," said Jim.

"Hazards?" she gasped breathlessly as she tried to keep up with his long strides. His strong hand gripped hers tightly as they scrambled down the steep slope to the others.

"Deep holes, logs washed down, even broken glass sometimes. Have to be careful with rivers, and we haven't been here since last summer."

Apparently, the children were used to this first inspection of the waterhole for safety. They sat on a ledge and dangled their legs in the water while Will and Jim waded in and swam and dived for a few minutes.

"The water gets pretty deep over there." Jim pointed a few meters downstream. "So stay up at this end and you'll be safer."

Robbie let out an Indian warwhoop and jumped in. Gail sprang back, but some of the water splashed on her.

"Robbie, you beast!" wailed Jacky as she wiped some water from her eyes. "Wait for me!"

Gail was delighted to see they both could swim quite well. She sat down on a grassy outcrop and slipped her feet into the cool water. After a brief swim, Jim came back and hauled himself out and perched on a log near her. Suddenly, she felt self-conscious. Except for that brief moment in her room, this was the first time they had been alone since the previous night, and she wondered how she could apologize for her breakdown.

Jim sat watching the antics of Will with the two squealing children. The silence became a little strained.

"Jim, about last night. . . ," she at last blurted out.

He turned his head. His face had lost all its twinkle and sadness filled his eyes. "You don't have to worry about that, Gail," he said quietly.

Suddenly, it became important to make him understand. She heard her own voice saying, "But I'd like you to know why. . .why I was upset. Why I've been so silly. . .working so hard."

The blue eyes went very dark. He turned his gaze back to the swimmers. "You don't have to if it upsets you too much. But sometimes it does help to talk it out." He hesitated, and then continued slowly. "Mum told me your brother was killed in a car accident. You limp sometimes at the end of a long day. Although I think not as much as when you first arrived." He paused again. "Were you driving the car?"

The soft query shook her. How dreadful if she had been! She swallowed hard.

"No," she said softly at last, "my father was driving."

He stiffened, but was silent. She took a deep breath and closed her eyes.

"I was the only survivor."

Even as the whispered words escaped, she realized for the first time that this was what haunted her the most. She felt guilty for still being alive.

Jim bit off a soft exclamation and, when she opened her eyes, he was watching her. There was no condemnation there, only compassion, and some other expression she could not quite make out.

Will and the children had moved closer to them. As he stood up, Jim reached out and pulled Gail to her feet.

"Let's go for a walk," he muttered.

He released her while they slipped their thongs back on, and then led the way with brisk strides along a track that followed the river bank until it curved out of sight of the waterhole.

Gail wished he would grab for her hand again. There had been something comforting and strengthening about that firm grip. Even when the track suddenly led up a steep incline, he did not touch her. He stood at the top and waited for her, staring down at the river that was flowing gently below the high bank at this point.

"Do you think you could tell me about it?" he asked softly at last. "Sometimes it helps." He carefully refrained from looking at her as he continued. "There were others in the car?"

She stood silent and still, trying to find the right words, the right place to start.

At last Jim turned abruptly and she saw him swallow as he looked at her. His eyes lingered on her hair, her face, as though he were seeing them for the first time. Then his blue eyes were probing and searching out the very secrets of her innermost being.

She had the absurd thought for a moment that his hands had begun to lift to reach out and gather her to him, but he only moved them behind his back as he leaned against the trunk of a river gum.

Her eyes jerked away from him. And then the words were there. Jim stood like a statue as they began to stumble out.

"Mum and Dad and Bill had come down for my graduation from nursing school." Gail did not see the startled look on Jim's face. "We were on the way home. Wayne. . . ," her voice choked.

She swallowed painfully, and turned her head and looked at him. His eyes were filled with pain. She licked her dry lips and forced herself to answer his unspoken question.

"Wayne. . .he was my fiancé."

Later, Gail was to remember the look of desolation that flashed into Jim's eyes with wonder.

"Was?"

"Yes."

Jim turned and moved along the track; his hands were clenched fists. Gail slowly followed him. It had helped to say their names out loud. Suddenly, she wanted to tell Jim about it all. It had been bottled up for too long.

Jim at last stopped and sat on the ground, using the trunk of a tree for a backrest. As he looked up at Gail, his tight lips hinted at his stern self-control. He invitingly patted the ground near him and she slipped down beside him. This time, he did reach out and take her hand gently. Then, he waited.

"The. . .the car was exactly the same color and model as yours," she began softly, and felt his hand tighten for a moment.

Once, started, the words flowed out in a torrent. With them, fled the last of the tension built up over those long, weary months. He listened quietly, except for an occasional soft question. She still could not remember the lead up to the actual smash, or her brief bouts of consciousness she had been told that she had had before coming to in the hospital. Jim shared her anguish as she told him of those first dreadful days of trying to cope with the realization that they had all been killed.

He was angry when she told him about that last confrontation with Aunt Harriet. But, not once did she mention the still-hospitalized driver of the truck, except to briefly state that he was "only injured."

"So you're one of Aunt Jean's girls as she calls you," Jim mused as she at last fell silent.

Gail caught her breath. She hadn't mentioned her last visit to Sister Drew's office. She knew now she would have to tell him her real name. It didn't really matter anymore. Perhaps he wouldn't think too badly of her now that he knew what had prompted it.

"Well, I didn't want to talk about any of this," she began slowly. "Jim, there's something else. Your Aunt Jean—"

"Jim! Mum says it's lunch time!" Will was waving to them from a short distance away.

Jim waved back. "Coming." He scrambled to his feet and looked ruefully at his grass and dirt-covered swimmers. "I'll have to wash these off before lunch," he said ruefully. "Come on, let's run. We can finish talking another time."

Gail hung back for a moment. "Jim, I'd rather you didn't mention this to anyone, not even your mother. She has enough to worry about with Beth and I—"

"I won't mention a word."

His eyes flashed with a strange expression, and Gail received a jolt as she had the sudden absurd feeling that Will's waiting figure was preventing Jim from reaching out to her. He turned away abruptly with a smile that didn't reach his eyes. "We'd better hurry up or they'll have eaten all the food."

Marian looked intently at Gail when she arrived a little breathless after having run nearly all the way.

"Jim sat in the dirt in his wet togs and is washing it off."

Gail felt the color pour into her face at the suddenly quizzical expression in Marian's eyes, and hid her face as she busied herself getting out the cups and drinks from the cooler.

They were all hungry and set to demolish the huge pile of food. As she ate, Gail was feeling almost lightheaded with relief at being able to talk as she had to Jim. She wasn't even worried anymore about that ridiculous name change business. Later, Jim had said.

After lunch, Jim and Will insisted on taking the children for a wander along the river bank.

"You two women make sure you try and have a sleep while it's quiet," was Jim's parting remark as he made to follow the others.

The two women grinned at each other and, as Jim walked away, two loud snores obediently came from the reclining figures on the rugs. Through her half-closed eyelids, Gail saw him pull a face at them before racing off with a smile.

Marian and Gail opened one eye each as the silence descended around them again except for the warble of a couple of magpies nearby. Marian sat up and cautiously looked around, and then they laughed at each other and relaxed again on the rugs. There was a comfortable silence.

Gail rolled onto her back and looked up through the gnarled branches of the old gum tree. The two black and white magpies flew up through the topmost leaves.

Just as well they are friendly today, she thought idly.

Briefly she remembered another picnic when she was a child. A magpie had swooped down and viciously pecked at her head. It had repeated its attacks until her parents had at last packed up and moved to another part of the park.

Gail closed her eyes. A tear slid out and slipped slowly down her cheek. She knew it was not just a tear for the past, but because she had at last actually been able to let herself dwell on a bittersweet memory. There was still the ache and the sense of loss, but the sheer agony had gone. Deliberately, she recalled other picnics. Wayne had only taken her once. He had claimed that he didn't like to share his food with the flies and the ants. That picnic had always stood out as a dismal failure, and the first time they had ever had a serious argument.

Gail thought of Jim. She had never met a man who showed such sensitivity and understanding of her needs. He was wonderful with the children. With wonder, she realized there was an integrity and quiet strength about him that she had never before seen in a man, not even Wayne. Many times she had sat quietly, listening to the exchanges between the three Stevenses. They all hated deception and double-dealing of any kind. And yet, she now recognized, they never really hated the people who behaved differently from their standards. They said what they thought to folk like Hilda, but always were kindly in their attitudes toward them.

"You awake, Gail?" Marian whispered softly.

Gail rolled onto her side and smiled at her. "You're not doing what you were told, either?"

"No." Marian's voice sounded husky.

Gail pushed herself up on one elbow so she could see the older woman's face better. "Are you all right?"

"Oh, yes," Marian answered. "I just didn't want to lie here thinking any longer."

Her voice cracked on the last word. Gail saw her teeth grip her bottom lip before she flung an arm up across her eyes.

"Would you like another cup of coffee? I think there's some hot water still in the thermos," Gail said gently after a few moments when her companion hadn't moved or spoken again.

"No, thanks, Gail." She turned on her side suddenly to face Gail. "I've been feeling a bit down since getting Beth's letter yesterday."

Letters from Jim's sister had arrived regularly for the children and their grandmother but their contents were rarely mentioned. She had felt it a little strange that neither of the children ever spoke about their father except to automatically ask God to "bless Daddy" in their prayers.

Gail had never seemed to get around to asking how long they expected her to stay or how the sick man was progressing. She knew how remiss she had been, and felt ashamed.

"How is your son-in-law, Marian? Somehow I've never had the chance to ask before," she said apologetically.

"He's not showing any improvement at all. Beth said in this last letter that he has withdrawn right into himself and hardly ever talks, even to her. Before this he was a very difficult patient. The doctors say that the. . .the accident is preying on his mind. Beth wants Jim to fly down again. And that's what's worrying me."

The older woman sat up and rested her chin on her knees, avoid Gail's eyes.

"I haven't told Jim about that part of the letter, and I'm not sure if I should or not. He has spent so much time and money on trips to Sydney recently. The harvest gets underway next week, and he has so much on his mind. I've been lying here praying for wisdom. Jim has been the only one who seems to be able to get through to Arthur."

She hesitated, about to speak again, when Gail quickly asked the question that had crossed her mind several times. Until now she had never felt free to ask.

"What are his actual injuries, Marian?"

She raised her head and looked steadily at Gail. "The first few weeks they had to concentrate on second degree burns on his back and legs. He also had a spinal injury. Has no one ever told you that he's paralyzed from the waist down?"

She waited tensely for Gail's answer.

"Oh, no!" Gail was appalled. Several things fell into place. This alone explained his protracted stay in the hospital, and Beth's determination to be near him. She stared silently at Marian, who was watching her intently with a strange expression.

"You see, Gail, there's someone who should go and see him." She spoke very slowly and with a peculiar intonation. She hesitated as Gail began to feel rather mystified. "This. . .this person should assure him that the accident wasn't his fault. The courts haven't cleared him yet, but—"

"Are you girls talking instead of sleeping?"

Jim was striding toward them with a mock scowl creasing his face. It seemed to Gail that Marian took a moment to recover and find her voice before finally saying with a forced laugh, "Oh, dear. Gail, we've been sprung."

Although her voice was determinedly cheerful, she was still on the receiving end of one of Jim's quick penetrating glances. He stood with his hands on his hips, legs astride. He shook his head at his mother.

"Sprung? What kind of word is that, may I ask, Mrs. Stevens?"

"Will's talk, young man—and yours, too, unless my ears have deceived me a few times." She reached out her hands and he hauled her up. "Ouch! I'm stiff. And I like talking to Gail, you bossy bully. She's my kind of person." She smiled gently at Gail as she scrambled to her feet. Before Jim could retort, she whipped up the rug and began shaking the grass and dirt from it as she continued swiftly, "Gail, if you'd like to stretch your legs and chase those other children away from that patch of sand, this bossy old thing can start packing all the stuff away in the car."

Gail laughed at the slightest emphasis on the word "other." Jim's lips were smiling, but he eyed her steadily before she turned away. As she disappeared down the bank, they heard her gaily call out. Mother and son looked at each other.

"She's a lovely girl, Jim," she said softly. He nodded abruptly, and she added hesitantly. "Jim, dear." She stopped, and took a deep breath. "Do be careful, though. I'm afraid there could be a hard streak in her and I don't want you to be hurt."

"Mum!"

Jim's disapproving exclamation of utter amazement was heard by Gail as she came swiftly back to them. She wondered briefly at the slight constraint they showed toward each other as she helped them pack up and she wished she had had a chance to find out more about what was happening in this delightful family.

The sun was almost at the horizon and the cool air flowing into the car lifted Gail's curls as they sped home. Jacky had triumphed over her brother and now sat between Jim and Gail.

Robbie chattered away in the back to his grandmother about the great dam they had been building in the river, but Jim was very silent, letting Gail respond to Jacky's conversation. She found herself watching him a few times.

Jacky's head at last drooped onto Gail's shoulder, and Marian told Robbie to be quiet while Jacky had a rest. Soon, a peaceful silence reigned. Gail was almost asleep herself when Robbie began softly humming a tune. Will soon picked up the melody and began to sing the words. Gail listened lazily as Jim joined in. Then she realized they were singing about a deer panting for the water like the soul panted for the Lord. It was a haunting melody and Gail strained to hear the words as she stared blindly out the window at the golden paddocks of wheat already being harvested in some places.

One song led to another. Marian joined in a couple of times and it became obvious to Gail that this was a regular feature of car trips. Even the sleepy children even suggested a favorite or two. Gail recognized some of the tunes from her own far-off days at church. Once, she even ventured to hum the melody of one whose words she had forgotten.

Jim must have heard, but didn't glance at her. The next song he chose was an old, very well known hymn, "What a Friend We Have in Jesus."

They all sang it enthusiastically. Gail ventured to softly murmur a few words until suddenly the meaning of what she was singing stung her. She stopped abruptly.

She was not sure if she had ever taken anything "to the Lord in prayer." By these people's standards, she certainly had plenty of reason to pray. And she wasn't quite as sure any more that all religion was a waste of time. It certainly seemed to work for people like Jim and his mother.

Gail did not realize just how the daily evening readings from the

Bible had subtly begun to influence her. The stories of the ancient heroes told in the first part of the Bible had been replaced by stories of Jesus Christ. Quite a few times, Gail had stood and stared at the painting over Jim's bed and wondered. She had gradually become used to hearing herself mentioned specifically in the prayers. It no longer embarrassed her. Instead, she felt warmed and included in the family circle.

The sun had at last slipped below the distant horizon, and it was all so peaceful that Gail was sorry when the car slowed down and swung into the long driveway. Through the dusk, she could see the top of the red corrugated iron roof peeping above the clump of pepper trees.

Gail's heart gave a sudden leap at the sense of homecoming. This place and these people were becoming very familiar and dear to her. She felt a tinge of fear. Loving people could hurt too much. Suddenly, she wondered if she should stay much longer.

But as the car pulled up beside the house, she turned and looked across at Jim as he glanced at her. He smiled gently, and she caught her breath.

She could not leave, yet.

Not yet, her treacherous heart pleaded. *Not yet.*

Chapter 7

S unday morning breakfast was well underway by the time Jim
entered the kitchen. A rather embarrassed Gail glanced up at
him as he said his usual cheerful "good mornings" and poured
himself a cup of tea.

"You have to hurry this morning, Uncle Jim," said Jacky importantly. "We're all helping because Auntie Gail's coming to church,
too."

Gail was busy making toast and didn't see the look of delight that
flashed across Jim's face. His mother did. She frowned suddenly.

"Now, who told her it was my turn to preach?" Jim sounded
severe, and Gail swung around quickly.

She saw the grin on his face and said stupidly, "Why, no one. I. . .
I just thought it was time. I. . .I mean. . ." She took a deep breath and
turned to rescue the toast. "I didn't even know you did preach. Don't
you have a minister?"

"Oh, yes," piped up Robbie. "Only he's boring and they don't
have him every week."

Gail stared, and then smiled weakly as Marian and Jim chuckled.
Will roared. Jacky, however, was scandalized.

"Robbie! What a thing to say! It's just because Uncle Jim is ours
that he's better!"

The children looked curiously at the convulsed quartet. Jacky's
bottom lip began to tremble. A dark tide of red had darkened Jim's
tanned face. His mother came to the rescue.

"Stop! Gail won't know whether to come to church or not." Her
eyes twinkling merrily, she went on to explain. "Rev. Telford is the
minister in Toowoomba who comes and takes the services as often as

he can. Otherwise, a few of the members are rostered. Now, come on, finish your breakfast. We're all making our own beds, too, and then it'll be time to go."

The church was a small weatherboard building in the corner of a paddock not far from the huge grain silos next to the railway line. Trees and shrubs had been planted around the grounds and the grass was neatly trimmed. It gave the general impression of a place well-used but lovingly looked after.

A group of people were standing, talking on the path near the front steps. They called friendly greetings and Marian quickly introduced Gail to the group as a whole.

"Everyone, this is Gail Brand, who has been helping us out. Please tell her your names after the service because we'd better go in now."

That name thing again, thought Gail as she responded a little shyly to the chorus of "hellos."

How she wished she had been able to speak to Jim alone after they had arrived home the night before. She had gone to bed wondering if he was avoiding her by going off to his room so early. Common sense told her now that it had probably been to finish preparing for the service. She frowned. There had still been something this morning. She thought they had been so close on the riverbank, and now he seemed to have retreated.

The inside of the building was as unpretentious as its outward appearance. It was bright with bowls of attractively arranged flowers and the sunshine that streamed through the open windows. As they filed in, a slight, gray-haired man was playing softly on the small electronic organ. A hush and stillness gradually descended on the people. Even the row of young children in the front settled down. A table on the platform was covered with a white throwover and, after a few moments, Jim came through a door at the side and moved quietly to sit on the chair behind it.

During the service that followed, Gail couldn't help making continual comparisons between the simplicity and sincerity of these people with the pomp and ceremony of that other service with Aunt Harriet. Perhaps both types of services were needed by both types of people to draw them to worship. If that were the case, these farmers and their families were her kind of people. Later, she was a little surprised to learn that about half of the congregation that morning were employed in many occupations. Even the local bush nurse had been there.

Gail was ashamed afterwards to realize how her mind had wondered during Jim's sermon after the simple communion service. To start with, she had listened intently, as he spoke with a deep conviction about the importance of knowing Jesus Christ. Jim urged them all to open their Bibles regularly and read and study it that the Holy Spirit could show them Jesus Christ. The idea of Christ's being the one theme of the whole Bible was a new one to Gail. In fact, a good deal of what Jim said she had never remembered hearing before, and she found she couldn't really understand some of it.

As the moments passed, Gail found herself dwelling more on the speaker than on the message. He was wearing the same suit she had seen him in that first time in Sister Drew's office. His face was alight with belief in the truth of the words he was using to convince and encourage his listeners.

What a fine man he is, she thought dreamily. *He not only tells other people to do these things but he does them himself.*

She had often seen his Bible left open on his desk beside other study books. One morning, she had been a little early doing the bedrooms, and his mother had stopped her from going into Jim and Will's room. Jim was running late and would probably still be having what she had called his "devotional time," she had explained matter-of-factly. Perhaps this was another one of the reasons their religion seemed to be so different from Aunt Harriet's. Never once had she seen a Bible in that cold house except carried in the hand to church.

After the service, the conversation seemed to be mainly about the harvest, about bags and bushels of wheat per acre, and the never ending topic of the weather.

"Why, hello, Gail. How are you surviving?"

Gail swung around to face an unsmiling Hilda Garrett. Her own polite smile faded at the hostility she could see in Hilda's face.

"So glad the Stevenses talked you into coming to church at last.

Or did you come because Jim was preaching?"

The venom in the low tones made Gail's cheeks burn. Her chin tilted, but before she could answer, she realized Marian had broken off what she was saying to turn and slip a hand inside Gail's elbow. She gave it a little warning squeeze. Gail glanced at her as Marian gave a light laugh. The faded blue eyes glinted at Hilda.

"Oh, dear, Hilda. Don't make me feel any worse than I do. I'm afraid Gail had to ask if she could come this morning because we neglected to ask her. I think she nearly changed her mind when she found out Jim was preaching." She adroitly changed the subject. "And how are those puppies of yours? Gail says she used to have a dog herself when her father owned a farm. So we think perhaps we might be able to have one for Robbie after all."

Gail felt warmed, protected, and suddenly very much an accepted member of the Stevens family. She wasn't aware that Jim had joined them until his deep voice came from behind her.

"Mum, you villain, have you been conspiring against me?"

He rested his hand casually on Gail's shoulder, and cocked an eyebrow at her. She hoped he couldn't feel her trembling. He looked annoyed and, for a moment, she thought he might be angry with her for obviously having mentioned the pup to his mother. This his hand tightened on her shoulder and she knew he, too, must have heard Hilda's spiteful words.

She forced herself to smile up at him. "We think the pair of us could handle one small boy and his puppy."

"Why don't you come over this afternoon, Jim, and pick it up," Hilda said a little too quickly.

Jim shook his head decisively, "No, Hilda. I'm afraid I have to finish overhauling the header this afternoon. It would be best if Gail drove Mum and the children over after lunch."

"You're working this afternoon?" Disbelief rang in Hilda's voice. "But you never do that on Sunday."

"I never work if it means missing out on church activities," Jim corrected her. "Yesterday, something cropped up and I didn't get it finished."

Gail looked at him, and opened her mouth to speak, but Marian slipped in smoothly with "We'd better get moving, Jim. Gail, would you mind calling the children for me, please?"

When they were at last on their way home, Gail turned to Jim and said quietly, "Jim, I'm sorry you had to leave that work yesterday. We could have gone another day."

He looked gravely back at her. "No, I'm so very glad we. . .we. . ." Very quickly he turned his head away and, after a brief pause, continued more cheerfully, "We all needed that break. I can quite easily finish this afternoon. God knows how important that picnic was and He understands." He hesitated again, and then added slowly, "I try to keep Sunday as the one day in the week different from the others because it's common sense that we need one day of rest. It's not because I believe Sunday is any holier than any other day in a week lived in His presence."

Gail was silent and thoughtful for the rest of the short trip home. That had just about explained the difference between Aunt Harriet and Jim. Her religion was something to be observed on Sundays and all her activities the rest of the week were more for her own gratification than anything else. Jim lived every day as though in God's continual presence. His God did not seem too impressed, either, with outward show. Yet, Jim's intimate relationship with God dictated his very lifestyle.

When she drove up to the Garrett house that afternoon, Gail couldn't help feeling apprehensive about Hilda. However, the man who had been playing the organ that morning came out to the car and was introduced to her as Mr. Garrett.

"I'm sorry I didn't get a chance to speak to you this morning, Gail. Welcome to the Plains." As he took her hand, his face crinkled into laughter lines at her surprised look. "I should have said 'Darling Downs you reckon? The old-timers often call this the Plains—the black soil plains."

The children had said their greetings and raced off to a shed beside the house where there was a chorus of yappings.

"I'm afraid Hilda had a couple of things to do inside. Why don't you join her, Gail, while we follow the children."

Gail only hesitated briefly before smiling brightly to ease Marian's sudden frown and moving towards the house.

The sullen greeting from Hilda was not very encouraging, but after a carefully worded question from Gail, Hilda began telling her about Polly, the puppies' mother, and her successes at local dog shows as she continued with her preparations for afternoon tea.

When Gail showed how impressed she was, Hilda suddenly beamed and pulled out a drawer full of show ribbons and photographs. As she went on preparing a plate of home-cooked biscuits and as Gail examined the contents of the drawer, Hilda explained some of the various points that the judges looked for.

"I'd love to breed and sell collies." Her busy hands stilled for a moment, and then she added in a slightly louder voice, "When Jim and I are married, I'm hoping I'll eventually be able to go in for them in a big way."

"Married!" Gail felt a wave of devastation and shock hit her.

Hilda put a hand up to her face, and her eyes opened wide. "Oh, dear, I shouldn't have said that," she said in a rush, a rather peculiar look of pleading in her eyes. "It. . .it's a secret. Please Gail, forget that I said that."

Gail felt bewildered. "I don't understand," she managed through suddenly dry lips. "Are you and Jim engaged?"

Hilda hesitated. The shrieking whistle blew on the electric kettle as it began to boil. As she poured the water into the teapot, her face was hidden from Gail's searching gaze as she spoke very quickly.

"Well, nothing is official you see. With. . .with Beth's troubles and then his mother. . .well, you see nothing can be said, yet. But Jim and I. . . Please don't tell Jim I said anything, Gail. He'd be very annoyed." She swung around and there was apprehension and fear in her watchful eyes.

Gail swallowed, but her strained voice made Hilda's eyes narrow. "Of course. I'm sure I wish you all the best and I hope—"

When her father came into the kitchen, Hilda thankfully broke off her stumbling words.

The rest of the visit passed for Gail in something of a haze. She didn't see the sharp look Mrs. Stevens gave her and the frown that creased her forehead as she looked thoughtfully at the hectic flush on Hilda's cheeks and her slightly agitated chatter as she served them their afternoon tea.

On the way home, Gail had to force herself not to think about her reactions to Hilda and Jim's plans to marry, and tried to concentrate on the children's excited talk about the puppy, Bonnie.

Gail was helping the children get ready for bed when Jim at last came in for his late tea. It had been hard to wrench the children away from their new pet and Jim was watching television by the time they were settled.

He looked up and smiled at her when she paused in the doorway. It wasn't his usual relaxed grin. To Gail's watchful eyes it held that hint of reserve she had noticed the evening before. Unexpected pain knifed through her.

"Finished at last? Are you going to watch television for a while? I think Mum has headed for bed."

Gail suddenly knew there was no way she could bear to be alone with him just now.

She yawned widely. "I think your mother has the right idea, Jim. Good night."

She thought a look of relief flashed across his face as he murmured good night before turning back to the television. As she showered and prepared for bed, she could no longer stop her mind from dwelling on what Hilda had said. When the light was out and she was staring into the darkness, she recognized at last what her reactions had really been to the news that Jim and Hilda would marry. There had been searing agony and savage jealousy.

She began to tremble, curling up in the bed, clutching the sheet to her tightly.

No. It couldn't be. She mustn't be. Love was pain and grief and sheer hell.

Wayne. Tears trembled on her closed eyelashes. She had loved him dearly. Perhaps in a sense she always would. There was no way she could compare him with Jim. He seemed only a boy compared to the man who had been the mainstay and support of his mother and family for so many years.

And she herself was no longer that same young girl who had so happily planned a future with Wayne. As she thought of him now, she realized it was without the same depth of agony and loss that had enveloped her only a few weeks before. Now, she admitted that was only possible because Jim had begun to fill that special, empty place in her heart.

Suddenly, she sat up and turned on the bed light. Opening the drawer jerkily, she pulled out the photographs. With trembling hands she unwrapped them. She studied the happy family group. Tears blurred her vision. She brushed them away impatiently. Always there would be this sense of loss, but she knew with an overwhelming feeling of relief that she could at last accept that they were gone.

She caressed the edge of the frame for a moment, and then reached over and stood it carefully on her bedside table. Then, she turned her attention to the engagement photo of herself and Wayne. Her smiling, excited face looked plump and girlish, and Wayne seemed so much younger than she remembered. She arranged it beside the other and thought of the last time she had looked at them. Winter was a long way off, spring had leapt into summer, and now she at last could look at the faces of her loved ones and know that the sadness in her heart would lessen as time passed.

"Only because my heart is daring to love again, my darlings," she whispered softly.

She lay back on her pillow and thought long and deeply about Hilda and Jim. She went over every word, every tone of voice that Jim and his mother had used when mentioning Hilda. There had certainly been anger, but perhaps it had been more like affectionate exasperation with someone they had known all their life. The more she dwelt on Jim's attitude to Hilda though, the more bewildered she felt. There had never been the least sign of any love between them that she could remember. Gail's heart lightened a little. Perhaps it had all been a figment of the poor woman's imagination. She would somehow ask Jim despite the promise made to Hilda. There was no need to let Jim know it had been Hilda herself who had mentioned their relationship.

She must have dozed off with the light on, she realized later when a persistent yapping roused her. Her eyes blinked open and the first thing she saw was the smiling faces in the photographs. She smiled sleepily back at them, then was suddenly wide awake. Bonnie was whimpering for her mother.

Gail jumped out of bed, quickly put on her bathrobe over her nightgown, and ran out into the corridor—and straight into a tall, solid figure!

"Oomph! Where's the fire?" said Jim's voice as he grabbed at her to stop her from falling.

"Oh, I'm so sorry," she gasped. "It's the puppy. I was afraid she'd wake everyone up."

"That's where I was heading, too. Only I haven't been to sleep yet. Come on, there he goes again."

"She."

Jim didn't pause in his stride as they hastened towards the pitiful sounds now getting more and more frenzied.

"What do you mean?"

Gail wished he would stop holding her arm. All she could think of was the warmth running straight through her like an electricity charge.

"Gail, what did you mean—she?"

"Oh," she gave a nervous giggle as she realized she had forgotten her instinctive correction. "I'm afraid we were misled about the dog. He's a she and called Bonnie, not Bennie."

With relief, she felt him release her as he reached up to switch on the patio light. "On, no! Beth will want to shoot me as it is. She'll just love having all the problems that go with a female dog around the place. Thanks Hilda!"

Well, that certainly did not sound like a man in love!

Gail's heart was doing all kinds of peculiar things as they entered the laundry and were greeted with a rapturous welcome from Bonnie. She bent to pick her up, but Jim stopped her.

"Please, don't make too much of a fuss over her or she'll demand us all night. Look in that cupboard for a hot water bottle, please, Gail. I think Mum keeps an old one in there."

They stayed, trying to settle the pup down, until at last a thoroughly exasperated Jim said, "We're wasting our time—and our sleep. Every time we make for the door, she starts again. I'm afraid we're just going to have to leave her."

She looked up at him rather pleadingly but, before she could say anything, he creased his forehead fiercely, but his eyes twinkled at her as he said firmly, "And no, he can't go to sleep in your room, or he'll end up on Robbie's bed and then my dear sister will certainly murder us both!"

He ushered her to the door and turned the laundry light off as he added, "Let's just hope she doesn't do this for too many nights in a row."

He pulled the door closed as Gail went ahead of him down the path. The light from the patio was cut off by the corner of the laundry and the ground was only dimly lit for a few paces.

As Gail went to take a step, something slithered quickly across the path. She screamed and jumped back, bumping into Jim. He grabbed her around the waist and pushed her aside.

"What is it?" he said sharply.

Gail was shaking. "I'm not sure. I. . .I think a snake just. . .just. . ."

"It didn't bite you, did it?"

"No, no. I nearly trod on something as it went across the path."

Jim quickly moved to turn on the laundry light again, much to Bonnie's delight, and peered out across the uncut lawn.

"I can't see anything, now. You run onto the patio while I leave this light on."

Gail fled. Jim joined her a moment later. Her face was still very pale her lips were trembling as she faced him.

"I hate snakes!" she said passionately.

"Don't we all! Oh, Gail, you poor dear."

As though of their own volition, Jim's arms reached out and pulled her into that comforting haven she had known before. Her body was still trembling and he held her closer as though to stop it with his own strength. It suddenly had the opposite effect—her trembling increased.

Gail felt Jim's body tremble in response. She lifted her head and her eyes searched his. Unmistakable passion filled his with a brilliance she could hardly believe. Then his head descended and she gasped as his lips captured hers.

The kiss was timeless. Warmth flooded through Gail's body and she felt as though her whole being was quickening with new life—with love.

Then, suddenly, the spell was broken. Jim wrenched himself away. Gail swayed at the sudden loss of support. She murmured an automatic protest and would have moved towards him.

His agonized, convulsed face stopped her. He opened his mouth to speak as a chill crept over her. He clamped his lips shut, and she saw him close his eyes tightly and swallow before trying again. She stood frozen and watched him with a dawning anguish of her own.

"I'm most terribly sorry, Gail. I. . .I had no right to kiss you like that. Would you please forgive me? It won't happen again."

The words seemed torn from him. And then the screen door banged and he was gone.

Chapter 8

The harvest commenced the next day in sweltering heat. After a sleepless night, Gail forced herself out of bed when the alarm rang. Her first desire after going to her room had been to pack her bags. The confirmation of Hilda's claim hurt unbearably. But, there was the harvest. There was Marian and the children. Heavy-eyed, she made her way to the kitchen to find Mrs. Stevens already in control.

"Good morning, Gail. I believe you had trouble with Bonnie last night?"

"Did. . .did Jim get up to go to her again? I'm afraid I just stayed in bed and listened to her yelping."

She avoided the sharp look Marian flashed at her while she continued making the children's lunches. "You. . .and Jim, too, for that matter, certainly look as though you didn't get much sleep last night."

Gail felt a wave of warmth creep into her cheeks. She busied herself pouring out a cup of tea before answering in a deliberately casual voice. "I did get some sleep." She didn't add that it wasn't until dawn before she had been able to drift into an unrefreshing doze. "Has Jim slept in?" she said instead.

"Oh, no. He's been up for ages. We won't see him now until smoke-o time."

"Smoke-o?"

Marian grinned. "Not heard that one? Morning tea to you. The header will be rolling as soon as the moisture content allows."

"Oh, yes, I think I remember Will telling me once that with bulk handling it was no good starting until the dew had dried off the grain. Phew! It's so hot I shouldn't think it will take long today."

"Yes, that's right," Marian said a little absent-mindedly. "Gail,

91

once you get back from taking the children up to get the bus, we'll have to start packing the smoke-o things. I'll go out with you today, but in the future it will be your job to take it out to the men. I'm afraid my silly old asthma doesn't like all the dust stirred up. Now, I think it's time the children were up."

There was apparently going to be no time for leisurely cups of tea with breakfast while the harvest was on, Gail realized as she quickly swallowed the remainder of hers and raced off to see to the children.

That day set the pattern for the next couple of weeks. In blistering heat, the paddocks were reaped one by one. Jim had employed a couple of truck drivers and someone to relieve him on the header at times. Jim and Gail managed to avoid each other as much as possible and only exchanged such stilted conversation that Gail noticed Marian frown in bewilderment at them a few times, although in some strange way she also seemed relieved.

Except when the whole family went to church each Sunday, Marian never left the house during those hectic days. Gail ferried the thermos flasks of tea as well as cool drinks with boxes of food to and fro over the denuded paddocks. She learned to carefully drive the Holden in the tracks made by the trucks and utility as she made her way across the stubble to where the header was eating deeper and deeper into the golden wheat.

She had little time to think during the day. At night, she was too exhausted to lie awake for long brooding on her growing love for Jim. For, try as she might, day by day she found her feelings deepening. The memory of that kiss could not be banished. No matter that after his distressed apology there had been no need to ask about Hilda. Although there had been no occasion for them to be alone since that night, sometimes Gail had caught him looking at her. But, he had avoided her eyes, and now she was more and more sure the agony she had seen in his face had been because of his shame at having yielded to a momentary temptation.

Gail suspected that Jim's devotion to Christ would have made him feel his failure toward Hilda very deeply. She knew that even on the most demanding day he still managed to have his devotional times.

Once, she had gone to put away some of his washed and ironed clothes after tea when she had thought he was still watching the news on television. Without knocking, she had pushed open the door of his room only to retreat very quickly as she caught a glimpse of the dark figure on his knees beside his bed. That had disturbed her as nothing else did during that time.

Table devotions each night were continued even when Jim was unable to share the evening meal with them.

"Gail, would you mind reading the Bible for us tonight?" Marian had asked one evening.

Gail had glanced at her drawn, pale face and readily agreed. After that, she found herself actually offering to read. She had been ashamed of how awkward and shy she had felt that first time but, without her even being aware of it, she had grown to enjoy those times. At first, she had tried to tell herself it was because it was all part of feeling like a member of a family again. Then, she knew that the Word she had heard and had read herself was beginning to challenge her.

Once, she had not understood a passage, and had finally plucked up the courage to ask Marian what it meant. She had been answered so matter-of-factly and without the least hint of preaching at her, that she had been encouraged from then on to continue asking at various times about things she had heard at church as well as from the readings.

Little did she know how the older woman quietly rejoiced at Gail's increasing interest in spiritual things.

Gail had eventually written to Sister Drew.

"I haven't mentioned that silly name change business, yet," she had written briefly. "There just hasn't seemed to be an appropriate time, although I was able to tell Jim about the accident. It doesn't really matter anymore, but if it worries you, I promise to tell them after the harvest."

She did not add that she shrank from forcing a private conversation with Jim because of the tension between them. She knew that after the harvest she would have to leave anyway. There was no way she could bear to be there when Hilda and Jim announced their engagement.

And then, one day, more letters from Ann Green and Sister Drew arrived.

The day had started badly. Gail had forgotten to wind her alarm clock. Marian had banged on her door, and then put her head around the corner and grinned as Gail raised a dazed face.

"You're late, sleepyhead. You've only half an hour to get up and leave for the school bus."

It was a mad scramble, but they just made it, Gail pulling up the car with a crunch of gravel and slight squeal of brakes as she saw the bus waiting.

"Phew! Nice going, Gail," said Will as he hopped out of the car. "You'll make a rally car driver after all," he yelled over his shoulder as he took off after the children.

Gail waited to wave the bus off before starting back. To her utter dismay, about two kilometers from the farm, the engine suddenly cut out. Gail managed to steer the car onto the grass before the vehicle stopped rolling.

She turned the ignition and tried to start the motor. Then she remembered, and glanced at the petrol gauge. Yesterday morning Jim had warned her to take the car down to the sheds and fill the petrol tank from the farm's barrel.

"Rally driver! Like fun!" she fumed as she began the long, hot walk across the paddocks to the house.

Fortunately, Jim was the sheds, and she was grateful for his restraint when he quickly filled a can of petrol and drove her back to the car.

When he had finished pouring the petrol into the car, he straightened wearily and turned toward her. Suddenly, she felt breathless, and couldn't look away from that blue gaze. A grease-stained hand left a smear on his cheek as he wiped his hand over his face.

"Look, Gail, we've got to talk," he suddenly said urgently, "not now, but soon."

They stared at each other silently. Then she nodded abruptly and managed a brief smile before driving away. For the rest of the morning, she thought about what they might say to each other.

It had been a bad start to a day that gradually went from bad to worse.

After returning from delivering a hastily prepared, but still late smoke-o to the disgruntled header driver, Gail noticed that Marian was pale and she insisted that she lie down for a while. She flew at the preparations for lunch, determined that there would be no more cause for complaints, but had just finished making the tea when she heard a vehicle stop outside.

"Anyone home?"

"Oh, no!" she muttered to herself as she recognized Hilda's voice. "In the kitchen," she called out.

"Oh, it's you." Hilda's lilting tones went flat as she saw Gail. She peered around the kitchen.

"Mrs. Stevens out?"

"No, she's resting."

"Oh, the poor dear! She must be exhausted! I'll go and see what I can do for her."

Before Gail could remonstrate, she had disappeared down the hall in the direction of the bedrooms. She hesitated for a moment and then shrugged. If anyone could handle Hilda, her future mother-in-law could.

The thought stabbed at her and unexpected tears sprang to her eyes. She brushed them away angrily. Silly fool. Only, how she would have loved having Marian for her own mother-in-law!

The screen door banged. It was the truck driver with a message for Jim. She had to race into Toowoomba for a spare part for a broken-down header.

Gail was away for most of the afternoon. It was a quick trip in and straight back to where Jim was working on the header, but it was nearly three hours later before Gail found herself back in the kitchen.

Apparently, Hilda had long gone home. Marian took one look at Gail's exhausted face as she entered the kitchen and made her sit down straight away.

"I'll make you a cup of coffee, love, while you sit there for a few minutes. "I'm afraid it's nearly time for you to meet the school bus, too. But the kids can wait a couple of minutes while you recover."

"Is it always as hectic as this at harvest time?" Gail asked in a tired voice, and then added, "I think I'd better make myself a sandwich, too."

"Gail! You did have some lunch, didn't you?"

She was horrified when Gail confessed there had not been time before, and insisted on Gail finishing every crumb of the food she placed in front of her.

"It won't be the first or the last time the children have had to walk part of the way home," she said. "I wish Jim would let me drive, but I'm afraid that rotten arthritis is making itself felt today." She smiled at Gail's murmur of sympathy. "It's just one of those things I can expect to get gradually worse. On your way back, don't forget the mail, will you. I'm hoping for a letter from Beth today."

Mrs. Stevens had at last told Jim about Beth's request for him to go down to Sydney again. They had both agreed that another trip was impossible until after the harvest unless there was a marked change in Arthur's condition. There had been a brief phone call from Beth after that, assuring them that the doctors said there had been no actual worsening of the paralysis but his whole attitude toward the possibility of being a permanent invalid was causing increasing concern.

Gail picked up the three children almost halfway home from the bus stop. Will was very quiet, but the children were decidedly grumpy from the heat and their tired feet. She stopped and picked up the mailbag, but they were all too busy with the evening chores to be able to open it.

The three youngsters were roped in to assist with the clearing away of the meal. Jim's tea was put aside to be heated up in the microwave, so Marian went to the lounge room with the mailbag. When Gail at last joined her, she raised a strained face from reading a letter.

"There's a couple for you, Gail," she said abruptly, and buried her head again in her letter.

Gail hesitated, hoping nothing had happened in Sydney; then she glanced at her own mail, knowing she would see Sister Drew's handwriting.

"I'm so tired I think I'll see that the children are okay and then go straight to bed," she said slowly. "Have you any idea how long Jim will be?"

"What's that, Gail?" Marian raised her head and looked blankly at Gail for a moment. "Oh, Jim shouldn't be much longer. He has to finish welding in the shed. The rest will have to be done as soon as it's light enough in the paddock." She gave herself a slight shake, and looked at Gail intently. "Look, why don't you go to bed right away. I can keep an eye on the children and fix Jim up. You look exhausted."

Gail ran her hand through her hair. "If you're sure you aren't too tired, also, I'll do just that. In fact, I think I'll race everyone else to the bath now."

Gail waited until she was lying on her bed before opening her letters. She opened the one from Ann first. Gail had answered her last one briefly by saying that she was helping out some old friends of Sister Drew's, and would contact her again when she eventually went back to Sydney.

This letter from Ann went to the point very quickly. A friend of Ann's was nursing the truck driver who had been left paralyzed. The doctors and nursing staff were becoming increasingly concerned about his mental state. Apparently, he had begun to refuse some of the treatments just when there had been several indications that the paralysis may not be as permanent or as extensive as originally thought.

Ann's friend had managed to get closer to him on night duty than the rest of the staff. From several things he had let slip in the quiet hours of the night, she was convinced that Gail held the key to his depression.

So far they had been fairly successful in keeping from his wife how alarmed the staff was becoming about him. It couldn't be long before she would have to be told.

Ann's closing comments were blunt. "Rightly or wrongly, Gail, you blame Art Smith for the death of your folk. When the court case comes up he may be punished or cleared of negligence. If you do not go and see this man, you yourself may very well be guilty of depriving that woman and her two children of an active husband and father.

In fact, Liz was warned to be extra careful with any drugs in his room and to be watchful in case he tries to harm himself. Could you ever forgive yourself if he committed suicide?"

Gail read and reread that last sentence. She had not known the man had a wife and two children. Her hand clenched on the letter with dawning horror.

Beth had two children. Beth's husband was paralyzed. Beth was worried because the accident was preying on his mind.

Gail closed her eyes and saw Marian looking the way she did the day of the picnic when she had lifted her head and looked steadily at Gail. Jim had interrupted them and Gail had been so aware of him that she had not taken in what his mother had been saying.

It couldn't be. It must not be. She had to know for sure.

In a daze, Gail stood up and walked from the bedroom. The lounge was empty. She hesitated, undecided whether to follow Marian to her room.

No. Jim. She had to find Jim.

Jim had only sketchily washed his face and hands before getting his tea, and was sitting wearily at the kitchen table eating his late meal. He looked up with bloodshot, dust-filled eyes at Gail as she stood in the doorway.

"Sorry about the filthy clothes, Gail. I was starving and—"

"Jim."

He stared at her curiously as she interrupted him, and waited.

"Jim," she said again, and this time something in her voice and face reached him through the haze of exhaustion. "Jim, what's Beth's husband's name?" Gail put her trembling hand to her mouth and waited.

"Beth?" replied Jim in a puzzled voice. "She's just plain Smith. I believe Arthur's name used to be Canley-Smith at one stage, but he's always just called himself Smith."

She was like a statue. Her lips felt stiff. Then, as she saw the growing concern in his face, she forced herself to say, "Isn't that strange. All the weeks I've been here, I've never once heard. . .heard the children's surname. . .or Beth's. I didn't know her name. I just didn't know, Jim. Will. . .will you remember that? I just didn't. . ."

She turned and walked slowly back to her room on shaking legs. She stood beside her bed with the letter still crushed in her hand. Sister Drew's letter was still waiting to be read. She opened it slowly, knowing what she would read.

It held a direct request from the doctor in charge of Art Smith to go and visit him as soon as possible. Written about the same time as Ann's, the letter contained the information that, after numerous infections, he was building up the resistance to antibiotics that paraplegics sometimes did. His last infection had taken a long time to control and they were fearful for him if he should have another. He was in a very depressed state and the nursing staff was finding it increasingly difficult to make him take any medication and treatment.

Gail was a little puzzled that Sister Drew seemed to take for granted that Gail already knew she was living with Arthur's family. The general tone of the letter was abrupt. Sister Drew did not know how Gail could continue with her bitter attitude towards Arthur when she professed to be so fond of his in-laws and, above all, his delightful children. The letter ended abruptly. If she would let her know when she was arriving, she would meet her at the airport. She was only "yours faithfully" at the conclusion of the letter.

As Gail stared blindly at the letter, she heard a gentle rap on her door.

"Are you all right, Gail?" Jim called softly.

It took her a moment to find her voice.

"I'll be fine, Jim."

There was a brief pause and then he called, "Good night then," before she heard his steps moving away.

Gail knew she had no choice. She had to leave as soon as possible. Her suitcases were stacked on top of the large wardrobe. Jumping to her feet, she feverishly grabbed a chair and climbed up on to it so she could reach them. The chair tilted and she almost lost her balance as she lifted them down. Her heart pounded with shock and fright at the thought of hurting herself and not being able to leave the next day.

She collapsed on the bed, gulping in deep breaths. The suitcases were sprawled across the floor. She looked at them and felt the wetness of tears and realized for the first time that she was crying. What was she going to do? Where would she end up? She was homeless again.

The words of the hymn flashed into her mind, "Take it to the Lord in prayer." Without afterwards knowing quite how she got there, she found herself on her knees, beside her bed, for the very first time. She couldn't even remember afterwards if she had actually articulated any words. Her whole being just seemed to reach out to God.

Gradually, her tears stopped; a long time later, she stood up. Her mind was functioning again now. She thought about Arthur Smith. The fact remained that he was still responsible for her family's death.

She looked across at the photographs. If it had not been for him, they would still be here. But, even if she did go to see him, could she assure him that she had really forgiven him?

She suddenly realized that he was not only responsible for the death of her family, but he was also the reason she had to leave this place of refuge. But then, if he were not in the hospital, she would probably have never met Jim.

And never learned to love him, she thought bitterly.

Her mouth set firmly. One thing was sure—she had to return to Sydney at once. She could not stay here another day. The Garretts had already finished their smaller acreage of wheat to be harvested. If help was needed, Marian would have to put up with Hilda for the last few days of harvest.

She began to pack the cases.

Chapter 9

Gail managed only a couple of hours of deep, exhausted sleep. As she at last stumbled out of bed, she refused to allow herself to think. The morning was considerably cooler and so she dressed quickly in the slack suit she had worn to the farm. It brought back memories of Jim's gentleness when she had been sick beside the car.

Without realizing it, she slipped into the pattern so recently conquered of forcing her mind not to dwell on hurtful memories. So, she began planning all that had to be done before she could leave. She knew there were several flights out of Brisbane for Sydney every day. The main thing was to leave as soon as possible. Someone would have to take her to Toowoomba at least, and then there would be buses or. . .

While she was decisively stripping her bed, she heard the phone ringing. She glanced at her watch. It was still very early. Who could be ringing at this early hour?

The phone was located a little way up the corridor from Gail's bedroom. When she left her room, she saw with surprise that it was Jim who had answered it. What even surprised her more was that he was still in his pajamas and bathrobe. Usually, by this time, he had long since gone down to the sheds to check everything for the day's work.

As she saw him, he put down the receiver and turned toward her. His face was alight with happiness that dimmed a little as his gaze swept over Gail.

Moving towards her he said, "That was Beth and—who told you this is the day to get on our good duds to go to town?"

Gail blinked. "This is the day we go to town?"

He began to laugh at her, and then stopped and looked a little puzzled.

"Isn't that why you're all dressed up? When it rains, we usually grab the chance to race into town."

"When it rains?" asked Gail stupidly.

"Didn't you hear it teeming down in the early hours? Boy, you must have been sleeping the sleep of the just! Lady, it really rained last night!"

Gail winced. She saw a swift frown momentarily crease his forehead. "Does that mean the harvest can't be finished?" she rushed to say, "And doesn't that mean you'll lose a lot of money?"

She was relieved to see the twinkle of amusement sweep back into his eyes. "You city slicker! If it keeps raining, the harvest may very well be finished, and, yes, we would lose a lot of money. But the sun is shining this morning. It just means that for today we don't work." He looked rueful. "I was thinking of all that hard work yesterday to get the header working again. It could have been done today."

Gail was watching him intently as he talked. It passed through her mind that this might be the last time he talked so freely to her. He would soon know. She caught her breath sharply. Perhaps now was the time. But suddenly she couldn't bear the thought of his knowing how bitter and unforgiving she had been.

Jim had been studying the changing expressions on her face as he talked, and must have seen the bleak look flash into her eyes.

"You are really taking this harvest to heart, aren't you, Gail?" His eyes were tender. "That storm just means the black soil will be too sticky for at least today for the trucks and header. The grain will have to dry out, too, before we start again."

He paused, and impulsively grabbed her hand. She snatched it away as though he had scorched her. The bright expression on his face disappeared.

"Anyway, we have to make a trip to Brisbane today as it happens," he said briskly. "Beth's coming home."

Gail froze. Her mouth went dry and she couldn't think of one word to say. Was this just a coincidence? She suddenly remembered what Marian had said once about coincidences.

"So many things happen in a person's life that appear to be

coincidences. But some people can see God's help and direction in them and in those apparently 'lucky breaks.' "

And she had pleaded for God's help last night.

Gail mentally shook herself. It must be just that Beth wanted to see the children. Jim was directing one of his soul searching looks at her.

"That was a phone call from Beth," he began slowly, "Arthur has insisted she come home for a few days and so she's decided she can't last another minute without seeing her two offspring again. She's catching the midday plane. Gail, is anything—"

"Jim! Who was on the phone so early. Is everything all right? It wasn't Beth, was it?"

Jim swung around to his mother and began telling her about Beth.

Gail closed her eyes. It didn't make sense. Why was Arthur sending his wife home? Those letters from Ann and Sister Drew had taken a few days to reach her. Was the hospital staff right to be worried about the depression? Or was he starting to improve? Beth would never have left him unless he had persuaded her. . .convinced her. . .

Something was wrong. A sense of fear and urgency began to surge through Gail. She had to get to Sydney before tonight.

Jim had been explaining to his mother and Gail heard her delighted exclamation. They came towards Gail and Marian stopped and looked with a puzzled frown at Gail's clothes.

"What are you dressed up for, Gail? I didn't know you were planning on going anywhere."

Gail looked at her speechlessly. She didn't know where to begin or what to say.

Marian Stevens stared back. She suddenly stiffened. Gail saw an eager, excited expression fill her face.

Gail's legs felt weak. She knew. Somehow, Marian knew.

"Gail?" All the pleading and hope she couldn't put into words were in the slightly husky voice.

"Yes," said Gail simply.

"Hey, you two! What's going on?"

Jim had caught the inflection in his mother's voice and was looking from one to another with a worried expression.

Marian kept looking steadily at Gail. She answered him very slowly, relief beginning to glow in her face.

"I believe Gail has decided she has to go back to Sydney today. Is that right, Gail?"

"Yes," was all Gail could still find to say.

"Back to Sydney! Today? Are you both crazy or something? Beth's coming today and you're leaving? What on earth's going on?" Jim's face was a picture of bewilderment and dawning anger.

Gail looked at him, and found her voice at last. "I've just got to go today," she managed to say quietly and firmly. She hesitated and her eyes locked with Marian's again.

"And apparently your mother knows why," she finished appealingly.

"Well, why then?" Jim snapped. He ran his hand over his face and Gail began to tremble.

"Oh, please. Please, Jim. I don't think I can tell you. I'd rather you didn't know until I'm gone. Please, Marian. . ."

"It's all right, Gail." She moved forward quickly and placed her hand on Gail's arm.

"It's not all right!" Jim began furiously. "I demand an explanation. What could be important enough to make you leave us in the lurch in the middle of harvest? And when will you be back? You do intend to come back?"

The increasing anguish on Gail's face brought him to an abrupt halt. He looked helplessly at his mother, some of that anguish dawning in his own eyes.

"Mum? We can't lose Gail. Not now. Not yet." His voice was quieter, pleading now.

His mother looked at him gently. She attempted a smile. "God knows best, son," she reminded him. Unquenchable faith shone in her face.

He stared at her dumbly. She looked back at him with compassion.

Gail glanced from one to the other. They were communicating without words. There was pain in Jim's face. Her heart leaped. For her?

Jim closed his eyes. He rocked gently on his feet for a moment. Gail saw his lips move. For one incredible moment, she thought he was praying as she had seen people silently do so at the little church as they had been handed communion.

Then he opened his eyes and looked at Gail. Her hopes died as she saw him square his shoulders. The anger was completely gone from his face.

"We'll just have to leave it to Him to sort out then, won't we?" he said steadily, and then turned and strode down the hallway to his room.

I don't know how God could work any of this mess out, Gail thought off and on during the next hectic hour or so. A phone call had secured a seat on a plane for her and then it had been decided, to Gail's relief, that the two excited children would accompany her and Jim to Brisbane. Marian decided not to go. She said it would be better if she did some of the necessary preparation and work for when the harvest resumed.

Gail looked at her doubtfully. There had been no return of any chest problems and she seemed very well, but Gail knew how tired she still was some evenings. She suspected there would be a marathon of baking as soon as they were gone. However, there was nothing she could do except work as hard as she could in the few minutes left and try to leave as little as possible of the housework undone.

The children were more excited and thrilled than Gail had ever seen them. She had not realized how much they had missed their mother. They had spoken to her on the phone quite often and, as Gail thought over the past weeks, she wondered how she could have been so blind as not to realize before that Beth's husband and children's father was the same man that Sister had been so concerned about.

For the first time Gail found herself thinking of Art—or Arthur—Smith as a person in his own right, and not some drunken monster who had been responsible for all her misery. She wondered about him now. What had he and Beth quarreled about so bitterly that he had walked out? Now he was an invalid. Would this be a permanent reconciliation?

The brief time left on the farm flew by. The children's joy at seeing their mother again had been blunted when they found out that Gail was leaving. For a moment, Robbie's bottom lip quivered. Marian quickly reminded him that they had Bonnie to introduce to his mother. At that he brightened up and dragged Jacky out to make sure Bonnie's coat was brushed until it shone. After that, there was plenty to do to keep them—and Gail—busy until it was time to go.

At last, Jim—a quiet, stern Jim—began to pack Gail's things in the car. Gail was in her bedroom when he returned for the last case. They stood and looked at each other for a long moment. She longed to tell him that Hilda was not good enough for him and that she, Gail, needed his strength and his love. Once, she thought he was going to speak. But then he set his lips grimly and turned away without a word.

Gail crossed the room and stared out of the window across the forlorn looking paddocks. All the wheat within her view had been reaped. She had often wondered what it was like here when the frost was on the ground. Stories had been told to her of the frozen pipes that had burst, of the radiators on vehicles that had to be protected.

She wanted to see those grim paddocks softened by the gentle green of the newly shooting wheat. She wanted to be able to see the seasons come and go. Jim had told he was planning to plant sorghum for the next crop. She had told him she wasn't sure if she knew what that looked liked. He had laughed at her a little and told her that she still had a lot to learn.

Now, she yearned to live all her tomorrows here with Jim.

The sun's rays were glinting on a few puddles of rain water. It seemed impossible that she had slept so soundly that the drumming of the rain on the roof had not awakened her. *If only tomorrow would come like that*, she thought. *A deep, peaceful sleep while the storm blew itself out. Then, when you woke, the sun would be shining again.*

They were all outside near the Holden when Gail let the screen door bang for the last time.

"Come on, Gail," called Will impatiently. He was being dropped off at the school bus stop on the way.

There had been no chance for Gail and Marian to speak privately. She went over to Gail, standing on the path beneath the trees.

Once, it would have been natural for Gail to lean over and kiss the lined cheek goodbye. Now, Gail stood looking at her uncertainly. Jim glanced at them briefly and made a business of settling the others in the car.

Gail blinked the ready tears away as she realized there was little likelihood she would see this fine woman ever again.

"I hope you don't hate me too much," she whispered.

Marian's eyes widened in astonishment. "Hate you?" she exclaimed in distress. "Have I given you the impression these last few weeks that I have hated you?"

It was Gail's turn to be surprised. "You mean you've known all that time? I thought your mail last night—"

"No, No! Jean phoned me that first Sunday, while you were still asleep. You looked so pale and strained that evening that I couldn't say anything. Then, when I thought about it, I wanted you to get to know us better. I kept hoping you would feel free to tell us of your own accord. That day of the picnic. . .I. . .I was about to say something when Jim interrupted us. I had faith in your own basic character, my dear. We are kindred spirits in so many ways. I really enjoyed being your. . .your mother for a little while. All this time you've been recovering from the shock of it all. I've prayed that healing would come and. . .well, I knew God would work it all out in His good time."

A warm glow had begun to spread through Gail's body. Until then she had not realized how cold and numbed she had been throughout the hectic rush of the morning.

"You knew," she murmured, "all this time you've known. You've put your arms around me and. . .and. . ."

Those warm, loving arms were holding her close again.

Gail did not see Jim looking across at them. He was looking at his mother with love and pride. He had been too far away to hear their conversation. He took a step as though to go to the two women. Then his hands clenched. He paused, and opened the car door instead. He climbed in and slammed it shut with unnecessary force.

The sound made Marian let Gail go. They both had to brush the tears away. Each gave the other rather watery smiles as they did so. The frozen look was gone from Gail's dark brown eyes.

"Jim's getting impatient. You must go. But Gail, my dear, we won't lose touch."

Gail found there were no words to express how she was feeling and turned and went across to the car. She dared not look at Jim as they moved slowly down the rough driveway made even worse by the heavy trucks. She waved goodbye to Marian Stevens until she was out of sight, knowing also she was saying good-bye to the house and farm that had become home for such a brief time. She choked back the tears that threatened. Merely keeping in touch but no longer being such an intimate part of all of this would be unbearable. She would, no doubt, write to them a few times. But she would never be back because of Jim, and especially not because of Hilda.

There was very little conversation between Jim and Gail on the trip to Brisbane. When they were driving past the beautiful Queen's Park in Toowoomba, Gail felt sad because there had been no time to really explore this lovely city perched on the top of the mountain range.

"We never did get a chance to bring you to Toowoomba for the day. I wanted to show you the view from Picnic Point—" Jim stopped abruptly, as though regretting his words.

Gail murmured something in response and, for a moment, their glances met. Her own sadness was reflected in his eyes. After that, she avoided looking at him and was bitterly aware that he never glanced at her once. She knew that Jim would be too courteous to show her how annoyed and dismayed he was with her for letting him down. But Beth might be able to stay and help until after the harvest. And there was always Hilda.

There was much she longed to say to him, but she was silent, and let the children's chatter go unchecked. They stopped only once for a refreshment break, and were just on time at the airport.

However, to Gail's dismay, her flight was delayed. It had been scheduled to take off a few minutes before Beth was due to arrive. She did not want to meet Beth. She had not asked Marian if Beth knew who she was, but she probably did by now. Perhaps that was even her main reason for coming home.

Beth's plane arrived a few minutes later.

Gail watched Robbie and Jacky race over to the slight, unexpectedly fair-haired woman who knelt down to hug and kiss them. Beth stood up and kissed Jim. The tears were still glistening on her cheeks when she turned to Gail. They stared at each other. Although she was fair where Jim was dark, her eyes were as blue as his.

To Gail's absolute horror, she saw all the warmth start to drain from them as Jim's sister stared at her.

The loudspeaker sprang into life, announcing Gail's flight.

"Oh, Gail. What a shame. You've got to go," said Jim quickly. "Beth, I'm afraid you'll have to say a very quick hello and good-bye to the friend of Aunt Jean who has been helping us out."

Beth's smile had completely disappeared while Jim was talking. Her lips tightened. Gail saw recognition and bitterness fill her face.

"You! So you were here all the time. I suppose you've been gloating all this time over Arthur's punishment."

"Beth!" Jim was looking at his sister in disbelief and horror. "What on earth's the matter with you? This is Gail who—"

"I know who she is! Abigail Brandon! I've studied her photo often enough, wondering how anyone so beautiful on the outside could be so hard and unforgiving on the inside. You should be thanking God you are alive, or not still in the hospital, like my husband."

Gail dared to glance quickly at Jim. His face was a mixture of bewilderment and dawning comprehension. He put his hand on Beth's arm and tried to stop the flow of brutal words. She shook him off and turned on him. Her face was pale and anguished. Her eyes shot sparks of fire.

"How could you, Jim!" she spat at him. "How could you have her looking after my children. Abigail Brandon! The girl who refuses to—"

Gail heard with relief the final urgent call to board the plane. She knew she couldn't take anymore. She felt sick and shaken. Her eyes locked with Jim's as she desperately interrupted the angry words.

"I've got to go, Jim. To. . .to see Arthur. And. . .and. . ." Tears blurred her last sight of him. "Please, don't judge me too harshly. Your mother, she'll tell you. . .tell you. . ."

Gail turned and ran towards the gate where the hostesses were already on their way to the plane. She thought she heard Jim's voice shouting after her, but she kept running.

Vaguely, she knew people were turning and watching her curiously. All Gail had mirrored on her mind was the horror in Jim's eyes.

Chapter 10

The hour that passed before the Boeing jet touched down at Mascot always remained a blur of pain in Gail's memory.

She spent most of the flight hunched miserably in her seat. Vaguely, she realized that the passenger next to her and the hostesses were concerned about her. She looked at them with dazed eyes and numbly shook her head at their offers of cups of tea and magazines, until they left her alone.

How Jim must be despising her! To have her time with that delightful family end like this was devastating.

And the children! They had been clinging to their mother's hands. Their eyes had grown huge with fear and dismay at the angry words directed at their beloved Gail. Their much awaited reunion was thoroughly spoiled.

Beth. Never before had anyone stared at Gail with such bitterness and hatred.

And she was Jim's sister.

The gentle jolt as the wheels touched on the tarmac and the increased roar of the jets brought Gail back to an awareness of her surroundings. She turned her head and caught the concerned look of the elderly man sitting beside her.

"Ah. That's better, my dear," he said softly.

Gail stared at him blankly, and then a tinge of color swept into her ashen cheeks as she realized the spectacle she must have made of herself.

"It's all right. You don't have to be embarrassed." The stranger's voice was gentle and sympathetic. "We all have times of pain and anguish in this old world."

The plane began to taxi along the runway to the terminal buildings. The hostesses began moving up and down the aisles again. One of them paused and glanced keenly at Gail. She gave her a relieved smile before hurrying on.

"We've been concerned about you," the gentle voice beside her went on.

Gail's throat was dry and sore. No tears had fallen, but her eyes were burning. "I'm sorry," she began in a hoarse whisper.

"No, no, my dear. You don't have to apologize." The man paused. Gail turned and looked at him again. He was very old, and watching her with a considering look.

"I've been hoping though that I might have an opportunity of saying something to you." He hesitated again. The plane was drawing to a stop. The man continued speaking with an urgency that caught Gail's attention. "My dear, I'm an old man now and have known much sorrow. I just want to tell you that God longs to be your friend and comfort and strength in times of pain and despair. He has been my constant companion and friend for well over sixty years and has never let me down. He loves you and longs for you to turn to Him. He—"

"Come on, Dad. Time to go."

Gail watched dumbly as the smiling, gray-haired lady released the old man's seat belt and helped him to his feet. He resisted the pull on his arm for a moment and looked back at Gail. Love and longing reached out to her. "Oh, I do pray that you will reach out to Him. He'll be there—always!"

For a few moments, Gail sat very still as the passengers moved slowly down the aisle. At last, she stirred and joined the stream of people.

There was some delay with the unloading of the plane. Gail made her way to a coffee lounge, suddenly realizing how little she had managed to swallow all day. Mechanically, she ordered some sandwiches and coffee that she forced herself to eat. As she began to feel a little better, she realized it was the same place she had been before going on the trip north. Only a few weeks had passed since she had waited here, wondering and worrying if she were doing the right thing.

Gail suddenly remembered how Jim's warm smile, just before he left her to find his own seat on the plane, had somehow given her hope that perhaps she had found a new life and reason for living. And she had found a new life. The love and acceptance she had found had brought healing to her wounded heart and mind. But now new sorrow had replaced the old.

"He loves you and longs for you to turn to Him."

Somebody else besides the old man had said those same words. Gail thought back over the past few weeks. Then, she remembered. It had been the Reverend Telford who had said those words. He had at first seemed such a quiet, unassuming young man when she had met him just before the service, but his sermon had been unexpectedly full of vim and passion. He had gazed longingly over the congregation and said those very same words the old man had just repeated. "He loves you and longs for you to turn to Him."

She had been waiting for an opportunity to ask Jim or his mother about some of the other things he had also mentioned. And now she never would.

Gail's hand shook. She hastily put down the cup of hot coffee. Jim had said he was preaching again this coming Sunday, and she had been looking forward to it. Now. . .

Perhaps Sister Drew would know some answers to the questions that were burning inside her.

Sister Drew.

Gail straightened. She had forgotten to ring her and let her know she was coming. And Art Smith. She still had to make sure he was not planning something very foolish.

The taxi driver couldn't have been more helpful and even carried her cases up the steps of the Nurses' Home and into the front entrance before giving her a cheerful wave good-bye. Gail left the luggage piled in the corridor and went straight to the nurse educator's office. She took a deep breath before raising her hand and knocking on the door.

She felt like a different person than the one who had been about to knock on this door only a few weeks ago. She could think about the accident without that sick churning inside her. Other people now occupied her attention; before she continually thought only of her own circumstances. Only one thing seemed to be the same. Her lips tilted wryly. She was still just a little scared of Sister Drew.

The familiar voice called out to her to come in, and she opened the door.

Sister Drew's head was bowed over her desk as her pen flew over some papers. "Be with you in a minute, Nurse. I've nearly finished this report for you."

Gail hesitated, then said softly, "Good afternoon, Sister."

Sister Drew's head jerked up. "Gail!"

She jumped to her feet and hurried around the desk. Gail breathed a faint sigh of relief at the beaming smile that lit the alert face. Two hands gripped Gail's shoulders and she unbelievingly felt a kiss on her cheek. This was a welcome she hadn't dreamed of.

"Oh, my dear girl, I'm so glad you've come!"

It was too much. The tears started pouring down Gail's face.

Sister gave a startled exclamation and put Gail gently into a chair. The floodgates were open and she only vaguely heard the knock on the door and Sister Drew speaking softly to someone.

She tried to pull herself together and had partly succeeded when she felt a comforting hand stroking her bowed head.

"You poor girl. Has it been that bad?" A box of tissues was offered, and the sympathetic voice continued. "Jim rang me a little while ago. He was worried about you."

"Jim rang!"

"Yes. From the Brisbane airport. He told me what had happened."

Gail swallowed on more tears. "Beth, she. . .she hates me. She thinks I went up there on purpose. To gloat. She—"

"Oh, no, no. Of course she doesn't. Not now anyway. I told Jim it was all my idea. That you didn't have the faintest idea. He had already told Beth that anyway before he rang."

"He told Beth that?"

"Yes. Apparently you asked him last night what Beth's name was and he guessed the rest."

"Oh. Yes, so I did."

Sister Drew perched on the edge of the desk; she looked puzzled. "But I don't understand. You must have known before last night that they were Arthur's folk. When I wrote to you that first week I thought I said something about it then."

"I've been so dumb. You only said that by then I'd know what the rest of your plan had been. I. . .I thought you meant something else. And somehow I just never even heard what Robbie and Jacky's surname was.

There was a knock on the door and a nurse entered carrying an afternoon tea tray. She looked curiously at Gail.

"Thank you, Nurse. And now you can deliver this report to Miss Fisher for me. And don't dawdle, girl!"

The old familiar battle-axe bite had crept into the Sister's voice. Gail grinned weakly as twinkling eyes were turned on her after the flustered nurse had shot out of the room.

"Got to keep them up to the mark," Sister Drew said cheerfully. She poured out the tea and waited until Gail had managed a few sips and felt her trembling gradually ease.

"And what do you want to do now, Gail," she asked with a hint of anxiety.

"I'm not sure." Gail rubbed her eyes again. "I think I've been in a daze ever since reading those letters last night."

"Letters?"

"Yes. Ann Green wrote to me, too. Her friend is one of the night nurses looking after Art—Arthur Smith." Gail hesitated, and then said slowly, "I think it's really her letter as much as anything that made me know I had to come as soon as possible. Do you know if the doctors think he is so depressed he could. . .would try and deliberately harm himself? And I don't understand why Beth went home when she did. Is there a marked improvement in him by any chance?"

Sister Drew looked startled. "I haven't heard any suggestion about that, Gail." She thought for a moment. "Perhaps because they know I'm a personal friend of the family they may have been afraid to say anything in case I mentioned it to Beth." There was a snort. "As

114

though any nurse worth her salt would discuss something like that with a relative."

"Ann asked me if. . .if I would like a suicide on my hands."

There was silence. They looked at each other. Sister Drew's face lost some of its color.

"His condition hasn't improved since I wrote to you," she said slowly. "In fact, I couldn't understand his encouraging Beth to go home. I even tried to talk them out of it last night, but he. . .he became upset and went on about having been selfish long enough." She stopped abruptly. Jumping to her feet, she said decisively, "I don't like it."

"I don't either," admitted Gail. "I just knew I had to get here as quickly as I could." She looked at Sister Drew with a hint of wonder. "It's funny, but getting to know his children and family made him somehow a person who could love and grieve, too, instead of being the murdering monster I've thought him." Her expression changed, and she added grimly, "But he still killed them all."

Jean ignored that. "Will you come cover and see him with me?" she asked bluntly.

Gail hesitated. "I guess that's what I have to do. But I still don't know if I can assure him that I don't blame him, or if I can forgive. . ."

Her voice had hardened. That had been her biggest worry about going to see the man. Would it make his depression worse if she couldn't. . .couldn't. . .

She looked up pleadingly at Sister Drew, who said thoughtfully, "When he first became obsessed with the idea of seeing you, I did not really think that forgiveness was what he wanted from you. Since then, I've often thought there was some other reason."

Gail stared at her in surprise. "But what other reason could there be? He was drunk and they—"

"He was *not* drunk!"

"Oh, I know the police tried to tell me something like that, but I heard—"

"I don't care what you heard! Arthur was not drunk! Merciful heavens, don't tell me all this time you've thought that?"

Gail had never see Sister Drew so angry. She gaped at her.

"That was only one senseless observation made by some stupid idiot glory-seeking in front of television cameras—trying to make out he was first on the scene. It was emphatically denied by the police at the time. I repeat, Arthur had not been drinking. He had been driving trucks for years, and although he has a heap of faults, drinking has never been one of them!"

Gail was dazed. "But all this time I was sure—"

"All this time you've been sure of nothing. And we've all been a pack of senseless idiots trying to protect you while you've been so shocked by the whole wretched business!"

Sister Drew stood up and strode over to the window. Her rigid back gradually relaxed as she let the anger drain out of her. At last, she turned to Gail, who stared back blindly.

Gail was trying to remember. She had never before tried to deliberately remember those few minutes before the smash. She had always shied away from trying to remember anything after getting into the car and waving good-bye to Ann. There had been something, though. If only she could remember!

"It will all come out at the long delayed inquest eventually," Sister Drew said firmly. "Gail, the brakes on the truck failed. Apparently they had been checked before taking on that load, but they failed a couple of minutes before your father's car came around that curve." She went to add something else and thought better of it. "It's well past the time when you should have gone to the police and asked them for a few facts yourself. Now, I don't think we should waste any more time before going over to see him."

Gail stood up. She was still very pale. Sister Drew hesitated for a moment and then compressed her lips together and moved to the door.

When they reached Arthur's room, they paused.

"I think it might be best if I saw him by myself, Sister."

"No way," Sister Drew said in her best battle-axe voice and pushed open the door.

"Good afternoon, Arthur," she said loudly as she strode into the room, "I've brought you a visitor."

"Oh, no, not another of your 'cheer up poor Arthur' games, Sister Drew," a tired voice said rudely.

Gail had nursed paraplegic patients so she was quite prepared for all the paraphernalia in the room needed by someone whose body couldn't move from the waist down. What she wasn't prepared for was the thin, drawn face with Robbie's mop of curly blond hair and Jacky's hazel eyes.

He had lifted his head to see who was entering the room, and then very slowly he let it drop back onto the pillows without taking his eyes off them. Those strangely familiar eyes clung to Gail's face. A faint spark of interest lit them for a moment before he turned his head away.

"For a moment I thought I knew you," he muttered.

Sister Drew opened her mouth to say something and then resolutely closed it again.

After a few moments, when neither woman had spoken—Gail because she could not—Arthur looked at her again. A slow flush crept into his yellow cheeks. "I do know you. It's Abigail Brandon, isn't it?"

She nodded wordlessly.

"So you've condescended to visit the poor scum after all, have you? Well you can get out! *I* don't want to see you! It's too late," he suddenly snarled at her.

Gail's heart plunged.

Sister Drew put her hands on her hips and glowered at him. Inwardly, she began to feel excited. Arthur was more animated than he had been for weeks.

"She's not going anywhere. She's just flown about a thousand kilometers to see you, and the least you can do is say hello for a couple of minutes." She reached out and pulled Gail closer to the bed, pushed a chair next to her, and plonked her down in it.

She's getting quite expert at sitting me down, Gail thought a little hysterically.

"You have a lot to talk about. She's got some crazy ideas about the crash and I want you to tell her what happened. You made such a fuss for so long about seeing her I suggest you stop acting like a two-year-old boy and sort some things out." She marched to the door, turned, and unexpectedly smiled lovingly at them both before disappearing.

"Phew! I didn't know she could blow up like that," Gail said.

Arthur had lifted his head and watched the proceedings with grim astonishment. He looked at Gail searchingly.

"You. . .you should have known her when I was one of her students," Gail said huskily, hardly realizing what she was saying. "You look amazingly like Robbie," she blurted out irrelevantly.

He looked startled. "Robbie? When did you see him?"

"I've just spent several weeks looking after him—and Jacky."

An intense yearning flickered into his eyes. He opened his mouth to say something, and then tightly clamped it shut. A wary look came over his face and there was an uneasy silence while they studied each other.

"How did you know who I am?" ventured Gail at last, then remembered, and bit her lip. "I. . .I suppose you've seen the same photograph your wife has. The one in the newspaper after. . .after the accident."

"Photo? Oh, no. Everyone has tried to spare the poor paralyzed patient. No one let a newspaper near me for a long time after the accident." His voice was very bitter.

Gail muttered, "Me, too." He narrowed his eyes at that, and she rushed on to ask, "Then how did you recognize me?"

He looked at her blankly, and then said with amazement, "You really don't remember, do you?"

"Remember? I know very little apparently!" It was her turn to sound bitter. "I wouldn't let anyone tell me anything, and so, according to Sister Drew, I've got some crazy ideas."

Arthur studied her closely for a few minutes, and then closed his eyes and moved his head restlessly.

"Oh well, nothing matters now," Gail thought she heard him mutter to himself.

Alarm touched her but, before she could respond, he spoke again in a very quiet, controlled voice.

"What do you want me to tell you?"

Gail stared at him silently. Nothing. She wanted him to tell her nothing. Perspiration began beading up on her forehead. She just wanted to be able to go and forget him and the smash and everything. But at the same time. . .there had been something in his voice a moment ago. She knew she had to try to get him talking, find out if he was planning anything.

Her tongue moistened her suddenly dry lips before she said, "I want to know why you were so obsessed about seeing me."

A harsh laugh broke from him. The eyes turned to her were filled with contempt for her, for himself, for the whole world. Gail caught her breath.

"Obsessed! I suppose I was. And that's funny, now. Really funny."

But not even the hint of a smile reached his hazel eyes. They were cold as ice. He studied her carefully. She shivered.

"You look as though you've recovered enough now. There doesn't seem any need to tell you anymore." With little interest, he watched the puzzled expression that entered her face with little interest. The same harsh excuse for a laugh twisted his lips and then he turned his head and stared at the ceiling again.

"Tell me. Tell me what?" asked Gail.

He was so still for so long that she opened her mouth to insist on an answer but, at the same time, he suddenly stirred and spoke as though each word was forced out.

"I was so terribly sorry for you. Your whole family gone. Wiped out. But I needed to tell you. . ." He paused.

When he continued, his voice had become harsher as though he, too, hated having to remember.

"It wasn't my fault. The brakes on the truck had failed just before that last bend. Sure, the truck was going too fast. But I know that stretch of road. There's a safety ramp just a few yards farther on. I had to use it once before to stop a runaway. I'd have made it this time, too, only for that car—" He broke off again and suddenly pushed himself onto one elbow and glared at Gail. "Do you have any idea why your car suddenly swerved right into me?"

For a moment, the question did not register. Gail stared at him. Her silence seemed to infuriate him.

"Well, do you?" he snapped at her.

She numbly shook her head. That acted like a time fuse. Suddenly, his words were hitting out at her, savage fury in every part of him.

"I've been lying here all these months doing nothing but think and think. Was there anything else I could have done? It all happened so fast. The brakes failed. That car coming over the double lines. A car full of people wiped out. All except one! And that such a poor specimen of a person that she wouldn't even let me see her, let alone breathe a word of thanks that I didn't let her burn to death—"

Gail was on her feet. He chopped off the last word, reprimanding himself for letting slip the one thing he had stubbornly refused to admit even to the police. With horror, he watched the effect his words had on the white-faced woman. Her body was starting to shake. She leaned against his bed as though she would fall without support.

"What. . .what are you saying? Burn to death? But that was only a dream. . .not real. . .no, no, no!"

Gail's voice had started off as though she had been running, and then, as the realization of what he had said struck her like a blow, she was screaming at him.

Arthur's horror-stricken face receded as a black mist came down. Her body slipped to the floor.

Chapter 11

A rthur's trembling fingers could not find his buzzer. It was
Sister Drew who burst into the room first.

"What have you done to her, Arthur? How could you!"
she roared at him while her hands were loosening Gail's clothing, feeling for a pulse, helping the other nurses to bring her out of the faint.

Arthur's voice was shaky and indignant. "I haven't done a thing!
She didn't seem to know anything about the fire. Just keeled right over after scaring the living daylights out of me."

Gail stirred, and felt a glass being held to her lips. Sister Drew's voice commanded her to swallow. She automatically obeyed and, after a while, opened dazed eyes and looked up at the concerned faces."

"Lie still for a bit, dear. You fainted."

Terror flooded Gail's eyes as she remembered. She struggled to sit up.

"No, no. Where's Arthur? He's got to tell me. Did they all die when. . .or. . .or. . .?"

Sister Drew yielded and helped her back into the chair beside the bed. With a curt nod she dismissed the nurses, who reluctantly went out, obviously longing to stay and watch the drama about to take place.

Gail was staring at Arthur. He saw the torment in her face. For the first time he caught a glimpse of the agony this woman had been through and his own expression changed.

"You poor kid," he said very softly, "you poor, poor kid."

"Tell me," she pleaded. "I've had nightmares. I could never remember what was in them that frightened me so much. But now. . . ," she brushed a hand across her eyes, "now I'm beginning to remember. The car was on fire, wasn't it? Someone was screaming. I. . .I tried to go back but he wouldn't let me. It was you, wasn't it? You. . .you. . .oh, tell me! Please!"

Arthur forgot that Sister Drew was still there staring at them with blank amazement. He reached out and gripped Gail's hand tightly.

"It's all right, it's all right. There was nothing you could have done. They were all dead. Killed instantly I guess. I knew that before I heard you moan. In fact, I thought at first you were all. . . Somehow, you were under the backseat. You were. . .were. . ."

His hand convulsed on hers. The stench of blood and petrol was in his nostrils again. Then the smoke had drifted by. He had increased his frantic efforts to free her trapped legs. He closed his eyes and could see again the horror he could never tell this woman about. The crushed body he had managed to drag off her. It had probably protected her—the reason why she had not been killed. He could never tell her any of that.

"You dragged me from the car. But. . .but. . .the screaming?" Gail's lips could hardly move, but she never took her eyes off Art.

He looked at her. "You were screaming. I think I might have been, too. But no one left in the car was screaming. I swear it."

Gail closed her eyes and sagged in the chair. Vaguely, she knew Sister Drew took over after that. She was insisting that Art could tell her anything else she wanted to know another time.

"There is a little more, I guess. But it can wait now," Gail heard Art agree.

Gail insisted she could walk. She stood up and swayed slightly. She resisted the grip on her arm for a moment and looked down at the man on the bed.

"You will be here tomorrow?" she whispered.

Shock made him freeze. The knowledge in her eyes left him speechless. Their eyes clung. At last he nodded. She relaxed, and let herself be led away.

Sister Drew took her straight to her own bedroom at the Nurses' Home. Not a word had been spoken until the door was closed.

"I want you to lie down on my bed and have a rest," Gail was told firmly.

She was only too thankful to submit to Sister Drew's gentle fussing. After careful questioning, she was stood over until she had eaten a small nourishing meal, which eventually helped to stop her trembling.

At last Sister Drew left her in peace while she raced down to her office to use the phone. Miss Fisher listened to her carefully and finally agreed to Jean's request for Gail to use an empty room in the Home.

"And you could tell her I would like to see her tomorrow sometime if she's up to it. A junior sister from Men's Medical has just handed me her resignation, and she might like to apply for the position. Oh, and there was a phone call concerning Sister Brandon. Just a moment." A brief pause, and Sister Drew heard the rustle of papers. "I intended to contact you later. It was a Reverend Diamond. Said he had only just returned from overseas and had been told about the accident. Was most anxious to speak to her."

Sister Drew carefully wrote down the phone number he had left for Gail to contact him.

The next call she made was long distance. Sister Drew spoke briefly to Marian Stevens and then listened intently. As she did so, her face began to light up, and when she eventually replaced the receiver, she sat for a few moments in deep thought.

Gail was sitting on the side of the bed when Sister Drew at last returned to the room. She looked up at her blankly.

"I've been remembering what happened in the car just before. . . just before. . ." She swallowed painfully.

Gail fought for control, closing her eyes tightly. "We'd been talking about the wedding. Bill was bored and watching Dad's driving. Mum always carried some sweets or biscuits. I was trying to get her bag when Bill suddenly yelled." Gail's eyes flew open. "Perhaps that startled Dad," she whispered. "Bill was leaning over the seat right next to him."

Sister Drew's arm tightened slightly, but she remained silent, allowing the memories to surface at last.

"I'd undone my seat belt and was right down on the floor. I don't know how it happened." There was another pause and then she concluded sadly, "There was something Wayne was going to tell me, too. When we got home. Guess I'll never know what it was now."

Sister Drew still waited patiently, and eventually Gail stirred and turned with sudden resolution to face her.

"Sister Drew, there's something I want to ask you. There was an old man on the plane this afternoon. He. . .he told me God loves me and longs for me to turn to Him. He said to reach out to Him and. . . and. . . I need Him so much, but I don't know how. . .or. . . I've been learning so much about God these past few weeks." Her eyes filled with a great yearning. "Jim. . ."

The way she choked on his name brought a gleam to Sister Drew's eyes that she hastily veiled as Gail stumbled on.

"Jim said once that he had handed over complete control of his life to Jesus Christ. Do you know if that is what the old man may have meant? Is that why you and Jim and his mother are so different from so many other religious people I've met? Like Aunt Harriet?"

There had been many times when Sister Drew had visited Gail in the hospital and had prayed and longed to talk to her about Christ as she did during the next half-hour or so. There were many questions from Gail and many answers found in the slightly battered Bible that Sister Drew picked up from the bedside table.

Gail carefully watched her as she talked and explained. The words she quoted from the Bible were burned deeply into Gail's heart and mind by the light that shone in her face and the ring of conviction and certainty that rang gloriously in her voice.

That same certainty and light had been Jim's the day he had preached. It had been Marian Stevens's when she had answered Gail's questions. And it had been in the old man—a total stranger.

Finally, Sister Drew rose to her feet and looked lovingly and longingly down at Gail.

"There's so much more I could share with you, Gail so much more God has to teach us both in the future. We don't know why God allows tragedy to strike at us, but we do know He loves us. Above all, remember that the proof we have of His love for all time is the death of Christ on the cross. God allowed that suffering, too. But He was also there—in the suffering. If you take that first step and ask Christ to come into your life, then He will become your teacher. I'm afraid it all boils down to faith. If you really believe that He is God's Son, and wants you to share an intimate relationship with Him, then you will do what He wants you to—you will obey Him. Only then will it be possible for Him to pour out His blessings and promises upon you the way He wants to. He will give you a whole new life and purpose for living. And you'll never be alone again."

She paused. Gail's face was very pale and drawn. She was looking down at her hands as they fiddled with a well-crumpled handkerchief.

"Now, my dear," Jean said gently. "I think you've had enough for one day. I've organized a room here in the Home for you and you can go and settle down there and think about it all in peace and privacy."

By the time Gail fell into bed that evening, she was too weary to try to sort it all out. As she snuggled into the soft pillow, her last waking thought was of the love on the old man's face as he told her that God loved her.

With her eyes closed, a deep, heartfelt prayer rose to her lips in the simple whisper of a child.

"Thank You, for loving me so much."

And then she slept deeply and without dreams until the early morning sun crept through her window.

Gail stirred and stretched luxuriously. It had been quite early when she had gone to bed, and she glanced at her watch to see that it was not yet time for the first shift of nurses to be up and scurrying into their uniforms.

She felt relaxed and rested as she had not felt for a very long time. A sense of well-being enveloped her as she turned over and looked around at the familiar bareness of the room. It was so typical of the other rooms she had occupied for years.

As she lay there, she remembered the way she had felt the day she had thought she had said good-bye to rooms like this. A slight smile stirred her lips as she thought of Ann's reaction to her sentimental tears.

That memory led to others. She got out of bed and went across to the window. It was a glorious new morning, the early rays of the sun just beginning to glisten on the trees in a nearby park. She stood there for a few moments, her heart full. Then she lifted her gaze a little and saw the small building tucked away among some trees.

Swiftly, she reached for her clothes and hurriedly dressed before making her way to that small building. It was the hospital chapel. She hesitated in the doorway. It was never locked and, as she sat down in a pew near the door, she felt ashamed that in all her years at the Nurses' Home she had never before ventured inside.

She looked around her. Soft lighting revealed the tasteful furnishings. There was a small platform with an altar. Gail thought briefly of the many people who, over the years, had come in here seeking God while their loved ones lived or died in the wards nearby.

She wondered if Beth and Jim had been here.

With a sigh, Gail leaned her head against the cool cement wall. She thought of Beth's angry, bitter words and then, with a feeling of relief and release, she remembered the love and acceptance in Marian Stevens's eyes and arms. She pushed thoughts of Jim away and dwelt on Sister Drew's words of the night before.

She closed her eyes, but the slow tears forced their way past her eyelids and trickled down her cheeks. Her whole body yearned for that God who loved her.

The minutes passed in that quiet place. Not even the hum of the awakening city intruded. Gradually, Gail began to feel that she was not alone. The sensation became so strong her figure tensed, her eyes flew open, and she glanced around. The chapel was empty.

"You'll never be alone again."

Sister Drew's words. Wonderful words.

When eventually Gail moved again and raised the head that had been bowed for countless moments, she did not realize that in her face shone the same brilliance that had lit up Sister Drew the night before. She only knew a great sense of peace and relief.

Reluctantly, she at last rose to her feet and, as she turned towards the door, noticed for the first time the painting hanging on the back wall. She peered at it for a moment, and then abruptly moved closer.

She was right. It was the same portrait of Christ that hung in Jim's bedroom. The beads of sweat glistened on the strong forehead above the eyes that she had often thought about when Christ had been mentioned.

Whether it was the soft lighting or her own imagination she was not sure, but it seemed that this painting reflected even more of His strength and tenderness as He looked at her.

When Gail at last emerged from the chapel, the sun had strengthened and hurrying nurses were making their way across to relieve the tired night staff. She lingered for a while, under the trees, looking about her. Perhaps this was where God wanted her to be. She had an appointment to see Miss Fisher later on. For a moment, a great longing for those sun-drenched black soil plains swept through her.

And for Jim.

She lifted her chin and straightened her shoulders. The old man's Friend had not let him down for over sixty years. Her new Friend would give her the strength to cope.

Later on in the morning, Sister Drew looked keenly at Gail as she walked into her office. The strain was gone from her eyes. She was at peace. There was a spring in her stride that told of purpose and hope. For a moment, she wondered if the change in her was merely the result of a good night's sleep and the release of tension. Then, with an endearing touch of bashfulness, Gail smiled gently at Sister Drew.

Gail stared in embarrassed surprise at the tears that began to slowly trickle down the lined face. Sister Drew brushed them away with the back of her hand, stood up, and walked around her desk to draw Gail close and kiss her gently on the cheek.

"I'm just so glad, my dear," was all that she said.

They looked at each other and Gail's lips at last twitched. Sister Drew gave a smothered laugh as she reached for a tissue and wiped her eyes. They beamed at each other.

"Well! I never thought the day would come when Sister Drew would cry all over me," Gail said daringly.

It was Sister Drew's turn to look a little embarrassed as she turned back to her desk. "It's the first time someone I have been talking to about the Lord has become a Christian," she retorted.

Her experience was still too new and wonderful for Gail to talk about, so she said swiftly, "Do you think I'd be allowed to see Art now?"

"Most certainly." Sister Drew's voice regained its usual crispness. "I've already rung the nursing unit manager and gained permission for you to go and see him at any time. And have you rung that Reverend Diamond yet?"

"No," Gail said reluctantly. "He was the minister at the church back home where Mum sometimes went." She paused, and then burst out with, "I want to talk to Art first. I realize now there's so much I don't know about the accident. Oh, Sister Drew, I'm so ashamed about my utter selfishness. If I'd gone to see him before, when you begged me to, so much anguish could have been avoided. Beth would not have been so bitter and. . .and Jim. . ." She stopped short and stared miserably at Sister Drew. "Art was right. I'm a poor specimen of a person. I. . ."

"You *were,* Gail. You were. Not now. Remember that now you're a new person. That's all in the past. Certainly the effects of the past can still be there, but you, yourself, have a new beginning."

Gail stared at her. A new beginning. A new Friend. A new Life. It was true. Sister Drew thrilled at the light that began to warm the dark eyes until they glowed with a deep fire.

"Thank you," Gail said softly. She made her way to the door and then turned and smiled at Sister Drew. "Thank you," she said fervently, and then was gone.

The door to Arthur's room was propped open when Gail arrived. A beaming nurse coming out of the room eyed her curiously, but cheerfully told her to go straight in as her patient had been fretting to see her all morning.

"I thought you'd be here ages ago," Art scowled at her as she approached his bed.

They eyed each other silently. Gail was relieved to see how friendly his eyes were behind the scowl. His face was less drawn and pale than the day before. Unexpectedly, he grinned at her.

"Sit down, please. And don't you dare faint on me again or darling

Sister Jean Drew will eat me for dinner."

Gail didn't move. She moistened her lips and began to say, "I want to say how sorry I am for—"

He scowled at her again as he rudely interrupted.

"Please, keep quiet and sit down."

Gail sat. She gripped her fingers together and tried again. "I can't shut up. I've behaved despicably and caused you a lot more pain than you already had and—"

Arthur raised a thin hand and shook it at her. "If you don't stop at once, I'll ring the bell and get you kicked out," he said ferociously.

She stared at him helplessly.

His face softened again. "There was plenty of excuse for you, you poor kid."

Gail looked down at her hands.

He straightened the sheet across his chest and cleared his throat. "Er. . .look, there's a lot to talk about and I don't want those nurses to know. Would you mind closing the door so they can't hear us?"

When Gail had sat down again, he was frowning as he examined his fingernails. She could not think of a single thing to say, and sat studying him until he shot a glance at her and said abruptly, "What did you mean yesterday when you asked me if I would still be here today?"

Gail tensed, searching very carefully for the right words. "Two days ago, I received a couple of letters that told me that certain people looking after you were afraid that you were becoming too depressed and might. . .might. . ."

He was still looking at his hands while she paused, hesitant to say more, and then he raised his head and looked at her. "And then I sent Beth home and after I spoke to you the way I did you were convinced they were right?"

She nodded slowly.

He sighed. "Nothing seemed worthwhile anymore. I was sick of pain. . .sick of being a cripple. . ." His voice was low and full of anguish. "I'd already made a mess of our marriage. I'll never know why Beth loves me. But she does, and she's a very fine woman. Too fine to have to put up with me. I could see what it was doing to her, having to choose between me and the kids, seeing me here day after day. I couldn't stand it any longer." He stopped abruptly.

Gail waited for him to continue, and then she asked softly, "And now?"

"Now?" He looked at her intently. "After you went last night I suddenly saw myself as the coward I really am," he said with self-loathing. "It was just the easy way out."

Gail swallowed and forced herself to say shyly, "Weren't you afraid of meeting God in such a way?"

He stared at her. "Don't tell me you believe all that religious stuff that Beth does?"

She nodded briefly.

"Well, how do you like that."

"It's all very new to me, I'm afraid, and I'm not sure if I can explain any of it yet, but—"

"And don't you try, either," Art exploded. "After we were married, Beth nagged me more than anything else about God and going to church. I can't believe in her God of love and that's final!"

Gail was so startled she blurted out before she stopped to think, "Well! If it wasn't for the way I've been gradually learning about God, I'd never have come to see you yesterday, and you could have been dead—oh!"

Gail gasped and put her hand up to her mouth and stared at him with appalled eyes.

There was a tense silence.

"I guess you could be right at that," Art at last said very softly in a shaking voice.

"Oh, I'm so sorry for saying that the way I did, I—"

"Please, stop saying you're sorry." He cleared his throat. Then, in a strained voice, he said, "Open that top drawer of the locker and find a hard-covered book shoved to the back."

Gail stared at him blankly until he glared at her and said fiercely, "Do it! Please!"

When she turned back to the bed with the book in her hand, she gazed down at him in stunned amazement. Carefully, between several pages of a large book, he had stored quite a number of tablets of different shapes and sizes.

"I'd worked it out—some are antibiotics that I didn't want to stop the infections. But I'd worked it out that, with the pain tablets and sleeping pills for last night, there should have been just enough. Instead, I swallowed the ones given to me last night and had the best sleep since I don't know when," he added shamedly. Then, in a mild panic, "Please throw those things down the sink. Quickly, before a nurse comes in."

Gail shook the book over the sink until she was sure all the tablets were gone, then turned on the tap and washed them away.

Art breathed a sigh of relief.

"I just don't understand how you could have fooled the nurses so many times!" Gail said incredulously.

He grinned weakly. "It wasn't easy. And some nurses I couldn't do it with—stood over me with beady eyes. And sometimes the pain was just so bad. . . . I made up for that by asking for them when I didn't really need them. So, it took a bit longer than I thought." His face sobered and, for a moment, he looked haunted as he added, "I didn't know how long a night could be."

Gail returned the book to the locker and sat down again.

"Let's not mention it again," Art said. "I've been in a panic to know how to get rid of them, but then I figured you might understand. . . . That's all over now. Finished." He swallowed and said slowly, "I guess you really came to see me to hear about the accident."

"I've been able to remember, since seeing you, the last few minutes before the smash," Gail managed to say at last. She still felt very shaken, and knew she would in the future always be one of those beady-eyed nurses!

Art looked at her speculatively. "Do you know, in some peculiar way, it was a relief to talk about it yesterday. Even though you fainted, I felt as though a great weight had gone after you left."

"Well, Sister Drew seems to think that now that I know what. . . ," Gail gulped, "what you told me about the fire, I'll probably not have any more nightmares. It's still very difficult to talk about it all, but there's something I've thought about since that doesn't make sense."

Gail paused. Neither took any notice of the heavy footsteps in the corridor. Gail had her back to the door, and Arthur had removed his eyes from her face as she spoke and closed them.

Neither heard the door pushed slowly open as Gail continued, "How could you have pulled me from the wreck when you were so badly injured yourself?"

There was silence for a moment, and then a deep voice spoke from the doorway.

"That's something I'd very much like to know, too."

Art's face lit up. "Jim!" he yelled.

Chapter 12

Gail froze while Jim took a few more steps into the room and came to the other side of Art's bed and into her line of vision. "How are you, Art?" His voice was polite, if a little mechanical.

Unfortunately, Jim wasn't even looking at the man on the bed. Blue eyes were locked with dazed brown ones.

Gail stared at the tall brown man in the familiar brown suit. It couldn't be. He was in Queensland. He was on the header.

She must have said so, because white teeth showed briefly for a moment, and it was Jim's voice that said gently, "I'm not, you know. Mr. Garrett is."

Hilda's father. Gail blinked rapidly, and then lowered her eyes.

"You didn't stop running so I had to come to you," the quiet voice said, and her eyes flew to meet his again.

Art had been looking from one to another in surprise. At last his eyes lit with amusement.

"Hey! I thought visitors to poor sick invalids came to see them—not each other," he said in a plaintive voice.

Gail blushed scarlet and tore her eyes away from Jim.

"We. . .er. . .didn't say good-bye properly," said Jim with a laugh in his voice. He pulled up a chair and sat down. With his chin resting on his hands as he leaned on the bed, he looked searchingly at Art. "You look a lot better than I expected after what Beth has said."

Art and Gail looked at each other. His eyes pleaded with her not to say anything.

"I guess it's the pretty visitor I have," he said quickly.

Jim looked suspiciously from one to the other. "You appeared to be having a very interesting conversation when I walked in."

Arthur looked embarrassed, and then suddenly alarmed.

"How long were you in the room?"

"I heard Gail ask you a question." Jim's eyes narrowed as Art relaxed. "Apparently, she seems to think that you pulled her from the wreck."

"Well," said Art a little too quickly and a little too casually, "I was just about to ask her what on earth she was talking about when you burst in."

Gail stared at him "But yesterday you said—"

Art interrupted her swiftly. "Yesterday you fainted, remember?"

"Fainted?" Jim exclaimed with concern.

"Apparently she didn't remember anything about the accident, and I'm afraid something I said shocked her."

"Was it about the fire?" Jim asked abruptly.

Gail's eyes widened. "How did you know?" she gasped.

"That nightmare you had, remember? You were yelling out something. I've given a lot of thought to that since I found out who you were." He stopped.

"I'm so sorry about all the deception, Jim," Gail said huskily after a pause.

Art watched curiously as Jim smiled at her and relief flashed into her face. "Hmm. It seems there are things I don't know," he complained.

"You'll no doubt hear all about it from Beth," Jim said rapidly. "Now, stop trying to sidetrack us. About Gail's question—what did you think Art said yesterday, Gail?"

Art started to protest again, but Jim ignored him and looked at Gail.

Something here was not quite right. Gail looked from one to another with a puzzled frown.

"Art said he pulled me out of the car just before it. . .it. . ." She swallowed. "I only vaguely remember anything at all after the impact. But someone was pulling me and. . ." She wiped a hand across her eyes.

There was silence. Art's thin cheeks were tinged with pink. Jim watched him closely.

"This interests me profoundly, Gail. You see, the police and doctors were rather puzzled. They didn't know how you could have received the type of injuries you had when Art kept insisting you must have been thrown out of the car."

"Thrown out! But Art, you said—" She stopped abruptly.

"What did he tell you, Gail?" Jim's voice had hardened.

She opened her mouth to answer him but Art suddenly cut in. "Please, don't make the poor kid go through all that again," he said roughly. "Okay. I acted the big hero."

There was silence. Art stared determinedly at the ceiling. He was very pale.

"You can't just leave it at that, I'm afraid, old man." Jim's voice was very gentle. "Couldn't you tell us a bit more?"

Gail held her breath and expelled it slowly as Art began to talk in a painfully disjointed voice.

It appeared that the car had been tossed off the huge bull-bars of the truck and then it had turned into the embankment beside the road. The truck had only jack-knifed and Art had merely been bruised and badly shaken. He had run over to the mess of glass and metal that had once been a car, not really thinking that anyone could have survived. The smell of petrol was strong and he had just noticed a wisp of smoke when he heard someone moan. He had managed to drag her only a few feet when the car burst into flames. Gail had come to a little and started to fight him. Suddenly, the petrol tank had exploded and something hit him in the back.

Art only told them the bare facts that morning. Later, when Gail talked to the police and ambulance crew, she found out that Art had fallen across her own body and shielded her from the fire. The grass near them had caught fire. The first rescuer on the scene had arrived just in time to beat out the flames as Art's clothes caught fire and prevented Art from being more severely burned than he had been. Even then, the burns had been bad enough to cause added problems in the treatment of his back.

When Art finished talking, he flung one arm up across his eyes and the two listeners saw his chest heave and heard one hard, dry sob burst from him.

There were tears running down Gail's own cheeks. Instinctively, she stood up and sat on the bed and put her arms around Art.

"Oh, Art," she murmured. "Thank you, so much. And I'm so sorry that you were so badly hurt saving my life."

Art tolerated her comforting arms for a few moments and then pushed her away. "I thought I told you to shut up about that 'sorry' business," he muttered.

Jim was the first to recover and adroitly changed the subject by starting to tell Arthur about the harvest. Some of his old truckie mates had been driving semitrailers carrying grain, Gail discovered as she listened quietly. Jim rambled on for a while until both Gail and Arthur had recovered and composed themselves.

Then, Jim looked at Gail and announced casually, "By the way, Gail, you'll be interested to know that while we were in Brisbane yesterday, Mum killed a large brown snake."

Gail exclaimed in horror.

"Where abouts, Jim?" asked Arthur with interest.

"Near the laundry door." Jim grinned at Gail's expression. "Don't look so frightened. Be thankful it wasn't curled up in a pile of dirty clothes when you were doing the washing. We think it must have been after some of the milk left out for Bonnie."

"I bet Mum broke her clothesline prop again," Art said with a grin. Jim nodded, and both men chuckled.

"She always grabs the longest weapons she can find," Art explained to Gail. "She reckons she's busted every prop she's ever had over the years killing snakes."

Gail thought of the clothesline prop she had often used. It had been at least eight feet long. "I don't think I could even get that close to a snake to kill it," shuddered Gail.

Jim's expression sobered. "If you knew it was around where the children played, and that next time it could bite one of them, you would."

They were all silent for a moment. Jim was looking intently at

Gail. "Gail hates snakes," he said softly to Arthur without taking his eyes off her.

Gail felt warmth creeping into her cheeks again. She lifted her chin and looked Jim straight in the eye. It wasn't she that had anything to be ashamed of that night she had nearly stepped on the snake.

Arthur glanced from Gail to Jim—they were absorbed in each other. His lips twitched and he began to laugh softly.

They both turned and stared at him as he muttered, "Well, well." He tried to turn the laugh into a cough behind one hand. "Er, yes. Interesting topic. . .er. . .snakes," he said very rapidly. His eyes were dancing. "Jim, do you remember the black one your dog, Toby, flushed out?"

He launched quickly into a snake yarn, giving Gail a chance to recover again.

After that, Arthur wanted to know all about Jacky and Robbie. His face softened while they told him about the chicken pox episode and their antics with the collie pup. Whatever the children's feeling about their father, it was obvious that he was hungry for news of them.

There was a shadow on Arthur's face as Gail assured him that Jacky had no scars on her face from the scabs. She wondered if the children's illness had not been the last straw for him in his already depressed state.

The physiotherapist arrived shortly afterwards to "do her torturing," as Arthur put it. Jim and Gail rose at once.

Gail reached out and gently touched one of Art's thin white hands. "I'll be back when I can to tell you all about my time up there," she promised with a sympathetic smile.

"I'll see you again before I go home tonight, mate," Jim said as he reached out and shook Art's hand.

"Yeah, you do that." A twinkle sprang to life in the eyes so much like his son's. "And then you can tell me when the wedding's going to be," he drawled softly.

Gail heard and nearly tripped on her way to the door. She didn't see Jim's look of utter amazement. Then, a dark tide of red swept over his face as he glared at his brother-in-law. Jim muttered something Gail didn't hear, but Art was chuckling out loud as he followed Gail outside the room.

Gail went striding off down the corridor and Jim didn't catch up with her until she stopped and jabbed the button for the lift. When she turned to face him, her chin was tilted, her eyes turbulent.

Before he could speak, she said quickly, "I'm afraid I've an appointment with the director of nursing very shortly. There's a job available for me. I don't think I'll have much time to see you before you go home. With uniforms and things to organize," she ended a little lamely.

"But Gail," he began urgently, "I came to see you. To take you back. Mum wants—"

The lift doors opened and several people crowded past them. He opened his mouth again, but she broke in, knowing her self-control wouldn't be able to take much more.

"I'm not going back, Jim. I'm sorry, but that was only a job to tide me over." She stepped into the lift.

He followed her and glared at a couple of unfortunate nurses who joined them. "Gail, we've got to talk," he began desperately as the lift doors closed. His hand smoothing over his face in the old characteristic way was the last straw.

"Not today, Jim," Gail's voice trembled. The lift stopped. "Nursing Administration is on this floor. Good. . .good-bye. I hope you and Hilda. . .your wedding plans. . .be happy. . ."

She couldn't look at him as she brushed past and raced off down the corridor, around a corner and out of sight. Tears were blurring her vision. She had once worked on this floor, and she went through a swinging door and then found herself in a linen room. It took her a couple of minutes to gain control, but she knew there was no way she could keep her interview with Miss Fisher. A nurse burst into the room; Gail straightened, murmured an apology, and retreated.

She headed for the stairs and on the next floor found a phone. After dialing Miss Fisher's office and asking for the appointment to be changed to the next day, she headed for the lifts again, trying not to think of Jim. She thrust her hand into the pocket in her skirt and felt the piece of paper on which Sister Drew had written Reverend

Diamond's phone number. She had met him several times over the years, and suddenly desperately needed to talk to someone who had known her family.

On the ground floor she made for the public phones.

When she at last hung up, the tears were pouring down her face again—but this time from utter wonder and joy. Outside, the sun streamed down as she lifted her radiant face and breathed deeply. She had to tell someone. Sister Drew would understand. But first. . .

It was late in the afternoon when Sister Drew, standing at her office window, breathed a sigh of relief as she watched Gail stride across the car park towards the Nurses' Home just like she had all those weeks ago.

She had been very concerned since Jim had erupted into her office, hours before, after their visit to Art, demanding that she help him track Gail down. For a moment, she watched the steady approach of the slender figure. As she got closer, Gail looked up briefly and Sister Drew smiled thankfully at her serene expression.

Gail paused for a moment outside the open office door and listened to hear if anyone was with Sister Drew. Then, she knocked and went in.

"Sister Drew, "I've got something rather wonderful to tell. . ."

A tall figure outlined near the window swung around.

Gail stopped, and then advanced slowly. "Why, Jim, I thought you'd be gone."

"Oh, did you? And I suppose that's why you've now turned up!" The words were cold and furious.

As he moved swiftly across the room, Gail looked into his face and took a step back at the fury and frustration glaring at her from the white, grim-faced, disheveled, desperate man. He reached out and grabbed her about the elbows, hauling her close.

"Where on earth have you been, Gail! We've turned the place upside down looking for you! How dare you run away like that when I've come so far to see you!"

"Me? But. . .but. . .Jim!"

The last word was muffled as hungry, urgent lips stopped his name on her mouth. It was a relieved, angry kiss. For a moment, she was too stunned to move. Then, her lips softened and began to respond as they always would to this beloved man.

Jim wrenched his head away. Gail stilled, waiting for she knew not what. He groaned, let his painful grip on her arms go and, for one dreadful moment, she thought he was already regretting the kiss. Then, his arms were around her, pressing her close to his body, his hand in her hair, holding her head against his as their lips joined again. This time there was no mistaking the tenderness, the love, that poured from one heart to the other.

At last, they searched each other's eyes, still clinging as though the other would disappear.

"I don't understand," Gail's voice was breathless with wonder and dawning excitement. "I thought you. . .you and. . ."

The anger had gone from his vivid blue eyes. There was no mistaking the light that blazed from them as he surveyed the rosy blush flooding Gail's bewildered face.

"I've wanted to do that ever since the night I made you cry," he murmured, then touched her lips briefly again with his as though he couldn't resist them.

Suddenly, with violence, she pushed him away from her. "Then why?" Anger and indignation started to rise in Gail. "Why did you kiss me and then be so dreadfully sorry! Why the *please forgive me, it won't happen again* drama," she spat at him.

One large hand wiped over his face.

"And don't *do* that!" she yelled at him.

He stared at her, the spot of color high on his cheekbones fading. "Do what?" he asked in a strained voice.

She turned her back and hunched her shoulders. "It doesn't matter," she muttered.

Gentle, hesitant hands touched her shoulders and he moved so he could see her face again. "Don't. . .don't kiss you again?"

She glared at him defiantly. "Yes! What about your wedding plans with Hilda? I do take it that was why you were so sorry?"

"Hilda?" Sheer amazement filled his face. "What on earth has she got to do with anything?" A thunderstruck expression swiftly chased the amazement away. "You mentioned her just before you ran off, didn't you? You don't think. . .? You do! Why?" His hands tightened on her.

"Because she told me!"

"Gail, we've got to talk," he said urgently.

"You've already said that!" she snapped at him, hardly daring to believe what she was thinking. "So, talk!"

He stared at her desperately. Then, he straightened. She held her breath when his hands let her go. A multitude of expressions flew across his face. Then, blue eyes were piercing her to the bone.

"Right! First, I couldn't believe my eyes when I first saw you. You were so angry and the most beautiful woman I'd ever seen. I knew from the beginning you were dangerous to my peace of mind. There was so much sadness in you, so much mystery about you. Above all, you didn't have a personal relationship with Christ. I guess I've almost developed a. . .a phobia about loving any woman who couldn't share my commitment to Him. I've seen what's happened to too many marriages where that one vital sharing is impossible. Even Beth. . . And then, when I was beginning to wonder about that, I found out about Wayne. You can hardly bear to talk about him still."

Gail's mouth had dropped open. Her hand went out to him as remembered anguish filled his eyes. He grabbed her hand and she winced as his hand tightened.

"Please, Gail, won't you come back with me," he pleaded hoarsely. "It'll give you more time to—"

"Jim," she interrupted the staccato words, still scarcely daring yet to believe what his eyes were telling her, "Oh, Jim, I do share your love for Christ."

"I know. Aunt Jean told me when I was so upset when you disappeared. But I meant more time to get over losing Wayne, more time so that perhaps you might learn to love again. To love me. . ."

She gasped. "Oh, Jim" she said wildly, "First Reverend Diamond tells me all my family, Wayne, too, had yielded completely to Christ's claims on their lives. There's absolutely no doubt I'll see them all again one day with Him. After lunch, I spent ages walking, sitting in the chapel, talking with God. And now. . .are you saying you. . .you love me? You want to be with me for all my tomorrows?"

"Of course I'm saying I love you. Of course I want to share with you all the tomorrows God gives us. The only wedding I'll ever be planning with anyone will be with you—no one else," he said furiously. "Surely, you must have known. Everyone else seems to. Even Arthur, after two minutes! I love you and. . ."

Sister Drew softly approached her office, hoping against hope that leaving Jim alone before Gail had arrived would have given those two dear people a chance to sort some things out. She poked her head around the partly opened door.

Well, well, she thought as she very quietly closed the door firmly on the two young people kissing so lovingly. As she walked away, her eyes were misting, her heart singing with joy, her lips gently moving with a loving prayer.

"Oh, thank You, Lord. Bless them! Bless them!"

SEARCH FOR YESTERDAY

To my delightful daughter, Gaylene, who has helped so much in the plotting and dreaming of my stories. Also in memory of our own beautiful Trixie—the Polly of this story—who died during the writing of this book.

Chapter 1

A nd that's when I pronounce you man and wife. Then you can lift the veil back and kiss Gail." The Reverend Rance Telford's deep tones were very matter-of-fact.

Hilda shivered. She heard Jim Stevens ask a question with laughter in his voice. Then he bent over and kissed Gail Brandon's flushed, smiling face.

Looking away from the group at the front of the small church, Hilda clenched her hands tightly. She swallowed painfully, forcing the tears back.

Why on earth didn't I suggest they pick up Dad for this rotten rehearsal? she thought despairingly, and then looked over at the slight, gray-haired man at the organ. *Because I knew he wouldn't be able to get home with them until much later, and he's really still not very well.*

But deep down, Hilda knew that was only part of her reason. She did want her father to be back home as soon as possible, but she had bitterly been forced to acknowledge the real reason to herself. She was too proud to let Jim and Gail think their wedding rehearsal would be so painful she couldn't be here. And she still had to survive the wedding itself anyway.

Jean Drew's soft voice made her give a little jump. "Are they nearly finished, Hilda?"

She glanced up at the older woman who had come to stand in the back aisle behind her. "I'm. . .I'm not sure," she said jerkily.

As she looked down at her, Jean's eyes narrowed. "Are you all right, Hilda?"

Hilda suddenly realized she had not managed to stop all the tears. Hurriedly she brushed at her cheeks with the back of a hand. "Just. . .

just feeling a bit nostalgic I suppose. I grew up with Beth and. . .and Jim."

Her husky words sounded forlorn, defensive, even to her own ears. She felt a blush creeping into her face, and quickly looked away.

"Yes, I know. You joined us on several outings the times I've managed to visit over the years."

Jean's quiet voice was full of compassion, and Hilda gritted her teeth. Of course Jim's mother's best friend from Sydney would know what an absolute fool she had made of herself over Jim last year.

"Are you sure you wouldn't like to help Marian and me with the flowers for the service?"

Hilda tensed.

Jean must have noticed her reaction and added swiftly, "I mean for tomorrow morning. Marian and I decided we just had to put at least one bowl of red roses in here for Good Friday even if they don't last until the wedding Saturday morning. But somehow that one bowl has grown." Her voice filled with amusement at her old friend who was making her way through the pews to join them. "The mother of the bridegroom is getting a bit carried away out there!"

"Oh, is she just!"

Hilda closed her eyes briefly, and then turned and managed a smile up at Marian Stevens. Pain lashed her as she saw the laughter in the familiar faded blue eyes disappear once they looked at her.

"It was good of you to drive Bob here, Hilda," Marian said briefly.

"He's still not really over the flu," Hilda responded sharply, looking back at her father. "He shouldn't even be out in the cool night air."

Her father must have heard her raised voice and glanced across at her. He looked anxious for a moment, and then smiled gently. She loved him dearly and even more these past long months for his wonderful support since Jim had told her he and Gail Brandon were going to be married. She forced an answering smile, and saw his smile widen and his lined face relax with relief.

Hilda thought she had come to grips with the fact that the dream she had nurtured for years of one day being Jim's wife was dead. But now pain knifed through her again as she looked back at the bridal party. Gail's attendants were Ann Green, one of her nursing friends from Sydney, and Jim's younger sister, Beth.

Beth was the same age as Hilda, and so they had always been in the same class right through school. An only child of older parents, Hilda had often been lonely and had loved spending as much time as she could wangle at the neighbors farm a few kilometers away across the flat black soil paddocks.

Through the years Jim had been like a brother. Then, within a few years, Hilda's mother had died and Beth had left home when she had married Arthur Smith. Hilda and Jim had been left a twosome, and as always, continued sharing transport to parties and outings in the farming community. But that had all begun to change early last year.

And then Gail had arrived.

There was a combined burst of laughter from the bridal party, and Rance Telford began ushering Jim and Gail toward the tiny vestry behind the platform.

"About time," said Jean with a relieved sigh. She turned and followed Marian quickly back to the kitchen to start bringing out the flowers.

"Well, that's all they need me for. We can go when you're ready, love."

Hilda started at her father's voice. She had been watching Jim's tall, dark figure towering over the slighter, fairer minister. She turned her head quickly, and then caught her breath.

"Dad, you look dreadful!" she exclaimed. "I wish you'd let them get someone else to play the organ, especially tomorrow, even if you do the wedding on Saturday."

Bob Garrett ran a hand over his weathered, lined face. "I am rather tired. That bout of flu certainly did a good job on me," he sighed and then shook his head. "But I'm feeling stronger every day, and I'll be fine. Besides, the only other musician is away for the weekend."

Hilda studied the pallor of his face doubtfully. He hated being fussed over, especially since her mother had died, so she bit her lip instead of protesting further.

"You did check with Rev. Telford about staying with us tonight, didn't you?" she murmured as she stood up.

"Botheration! I forgot all about it!" Mr Garrett hesitated, and then sighed heavily as he turned back.

"You go on out to the car, Dad. I'll ask him," Hilda said hurriedly, and then her heart sank. It would mean intruding on the group in the vestry.

Reluctantly, she knocked gently on the vestry door before opening it. Faces were turned toward her, and hurt slashed her as the radiant smiles on Jim and Gail's faces were replaced by wariness.

"Dad. . .Dad forgot to ask Rev. Telford if he had decided to stay with us instead of driving all the way back to Toowoomba tonight," she blurted out hurriedly, avoiding their eyes and looking at the minister.

"Oh, Hildie, I'm sorry. I meant to ring you." Rance Telford stood as he put up a hand to push back his already ruffled light brown hair. "Yes, please. I'd love to stay tonight, and tomorrow too if I could." He walked across to her, and then looked anxious. "Are you sure it won't be too much trouble, especially since your father's been sick?"

"Oh, no," she said hastily, "he's really hoping you can come."

A rather wry look crossed the handsome face looking down at her. Heat rose to her own face.

"And. . .and I have too, of course. I. . .I mean. . .we've been looking forward to. . .to having you stay," she stammered awkwardly, and not quite truthfully. The last thing she had felt like this dreadful Easter weekend was having a guest stay. Especially the minister!

A slightly rueful grin tilted Rance's well-shaped lips. She felt the color flooding her face even more. He knew.

"I. . .I wondered if you'd like to go for a picnic after church tomorrow. To the Bunya Mountains perhaps?" she added impulsively, and tilted her chin as surprise filled his face.

"Why, what a lovely idea," Gail Brandon exclaimed. "Jim took us there a few weeks ago."

A sharp pang shot through Hilda. She deliberately kept her eyes on Rance Telford's face, hoping he had not noticed her reaction. Once she would have automatically accompanied the Stevenses on an outing like that.

The amber eyes staring down at her were piercing all of a sudden. "We'll see how we go tomorrow, perhaps," Rance said briefly.

Somehow Hilda managed to smile broadly at the young couple. "Best wishes on Saturday, you two. I'd better get Dad home now."

As she started to turn away, she glanced at Rance Telford. All the way home, the look of surprised approval that she had seen in his eyes somehow comforted her, as at the same time it embarrassed her. So even their minister was aware of the rumours she had deliberately fostered last year about her relationship with Jim.

About fifteen minutes later, lost in thought, she stopped the car to let her father out before continuing to the garage.

She did not realize how quiet she had been until instead of opening his door, he reached across and patted her gently on her hand. "It will get easier, sweetheart. Just give it more time."

"Oh, Dad," she said miserably. "Everybody knows, even Rance Telford."

"No, I don't agree. Jim and Marian would never have said anything to hurt you deliberately. And since Gail made a personal commitment to Christ, she has lost all her old bitterness and anger. None of them would want to hurt you."

She stiffened. "Wouldn't they?" Her voice was harsh.

He sighed wearily. "I think you should know them well enough to know that, Hildie." There was quiet reproof in his voice, and she refrained from answering him as he opened his door. "I won't wait up for Rance. He'll be a while yet and you can look after him. Goodnight," he said briefly.

She watched him walk slowly across the rough gravel, lit by the headlights, until he stepped onto the area of lawn the outside light reached. As she watched his slight, stooped shoulders, bitter regret lashed her. Perhaps it would have been better if she had not blurted it all out to him last year when Jim and Gail had announced their engagement. He was hurting for her, and she loved him for it, but she doubted if he could really understand the depth of her own hurt and humiliation.

She had never really thought about her father's age. Now it hit her that he would soon be seventy. He was really an old man. As long as she could remember his hair had been gray, but now it was much whiter.

When her mother had died, something seemed to have died in him also. Although he was still the gentle, loving man he had always been, he had never really regained his old exuberance and drive. And this bout of illness had taken such a lot out of him.

She garaged the car in the large shed a short distance from the house. As she strolled back to the house, weariness dragged her feet. Suddenly she wished she could just curl up on her bed, wake up in the morning to find the wedding was all over, and somehow discover her heart had stopped aching. But sleep had only come easily lately when she had been totally exhausted. And that had been most nights since her father had been sick.

With a sigh she sank onto the cane lounge on that part of the verandah only faintly lit and stared out across the yard where the outdoor light had changed the garden to a mysterious place of softly swaying shadows. There was a movement beside her, and a soft, moist nose nudged her arm.

"So there you are, Polly," she murmured to the brown and white collie, as she turned to fondle her. "And how are you tonight, hmm? Too lazy to greet us at the car?"

The dog whimpered softly, and sat beside her. One paw came up to rest on her lap. Hilda stopped rubbing the spot behind the drooping ears, and lifted the long nose to examine it in the faint light. "And are you still dribbling that rotten pink stuff from your nose, I wonder?"

Another reason to be worried. Polly had developed a slight lump on the nose, just between her eyes. And just that morning Hilda had noticed a discharge had started.

Hilda sighed. "Well, it's probably only a cyst of some sort, but it's to the vet for you. Right after Easter."

The dog settled down beside her feet, and Hilda felt a little comforted as she relaxed, her gaze returning to the shadows.

It was the crunch of gravel under swift strides that brought her awake. As she stirred and sat up a little stiffly, Polly rose and ambled over toward the steps. The man stopped with one foot on the bottom step.

"Hi, Polly. Not going to eat me tonight?" Rance Telford's deep voice murmured.

The dog's tail moved enthusiastically from side to side and she bounded down the steps. Then, to Hilda's astonishment, she opened her mouth and "talked" to him as only a collie could. When Polly had been a small puppy they had tried to train her not to bark when they arrived home, and she had ever since greeted them by what a very young Hilda had called "Collie lingo."

"Well! I've never heard her do that to anyone except Dad and me. . .and Mum," Hilda exclaimed as she stood up. "Not even Jim—" She broke off, biting her lip.

Rance paused in stroking the dog and peered toward her as she moved out from the shadows of the verandah. "We've become good friends since I've spent so much time with your father these past weeks." He studied her face. "I've kept you up," he said regretfully and joined her on the verandah. "You look very tired."

"I was out on the tractor at dawn," Hilda said abruptly, self-consciously tucking a strand of her dark copper hair behind one ear. "With Dad being sick, it's a battle to get the sorghum stubble ploughed in and the other paddocks ready for the wheat planting."

He stood stock still. "I knew you'd been working on the tractor, but you haven't been doing all the work by yourself, have you?"

"And why not," she snapped, feeling suddenly defensive. "I've always helped where I could on the farm, including driving the tractor when Dad would let me. And since he's been sick there's been no choice. The ground has to be ploughed and fertilized, ready for planting at the end of May or beginning of June. As soon as it rains. It might be between seasons and the sorghum harvest finished, but it's still a busy time. And with Dad being sick there's still a lot to do. I've got to finish before the forecast storms come and make the black soil bog down any foolish vehicle daring to venture onto it."

"But wasn't there anyone you could employ? I'm sure someone from church would have helped."

Hilda tilted her chin and glared at him, not for a moment prepared to admit she had gone very much against Bob Garrett's wishes by taking over the tractor completely, working from sunrise to sunset.

"Any men who've helped out in the past are already working flat out," she said defiantly. "The cotton farmers on the Downs are in the middle of their harvest now." Then she paused, and for some inexplicable reason she found a grin twitching her lips at his horrified face. "We farm girls are tough, you know. Not like your city-slicker ones."

An answering smile touched his face. "Not so much of the 'my' city slickers, thank you. I was reared on a farm, too. Admittedly it was a dairy farm closer to Toowoomba and a much smaller acreage than the farms out here." The smile disappeared. "But Mum certainly never had to drive the tractor, and I had no sisters." The expression on his face changed again. He hesitated for a moment, and then tilted his chin and added steadily, "I thought you of all people would have learnt not to underestimate girls from the city, Hildie."

All amusement was wiped out of Hilda at his sharp response. She fought for control as she stared at him. So even their minister condemned her.

"Did. . .did Dad tell you. . .?" Her throat seized up.

"No. Except to ask me to pray for you because you were going through a rough time," he hastened to assure her. "I can't understand why Bob didn't tell me there were no men helping you." Rance hesitated, but then continued quietly, "Jim and Gail told me at Christmas time when they first saw me about the wedding. All they said was that they were concerned about an old friend of his who had made mischief by telling Gail he was secretly engaged to her. He wondered if he should confront her. It didn't take much to put two and two together, but they didn't mention you by name."

"Big of them!" She stared at him defiantly.

His face softened, and he said very gently, "It's very hard to face up to our failures, isn't it? Let alone accept them!"

Suddenly, the pain and misery of all the long months overwhelmed her. "Failures? What would you know about being a failure? Oh, I know everything there is to know about being a failure! Failing to win Jim is only the last of a very long list." She laughed harshly and without mirth. "Failing to be the soft, gentle, domesticated female—the daughter my mother always wanted. Failing to complete the science degree at university. Failing to have boyfriends. Failing to be like all the other soppy, hypocritical Christian women at church. . ." Her voice rose hysterically. "And telling outright lies is just what could be expected from a failure! Well, isn't it?" The tears started streaming down her face.

"I sincerely hope not," she heard him mutter. He sighed deeply.

Warm hands grasped Hilda gently by the shoulders. And then her trembling body was being held firmly against him. His shoulder was just the right height for her aching head, and she leaned into him as the sobs shook her.

Hilda didn't know how long he held her, soothing her with a soft hand on her back and murmuring comforting words. It was the first time she had really let go, not wanting to upset her father any more than he had been. When the sobs died down, she pushed away from him. He released her, produced a handkerchief, and started mopping her up.

She numbly let him wipe her saturated face, but when he held it to her nose and ordered her matter-of-factly to "blow," she found herself giving a choked sound and snatching it off him. He stood silently until she had finished. Then she felt his warm gentle fingers enclose her face. Reluctantly she raised her wet eyes.

"You're. . .you're very kind. . . ," she faltered.

"Kind!"

Her eyes widened at the bleak expression that filled his face.

There was a wealth of self-contempt in his face and voice as he continued, "No, I'm not being kind. My old girlfriend could certainly have told you she didn't think I was kind. And you're very wrong about my not knowing about being a failure, Hildie, my dear."

His voice was harsh. Hilda stared at him and took a step back. Deep in his dark eyes was a depth of anguish that more than matched her own.

"I'm perhaps one of the worst failures there is." His voice choked, and she watched with fascination as he swallowed painfully. "My mother believes I've failed as a son. I'm failing as a father. I've failed in my relationship with the woman I asked to marry me, and. . .and. . ." His voice sank even further, and Hilda had to strain to hear him. "I've failed as a minister of the Gospel of Jesus Christ."

Chapter 2

Hilda stood frozen as Rance stooped, picked up the small bag he had dropped, and strode past her. He wrenched the screen door open, and stood holding it for her.

"Let's get to bed," she heard him say wearily. "I've got to get up early to finish preparing for tomorrow's service."

She moved slowly toward him, and then stopped. "Rev. Telford, what do you mean, you—"

"Oh, Hildie, call me Rance," he said impatiently, "And I shouldn't have said what I did to you. I don't want to talk about it. Now, let's call it a night. We can talk more tomorrow. And about your problems, not mine," he added sharply."

Hilda hesitated for a moment, but he looked her in the eye and glared at her so angrily, she strode past him quickly. After she had briefly shown him to his room, he muttered an abrupt goodnight and closed the door firmly in her face.

She stared with amazement at the closed door. He hadn't even let her offer him some supper. Never had she known he could be like this! What on earth did he mean? The quiet, unassuming, respected Rev. Telford a failure?

Her shoulders slumped wearily as she turned away and automatically began switching off the lights before heading for her own room. At least he knew the layout of the rest of the house and could get a drink if he wanted anything. They had been on the church roster to provide meals for him and his fiancée at various times, but he had never stayed overnight with them before.

Hilda knew he was actually employed by a large church in Too-woomba. They had made an arrangement with the small bush church on the Darling Downs to release him to preach there once a month and do any other services for the smaller congregation as needed.

With a sigh of relief that the long day was at last over, she entered her bedroom and went over to close the curtains at her window. As she reached for the cord she paused and then frowned.

Come to think of it, when was the last time his fiancée, Maree Sadler, had been with Rance? Why, she couldn't remember seeing her since those busy harvest days well before Christmas. Suddenly she realized that it must have been about then he started accepting offers from various members of the church to stay overnight.

As Hilda prepared for bed, she acknowledged with a sense of shame that she had been so absorbed in her own misery and guilt that she had never once enquired about Maree, even though Rance had visited them quite a lot lately. Not that Hilda had ever liked his tall, sophisticated fiancée very much. Maree had never actually been unfriendly, just rather cool and aloof.

The last few weeks, Hilda had come in from the paddock several times to find Rance with her father. He had always left soon after, and she had taken for granted he had been keen to get home to his beautiful fiancée.

It wasn't until she was in bed that she remembered he had also said he'd failed as a father and a son. She shook her head. She must have heard incorrectly. She could understand only too well how he could feel he had not lived up to his mother's expectations, but how could he be a father when to her knowledge he had never been married? Her eyes widened. Unless of course. . .

She suddenly realized how little she really knew about Rance Telford. He had shared briefly once in a sermon that when he had accepted Christ as his Savior while at university, he had been saved from a wasted life by the grace and power of Christ. He really wasn't much older than Jim, and his handsome, dark blond looks had caused quite a stir among the girls at church until he had produced a fiancée.

She puzzled about it for awhile, and then decided if she was going to have to spend time with him tomorrow, she had better ask her father if he knew why Rance had been so abrupt and blurted out what he had.

Then sheer exhaustion sent her into a deep sleep.

———

"Hildie! Rise and shine or you'll be late!" As he knocked sharply. Bob Garrett's voice rang cheerfully outside her door.

Hilda jerked awake and glanced at the clock. She groaned.

"I'm leaving in a few minutes with Rance to unlock the church and set up. See you when you get there, sleepyhead!"

As she sprang out of bed, she heard his footsteps moving quickly away and then the faint murmur of voices. There was only time for a very quick cup of hot, steaming tea to wake her up properly before having a quick wash and scrambling into a cool shirtwaister cotton dress.

She scowled at her pale face and the bruises under her eyes and wished fervently that she could stay home. But, as long as she could remember, they had gone to Easter services as a family, and it would upset her father considerably if she did not turn up.

Makeup could not be neglected this morning or everyone would think she had gone into mourning! The eye shadow and touch of blusher she hurriedly applied helped. The white dress emphasized the dark golden tan of her neck and arms that had deepened from her hours on the tractor.

Satisfied at last, she glanced at her watch and groaned. Grabbing her bag, she raced down to the garage. She fervently hoped there would be a spare seat in the back row, or she would have to feel all those eyes on her as she walked down the front. It wasn't until the neat weatherboard building came into view that she realized she would now have very little opportunity of asking her father about Rance.

The church was comfortably full, and Hilda reluctantly had to take a seat almost near the front. Fortunately, Rance rose to his feet as she moved rapidly down the aisle, and attention was diverted to him as the rustling and murmurs were hushed.

She watched Rance with new eyes as his gaze swept over the congregation, welcoming them all to this Good Friday service. For the first time she noticed that he had lost weight, and the lines near his mouth were surely more marked.

"Let us take another look at the cross, this morning," she suddenly realized he was saying in a quiet voice. "Let us look at the battered, bruised Man hanging on that cruel thing, suffering the taunts and jibes of His enemies, and remember this is our God there, in human form, suffering and dying in your place and mine."

Then he announced the first hymn, and the organ began playing very softly. Hilda glanced across at her father. This was one of his favorites, and suddenly she was fiercely proud of him, loving him as the music swelled and they stood to sing. She knew how softly he would throb out the first and second verses of "When I Survey the Wondrous Cross," and how the third would be a little louder, and how he loved to boom out that last triumphant declaration of commitment and love.

The tears were burning her eyes by the time the voices reverently, but loudly, started that last verse, pouring out the faith and commitment of the people. Her own voice choked with tears as she realized what she was singing as she never had before. God's demand on her life was that she give Him complete control of every aspect. How she had failed to do that!

She looked up swiftly. Rance's loud, rich tones had faltered, and faded to a complete stop. His eyes were fixed on the hymnbook in front of him. Then he moved jerkily, and she saw his hand clench tightly on the edge of the lectern. The triumphant voices and music finished together, and for a moment there was absolute stillness.

Hilda's eyes remained fixed on Rance. He opened his mouth and then closed it again, swallowing convulsively. "Let us join in prayer," he managed huskily at last with an obvious effort.

As the heads bowed around her, Hilda continued to stare worriedly at him. One lean hand passed over his mouth and she heard him clear his throat. He then clasped his hands very tightly in front of him and briefly and simply asked God to bless each one present and accept their worship and praise. Hilda was still staring at him as he said a fervent "amen."

As she sat down with the rest of the people, she felt guilty—and rather foolish—that she had not really heard what he had prayed!

Hilda found herself suddenly offering up a brief, earnest prayer for

Rance. Whatever had happened to cause his anguish, so briefly revealed to her the night before, had not stopped him from serving the church this weekend. She had just caught a brief glimpse of the effort it was costing him to remain calm, clearheaded, and stand up there in front of them all.

Whatever he thought of himself, whether he was actually the failure he claimed or not, suddenly a wave of admiration for his strength and dedication swept through her. If he really believed he was failing in all those areas, her own problems suddenly seemed minimal in comparison.

But when Hilda was standing waiting for her father after the service, those same problems surfaced savagely and she began to wish she had stayed home after all. A few folk wished her a quiet good morning, but she sensed many others weren't quite sure how to greet her. A pair of young teenage girls were obviously avidly curious about how she was taking the wedding the following day. Then a couple she knew very well walked right past her as though she was invisible and joined the crowd of well-wishers around Jim and Gail.

Her feelings raw, she turned away and spotted Beth hurrying toward her. She started to smile with relief at her old friend, but froze as Beth merely nodded tight-lipped at her before hurrying past to grab her two small children, Jacky and Robbie.

"She'll get over it, Hildie," a deep, compassionate voice murmured softly behind her. "She's very worried about her husband at the moment."

Hilda kept her face averted. "Beth hasn't spoken to me since . . .since. . ." Then what Rance had said sank in and she turned abruptly to him. "Worried about Arthur? I thought he was doing very well since they moved to Brisbane," she said anxiously.

Those compassionate eyes studied her thoughtfully for a moment, and then softened even more. "I saw him a couple of weeks ago at their house in Brisbane. He's going through another bout of depression. I didn't really get a fantastic welcome!" A wry smile crossed his face. "Told me bluntly just because he still can't walk it doesn't mean he suddenly wants anything to do with religion!"

The thought of Beth's rough diamond of a husband being suddenly confronted by a visit from Beth's home church minister brought a touch of amusement to Hilda's strained face. "And I suspect he didn't say it quite as politely as that to you!"

Rance laughed. "You suspect right!" Then he sobered, and sighed. "If ever a man needed to have a personal relationship with the Lord to get him through each day, Arthur does."

"Oh, dear, his paralysis hasn't gotten worse, has it?" Hilda asked anxiously.

"No, no," Rance hastened to reassure her. "He's still getting about in his wheelchair okay. But he's still not reconciled to being so dependant." He smiled ruefully. "I don't suppose I'd handle being partially paralysed from the waist down very well either."

Before Hilda could respond, she noticed her father approaching. "Rance, I'm going to take Dad home," she said hurriedly, "He looks so tired!"

"Right," he agreed briskly, "I'll see you both later after I've locked up."

But by the time he arrived at the farm, only Hilda greeted him. "I insisted Dad go and lie down," she said to him quickly as he entered the kitchen where she had just finished serving out a cold meal for them both. "Afraid our picnic is off," she added abruptly. "I don't want to leave him."

Rance looked concerned. "I tried to get him to let me bring someone from town to play for at least today, but he insisted he'd manage."

"I tried too," Hilda said grimly, "but my father has always done exactly what he wanted to when it comes to playing his music!"

They shared the meal almost in silence. And yet, it wasn't an uncomfortable silence, Hilda mused as she ventured a glance at him from time to time. A few times his lips were a straight line and his expression so grim, that she knew his thoughts were a long way from the peaceful farm house. She was still feeling weary and concerned enough about her father not to be interested in talking too much, even to bring up their conversation of the night before.

However, to their immense relief, after a few hours, Bob Garrett declared he was fine and insisted on joining them for the evening meal and then a game of Scrabble later. His color was much improved, and Hilda found rather to her own astonishment that she enjoyed the fun of Rance and herself being thoroughly beaten by him.

"Well!" Rance declared rather wistfully as Bob gleefully added up their scores, "It's been a long time since I enjoyed a game of Scrabble. Especially so well-matched!"

"Well-matched? Against this old rogue!" laughed Hilda, "He's always coming up with words I've never even heard! And you had a few yourself. I think you're just a pair of cheats!"

Rance's eyes danced, but he intoned piously, "Oh, no, never let it be said of two Christian gentlemen. We just read the right kind of books!"

"Yeah," she laughed back at him, "real heavy old theological tomes!"

"Tomes! Now that's a word I could have used—"

Rance and Hilda groaned together. Bob Garrett stopped and then laughed with them.

"No more!" chuckled Hilda. "I need some supper. Any takers?"

Both men chorused their approval cheerfully, but as Hilda bustled off to the kitchen, she missed seeing the thumbs up sign her suddenly grave-faced father gave his friend behind her back. Rance nodded with a slight, sympathetic smile. When Hilda returned they started teasing her, and it was with some satisfaction they eventually said goodnight to her prettily flushed, smiling face.

For some reason Hilda found it hard to explain to herself, the wedding the next day was not the traumatic time she had expected. Perhaps it was because the sheer radiance of the bride and groom left little space for regret and dwelling on "the might have beens." Perhaps it was because Hilda found herself watching Rance with new eyes again.

He had really relaxed last night, and been good fun. She had never before seen him as an ordinary man, and not in his position as "the minister." Whatever had made him blurt out his belief that he had failed as a minister, she could see no sign of that as he led the marriage service.

As she watched him smiling lovingly at the pair before him, it suddenly struck Hilda that he was a very good minister, indeed. She thought of the favorable comments she had heard expressed about him by folk he had visited in their homes when they had been facing difficult times.

"He has a pastor's heart, that one. He really cares," she had overheard said by an elderly gentleman, who had been in the throes of the heartache of having to leave his farm to live in the city. His listeners had chorused their enthusiastic agreement.

Although he had always given her the impression of being a quietly spoken, gentle man, the sermons Rance had preached with fire and passion had often made her wince, and stirred her up to determine to be a better Christian.

But my good intentions didn't amount to much. She forced a smile as her father glanced at her.

The wedding reception was being held at a large hall in the small township of Cecil Plains, about half an hour's drive from the church. Hilda drove slowly, reluctant to arrive too early.

Her father was quiet also, absorbed in his own thoughts, until he said suddenly, "Hilda, after the wedding, I. . .I have to tell you something."

His voice sounded so strained that she glanced at him sharply. "Are you sure you're up to going to the reception, Dad? I could take you home, and then return myself. I know everyone would understand."

"No, no," he said swiftly, "I am a bit tired again, but my part's finished now and I'll just sit quietly. It's just. . ." He paused, and then added steadily, "I've been talking a lot to Rance lately about something that happened a long time ago. . .a very long time ago. Ever since your. . .your mother died I've been wondering whether I should tell you. He's convinced me that you have a right to know."

"Goodness, Dad, what deep, dark secrets could you have?" Hilda said with a smile as she glanced fondly at him. Then she saw the way he was sitting rigidly in his seat, his hands clutched together. "Dad! What on earth?"

He turned and caught her worried expression. "No, not now!" he interrupted her sharply. "Later. I just had to put the decision I've made into words so I don't chicken out again. We haven't enough time now. It's kept all these years. Another few hours won't matter."

Hilda bit her tongue, stifling the questions that began to seethe. She had always known that her parents' relationship had not always been rosy. Her mother had been a very fussy, nervous person who could suddenly erupt over seemingly trivial things that displeased her.

And then in her early teens, Hilda had realized there was something important in her past she had not wanted her daughter to know. One time when she had overheard them arguing, her mother had become almost hysterical, screaming at her father that he was not to tell Hilda. As had happened so many times, he had given way to the small woman whom Hilda had always known he loved more than anyone, even his own daughter.

"You. . .you've grown very close to Rance, haven't you, Dad?" Hilda said quietly after a long, tense silence.

There was another silence for a moment, and then Bob Garrett muttered, "He's a man with an immense problem to sort out, Hildie, love. Maree couldn't cope with it and broke off her engagement to him last year."

"Broke off their engagement! But why didn't you tell me? Does anyone else know?"

"No!" he said sharply, "and he doesn't want it broadcast just yet. He had to tell the leaders of the church in Toowoomba about it all, but he doesn't want the folk here to know until a decision has been made about—"

Bob Garrett broke off and drew in a sharp breath even as Hilda slowed the car to turn into the car park. "But it's not my prerogative to talk about that. We've been doing a lot of praying and sharing the Word together to help him find his way. Things still aren't resolved for him by any means, but I think it's me who's at last found my way."

He was silent as the car rolled to a stop, and then smiled gently at the worried, bewildered face Hilda turned towards him. "Hildie, daughter-dear. . ." He reached over and touched her gently on her nose with his forefinger in the familiar way he had as long as she could remember. "I. . .I. . .you know that I've always loved you very, very much, don't you?"

She nodded, her throat choked up with emotion. He had not called her his "daughter-dear" for a long time. Then the grave expression on his face was blurred by the sudden mist that covered her eyes, as the usually undemonstrative man leaned over and kissed her gently on the forehead.

Before Hilda had got over her absolute astonishment, her father was out of the car and calling out to folk who had also just arrived. She followed him slowly, trying to behave as though the last few moments had not happened.

As the hours passed, Hilda joined in the festive activities of the reception as best she could. She had to force herself to eat the delicious meal, though, and constantly found her eyes drawn to where Rance was seated at the head table. Her thoughts were in turmoil. They swung from Rance to her father's unusual behavior and back again.

There was a burst of laughter from the bridal party, and Hilda glanced across at them automatically, her thoughts still worrying over her fathers words. What could he possibly need to tell her that distressed him so much?

"Hildie!" her father suddenly whispered savagely. "Stop scowling, and at least give the impression of having a good time! You'll spoil the day for Jim and Gail."

Hilda turned to him in astonishment.

"People are watching you," he added under his breath, and then turned to the people on his other side and engaged them in conversation.

Hilda felt the hot tide of red that swept into her face, and applied herself to the food in front of her, not game to look up. She'd hardly given a thought to the bride and groom! It was the minister taking all her attention, she realized with something like a touch of horror.

She turned a little desperately to the middle-aged lady seated on her other side and engaged her in inane conversation. Afterwards, she could never remember even the woman's name, and certainly nothing that they had talked about.

When the delicious pavlova with its topping of fresh strawberries, kiwi fruit, banana, and whipped cream was served, Hilda noticed that her father had hardly touched the roast lamb and vegetables of the first course. But his face was animated and he was enjoying himself, she told herself, trying to stifle the pang of fear for him.

She wondered briefly again what it was he had decided to tell her. Probably some old skeleton in the cupboard from his past or, more likely, her mother's. Her parents had never talked very much about the days before she had been born. Her mother had been well into her forties when Hilda had made her appearance, and they had told her many times over the years what a difference her late arrival in their marriage had made.

So it was that, when the master of ceremonies called for quiet and the usual speeches commenced, it was with a small sense of shock that Hilda realized she had hardly thought of Jim and Gail as actually being married.

Hilda studied Jim thoughtfully when it came his turn to stand up and respond. He was certainly a very handsome man. He was also a very nice man, a good friend to have. She glanced back at Rance. He was watching her intently, and for a moment their eyes locked. Then his beautiful, kind smile transformed his face, and she found her own lips twitching in response.

Suddenly it was as though a tremendous burden rolled from her, and her tentative smile became a sudden beam. She saw Rance straighten and the smile was wiped off his face. Hilda looked quickly back at Jim, feeling suddenly ridiculously shy.

She knew with sudden clarity that a part of her would always love Jim, but as the brother she had never had. He had been so right about their relationship all along.

As Jim sat down and Hilda joined in the enthusiastic clapping, she glanced at Gail and found her looking at her a little anxiously. Hilda found herself smiling a little mistily and apologetically at her. She saw Gail catch her breath slightly. Then suddenly Gail's whole face lit up as she smiled radiantly back at her.

Message received and understood.

The rest of the evening passed in something of a blur for Hilda. What stood out much later was the feeling of utter relief she had felt as she hugged Gail good-bye. The bride had changed out of the breathtakingly beautiful lace wedding gown into a smart suit and had topped her shining, honey blond curls with a frivolous piece of net that could have been called a hat.

Hilda had murmured a fervent, "I'm so sorry, Gail," and received an extra generous hug and kiss of understanding from the radiant bride. Jim had beamed at her with relief and given her one of his old brotherly hugs, before passing on to the next well-wisher to say good-bye. Then they had driven off noisily in Jim's Holden. It had been decorated with tin cans and all kinds of weird and wonderful things by Jim's young brother, Will, and some of his friends.

But all of that was overshadowed and wiped away when the touch on Hilda's arm made her turn a laughing face from watching the departing car toward Rance Telford. Something clutched her heart when she saw his pale face and anxious expression.

Then she knew, even as he spoke.

"Hildie, dear, it's your Dad. He's not at all well. Complaining of chest pain. Jean Drew's with him. We're organizing a car to get him to the doctor."

"Oh, no, oh, no," she moaned continually as she rushed back inside. But she was too late.

Bob Garrett was no longer breathing. His face was gray. Jean Drew, a very experienced nursing sister, had already started cardiac pulmonary resuscitation. Rance raced to join her, but it was to no avail.

The father Hilda had loved so dearly all her life had gone Home for eternity with his best Friend.

Chapter 3

I n direct contrast to the warm sunny weather of the Easter weekend just past, the day of the funeral was overcast and cold, a
reminder that winter was not too far away.

Hilda had come out of her anguished daze enough that first
evening to state vehemently to a devastated Marian Stevens that Jim
and Gail were not to be told. It would only spoil their honeymoon, and
she had already caused them enough heartache. At that, Rance's beautiful, gentle smile had briefly reached through to the part of her that
had frozen. It brought some semblance of warmth, but she had turned
away from him.

Rance had never been far away that first night. Dry-eyed, Hilda
had wandered aimlessly around the house and then outside to sit with
Polly crouched close beside her, until Rance had at last persuaded her
to lie down in her room.

Later she realized that Jean Drew had been there with them too,
preparing the endless cups of tea and then the supper she had not been
able to swallow for the lump in her throat. She had bowed her head
when they prayed with her, but not even prayer had penetrated her
pain. God seemed far away.

During the long two days that had slipped by, Hilda functioned on
some automatic level of rigid self-control. She was vaguely aware that
people were being very kind. Jean Drew had moved in and stayed
night and day with her. Rance had come and gone, and then had slept
at the house again on Easter Monday before the funeral the next day.

He had gently organized everything, asking her wishes, but she
had let him make all the arrangements, only requesting they sing the
hymn from Good Friday, "When I Survey the Wondrous Cross."

The funeral was held in the little building her father had worshipped and served in all his life. Rance had offered to organize it in the bigger city church, but she had refused.

"There. . .there aren't any relatives who can come, Rance," she had faltered dry-eyed, feeling so dreadfully alone. "There's only Great-Aunt Lily, my mother's aunt. And she's in a nursing home in Sydney. We. . .we never kept in touch with any of her family. So there won't be a lot of people. And he. . .he. . .this was the place he loved. . ."

Rance had looked at her a little strangely, but made no comment.

In fact, Hilda was amazed at the number who came to say their last farewell to their friend, neighbor, and brother in Christ. There were far more folk than at her mother's funeral. Only when the crowd spilled out of the packed little church did Hilda realize Rance had been wiser than she by quietly contacting someone to set up amplification outside so the overflow could hear.

Rance spoke with conviction about the resurrection and the hope of the Christian. Hilda had heard it all before at her mother's funeral. Then she had been strengthened and comforted. But now she just felt cold, and nothing that was said touched her. As she steeled herself to composedly accept the hugs and tears afterwards, it was as though it was happening to someone else. It couldn't possibly be her darling father they were referring to.

And Jim and Gail were present. They had returned from their honeymoon at the Gold Coast after all. "We loved him, too," a sad-eyed Jim said briefly. "Mum had to tell us."

Jean Drew continued to stay with Hilda the rest of the week. Despite the older woman's protests, Hilda insisted on starting up the tractor the day after the funeral. Rance had gone back to Toowoomba straight from the funeral, causing Hilda to feel as though he had deserted her. She felt vaguely surprised how much she missed his quiet, accepting presence.

It had not rained as expected, and the days warmed up again. In fact it had become very hot and humid for April, and Hilda turned on the car's air conditioner as she drove herself and Jean to the Sunday morning service the following weekend.

"I'm glad there's not a lot of paddocks left to cultivate," Hilda observed, as a trickle of sweat ran down her face. "This hot weather will surely bring the rain."

"Perhaps," said Jean quietly. "But you've nearly exhausted your-self doing it."

"It. . .it's what Dad would have wanted," Hilda said just as qui-etly, but with clipped words. She added quickly, "We'll probably get a thunderstorm this evening if this keeps up."

"Bob would not like to see how pale and drawn you are, my dear," Jean persisted.

Hilda's grip on the steering wheel tightened. The car swerved a lit-tle, and Jean glanced at her sharply.

"I wish you'd let me drive, Hilda."

"And I told you I could manage perfectly well!" Hilda snapped irritably. Then she swallowed painfully on the hard lump that seemed to have taken up permanent residence in her throat. "I. . .I'm sorry, Aunt Jean. I. . .you didn't deserve that," she murmured with shame.

When Jean didn't answer, Hilda felt worse. Jean had gently sug-gested that morning that it might be too soon for Hilda to face every-one at church, offering to share a simple time of fellowship with her at home. Hilda had simply stared at her in surprise. Dad would have expected her to go. But ever since the tentative warning, Hilda had felt the tension building up in her, and now she wondered if Jean might have been right after all.

"It's good to hear you call me 'aunt' again, child," the older woman said softly at last. "I've always been especially fond of you over the years."

There was a faint tremor in her voice, and Hilda bit her lip. It had only been the last year or so that Hilda had felt it was too babyish to keep on using the honorary title the three friends had long ago be-stowed on this old friend of the Stevens family. She had never mar-ried, and to Hilda's knowledge had no close family. Never before had Jean made any comment on being just called "Jean."

One of the senior men of the congregation led the service and preached that morning. The first hymn had hardly commenced when

Hilda knew that Jean had been right. It was too soon to sit in this familiar place with a strange face occupying the seat at the organ.

Hilda sat rigidly during the long hour that followed. She found she dared not open her mouth to sing, and she couldn't pray. Immediately after the benediction, she was immensely relieved when Jean grasped her arm and hurried her from the building before anyone could do more than smile sympathetically at her desperate, strained face. Without a word, Jean held out her hand for the car keys, climbed into the driver's seat, and drove them quickly home.

Hilda's rigid self-control lasted until they stopped at the house. As Rance's familiar figure rose from the old chair on the verandah, the volcano of emotions seething inside her erupted. It never entered her mind until a long time later to wonder why he was there and not at his church service in Toowoomba.

She sprang out of the car and slammed the door viciously. Jean followed her hurriedly. Hilda ignored Jean's tentative, "Hilda, dear. . ." and strode angrily up the steps to the quiet figure waiting for them.

"It's not fair! It's not fair!" she stormed. "Why did he have to go and leave me too? He said he loved me. If he did, why did he leave me like that? Why! Why! I. . .I didn't even have time to say good-bye. There's no one else, now. No. . .one. What am I going to do?"

Her tight fists were thumping on Rance's solid, muscular chest. She felt her knees suddenly buckle. Then she felt strong arms sweep up her shaking body. She buried her head against his warmth, clutching wildly at him. As she felt him turn and carry her inside, she heard Jean's tearful voice saying from a distance, "I've been afraid of something like this."

But then the wracking sobs came at last. Hilda cried as though she would never stop. Vaguely she realized warm arms cradled her. Rance's cracked, broken voice tried to soothe her. Moisture touched her face from his as she clung to him.

There was a faint murmur of voices. Rance moved, and she felt the soft mattress beneath her. The protective arms left her and she curled into a tight ball of agony, feeling desperately alone once more.

Rance's choked voice whispered, "God's here, sweetheart. He's loving you." Then a large gentle hand pushed her tumbled hair away from her face and stroked and soothed her.

Rance murmured something she couldn't quite hear over his shoulder to Jean, something about someone dying. There was a shocked exclamation, and then a woman's voice, like Jean's and yet not like Jean's. Briefly it broke through the pain that wracked Hilda. It was filled with such emotion. . .praying. . .

"Oh, loving God! Oh, Father! Be near and bring these tortured hearts Your comfort and Your peace. . ." The tearful voice continued to pray softly, but Hilda's sobs drowned out the words. Timeless moments later, Hilda's agony gradually died away and her exhausted body slept.

When Hilda at last stirred, for a moment she wondered why her eyes felt so sticky as she opened them, and why she had gone to bed in her clothes. Then she remembered, and gave a deep, quivering sigh. It was real. Her father really was dead.

There was a rustle of movement, and a quiet voice asked, "Would you like a hot drink, Hilda, dear?"

Hilda peered up at Jean. As the older woman's tender hand pushed back a heavy lock of dark hair away from her face, she suddenly remembered the feel of a larger, stronger hand, and pushed herself up on one elbow, glancing swiftly around the room. "I. . .I'm sorry, Aunt Jean, I. . ."

"I'm not, love. Tears are one of God's precious gifts. We've been so worried because until now there weren't any."

Hilda sat up slowly. Tears burnt behind her eyes again, but suddenly she knew Jean was right. Her head ached a little but that hard lump in her throat had dissolved. Although that crushed, helpless feeling was not completely gone, it was definitely a lot easier.

She looked around the room again. "Did. . .did I dream it, or was Rance really here?" she asked huskily.

Jean turned away quickly. "Yes, he stayed as long as he could, but he had to go. Some. . .some urgent matters were waiting for him. I'll get that drink for you. And you must be hungry," she finished a little abruptly before disappearing through the doorway.

Hilda swept her hair back from her face and swung her legs over the side of the bed. She frowned, disappointed that Rance had gone again so soon. There had been so much she needed to talk to him about.

For the first time since the wedding reception, Hilda actually enjoyed the food that Jean set before them that evening.

"It's good to see you with some color back in your cheeks," Jean said with a hint of buoyancy in her voice as she smiled gently at her. Then her expression changed. "Hilda, I'm very sorry, but I'm afraid my holidays from the hospital finish in another few days."

Hilda looked up at her blankly, and Jean added hurriedly, "I was going to ask for an extension of my leave in the morning. But now I'm wondering if you think you'll be able to cope on your own. Marian said she could come over for a few hours most days for awhile, but she has Will to think of, and the farm, while Jim's away.

Hilda reached across the table and took Jean's hand. "Oh, Aunt Jean, I don't know what I'd have done without you this last week." Tears choked her for a moment, but she resolutely forced them back. "I just haven't been thinking straight since. . .since. . ."

"Yes, yes, I know that, dear," Jean assured her quickly, "but there are certain business matters as. . .as well as other things that you need to think about, aren't there? Marian said to tell you that when you're ready, she'll help you all she can. She went through this when her husband died, and she'll be able to advise you."

"Oh," Hilda said blankly, "yes, of course. I. . .I suppose there's the bank, and. . .and Dad's will. He. . .he. . ." She fought for control.

"Now, now," Jean said rapidly, "don't worry about it anymore tonight. Try and get some more rest. We'll talk about things tomorrow."

But much later that night, after they had gone to their bedrooms, Hilda couldn't sleep, and eventually turned on the light again and started making a list of all the things she could think of that would need attention in the days ahead. The list grew ominously long. She had not ventured into her father's bedroom since he had gone. There were her father's clothes, his personal papers, his war plane collection, bills to pay. . .

The tears crept down her cheeks again. "Oh, God, I need You!"

she suddenly cried aloud. "Where's the comfort and the peace You're supposed to give at times like this to someone who believes in You?" she accused angrily.

She flung herself down on the pillow, and a flood of tears came again. Impatient with herself, she sat up after a while, fighting for control. Reaching for another tissue from the box on her bedside table, her hand bumped the book lying there. With a quivering sob, her fingers closed on it and she picked it up.

The burgundy leather cover was thick with dust. With a sense of shame she wiped it off. Since her father had been sick there had been so much to do that there had seemed no time to even have a token daily reading of her Bible. She rubbed at her wet cheeks and then she opened the book at random. It fell open at a bookmark. The words on it sprang out at her.

"Underneath are the everlasting arms."

She gave a soft sob and turned it over, knowing what she would see. A few days before her mother had died after her long illness, her father had given it to her. On the back he had written, "My daughter-dear, always let Him hold you safe in His loving arms too."

She cradled the Bible in her arms. It was almost like a rebuke directly from her father. She was crying out for help, but until now had not gone to the Source of all help and strength. She had not even opened up the Scriptures, or spent time on her knees.

In fact, she couldn't remember really spending time alone with the Lord since she had lied to Gail. Somehow it had seemed as though her prayers had bounced off the ceiling. And now, because of the faithful teaching she had been given by her parents and through the church fellowship, she knew deep down in her being what the problem was. It was only unconfessed sin that hindered her prayers and had taken away her desire to read the Scriptures.

With a sob of regret and pain, she tumbled out of bed and onto her knees. "I'm so sorry, Lord. I've been so nasty and horrible. . . and. . .and I've lied, and. . .Oh, please forgive me. Oh, Lord, I do so need to feel Your arms about me now more than I ever have," she murmured fervently.

A few more tears slipped silently down her face. She gave a deep sigh and felt herself relax.

Many times down the years she would remember those next few moments with a sense of awed wonder. The sense of God's presence was suddenly so real, so close, that it was as though He wrapped her up in His arms. She was never to forget the awareness of a great Love surrounding her. And with it came peace and the first sound, dreamless sleep for many long days.

More gentle, healing tears were shed in the next few days while doing all that had to be done. But each night in her room, Hilda opened the Scriptures and read and prayed and grasped hold of the promises she read with single-minded fervor.

"You've been really wonderful, Hilda," Jean said briskly the morning she said good-bye. "We're very proud of you."

Hilda smiled a little self-consciously at her. She knew that the "we" included Marian Stevens who had spent many hours helping out. All constraint between them was now a thing of the past.

"Hilda," Jean added a little hesitantly, "while you were outside with Polly this morning, Rance rang. He. . .he wanted to know how you were and to tell you he's sorry he hasn't been in contact with you."

Hilda refused to acknowledge even to herself just how disappointed she had been that she had not seen or even heard from him since Sunday, so she shrugged nonchalantly, and merely said, "I guess he's been busy." Before Jean could refer to him again, Hilda reached out and gave her a big hug. "Thank's so much for everything, Aunt Jean. I don't know what I'd have done without you."

"Rubbish, my dear. I wish I could have stayed and done more," Jean said a little unsteadily. "Your Dad was a very fine man. I've known him a long time and I'm going to miss him, too, you know. Now, don't forget," she added rapidly as she straightened, "let me know any time you can plan a trip to Sydney. I'd love to see you."

The house was quiet and empty after Marian had driven away with Jean. Hilda went for a stroll down to the sheds. She poked around the large machinery shed, mentally noting jobs still not attended to. Then she suddenly realized she had not seen Polly all morning.

She called and whistled, and when no collie came bounding out, her heart missed a beat. Anxiously she moved over to the small garden shed near the house. Here the dog always settled for the night beside her bowl of water and food dish. She called loudly again, and a surge of relief filled her when the collie appeared in the doorway.

"Oh, Polly, you had me worried there for a moment," she exclaimed with relief as she knelt to hug and pet the animal. To her relief the lump on the nose didn't appear to be any larger, but the dog seemed much quieter as Hilda let her inside the house and fussed over her.

"We'd better get you to the vet, I'm afraid," Hilda muttered anxiously. She thought for a moment and then went to the phone.

The vet she normally went to was out of town, but had a late appointment free the next day. After she had hung up, Hilda hesitated, and then picked up the phone again and tried Rance Telford's number. Perhaps she could call in and see him while she was in Toowoomba.

As she heard the ringing tone, sudden heat flooded through her as she remembered the way she had flown at him. And then she remembered also that his tears had mingled with her own, and she felt comforted knowing he too had thought very highly of her father. Suddenly, Hilda was fiercely grateful that he had spent so much time with her father so recently. Her father had enjoyed his company so much.

No one answered, and her disappointment was more than she had expected. She frowned at herself as she hung up and took Polly outside to give her long hair a good brush.

At first it had been too painful to dwell on that last precious day with her father. Now she let her thoughts linger on events the day of the wedding. Suddenly she remembered what her father had told her about Rance Telford and his fiancée, or rather, ex-fiancée. Her hand paused in its rhythmic brushing.

Polly objected and lifted a paw to Hilda's lap. For once, Hilda didn't smile and make her usual fuss of the dog. She resumed the brushing automatically as concern for Rance filled her.

He had been really down. Called himself a failure. Her hand paused briefly again. More than that, he had also said something about failing as a father. She dismissed his claim of failing as a minister, although to feel so, that undoubtedly dedicated man must have been feeling very down. Hadn't her father said Maree Sadler had broken off their engagement because of some immense problem Rance had that she could not cope with?

Hilda gave in to Polly's short bark of displeasure that expressive paw treatment had failed to restart the soothing brushing. But as her hand continued to untangle the dog's long hair, her mind was still with the man who had somehow begun to occupy so much of her thoughts.

Rance must have been married before, or else. . .or else their minister, who had often warned the young people about letting their boy-girl relationships get out of hand outside of marriage, might have known what he was talking about from bitter experience. She wondered sympathetically if the problem her Dad had mentioned had affected Rance in the ministry in Toowoomba.

Then, as she had many times these past few days, she pondered sadly about what her father could possibly have been going to tell her later that night. There had been no hint of anything in his private papers to give her a clue.

Her hands stilled. Polly nudged her again to continue, but this time the dog got no response. What if, Hilda mused, her father had told Rance?

"Where are you, Rance Telford?" she muttered crossly, acknowledging how disappointed she had been he had not visited her again. "Don't you know I've got so many questions you may be able to answer?"

References in the Scriptures about life, death, and the resurrection that she had never really studied in depth before, she badly wanted to ask Rance about. Now she admitted a little reluctantly that she also needed to see him again as much for his strength and compassion.

Marian rang that evening. On being told about the trip to Toowoomba she immediately offered to go with Hilda.

"No thanks, Aunt Marian," Hilda said gratefully. "I've also managed to get an appointment with Dad's solicitor." She hesitated, but for some reason she couldn't understand herself, she refrained from mentioning her intention to try and see Rance as well.

The appointment with the solicitor went smoothly. He assured her that her father's affairs were all in order and there would be no problems transferring everything over into her name. There would just be the usual numerous forms to fill out and government requirements to fulfill. It all seemed unreal, and Hilda was glad of the excuse to rush off to keep the appointment at the vet.

"It could be one of three things," the vet told her after examining Polly. "A simple infection which long-nosed animals are susceptible to, a fungal infection, or. . .or a tumor, I'm afraid."

An appointment was organized the next day for the dog to have tests under a general anaesthetic. A shaken Hilda gave Polly an extra hug once they were back in the car. "Oh, Polly, dear. It has to be just an infection. It has to!"

On an impulse, she decided to see if Rance happened to be home. The brick veneer house next to the old church on a busy road was easy to find with the sign "Church Manse" prominently displayed. She had never had cause to visit there before, and as she opened the small, wrought iron gate, she felt a tinge of disappointment at the ill-kept lawn and gardens. Surely the grounds of a minister's residence should be better maintained than this. In fact, the whole place looked deserted. She was disappointed, but not really surprised, when no one answered the door.

As she drove home into the setting sun she wondered if Rance was living somewhere else. She fervently hoped that he had someone to help him through his problems the way he and Jean Drew had been there for her.

The sun's legacy of pink-tinged clouds was fading rapidly, and the stars were starting to peep out as Hilda drove slowly up the long driveway from the road to her home. A slight feeling of panic touched her at the thought that from now on, she would be coming home to an empty house.

She did not bother to garage the car, pulling up near the house to let Polly out. It was only as she nearly reached the house herself that she simultaneously noticed a car parked down near the garage, and realized someone was waiting for her after all.

"Hello, Hildie. I hoped you'd be home tonight soon," familiar deep tones said to her from the verandah.

Her face lit up. "Oh, Rance. I'm so glad you're here! I just called to see you in Toowoomba."

She ran up the steps, and somehow both her hands were clasped tightly in his. And someone had called her "Hildie" again! In her early teenage years she had decided she absolutely hated her old-fashioned name. Her father had started calling her "Hildie" despite her mother's strong protests. And she had been "Hilda" for so long, people who had known her since birth never had become used to "Hildie."

She heard Rance give a deep sigh of relief. "You're better."

The smile on her face wobbled a little. "Not. . .not completely, but I no longer feel so. . .so spaced out."

She was a little surprised at just how thrilled she was he had come to see her, and feeling a little embarrassed, she tugged her hands from his and moved past him to open the door. She switched on the lights and then threw down her handbag on the hall table as she heard him follow her inside.

"Have you had tea yet?" she asked over her shoulder on her way to the kitchen. When he didn't answer her, she turned toward him and then was still. "You look dreadful!" she whispered at last.

His face was pale and drawn. He obviously hadn't shaved that day, but worst of all were the red-rimmed, sunken eyes. He was wearing a crumpled, stained tee-shirt and a pair of battered jeans.

He gave a harsh, mirthless laugh. "I guess that's all part of the scene that goes along with your world falling around you. We seem to be in the same boat, don't we?" His eyes swept over her, and then returned to study her face. "It's good to see you're coping so much better. Have you come to terms now with the fact that you were adopted?"

Hilda stared at him speechlessly. She opened her mouth, and nothing came out. She tried again, even as she saw Rance's face change to an expression of horror.

"A. . .adopted?" she managed to croak. "Are. . .are you crazy?"

Chapter 4

H e didn't tell you." Rance's voice was flat. He closed his eyes tightly for a moment. When he looked at her again, regret, bewilderment, a myriad of emotions had filled his pale face and red-rimmed eyes.

Neither moved.

Every drop of color drained from Hilda's cheeks as she read the truth in his eyes. She forced her legs to move and almost fell into the nearest chair.

"I wonder if there's any other way to stuff up this week?" Rance muttered angrily.

His long strides took him past her. When he returned a moment later with a glass of water, he crouched down beside her. She was shaking so much he held the glass to her lips. Her teeth clattered briefly against the edge as she obediently swallowed a mouthful. Then suddenly she pushed his hand violently aside. The water sloshed over his hand and onto the carpet. He ignored it, holding her gaze steadily.

She searched his eyes pleadingly. Wordlessly.

"Your father told me he had decided to tell you. Or rather," Rance hastened to add rapidly, "he said he would try to tell you."

"He didn't." Hilda heard her voice as though it was coming from a vast distance. She shook her head slightly, and then rubbed one hand jerkily across her forehead. "On. . .on the way to the wedding. . .no, no. . .it was the reception." She stopped and tried to moisten her suddenly dry lips.

O God, O God, her mind screamed. *It's not true. . . It can't be. Help me!*

"He said he wanted to tell me something later," she said at last in

179

a carefully controlled monotone. "He said it had happened so long ago, another few hours wouldn't make a difference." A sound—half laugh, half sob of anguish—tore from her. "He. . .he was wrong, wasn't he?"

"Oh, Hildie, I'm so sorry," Rance murmured brokenly.

"Tell. . .tell me. Please."

Rance didn't move for a moment. Then he stood up. Deliberately and carefully he turned away, putting the nearly empty glass on the table. He stood rigidly with his back turned to her.

"Did. . .did he tell you about Maree and. . .and Nathan?"

For a moment the switch in conversation confused her. Maree? Who was Nathan? What did they have to do with—?

"Did he tell you about our broken engagement?" he insisted more forcefully.

Hilda nodded, and then dazedly realized he couldn't see that, and moistened her lips again and managed to say "Yes."

She saw him straighten his shoulders and then turn slowly to face her. His expression was remote. "Have you told anyone else?" he asked sharply.

"Of course not!"

He relaxed a little, and then picked up a chair and moved it directly in front of her. "Thank you," he said simply as he sat down. "The church leaders in Toowoomba know now, but your father has been the only one I felt free to talk with about the whole situation." He looked down at his hands. "He was wonderful to me, and we grew very close. So much so, that one day when I was feeling particularly down, he told me he also had a problem he wanted to talk about. I think he was really trying to get me to come out of. . .of wallowing in self-pity."

Rance raised his head, and then reached over and picked up one of Hilda's hands with both of his. "He. . .he was very worried about his daughter-dear, whom he loved very much."

Hilda moved convulsively, and then was clinging wordlessly to Rance's hands.

"I felt very honored when he said he had never spoken of this problem to anyone except your. . .your mother since you were born." Rance looked down at their entwined hands. "And now I've even betrayed that confidence," he added bitterly under his breath, his grip tightening painfully.

Hilda winced. "No. . .no, you haven't, not really," she whispered, swallowing painfully, and then managed to say in a stronger voice, "I was going to ask you if you knew what. . .and he was going to tell me anyway. Did. . .did he really say those exact words? That I'm. . .that I. . ." She couldn't voice the incredible, the unbelievable.

Rance looked at her steadily. "He didn't tell me very much. Just that you were not their natural daughter."

Hilda closed her eyes for a moment. Not their natural daughter!

"Your mother had always insisted there was no need to ever tell you that you'd been adopted," Rance continued in a low, compassionate voice. "Bob had wanted you to grow up with the knowledge, but she had. . .had an obsession that you would hate them. The older you grew, the more he was convinced she was wrong, but she. . . Apparently when she found out she had cancer, she made him promise never to tell you. And breaking that promise was what he wanted to talk about."

Hilda stared at him for a moment longer. He stared back at her steadily, and then she closed her eyes.

"So that's what it was," she said harshly at last. A shudder shook her body, and she pulled her hands away from his gentle grasp. "They should have told me," she said numbly. Then another emotion began to stir and strengthen. "Mum was right in a way. I think I do hate them. Not for adopting me, but. . .but. . . How dare they not tell me!" Her voice had gradually risen, and suddenly she sprang to her feet.

"Hildie, don't—"

She didn't hear the pleading in his voice. Rage drowned everything out. Rage against her mother. Rage against her father for leaving it too late to tell her. Rage against them both for dying. . .for leaving her alone. . .

"How could they not tell me! How could they! For over twenty years I've thought I was Hilda Garrett. But I'm not, am I? I'm not their daughter. They've lived a lie all these years! And if I'm not Hilda Garrett, who am I?"

She stumbled across to the side table and picked up a smiling family photo. Rance sprang to his feet, but he wasn't fast enough. It smashed in a tingle of glass against the nearest wall.

"Stop it, Hildie!" Rance roared.

Two strong hands descended violently on her shoulders, forcing her to stop as she blindly went for another photo. She fought against him for a moment, but he shook her, and then folded her tightly in his arms.

"Don't. . .don't. . . ," he said over and over so brokenly that it penetrated the white heat raging through her, and her body at last went limp.

"They are your mother and father in every way that really matters. Think about it. They made a mistake not telling you they adopted you. But they did love you! And no one can ever take that away from you," Rance insisted in a strong, passionate voice.

Then he pushed her far enough away from him to give her another shake, gentler this time, and to look her in the eye and glare fiercely at her. "And, oh, there've been times I've envied you," he added with fervent longing. "I've envied you having a father that loved you as much as Bob did, for having parents who gave you such a rich Christian heritage. And I've often longed that my father had loved my mother and been faithful to her even. . .even half as much. . ."

His voice faded, and he let her go slowly and stood very still for a moment. Then he added earnestly, sadly, "Watching Bob and listening to him taught me more about love and sacrifice and commitment than I ever dreamed possible. It made me realize how weak my own has been towards my parents, my. . .my Lord. . ."

Slow tears trickled down Hilda's face. "They should have told me," she whispered at last. She turned away from him.

"That's what I told your dad. He said he very nearly did just before you started school, but he didn't. He couldn't risk upsetting your mother." Rance hesitated, and then added firmly, "He also said that he rarely even thought about the fact that you weren't actually their flesh and blood. But after your mother died, he was worried in case something happened to him, too. But his promise to her worried him even more."

Hilda didn't move. After a few moments, she heard him move, and when she turned around he was carefully picking up pieces of glass from the floor. She hesitated and then stooped to pick up the shattered frame.

"I'm. . .I'm sorry," she whispered, staring down at the smiling, happy faces. "Please, don't. . .don't worry about the mess. I'll clear it up."

Rance straightened with shards of glass in his hand. "Hildie," he commenced, and then broke off. "I'd better get rid of these first," he muttered and strode from the room.

He was gone a few minutes. Hilda heard the rustle of paper and knew he was wrapping up the glass before discarding it in the garbage. When he returned, she was sitting down, still holding the photo, staring blankly into the distance.

"Rance," she began without moving, "surely their friends, like Marian Stevens, must have known I was adopted?"

Rance sat beside her again. "He said no one else knew besides him, your mother, and the authorities in Sydney who organized the adoption."

That startled her, and she looked at him wide eyed. "Sydney!"

He nodded abruptly. "One of the reasons he didn't—" He stopped and then said wearily, "Hildie, he did tell me a little more, but do you think we could have a cup of tea or something while we talk? I. . .I've had a rough few days, and I've just driven up from Sydney from—" He broke off abruptly, and dropped his eyes.

Despite her distress and bewilderment, something like relief stirred in Hilda. He had been away. He had not forgotten about her after all.

She stood up slowly and took a deep breath. "Yes, of course. Though I. . .I do want you to tell me everything you can remember he said," she warned him in a suddenly firm voice.

He raised his head, and a sudden glint of admiration lightened his exhausted face. "There isn't really very much, but I will tell you all I know," he assured her without hesitation.

Between them they heated some soup, made some toast, set the table simply with some place mats, and sat down. Hilda automatically bowed her head and waited.

There was silence, and then Rance muttered, "You can say grace for us."

She glanced up at him quickly. His head was bowed and his eyes closed as he waited. She hesitated for a moment, and then prayed in a faltering voice, "O, Lord, we do thank You for. . .for all Your goodness and this food, and. . . ," she swallowed, and added earnestly, "and we do need Your strength, and Your help so much. Amen."

"Amen!" Rance's voice held a hint of desperation.

As they silently started to eat, Hilda looked across the table at him curiously. "How long were you waiting for me this evening?" she asked at last as the silence lengthened.

He hesitated and then smiled a little crookedly. "About an hour or so, I guess."

Her eyes widened. "Why on earth didn't you go over to the Stevens's?"

He looked down swiftly, and he hesitated before he said softly, "I was enjoying the peace and quiet here too much. There's something about the silent spaces that brings me closer to God. It helped," he added simply.

Then she remembered, and put down her own spoon. "Rance! You said something before about your world falling down around you? Has something else happened?"

He looked up at her briefly and then away again. "I don't want to talk about it," he grated out.

There was a great sadness in his eyes, and she remembered the night of the wedding rehearsal. She hesitated, and then fearing another rebuff, resumed trying to swallow food that could have been sawdust for all she tasted it. They ate in silence, and then Hilda made a pot of tea.

She couldn't quite bring herself to ask him more questions, even about what her father had said. "Rance, I'm so sorry about Maree," she said softly instead, as she handed him his steaming cup of tea.

He started, the tea slopping over the side of the cup. She bit her lip and waited, not sure what to do or say.

He was silent, looking down at the cup, running a long, lean finger along the edge of its saucer. "Thank you, Hildie, but I can't talk about it yet," he said at last very quietly and sadly, "especially at the moment."

As she took a sip of the fragrant beverage, Hilda silently watched him over the brim of her own cup. She suddenly remembered he had also said something about someone called Nathan and was about to ask him who he was, when Rance suddenly put down his own cup, took a deep breath, and said abruptly, "I promised to tell you what Bob said." Hilda tensed.

"You know they were both in their late thirties before they married?" Rance began slowly. She nodded briefly, and he continued. "They very much wanted a child and were very disappointed for years."

Hilda nodded again. Tears blurred her eyes. "They often told me about those years," she said in a choked voice, and then added bitterly, "but they also said how delighted they were, but scared too, because she was well over forty when they found out she was pregnant. But that wasn't true, was it?"

"Yes, it was true," Rance said softly. She stared at him, and he continued hurriedly. "The baby died."

Rapidly he told her how, late in her pregnancy, they had received word of the death of Mavis Garrett's mother in Sydney. She had insisted on going down to the funeral, but while down there, she had slipped and broken her leg.

"Your father didn't say what happened any more than at the same time a baby girl was born prematurely and died a couple days later. They both took it very hard. It had been a difficult pregnancy from the start, and your mother apparently ended up on the verge of a breakdown."

Hilda gave a slight exclamation. "Dad told me once when she really went berserk at me in my teens that she'd once almost had a nervous breakdown," she said slowly.

Rance nodded. "I think it must have been touch and go, from what he said. She was still in the hospital with her leg in traction when she overheard the staff talking about a baby who had been born the same day as their own baby and was up for adoption."

"Did. . .did he say anything about the. . .about my real mother?" Hilda whispered.

Rance shook his head gently. "No, he didn't. He told me that it became an obsession with Mavis to adopt you. It apparently took some time to persuade the powers that be."

"But they succeeded," Hilda said thoughtfully, "and I suppose they came home and never told anyone."

Rance hesitated, and then said slowly, "Your father didn't say, but it would seem so."

Hilda was silent, thinking back over the years. Now that she knew, it did explain a few times why her mother had been abrupt with her, even furiously angry, yelling, "How on earth do I know where you got your red hair from, but I'll have white hair if you don't stop asking such stupid questions!"

It explained so many other little things.

Rance's light touch on her hand brought her back to the present with a start. She looked at him inquiringly.

"I said I'll have to be going soon," he said softly, "My mother and stepfather are expecting me tonight, and they'll be worried if I don't turn up soon. Will you be all right by yourself?"

"Oh," Hilda said blankly, suddenly remembering what he had said. "You've driven straight here from Sydney? No wonder you look so terrible!"

A rueful grin tilted his lips. "I look that bad, huh?"

No, you look like the nicest man I've ever met, suddenly flashed into Hilda's mind, astounding her. She frowned and said bluntly, "You do look absolutely exhausted. Are you sure you should drive anymore tonight? Your mother lives the other side of Dalby, doesn't she? Wouldn't you rather stay here?"

"Jean's gone home, hasn't she?"

She frowned slightly, "Yes, but that doesn't matter, does—oh!" She suddenly felt heat fill her face.

"Exactly," he said with his twisted smile. "Think what the neighbors would think! Or," he added shortly as he stood up, "more what some church people would think!"

As he drove off, Hilda was still wondering about the bitter tone in his voice when he had referred to the church people. And suddenly she was sorry that he had not offered to pray with her about all that they had talked about. It had been the kind of thing she knew he had often done with her father.

And it wasn't until she had reentered the house that she remembered that she still didn't know who Nathan was, and that Rance had said something about "the world falling around you, too." Something more than the day's car trip from Sydney had happened to make him look so dreadful.

Suddenly Hilda wished quite desperately that she had insisted he stay despite any possible gossip. She had been so wrapped up in her own pain that she had been totally selfish of his own personal pain and needs.

Hilda slept little that night. For hours she lay awake going over every word Rance had said about her adoption. He had known so little. Why hadn't her real mother wanted her? Had she ever had another baby? Were there half-brothers and sisters somewhere?

And then the tears slid down her face because now she could never talk to her mother or father about it all, or rather, to the people she had always believed were her parents.

Chapter 5

I t was difficult to get an early start the next morning to take Polly to have her tests. But they made the appointment just in time, and Hilda left a forlorn collie to be ushered off by a nurse and drove to the other side of the city to the lookout at Picnic Point. It was a very popular tourist spot at the top of the cliffs looking down over the fertile Lockyer Valley stretching to the east.

She sat for a while in the sun, gazing out across the tops of the giant old gum trees. The sun glistened off matchbook-size vehicles on the highway that meandered its way down the mountain range. So many times over the years she had traveled on it, past the small villages scattered along the fertile valleys, the rich farmlands and the beautiful rolling hills that linked Toowoomba with the city of Brisbane almost one hundred miles away.

I wonder where my real mother grew up. Was it in Sydney or out in the country somewhere?

She jumped up restlessly and strode off along the paths that led to the large picnic areas looking down on the wide, flat, green surface of Tabletop Mountain a short distance away. The church youth group had organized a hike and spent the day climbing the relatively gentle slopes a few years before. Long before Rance had appeared on the scene.

Had her mother ever gone to church? Why had she given her baby away?

She deliberately tried to block off such thoughts and focus instead on Rance. During the long hours of the night, she had wondered again and again what was happening in his life. Why had he gone to Sydney? What on earth could that "immense problem" be that her father had mentioned?

A brisk wind sprang up and she shivered. She glanced at her watch. Still another few hours before she could pick up Polly. She had planned to do some shopping, but she wasn't in the mood now. Strolling over to the kiosk, she bought herself a hot drink and a meat pie. Reluctantly she returned to the shelter of the car.

As she ate her impromptu meal, it seemed strange sitting there by herself. It was the first time she had ever been to Picnic Point alone. Being midweek, there were fewer people about. Suddenly she felt very lonely.

Something I'm going to have to get used to. And although she managed to shrug off the gloomy thought, it returned with force as she later listened to the grave-faced vet.

"We'll have to wait for the biopsy result, but I'm pretty sure she has cancer," he told her directly.

A few days later, the diagnosis was confirmed, with the added news that it was considerably advanced and nothing could be done. Polly could live only a few weeks or months at the most. A course of cortisone tablets relieved any inflammation, as the vet had explained, and the beautiful creature started to brighten up, but Hilda knew it wouldn't last.

Hilda's heart was very sore. Over the years, she had shown the collie at various dog exhibitions and won several awards. It had been a dream of her's to one day start breeding and selling collies. Now, that could never be with Polly.

Hilda let Polly sleep inside the house, but the farmhouse was still often far too empty and lonely at the end of a day on the tractor. The preparation of the paddocks for planting wheat and barley had been finished, but there were still a few acres of sorghum stubble to plow in that her father had decided to keep fallow.

Several times in the lonely evenings she wished she could contact Rance. But the phone was never answered at the manse, and she had no idea how to contact his mother.

The days dragged by. Marian Stevens rang regularly and insisted she come to them for meals. Other folk from church also checked on how she was, but she gently refused most offers of help and hospitality. With Marian she could shed a few tears as they talked about her parents. That initial sharp pain of grief and loss gradually faded to a dull ache.

Then one day sometime after Rance's visit, Hilda asked Marian if she had known about her adoption. The shocked expression on the older woman's face told Hilda the answer. After asking Marian not to mention it to anyone, Hilda poured it all out to her wide-eyed friend.

"I remember vividly the day they brought you home," Marian said thoughtfully after a while. "Mavis had been in hospital quite a long time after you had been born prematurely." She stopped awkwardly, and then continued hastily. "You were a beautiful, auburn-haired mite, full of smiles. They were so very proud of you."

"Do you by any chance know which hospital I was born in, Aunt Marian?" Hilda asked wistfully.

Marian Stevens looked at her sharply. "Yes, as a matter of fact, I do," she said slowly. "Mavis insisted on going to the hospital she'd heard so much about over the years from Jean Drew and myself. That's where I met Jean. I didn't finish my nurse's training, but Jean did and stayed on there as a sister. She's always been very proud of the place's reputation. But unfortunately, she wasn't there at the time. In fact she had been overseas for a year or more doing more training or something. It was about then I lost track of Jean, for some years in fact. Anyway, the hospital was also in a suburb where Mavis had an aunt that Bob could stay with."

"Aunt Lily," murmured Hilda. "And the name of the hospital?"

Marian told her, and then hesitated as though about to say something else. Hilda rushed in, changing the subject, and it was obvious that Marian followed her lead reluctantly.

So, at least I know where I was born, Hilda thought wistfully as she drove home later that night.

The evening that the last paddock was ploughed for the time being, Hilda wearily trudged up to the house feeling depressed, filthy dirty, and thoroughly exhausted. Would she be able to keep on running the farm like this? At least there had been no mechanical breakdowns. That would have been something well out of her expertise and very costly to have done. As the days had passed she realized more and more how much work her father had done despite her increasing help the last couple of years.

Sadly she had to face the fact that she had to make a big decision about whether she could keep the farm or not. There wasn't enough money to really employ someone full time, probably not even part time, she thought a little bitterly. Even if the Lord gave her a bumper crop, there was no guarantee the Wheat Board would be able to find enough markets for it and the huge harvests from all the other hopeful, desperate farmers like herself.

She soaked for a long time in a luxurious full bath, despite the fact that the rainwater tanks needed a few storms to fill them. She was leisurely dressing in a comfortable pair of jeans and blouse when the phone rang. Expecting to hear Marian's cheerful voice, something leaped inside her when long distance pips sounded, and it was Rance.

"Oh, Rance, I'm so glad you rang. I've been wanting to discuss something with you," she started eagerly.

There was silence for a moment, and then he said a little huskily, "I should have rung you before I came back down here to Sydney. I'm sorry, there's been a lot to sort out, and Nathan's also been sick. He's had a bout of bronchitis and asthma, but he's well on the mend now." He paused again, and then asked in a firmer voice, "How have you been?"

Hilda closed her eyes. Nathan again. Suddenly she longed quite desperately to see him. "Polly's got cancer in the nose," she blurted out.

"Hildie, no!"

"The. . .the vet says he doesn't know how long. Cortisone helped at first, but now. . ." Her voice choked.

He asked her a few more questions and then, "Is that what you wanted to talk to me about, Hildie?" he asked quietly, after another pause.

Tears stung her eyes again, so glad there was one person who still called her that. Had her father ever told him how much she had always hated her name?

"I. . .yes. . .I mean, no," Hilda said at last.

191

She there and then made up her mind about something that she had been contemplating ever since his last visit.

She straightened, and tilted her chin. "I've decided," she began in as firm a voice as she could manage, "I've decided to try and find out who my biological parents are."

Rance was silent for a long moment. "I'm not too sure it's always a good idea to dig into the past, Hildie," he said slowly, and then added briskly, "I'll be home as soon as I can. We'll talk about it first. See you then," and hung up.

Hilda replaced the phone reluctantly. She frowned. What was there to talk about? After all, it was her decision alone to make.

"Have you really thought and prayed this right through?" a grave-faced Rance asked a defiant Hilda a few days later.

She looked back at him steadily. "I don't think I can honestly say I'm sure I know exactly what God wants me to do, but surely it can't be wrong just finding out who my mother was?"

"It depends what your motives are for finding out."

She looked away. What were her motives? Were they as simple as she thought? "Isn't just wanting to know who I am enough motive?" she snapped at last.

"No, I don't believe it is," he answered quietly. "Have you any idea what you'll do with the knowledge? Its effects on you and your biological parents must be considered."

They were sitting in a sunny, sheltered spot on the verandah, look-ing out across the dark paddocks that stretched far into the distance. The setting sun was turning a few clouds low on the horizon a golden delight. A drop in temperature the past few days had caused the win-ter slacks and jumpers to be hauled out of cupboards as the flat black soil plains braced itself for a cold winter.

Hilda shivered, and stood up. "It's too cold out here. Let's go into the lounge room," she muttered.

She busied herself shutting doors and checking that windows were closed before she turned on the reverse cycle air-conditioner. Soon its warmth started taking away the chill air in the room.

As she sat across from Rance, she observed as casually as she could, "Feels like winter may start early this year. I wish it would rain so we can get the wheat well up before any heavy frosts."

Rance remained silent, frowning down at his hands.

"I have to know who I am, Rance," she burst out. "It's as though suddenly I don't have any identity, any roots."

His gaze darkened as he looked at her. "When your parents adopted you, they not only gave you their name, but their roots as well."

"Oh, Rance, don't. . .please don't get me wrong! I've been one of the most fortunate people to have been given such a heritage, but I. . .I still need to know." Tears filled her eyes as she said rapidly, "I don't even know where my red hair and blue eyes come from. That was always one thing I used to pester Mum and Dad about when I was little, and the kids at school called me names. They always just said they didn't know, and that I was their very own, beautiful copper-headed princess.

"And there's my name. I've always hated it," she added with a touch of bitterness. "Is it the name my real mother gave me, and if so, why? It's such an old fashioned name, and I've always wondered why on earth I was called that. There were never any relatives in Mum or Dad's families called 'Hilda.' And. . .and it was one of the times Mum yelled at me when I kept pestering her about it. She went right off her head." She sniffed back a tear, and said forlornly, "I don't even have any close relatives now. What if there are grandparents somewhere, brothers, sisters?"

"But that's what I was just trying to say, Hildie love." Rance's voice was gentle and kind, his face filled with compassion. "Will you want to meet them? Will they want to have any contact with you? What if there's a veto on any contact?"

"A veto?"

He studied her large eyes for a moment, and then sighed. "Do you know anything about the adoption laws at all?"

"I know that a bill was passed allowing people to find out who their biological parents are, but I don't even know where to start," she admitted. "The. . .the only thing in our area phone directory was some adoption support group with a Brisbane number."

"Yes, I know there are such groups," Rance said slowly. "There are also groups that can act as mediators, but there are also Adoption Privacy groups that are opposed to the new laws. Some people are afraid of their privacy being invaded. There've been some sad cases where adopted children have turned up out of the blue and caused tremendous problems. And then mothers have tracked down a child. Imagine how more shocked you would have been if your natural mother had suddenly arrived claiming to be your real mother before you even knew you were adopted! Parents or children can lodge their names on a contact veto register, but there have still been problems where people have made contact illegally."

There was silence. "I wouldn't want to upset anyone," Hilda said at last in a small voice.

A skeptical look passed across Rance's face. Hilda suddenly remembered her lie to Gail about being engaged to Jim, and went scarlet.

"I. . .it's because I did cause so much hurt then, to Gail and Jim, as well as Dad and myself that I couldn't. . .I wouldn't. . . ," she blurted out in a stifled voice. Then she straightened, and looked at him steadily. "I've apologized to Gail for that lie, and I've asked God to forgive me too. I know they've both forgiven me and that's all in the past now."

Rance's expression softened again. "I'm sorry, Hildie. I wasn't referring to your past mistakes." He gave a sudden self-derisive snort. "I'm the last person to bring up someone's past! And I've seen a big change in Hilda Garrett since last year. You're a very beautiful woman, and I don't just mean on the outside."

Hilda gaped at him. He actually thought she was beautiful!

Something flickered deep inside Hilda. She wasn't sure what the feeling was, except she suddenly had an overwhelming desire that this man continue to think well of her.

My goodness, he's a wonderful man, she thought fervently. *If he were my fiancé, there would be no way I could ever give him up.*

Rance's expression changed again. Hilda suddenly realized their eyes were clinging, searching. There was something in his dark eyes she couldn't interpret. . .a heat. . .

Something melted inside her. She started to lean toward him. Then she gave a little gasp, and sprang to her feet. For a moment she had quite desperately wanted him to kiss her.

Rance stood up also. "I've got to go," he said shortly.

Hilda could feel the warmth in her face, and not for the first time wished her fair skin did not flush so easily. Trying to speak naturally, she said, "I was hoping you might be able to help me, Rance. I don't really know where to start. And. . .and I wanted to ask you who this Nathan is you've been so concerned about."

"You mean the grapevine that exists in our church in Too-woomba hasn't done its job out here?" Anger and pain filled Rance's face. He hesitated and then straightened his shoulders as though bracing himself. "Nathan is my nine-year-old son. I only found out he existed last year."

Speechless, Hilda felt her mouth drop as she stared at him.

"I thought your father had told you about him. You seemed to know about Maree breaking our engagement," Rance said slowly, the expression on his face changing.

With considerable difficulty Hilda found her voice. "Dad. . . Dad only told me about Maree, and on the way to the reception briefly mentioned that you had an immense problem. At the same time he said he had decided to tell me. . .tell me what I now know must have been about my adoption," she finished a little breathlessly.

"I don't know what I would have done if I hadn't had Bob to talk to about the whole sorry mess," Rance said softly. "He was more like a father to me than my own has ever been." He suddenly ran a hand through his hair as Hilda felt the still-too-ready tears gathering behind her eyes. "Perhaps it was so easy for him to be so non-judgmental and understanding of what I was going through because of his own past." A slight smile twisted his lips. "Looks like you and I both have yesterdays we have to sort out so we can cope with what God wants us to do today and tomorrow."

Before she could speak, he suddenly moved briskly towards the door. "I've just got to go. Afraid I can't go into more details about my past now," he added abruptly. "I'll tell you more some other time, if. . . if you're still interested."

Rance paused and turned back to her. He must have mistaken the disappointed look he saw on her face, and said firmly, "I'm sorry, Hildie. There's still so much to sort out about Nathan and a job for me, that I'm afraid I just haven't got the time to help you as I'd like to at the moment. Perhaps you can start by ringing that adoption group in Brisbane. I'm sure they can tell you more about what you have to do. If not, there are various government community and family departments that could help you."

He left rather abruptly, almost as though he were scared to get involved anymore with her, Hilda thought a little resentfully. He seemed to take it for granted she wasn't interested in his affairs. She scowled as his car disappeared down the long, bumpy track to the main road. How could he know she was becoming more and more vitally interested in everything that concerned Rance Telford?

There had suddenly been so many, many things she wanted to talk about with him. She longed to know more about Nathan. Nine years ago Rance would have been at university. And that was around the time he had been converted. And all this time since he had become a Christian and trained and been in the ministry, there had been a son he had known nothing about? But how come he'd found out now?

He had actually said she was beautiful. As she went back inside, a warm glow spread through her. It chased away some of her disappointment that he had not wanted to spend more time with her. And it was nice that he had been concerned enough about her to travel all this way to see her. She wondered if he had known that she had suddenly longed for him to kiss her. Perhaps that was why he had rushed off the way he had, she thought with dismay, and a sudden feeling of desolation.

He'd said nothing about where he was staying. Marian Stevens had told her he had resigned from the ministry in Toowoomba, which had explained the desolate air of the manse and his looking for a job. Her expression cleared a little. Perhaps he was still with his mother and stepfather near Dalby. And then she scowled again. She still didn't know where she could ring him.

It wasn't until she was tossing and turning unable to sleep late that night, that she faced up to her increasing sense of loss that he had not kissed her. She sat up abruptly in bed.

You stupid idiot! You're coming close to falling in love with the man! she berated herself. *The man has just become an instant father. The last thing he needs is to have to fend off a woman who thinks she's falling for him!*

Suddenly she found herself praying. "Oh, God," she pleaded foolishly, "don't let me like him too much." After a moment or two she calmed down, and then added beseechingly, "Please guard and keep us both. Show us what You want us to do."

She started to tremble as she tried to relax on the bed again. Suddenly she was scared—scared that it was too late. She had a sneaking suspicion she had already gone past liking to loving Rance Telford.

"If this is all part of Your will, please take away the fear and give me Your courage," she whispered at last.

Hilda rang the adoption support group in Brisbane the next morning. The woman who answered was very kind and helpful, although she too tried to warn her of some of the difficulties that finding her mother might create. To set the ball in motion, all Hilda had to do was apply for her original birth certificate. When she had been adopted, the Garretts would have filled out information for an amended birth certificate. To obtain the original she had to provide adequate proof of her identity.

She was sitting staring at the notes she had made as the woman talked, when the phone rang. It was Rance, and the sudden peculiar gymnastics of her heart shook her.

"I just rang the local Social Security office," he started briskly. "They said your parents would have had legal papers about your adoption. Even if those had not disappeared, you would still have to apply for your original birth certificate. You just need adequate proof of your identity."

"I. . .I know," she said in a husky voice, trying to pull herself together. "I've just rung that support group in Brisbane."

"Good," Rance said rather abruptly. There was a pause, and then he added a little more gently, "So, are you going to go ahead with it all?"

"Yes, I am," she said as firmly as she was capable of at that moment.

"Well, if there's anything I can do to help, I want you to know I really want to."

Hilda wondered why his voice had suddenly gone so deep and husky. She hesitated and then said quite sharply, "Well then, I should at least know where you're living now or have your phone number so I can reach you."

"Oh, I thought I told you I was staying with my mother. Bob had the number," he said with surprise in his voice.

"He probably did," she snapped through suddenly gritted teeth, "but I don't know your stepfather's name!"

"You don't?" He told her the name in a voice still full of surprise.

Hilda was struck dumb for a few moments, then she said in a strangled voice, "That man's your stepfather!"

The man was a well-known grazier and farmer, who also happened to be very wealthy and influential!

There was amused understanding in Rance's voice. "He certainly is!" Before she could say anything more, he said good-bye briskly and hung up.

Hilda was intrigued. She knew even less about their former minister than she had thought. And how had the stepson of such a prominent man come to enter the ministry of the church?

Well, it was none of her business, her sensible side tried to tell her. That other side of her she had discovered during the dark hours of the night wanted desperately to know all there was to know about this man who was becoming more and more important to her.

Chapter 6

No, I'm sorry, Lawrence isn't here at the moment. Who did you say was calling?"

Lawrence? Hilda bit her lip. She was bitterly disappointed that he was not home to share her news. Hilda gave her name again in a stifled voice.

The woman's voice at the other end of the phone became even more reserved as she said in a cold voice, "Oh, yes, Miss Garrett, my son has mentioned you. I'll tell him you called," and then hung up.

So that was Rance's mother. And now Hilda knew how Rance had come by his unusual name. It was merely an abbreviation of "Lawrence." Hilda replaced the phone receiver reluctantly.

She sighed as she glanced down at the birth certificate clutched in her hand. There had been several more calls from Rance, but it had been the first time she had yielded to her desire to ring him. He had usually sounded tired and discouraged, but, to her frustration and disappointment, steadfastly refused to talk about his problems. He always enquired after Polly and wanted to know about Hilda's search for her mother. So when he had not rung for a few evenings, she had not been able to resist the urgent need to tell him her exciting news. Much good it had done her, and for some reason, his mother had disapproved of her trying to contact him.

Hilda reached out to pick up the phone and ring the Stevenses. Then she hesitated and changed her mind. Jim and Gail had been back from their delayed honeymoon trip for some time now, but she knew they were very busy finishing off some plowing delayed by their wedding. Besides, she had pledged Mrs. Stevens to secrecy about her adoption and never even mentioned to her the decision to find her natural mother.

Hilda spread out the certificate again with a trembling hand. There it was in black and white. She had been named Hilda Louise. The woman who had given birth to her was a Margaret Louise Jones, and the line opposite "Father" said simply "Unknown." The address given for her mother was at a place called Paddington, an inner suburb of Sydney.

A great longing filled Hilda to pack her bag and get to Sydney as fast as she could. There was always a slim chance Margaret Louise Jones still lived at that address, or perhaps someone there or in the neighborhood would remember a pregnant woman. She caught her breath. Jones was a very common name. Had her mother given her real name and address?

But Hilda knew she couldn't leave Polly. The dog had been gradually getting weaker. She had started to refuse all food, even the special delicacies she had always loved. All she was taking was fluids.

And then, it was very likely the wheat would have to be planted any day now. Several evenings the storm clouds had rolled over without fulfilling their promise of rain. Once the ground had been soaked enough to give a reasonably moist subsoil, it would only take a few days to dry out enough for the tractor to be started again.

Hilda had very reluctantly approached a real estate agent to come and give her an estimate of what the place was worth. She was still trying to decide what to do, but even if she put the farm on the market, the next crop would have to be planted.

The phone trilled its urgent summons right beside her, and Hilda jumped.

"It's Jim here, Hilda. Could Gail and I come over and see you for awhile? We've got a proposition to put to you."

It was Friday. Hilda had been dreading another long evening by herself and eagerly agreed.

Jim and Gail had already been over a few times since their return, and to her own private surprise, she and Gail were well on the way to becoming good friends. The fact that they had both suffered tragedy in their lives had somehow drawn them closer together. Hilda also knew it was because she herself was letting God change her so much from the selfish girl who had always been trying to impress Jim and his mother with her abilities.

So when the headlights neared the house a few minutes later, Hilda went out eagerly to welcome them. But it wasn't Jim's Holden after all. Rance's lithe figure stepped from the car and strode along the lighted path toward her.

"Oh, Rance! What a gorgeous surprise," she called out, and impulsively rushed down the steps towards him. "I just tried to ring you!"

Her eyes were fixed on his gentle smile. In her haste she had forgotten her feet were bare and stubbed her toe on a cracked, uneven piece of the path.

"Whoa, there," Rance's amused voice exclaimed.

As she gave an exclamation of pain and stumbled, he grabbed her. It seemed the most natural thing in the world to feel his arms close around her and to raise her face for his kiss. His arms tightened convulsively, and then their lips met. Hilda felt a surge of heat and the delightful feeling that this was where she belonged, in this man's arms. She only came back to earth when she heard Rance give a muffled groan and suddenly wrench his lips from hers.

"Hildie!" he gasped in a breathless, appalled voice. "I'm so sorry, I don't know why. . ." His dazed voice broke off.

There was a crunch of gravel, and they both turned as they became aware of the sound of a car rolling to a stop. They stood frozen for a moment as the head lights surrounded them. Hilda suddenly realized Rance's warm arms were still holding her close and pushed him away.

"It's Jim," she said breathlessly.

Rance stiffened, and she saw him swallow as he took a step back from her.

"Gail's with him," she added defensively, hurt stinging her suddenly. "Jim just rang and said that they wanted to talk to me about something."

Jim and Gail called out their greetings. As she heard the amused speculation in their voices, Hilda knew she must be crimson with embarrassment. She quickly ushered them all inside, and the awkward moment soon passed. Gail had brought over a delicious chocolate caramel slice which she claimed was a new recipe she had tried. Soon they were relaxing with hot drinks.

"Not bad, not bad at all for a beginner cook," Jim teased Gail gently. At Hilda's raised eyebrow, Jim laughed. "Mum apparently had to teach Sister Brandon how to cook when she came to housekeep for us. They managed very successfully to keep it a secret from her boss!"

Hilda grinned at them both. When she glanced across at Rance, he was watching her with an indecipherable expression. She sobered quickly, and then felt relieved when his eyes suddenly lit up with his old sweet smile.

"Hildie's an excellent cook," he murmured softly.

She felt the pink rising in her cheeks and looked hastily away, still feeling confused by their encounter outside. "You said you had a proposition to put to me, Jim," she said hurriedly.

Jim hesitated and looked across at Gail. "It was Gail's idea really. You tell her, sweetheart."

A few minutes later, Hilda was staring at them wide-eyed. "You want to share farm this property?" she gasped, excitement clutching at her.

"I've got some capital from my father's estate that I've been wondering what to do with," Gail said quickly. "Jim heard yesterday that you were considering selling. There isn't enough money to buy you out yet, but there is enough to hire some workman and to come to some arrangement with you about using your machinery and everything. Jim's quite sure he could run the two farms as one, especially with some capital to start off with. You could still live in the house, or rent it out, but that would be entirely up to you. Of course, it all depends on whether or not you need the money from an immediate sale. We would like to have first option on it in the future if you want to sell in a few years. But Jim thought—"

"Oh, no!" Hilda said passionately. "The last thing I want to do is to sell the farm that Dad's family has owned for so long. But I didn't know what else to do. It. . .I. . ." She burst into tears of sheer relief. "Its. . .a. . .simply. . .wonderful. . .idea," she gasped between sobs.

It was Rance who reached her before Jim.

Neither noticed the delighted glance Jim and Gail gave each other as their ex-minister held Hilda tightly, murmuring soothing words until she had forced back the tears of relief and happiness.

She was still clinging to Rance's hands with both of hers, when she at last looked across at Gail and Jim with a rather damp smile. "I knew God would have a plan for me. And now it seems as though He's opening the way for me to go and find—"

She broke off, remembering that Gail and Jim knew nothing of her adoption. She hesitated for a moment, and glanced up at Rance. He started to withdraw his hands, and only then did she realize she was nestling into his side as though it was a perfectly natural place to be.

She sat up hastily, beginning to blush furiously. "I seem to be making a habit of crying all over you, Rance," she said with considerable confusion.

"Don't mind in the least," he said cheerfully and grinned at her, "especially when it's because you're happy about something for a change."

Hilda found herself pulling a face at him. A rush of embarrassment and nerves suddenly filled her. She turned quickly away from the sudden gleam in his eyes back to Jim and Gail.

They eagerly began to pour out the ideas they'd already come up with. Despite Hilda's protests, Jim insisted that they must get their solicitors to draw up a legal contract for them to sign. Rance showed his involvement and interest in Hilda's affairs by making a couple of wise suggestions, proving to Hilda that he was more familiar with the working of a farm than she had expected.

"Well, that's about all we can do until the legal boys get together," Jim said at last with considerable satisfaction as he surveyed the notes he had ended up jotting down. He closed the notebook with a snap and looked across at Rance. "And we still haven't asked Rance what he's doing with himself. We were very sorry to hear the church in Toowoomba voted not to continue to employ you, mate," he added gravely. "We're going to miss you very much."

Rance's face was suddenly grim. "Yes, I was very disappointed by their attitude," he said abruptly. He looked across at Hilda's shocked face. "Didn't you know I got the sack?"

"Aunt Marian just said you'd resigned!" she exclaimed in dismay.

"Oh, I resigned all right. But no minister could stay after being so roundly condemned for having a child out of wedlock. It didn't seem to matter to the majority of them that it was something that had happened in my life before Christ saved me and showed me how to live His way!"

Hilda was even more shocked by the bitterness and anger in him. She stared at him speechlessly.

"I actually stopped by here tonight on my way through to Toowoomba to stay the night there," Rance continued curtly. "I'm moving to Sydney for the foreseeable future, and it'll give me an earlier start for the trip. The church's ministerial placement board thinks there may be a church down there who'll contact me about a ministry with them."

A cold hand clutched at Hilda's heart as she stared at Rance. Jim said something about being sorry to hear that, and then Hilda found her breath.

"Your mother didn't say anything about you leaving when I rang you this evening," Hilda said in a strangled voice.

A shadow crossed his face. "That's right, you did say something when I first arrived about trying to ring me, didn't you? I'm afraid my mother isn't a Christian and was very disappointed when I went into the ministry. Now she's very angry and upset by everything. What did you want me for, Hilda?"

I want you to stay. I want you to help me. I want to help you overcome all the pain in you. I want you to need me as much as I need you, trembled on her lips.

Instead, she heard herself blurt out wildly, "I had news about my search, and. . .and wanted to know what was happening about Nathan."

"It's obvious that you two have a few things to talk about," Jim chipped in hastily. He stood up. Then he glanced at his watch and frowned. "Have you booked into a motel, Rance?" When Rance shook his head, he said urgently, "Look, it's going to be very late now by the time you get to Toowoomba. Most accommodations will likely be booked out. Why don't you come over after you finish talking to Hilda and stay the night with us instead?"

Hilda looked pleadingly at Rance as he started to refuse and was very relieved when he suddenly changed his mind and said simply, "Thanks a lot, Jim."

Rance accompanied Hilda outside to wave off the young couple. "I'm so glad about the farm, Hildie," he said quietly into the darkness after they had gone.

Hilda tucked her arm inside his elbow without thinking, her mind still on all the things they had thrashed out with Jim and Gail. "So am I," she said fervently. The strong body beside her tensed. She quickly withdrew her hand and turned back to the house. "I received my original birth certificate today," she blurted out. Her voice was unnaturally bright even to her own ears. She bit her lip.

Rance drew in a deep breath, but he was silent until she had led the way back inside and handed him the certificate. "So your name has always been Hilda," he mused softly. "What about Louise?"

Hilda folded her arms over each other as a tremor passed through her. "No, it's Mavis," she said abruptly, and as he looked up at her, she added with a nervous smile, "I think I was hoping it wouldn't be Hilda. I've always hated it."

A surprised look crossed his face. "Why? I've always thought it a unique name."

"Hmmph," she snorted, "that almost describes it, but I think the right word should be antique!"

A strange expression crossed Rance's face. He turned quickly away, but she thought he murmured, "unique. There's certainly only one Hildie."

She didn't know for a moment whether it was a compliment or not. *Probably not. Not with my past performance.*

"Where's Polly?" Rance asked suddenly.

"She spends all day in here now, and the nights out in the laundry. She. . .she's stopped eating these last few days, but she's still drinking," Hilda said sadly.

She thought for a moment Rance started to move toward her, but he stilled and then went toward the back door. She followed him slowly. He was crouched beside Polly when she arrived in the laundry doorway. Polly sat up slowly, and wagged her tail at them both, then she walked stiffly over to the water dish and drank thirstily.

There was nothing to do or say except to pat her gently until the beautiful dog settled down again with her head on her paws. Her once beautiful coat of hair was no longer glossy, and her ears drooped.

They turned off the light again and returned silently to the kitchen. Hilda gave a quivering sigh. "It's going to be very lonely here without her," she murmured huskily, "and you're not going to be around either, Rance. Are. . .are you really moving to Sydney permanently?"

He ran his hand through his ruffled hair. "That's where Nathan is," he said evenly. His face tightened. "I've been desperately wanting him to come and live with me, but they. . .he. . . Oh, Hildie, it's a dreadful mess!"

"Would. . .would you like to talk to me about it?" she asked hesitantly.

He searched her face, and for one tingling moment she thought he would lower his guard and talk about it all to her. But he said quickly "You've got enough problems of your own." He looked down at the birth certificate. "Are you going to continue trying to find your biological mother?"

Hilda swallowed her disappointment. "Yes, I want to—need to— very much." Her face lit up. "And sooner than I thought possible because of Jim and Gail taking over the working of the farm."

"I do hope you don't get hurt, Hildie."

"That's a risk I'm afraid I have to take," she said a little mistily. "Do you know where you'll be living in Sydney?"

His face closed up again. "Friends of mine from my theological training days have offered to let me stay until I can get a flat or house to rent."

His expression was so forbidding, Hilda dared not ask him if he would keep in touch. Instead, she said earnestly, "You've been so good to me Rance, and Dad thought of you very highly. If. . .if there's ever anything I can do to help you, will you let me know?" she finished in a rush as she saw him start to scowl.

"I'm not sure if that would be wise, Hildie," he said very softly after a brief pause. He straightened and added decisively, "I'd better go, or I'll be keeping the Stevenses out of bed too late."

Rance strode outside, and Hildie trailed miserably after him, wondering what he meant. At the top of the steps, he turned. When she reached him, they stared at each other silently. Then she saw him swallow convulsively. As though he could not help himself, he reached out his hand and slid a gentle finger down her soft cheek, leaving a trail of fire that ignited Hilda's senses.

As she drew in a sharp breath, he said very quietly, "Don't come down to the car with me."

She stood frozen, frantically trying to think of something to say that would stop him leaving like this.

He whispered, "Bye, Hildie love," and turned and disappeared into the blackness of the night.

Hilda spent a long, restless night. Surely that had not been a final good-bye? Surely Rance would contact her when he settled down permanently? It took a long time before she was able to commit her confusion and uncertainty to the Lord and fall into a sound asleep.

Polly's whimpering brought her wide awake not long after dawn. Shrugging on her warm bathrobe she raced out to the laundry. As she saw her, Polly cried out even more pitifully, trying desperately, and unsuccessfully, to get up on her back legs.

"Oh, Polly dear. Oh, Polly you poor darling. What is it?"

But the answer was obvious. Although Hilda tried hard to soothe her, the dog became more distressed and kept trying to struggle to her feet the moment Hilda made a move to go and phone the vet. Then she would rest for a moment, panting rapidly, and then the dreadful crying and struggling commenced again.

At last Hilda had to leave her, and as she stumbled back inside to the phone, the crying and whimpering increased in volume. The receiver was in her shaking hand when she paused and listened intently. Yes, it was a car approaching.

"Oh, thank You, Lord," she said tearfully as she raced outside.

It was Rance.

Hilda was in the driveway as the car stopped with a jolt and Rance flung open the car. "Hildie! What the—"

"Oh, Rance, Rance! It's Polly. . . ," she cried desperately as he grabbed her by the arms.

Together they raced back to Polly. The collie subsided weakly as they crouched beside her.

"I. . .I was just going to ring the vet's emergency number to tell them I was bringing her straight in," Hilda said softly, fighting back the tears as she once again stopped Polly's pathetic struggle to try and get up.

Rance placed a gentle arm around her shoulders. "Hildie, you do know what they have to do," he asked hesitantly.

She swallowed and said as calmly as she could, "Yes, of course."

"You stay with her, and I'll ring them. Is the number near the phone?"

She nodded briefly. His hand tightened for a moment, and then he disappeared. When he returned he said briskly, "I'll stay with her until you get changed. They'll meet us at the surgery."

"Us? But you. . ."

"Go on, love," he said so tenderly, she smiled blindly at him through her tear-filled eyes and did as he said.

It was a harrowing trip into Toowoomba with Hilda holding Polly as best she could, but on the silent trip home later that morning the car seemed sadly empty and Hilda's heart ached. She shed a few silent tears, but most of her tears for Polly had fallen as she had watched her weaken over the weeks.

As the car turned into the farm driveway Hilda burst out with, "I. . .I don't know what I'm going to do without you to be there when I need you, Rance."

"God will use someone else, of course, Hildie," Rance said in such a harsh voice, that Hilda couldn't say another word.

She opened her door as soon as the car stopped, but Rance gave a sudden slight groan and gripped her arm tightly. "Oh, Hildie, sweetheart, I'm sorry. I don't know just why I turned into your drive-way on an impulse at the last moment this morning. I certainly hadn't planned to, but I haven't been able to get the hurt look in your eyes last night out of my mind."

A firm hand touched her chin and turned her averted face toward him. "And now I've hurt you again. I should let you disappear out of my life for your sake, but I'm not strong enough, I'm afraid. Would. . . would it be okay if I rang you sometimes?"

She searched his eyes. Regret, confusion, and a hint of despera-tion stared back at her. Somewhere she drummed up the courage to put into words the wish that had come to her sometime during the long hours of the night.

"If you really mean that," she began slowly, watching him care-fully for his reaction, "then do you think there's any possibility I could hitch a lift with you to Sydney?"

She thought she saw something like hope flash briefly into his eyes, and then knew she must have been mistaken. His lips tightened and her heart sank. She looked swiftly away.

Rance let go of her and sat back. "To search for Margaret Louise?"

There was a fraction of a pause and then Hilda nodded. She wasn't ready to admit that perhaps that was no longer her primary reason.

"Have you somewhere to stay?"

Hilda nodded again. "Jean Drew said anytime."

She dared to glance at him again. Suddenly he shrugged, and grinned his little lopsided smile at her. Her heart leaped.

"Think you could be ready in half an hour?"

Relief swept through her on a surging tide. "You're on!" she beamed at him.

Chapter 7

I t was closer to an hour than thirty minutes by the time Hilda had thrown a few belongings together and made phone calls to the Stevenses and Jean Drew. Jim assured her he would organize planting her wheat if she had not returned in time. But, as they started off, it was the knowing amusement in Jim's voice that caused her to feel constrained and uneasy with Rance.

He picked up on her discomfort, and any conversation was kept to general topics and the surrounding scenery, anything but their own private lives. Because of her disturbed night and the trauma of saying good-bye to Polly, Hilda dozed off and on for the first few hours. Then she insisted on driving while Rance had a rest. They stopped to stretch their legs a couple of times and fill up the petrol tank. It wasn't until they stopped for a longer break at McDonald's in the city of Tamworth that the atmosphere between them eased.

Tamworth hosted the huge Australian Country Music Festival every January, and they were soon into a lively discussion of the merits of country western music. Hilda was delighted to find he shared her wide ranging taste in music.

Hilda thoroughly enjoyed the next part of the trip southeast down the range at Murrurundi and the beautiful rolling hills of the Hunter Valley. It had been dark for some time, and they were both weary by the time they reached the F3 Freeway between Newcastle and Sydney. They had continued to share the driving, but Hilda was only too happy for Rance to drive the last stretch.

Once on the freeway, Hilda had expected not to stop again until they at least reached the Normanhurst area, one of the northern suburbs of Sydney where Rance's friends lived. But they had been on the freeway for sometime when Rance slowed and took the exit to a brightly lit, huge service center.

Hilda had been enjoying the comfortable silence and the smooth, fast travel on the freeway. She yawned and stretched. "Getting too tired, Rance?" she asked sympathetically. "Would you like me to drive again after all?"

"Nope," he said in the quiet voice she enjoyed so much, "I've decided we'll be arriving too late to expect David and Kim to get us an evening meal, and I'm starving."

She laughed. "That Big Mac does seem a long time ago. But this complex wasn't here the last trip Dad and I took to Sydney."

She was looking around her with interest at the large number of petrol and diesel pumps and the dozen or more big transport vehicles. As he drove slowly over to the restaurant parking area, Hilda did not notice the quick glance Rance directed at her. It was the first time he had heard her so easily mention her father.

When Hilda returned from the rest room to the dining area, she saw Rance just hanging up the public phone. She looked at his smiling face inquiringly.

"Well, that's settled. Kim's quite happy for you to stay the night with them."

She opened her mouth to protest at his high-handed organizing on her behalf and paused as she saw the fatigue in his face. She suddenly realized that Jean lived at least another half hour from his friends' place, and he would have had to drive her there and return.

"Oh, I'm sorry, Rance. I didn't think what a nuisance I'd be."

His smile was the very gentle, beautiful one that so transformed his face. It seemed like forever since she had last seen it. As he touched her elbow and started propelling her into the restaurant, she caught her breath. Heat radiated along her arm.

"Never a nuisance, Hildie. I've really enjoyed your company. The last trip down here was long and lonely."

Hilda waited until they had started eating their delicious meal before she ventured to say, "Rance, that last trip to Sydney you mentioned, was. . .was that just after Dad's funeral?"

Rance paused with food halfway to his mouth and looked across the table at her. He put down his fork. "No, I flew down that time, late on Tuesday. I had intended to drive down on Easter Monday."

She stared at him. All that he had done for her that whole weekend flooded back. "I don't know what I would have done without you when. . .when Dad died," she said earnestly.

Rance's eyes darkened with emotion. "I'm missing him dreadfully. He was very dear to me, and so is his daughter, Hildie."

"Then if that's the case, do you think you could tell me about Nathan?" Hilda said quickly before she had time to get cold feet again. His face tightened, but before he could utter the sharp retort she saw on his lips, she continued very rapidly, "Something's eating into you, Rance. If Dad had been alive, you'd have been able to talk to him, wouldn't you?"

Rance stared at her. A suddenly wistful look filled his face.

"I've spent over twenty-three years being taught by Dad," Hilda said very softly. "I think some of his ideas would have rubbed off in that time, don't you?" He remained silent, and she continued earnestly, "Whatever it is, it's affecting your relationship with Jesus, isn't it? You didn't want to say grace that night, and you haven't once offered to pray with me the times you've visited."

"I tried talking to a couple of the church leaders in Toowoomba," he said bitterly. "All that accomplished was condemnation and my ministry there having to finish."

"Did Dad condemn you?"

The anger in his eyes faded. He looked down at his plate and shook his head.

"Do. . .do you believe Jesus condemns you?" she asked bravely.

He raised his head quickly. "No!" he said vehemently. "My de facto relationship with Val was forgiven when I asked Him to be my Savior. He gave me new life. That old past has been done away with. Since then, when I've slipped up again, I've claimed His promise to forgive me when I agree with Him about my sin."

A sharp pang shot through Hilda. So her name was Val. She swallowed quickly, and quoted huskily, "There is now no condemnation for those in Christ Jesus."

There was an arrested look in his eye. "Your Dad quoted that very passage from the book of Romans, too," he murmured.

A slight smile crossed Hilda's face. "I've heard him remind hurting Christians about that many times. As well as his rebellious daughter!"

"It's amazing, isn't it? I've preached from those words of Paul several times over the years, but its harder to put it into practice when I. . .when I'm feeling so guilty!" he burst out.

"Dad also used to say that after studying the life of the apostle Paul, he had come to the conclusion that he was a man who should have carried the guilt of persecuting and killing Christians to his grave. Instead, Paul wrote those words," Hilda said reminiscently. She looked down at the table, and unconsciously traced a pattern with her fork. "And Paul also wrote to the young man, Timothy, explaining how, despite all his past before he became a believer, Christ still gave him strength and appointed him to His service of ministry."

A strangled sound from Rance brought her eyes swiftly back to his face. He was staring at her with the strangest expression. A vivid blush turned Hilda scarlet. She dropped the fork, and stared at him with dismay. She had been preaching to the preacher!

She opened her lips to apologize, but Rance spoke first. "Thank you, Hildie. I needed to be reminded of that, and I think I can tell you about it all after all. But," he gestured at their rapidly cooling food, "not now, I think. We should get to Normanhurst as soon as possible."

Hilda found she had lost most of her appetite, but forced down the rest of the meal as best she could. She thought that the subject was closed, and as they resumed their journey, she quietly made irregular comments about the traffic and the scenery. Rance hardly spoke, and at last she lapsed into silence.

Unexpectedly, Hilda heard him say, "Hildie, I haven't just been feeling guilty about the immorality in my past. I've been feeling so bad about the type of upbringing my. . .my son has had. What you said about your father's ideas rubbing off onto you stung. I doubt very much if my son has ever been told that God loves him."

"But that's not your fault, Rance!" Hilda cried out indignantly.

"You didn't know of his existence."

"No, but I may have if I hadn't cut myself so completely off from Val and all my old friends of that era," he said quietly.

They traveled in silence for awhile. Hilda felt an overwhelming gratitude for the fact that she had always only known a Christian lifestyle. It had saved her from so many painful memories of a background like Rance had known.

"You know, at first I was so zealous about trying to win my friends for Christ," Rance said sadly, "but I was still very young, and even more immature in spiritual things. I found myself being sucked back into their drug scene and lifestyle again. I even. . .one night Val and I again made love. That's what I find so hard to forgive myself for. It was after that night I walked away from them all for good. A couple years later I started studying for the ministry. The years were so busy. I always intended to try and find out what had happened to Val, but then I moved to Queensland."

Hilda was afraid to move as the quiet voice continued. A thrill of delight shot through her. He was telling her at last about himself. He trusted her.

"Just before Christmas, I had a letter from Val's grandparents. They were very worried about Nathan because they had just found out Val had AIDS. As he was my son, wasn't it about time I did something to look after him?"

Hilda gave a choked exclamation.

He glanced briefly at her shocked face and added grimly, "You can imagine that at first I thought it was a hoax. Val came from a family background that. . .well, to put it gently, left much to be desired. Her father was an alcoholic, and her mother had just given up on life and didn't care what happened to her daughter. They kicked her out when she turned fifteen.

"Her grandparents weren't much better, but they did take her in. For years she had refused to tell them who Nathan's father was. They had reared one child, they informed her, and didn't want the responsibility of another. When she had become too sick to look after him, they kept threatening to hand Nathan over to Children's Services. So she gave in. They tracked me down at last."

There wasn't a thing Hilda could think of to say as Rance's abrupt explanation finished. At last, when she knew she had control of her voice, she asked softly "Have. . .have you found out why she hadn't contacted you when he was born?"

There was a tense silence, and Hilda wished she had kept quiet as she stared straight ahead, aware that he had tensed even more.

"Yes." That answer was a long time coming. There was so much pain in his voice, Hilda dared not say another word. After a few moments he added in a clipped voice, "She refused to see me until that Thursday before Easter. Then she had the nurse at the hospital ring me. It. . .it was just as I was leaving for the wedding rehearsal. I went down as soon as I could." His voice became husky, and full of self-condemnation. "She. . . she. . .Val told me. . .just before she died, why she didn't burden me, as she put it, by letting me know about Nathan. She thought it would harm me in the church. She. . .she didn't want me to be contaminated by her again because I was a good man, and. . . and it was good to see at least someone she loved escape. . .escape the hopelessness."

Traffic signs swept past, warning that the end of the freeway was imminent. Hilda saw them through a mist of tears, wondering if she could ever have been as noble as that poor woman. And what turmoil Rance must have been in that whole weekend! Hilda couldn't have said a word if her life had depended on it.

"We haven't much farther to go, and I have to concentrate now on finding the Mortons' house. If you haven't been turned off me by what I've just told you, we'll talk more some other time." Rance's voice was withdrawn and unexpectedly cold.

Hilda ached even more for him. So many people he cared about had rejected him because of what he had just told her.

"Nothing you could tell me could ever turn me off you, as you put it, Rance," she blurted out passionately. Anger had cleared her mind and even crept into her voice. Then she suddenly hoped she had not given too much away about her growing feelings for him.

Even as Rance eased his foot on the accelerator in obedience to the speed limit, he reached across and took hold of one of Hilda's tightly clenched hands. Her hand unfolded and then clung to his. Neither said a word as they arrived at the Mortons' home.

Hilda liked David and Kim Morton immediately. They were obviously concerned about Rance, and both gave him big hugs. She found herself included in their loving greetings and felt instantly at home.

It was very late, but at their hosts' insistence they had almost finished a quick cup of tea, when a little voice from the doorway said indignantly "Yous said Unca Wance wouldn't come 'til bweakfas' time!"

Rance's tired face lit up. He put his cup down and moved swiftly to scoop up a curly headed tot and a blue teddy bear almost as big.

"Well, I tricked you, didn't I, princess? Got a kiss for me?"

The gentle love and genuine delight in Rance's face made a lump form in Hilda's throat. He would be a wonderful father. She looked across and caught David's eye. He was watching her watching Rance. A small, surprised grin shaped his lips, and she blushed furiously and bent her head over her cup.

"Jodie, what are you doing out of bed?" Kim said with fond exasperation as she stood up.

The little girl peeped warily at her mother over Rance's shoulder as she hugged him fiercely around his neck. "Jus' wovin' Unca Wance, of course," she said indignantly.

The three watching adults smiled.

Rance chuckled, and his voice was filled with love and emotion as he said, "There, Mummy, a perfectly acceptable answer. But what about I carry you back to bed now so you can get more beauty sleep?"

While he had been talking, Jodie had been staring at Hilda. When Hilda smiled at her, she hid her face shyly and reached up and whispered in Rance's ear.

Rance swung around and stared at Hilda with a startled expression on his face.

A dainty hand pushed on his face trying to turn it back to her. "Well, is she?" the little girl demanded loudly.

"I think you may be one very clever little girl," Rance said very slowly, still staring at Hilda. Then he whispered something in Jodie's ear. He shot a grin of pure mischief at Hilda, and said out loud, "Come on, Miss Moppet, you can meet the pretty lady in the morning. I'd better carry you back to bed before Mummy gets cross with both of us."

"I not Mis' Moffet, silly," they heard her giggle as they both disappeared, "but you're Georthie Porthie!"

The three left behind looked at each other.

"Now, I wonder what that was all about," murmured Kim thoughtfully as she looked speculatively across at her husband. Some silent communication must have passed between them for her eyes widened suddenly, and then she stood up quickly and said, "You must be very tired, Hilda. I'll show you to your room. Rance won't get away from that little madam for awhile, and you can grab the bathroom first."

Hilda followed her obediently, although she too very much wanted to know what had brought that particular look into Rance's face. She was exhausted, but it took her a long time to go to sleep. Not the least of her worries was just when she would see Rance again after he had left her with Jean Drew the next day.

But there was no need to have concerned herself. Rance had worked that out already. "I've rung Jean Drew and told her you're staying here with me," Rance told her crisply after he had said a brief good morning. "David and Kim suggested it."

Hilda stared back at him crossly, even as tingles of relief swept her. "Without asking me?"

"It was the most sensible thing to do. How were you going to find that address on the birth certificate without transport? And I thought you might—" He paused, and looked uncertain for a moment. Then he lifted his chin and glared at her. "I thought that seeing I was so kind as to let you hitch a ride with me all that way, you wouldn't mind helping me with Nathan," he said with a challenge sparkling out of his eyes at her.

Inwardly, Hilda was thrilled. Outwardly, she tilted her chin right back at him. "And if I do mind?"

He looked taken aback, and she couldn't stop her lips from twitching. Relief flashed into his eyes. He started to smile, but then gave a mock scowl instead. "It'll be bread and water rations for a month!"

"Is this a private joke, or can anyone join?" David's amused voice broke into their shared laughter, and they sobered quickly.

"Just Rance flexing his male chauvinistic muscle," Hilda said cheekily, feeling incredibly lighthearted.

"Didn't get me far," Rance grumbled. He grinned at David and said, "The woman has submitted and will be staying, too. As long as you can put up with us both.

"Good," said Kim as she entered the room with Jodie tucked on one hip. She beamed happily at Hilda. "This is Miss Garrett, Jodie. She's Uncle Rance's friend who came with him last night."

She swung the small girl down. Jodie studied Hilda for a moment and then put her hands on her hips and confronted Rance. "You said she's Aunt Hildie," he was accused.

Hilda watched with amusement as a hint of color touched Rance's cheekbones. "I'm sure she won't mind if you call her that, princess." He took a long stride forward and tossed Jodie up into the air. "Will you?" he then appealed to Hilda a little uncertainly.

Hilda couldn't resist the two pairs of dark eyes so close together. She swept a deep curtesy. "I'm at her majesty's service."

"Ooooh," Jodie giggled with delight. "I not weally a pwincess! Uncle Wance's jus' bein' funny."

"Funny, am I!" Rance tickled his small captive to her great delight. He then carried her off, at her demand, to play with a new toy.

Hilda turned to David as she heard him sigh faintly. "He's always been wonderful with kids. It's a dreadful shame that—" He stopped abruptly, and bit his lip as he looked at Hilda.

"It's okay," Kim said softly, "Rance told me that Hilda knows about Nathan."

"He's told me some of it, but I think not all," Hilda said slowly, and then she burst out angrily, "How could that woman not tell him he had a son!"

"From what I remember of Rance when he first came to Bible

College, she may have been afraid to tell him," David said thoughtfully. "He was a very opinionated, everything's-black-or-white type of person."

"Well, he's certainly not like that now," said Kim fiercely. "He's allowing God to change him into a wonderful man, and a tremendous pastor. Maree's a fool, and the way that. . .that church treated him is a crime! It's really knocked him for a six. His self-esteem is about zero. Seems to think he's suddenly become unlovable and of no more use to God—or man."

"Oh," said Hilda blankly, "I hadn't realized. . ." She stopped short, suddenly remembering what Rance had said about being a failure that night that now seemed so long ago.

"He'll come through this," said David firmly. "I've seen his commitment to Christ stand many tests over the last few years. As long as he maintains his faith and relationship with Christ, he'll find his way soon. We just have to keep supporting him in prayer and any way we can."

Hilda looked at him doubtfully. She knew that all was far from well with Rance's spiritual health. But she said no more, and a little later Rance came back and suggested the worst of the morning peak hour traffic would be over and they should go and see Nathan.

"Does Nathan know you're coming to see him today?" Hilda asked as they neared their destination.

"I wasn't sure how long it would take to wind things up at the church and move my things out of the manse and store them at my stepfather's place. And then I couldn't be sure he would get a message from his great-grandparents anyway." Rance looked across at her, and she saw his jaw tighten as he added, "I hope you don't expect a loving father-son reunion, Hildie. He's a very confused little boy, and for some reason, whenever I go near him he retreats."

"What are his grandparents like?"

Rance didn't answer for a moment, and then said grimly, "I'll let you judge for yourself."

The house that Rance parked the car beside was in a very poor-looking neighborhood. The houses each side were almost sitting on top of each other. Several steps sagged from rotten timber as they approached a front door that had a panel of broken glass, haphazardly boarded up with a scrap of dirty timber.

There was no answer to Rance's first knock. After a few moments, he knocked a little louder. There was a sound of slow, light steps behind the door, and then silence. Suddenly a man's loud, harsh voice roared something out from somewhere in the house.

The door was opened the tiniest crack, and a scared little voice croaked, "Granddad said to go away. He doesn't want any today."

Rance caught the edge of the door and pushed it open a little more. There was the sound of a frightened gasp, and a little figure darted behind the door.

"Nat, it's your father," Rance called softly, "can I see you for a moment?"

There was silence, and then half a face peered around the partly open door. "Oh, please, go away," the boy whispered desperately. "He's sleeping it off, and he'll be so angry if we upset him."

"Then we won't wake him, mate," Rance said in a very controlled voice. "Why don't you just come outside. I want you to meet a very nice lady who's with me."

"No," the boy wailed, "I'm not allowed outside today."

"Rance," began Hilda with dawning horror.

"I know," murmured Rance between gritted teeth. "I saw him too."

He suddenly forced open the door and in one movement grabbed the thin arm of the boy as he started to back off. The boy gave a whimper of pain.

Rance gave a choked sound of distress and changed his grip to gently pull Nathan forward from the dark shadows of the hallway. "Oh, son," he moaned. "Who did this to you?"

One eye was almost closed from a huge bruise that stretched down one side of Nathan's small, tear-streaked face. Blood was smeared on the other cheek, perhaps from the grazes and bruising on both his thin arms.

Chapter 8

N athan cowered, trying to pull away. He was trembling violently. "No, no," his terrified voice begged in pitiful gasps. "Don't hit me. I'll be good."

Hilda moved forward and crouched down to his eye level. "We would never hurt you, Nat," she said earnestly. "We want to help you."

The pain-filled, childish eyes stared at her. Something flickered across his face and he stopped trying to pull away from Rance.

"Wouldn't you like to come with your father? He'll never let anyone hurt you ever again," she persisted very gently.

The boy looked at Rance and then quickly back to Hilda. "For real?"

She nodded earnestly, trying desperately to keep the tears from her eyes.

"And. . .and will you be there, too?"

"Yes," Hilda said firmly.

He studied her suspiciously for another long moment. Hilda could feel the tension in the tall, grim figure beside her and prayed that he would not let his fury show. Nathan glanced fearfully up at his father briefly and then back at Hilda. He nodded once, and then he staggered, all the color that was left in his face suddenly leaving it.

"I feel sick," he muttered.

Hilda's hand went out to steady him, but Rance was before her. His strong arms reached down to carefully pick up the boy. Nathan stiffened with terror again and then suddenly went limp.

Without a word, Rance took off with him down the steps. "Get in the car, Hildie. He's fainted. You can hold him. I'll drive." The words were staccato sharp.

Rance settled his burden as gently as he could on her lap. As he started to move rapidly to the driver's side, there was a sudden roar of expletives from the house.

"Hey, what'd ya think—" The words were cut off as the bedraggled, bleary-eyed, and bloated man in the doorway saw Rance turn toward him.

"Yes, it's me, you filthy old man," Rance shouted furiously at him. "And don't think I won't be back!"

Rance turned away, but Hilda saw the sudden fear that twisted the old man's face. He opened his lips and mouthed something back which Hilda could not make out above the sudden roar of the motor. She thought he had said, "It's not my fault." Hilda looked down at the still body in her arms.

As the car pulled away from the curb, Rance said sharply, "Can you get the street directory out of the glove box?"

Nathan was undernourished, but still a dead weight against her shoulder. "No, I can't Rance," she said urgently, "I don't want to move him."

"Right." Rance pulled up around the corner out of sight of the house and quickly found the directory. "I know there's a public hospital in this suburb somewhere," he muttered fiercely. "Ah, there it is. This should only take about ten minutes."

It was a little more than that before they pulled up outside the emergency entrance. As the car stopped with a jerk, Nathan stirred and tried to sit up.

"It's okay, Nat. It's okay," Hilda soothed him. "We're at a hospital. There'll be a doctor here to make you feel better."

Fear flashed into the dark eyes that looked up at her again, and Hilda understood why when the casualty nurse took one look at the boy in the arms of the tall, ashen-faced man, and greeted him by name.

"Well, if it isn't Nathan again. Been in a fight again young man?" she said suspiciously as she looked from him to the man carrying him.

"You might say that," the grim-faced Rance said so savagely the woman took a step back. "But it certainly wasn't with someone his own size!"

Her expression softened. "We thought that might have been the case before," she muttered softly.

"Before!" Rance snarled. He visibly controlled himself and deposited Nathan very gently on the examination couch. Then he said in a tight, sharp voice, "I need to use the phone immediately."

The nurse nodded, "I'll show you and tell the doctor. Be right back," she added to Hilda.

She waited for Rance to precede her, but he hesitated. A large hand reached out and touched the unbruised cheek so tenderly, Hilda felt the tears spill over the top at last. For Rance's sake, she was pleased that Nathan didn't shrink away from that loving touch. He just stared blankly up at his father.

"Don't be scared, mate. You are never going back to that house again, Nathan. Never!" Rance said fiercely, and then strode away.

By the time he had returned, a doctor had started to gently examine Nathan. "You the boy's father?" he scowled at Rance.

Rance nodded briefly, and as the doctor finished his examination, stood rigidly beside Hilda. Her hand crept out and touched his tense hand. He jumped slightly and then grasped her hand tightly, never taking his eyes from the small body. They both winced as bruise after bruise was revealed all over the thin little body.

All the time, the doctor asked Nathan soft questions. Some the boy answered, some he didn't. At last, Rance cleared his throat and took a step closer. The doctor paused. He frowned and looked up at Rance intently.

"Nathan, we want you to tell this doctor exactly how you got hurt. Then it will be easier to make you better and make sure it never happens again."

"But. . .but you said I'd never have to go back. You promised," the weak voice managed. "It won't happen if he never comes near me again."

"If who never comes near you, young man?" the doctor asked conversationally.

"Why, Granddad of course!"

No one moved for a moment. Then Hilda saw the doctor relax and look compassionately for the first time at Rance. Suddenly, Hilda realized angrily that he had thought Rance must have done it!

Rance crouched down and looked the boy straight in the eye. "Nathan, no one is allowed to hurt another person like you have been, especially a boy your age. Don't you know that?"

The boy just stared at him blankly.

Rance continued, "The police won't let them, and I've just rung them up. When you're feeling better, they'll want to ask you all about it, and you must tell them the whole truth. Do you remember what I said last time about coming to live with me?"

There was a faint nod. "He. . .he said you didn't mean it."

"Oh, son, I've already missed out on too many of your years. There's no way I'm going to miss out on any more!" Rance vowed in a cracked voice.

Then he bent over and placed a soft kiss on his son's forehead. Hilda felt the tears sliding down her cheeks again, and then caught her breath as a thin hand suddenly reached up and touched Rance on the cheek. When Rance stood up, he was smiling down at the boy gently.

"Okay, you two," the doctor interrupted briskly. "This young man needs a couple of x-rays, and then I think we'd better find him a bed here for a while." Instant fright flashed into Nathan's eyes. "You're still suffering from shock as well as feeling very sore," he added firmly, and then said quickly, "Oh, your Dad and this young lady can stay with you if you want them to."

Nathan looked anxiously from Rance to Hilda wordlessly.

"Of course, we're staying," Hilda said determinedly. "As long as you want us to."

The relief that filled his face before he wearily closed his eyes brought a choked sound from Rance.

"That's settled then," the doctor said cheerfully, "but now there's not much room in this little cubicle, so they have to wait just outside while the nurse cleans you up a bit. She's going to give you an injection too, so it doesn't hurt so much when we move you."

Once out of earshot, Rance burst out to the doctor, "The nurse said he's been in before?"

The doctor nodded grimly. "Not quite two weeks ago, an elderly woman brought him in. Claimed he'd been in a fight, but he was so scared that we were suspicious."

"Why didn't you report it to the police then?" Hilda asked angrily.

"We reported it to Children's Services for them to investigate. I had hoped they would have been out to the home by this." He sighed. "Like all of us, I suppose" he added wearily, "not enough staff and too many urgent calls."

Nathan was kept sedated for the next few hours but still slept restlessly. The moment his eyes opened, they searched anxiously for Rance and Hilda. Reassured by their smiles and touch, he would doze off again.

Once when he was asleep, the police called in briefly. It was obvious they had already talked to the medical staff. After introducing themselves, the officers explained that a warrant was being issued for the arrest of the great-grandfather.

Tight-lipped, Rance snarled, "Good!"

Hilda observed the darkness in his face with considerable worry. She had been silently praying during their vigil, as much for this anguished man as for his son.

Sometime later, Rance murmured to Hilda, "Do you mind staying without me? There are a few urgent things I need to do. Tell him I'll be back as soon as I can."

A little surprised, she stared up at him and then nodded. She felt the warmth of his lips brush her own and then he disappeared.

Rance was gone for longer than she had expected. When Nathan woke a few minutes after he left and realized his father was gone, Hilda would never forget the look of despair that filled his face.

"Look, he's got to come back and take me home, doesn't he?" she hastened to reassure him.

He stared at her for a moment with a flicker of hope, but then his face closed up again. His resigned look of disbelief nearly broke her heart. How many people all his life had abandoned him to cause that total look of unsurprised acceptance?

The color had returned to Rance's face when he did return. She turned swiftly to greet him and was relieved at the gleam in his eye.

"Oh, I'm so thankful you're back," she burst out.

It had been a long, exhausting few hours. Nathan had been awake for some time, but she had not been able to get a word out of him. She had tried to quietly talk about anything she could think of, but he had just turned his back on her.

"Hello, Nathan," Rance said with a piercing look at the face that had briefly turned to see who had entered.

Hilda thought she saw surprise, followed by relief, flicker across the battered face, but then he turned quickly away again.

"Sorry I was away so long, but I've been very busy—very successfully busy, I might add," Rance said with a quick smile at Hilda. He winked at her and raised his voice slightly. "Hildie, God's been looking out for us. What would you say if I told you I've just organized a fully furnished house to live in with Nathan?"

"Already!"

The previous evening, Rance had told the Mortons that after seeing Nathan, he intended searching for a flat or unit to rent so the boy could go and live with him as soon as possible. The Mortons had warned him that such a search could take some time. Anything worth living in was very expensive at the moment, and there were long waiting lists for any rented premises.

Rance smiled a little grimly at Hilda, and said quietly to her, "David was right. There's absolutely nothing decent enough to rent anywhere. So, for the first time in my life, I've rung up my stepfather and taken him up on his repeated offers of help. When he got over his astonishment, he made a few phone calls. It turns out he owns a holiday house that has just become vacant."

The tense little body in the bed suddenly turned over painfully, and stared at Rance suspiciously.

"Do you like the beach, Nathan?" Rance asked gently.

A faint glimmer of excitement touched the battered face. "I. . .I don't remember."

Hilda gave a little gasp. She saw Rance's hands clench tightly. Very few children in this land of sun and surf, living so close to the sea, could say that!

"Well, the house you and I are going to is right near the beach. As soon as the doctor says you're well enough, we'll go there," Rance said in a controlled voice. "It's a long way from here. It's down the south coast on the way to Wollongong."

"Will. . .will he know where we are?"

Rance moved closer and placed a hand on the boy's hand. "Nathan, the police have told me that your. . .your grandfather's been arrested. He couldn't get any bail money, and he's locked away in a jail cell. You don't have to worry about him ever again."

His voice was gentle, but Hilda heard the steel in it. She shivered. This was a Rance she had not seen before.

"Will you be there, too?" The dark eyes beseeched Hilda.

Hilda looked at the boy, and then up at Rance helplessly.

A hard light glinted at her from suddenly fierce eyes that dared her to contradict him. "Yes," he said firmly, "Hildie will be there, too." When her eyes widened and flashed back at him, he added autocratically, "Don't worry, there's a live-in housekeeper, according to my stepfather. You won't have to do anything."

"Exactly where is this house?" Hilda said stiffly.

"Near Stanwell Park."

The name meant nothing to Hilda. Darkened amber eyes clashed with clear blue eyes.

"It's on the south coast, but north of Wollongong. Its well-known for the hang gliding off the cliffs not far from there. The house is actually at a place called Wattle Point, but there's also a beach, even if it's only a small one compared to your Gold Coast standards." He paused and then pleaded softly, "It's obvious that Nathan's wary of me. Perhaps it's because he's only known unpleasant men. And who knows what he's been told about parsons! I need you, Hildie."

Hilda looked swiftly away, hoping her face had not revealed the suddenly desperate feeling that filled her. How she longed for him to need her for so many other reasons than to help with Nathan. She looked across at the tense little figure in the bed.

"Looks like we three stick together, then, doesn't it, Nat?" she said with a forced smile.

Nathan's face brightened with hope, but he didn't smile. He studied her face carefully and then doubtfully looked briefly at Rance. He closed his eyes and muttered listlessly, "I suppose."

Hilda glanced up at Rance, and saw him biting on his bottom lip. He would have a battle on his hands for Nathan to be convinced that he really cared what happened to his son.

The doctor called back late in the afternoon to tell them there were a couple of cracked ribs, but fortunately no other damage except the lacerations and bruising. When they told him about the house at Wattle Point, he agreed with some relief that Nathan could be discharged the next day as long as he was still doing all right.

Hilda felt emotionally drained by the evening. She felt relieved when Rance decided that rather than stay all night at the hospital, they would get a good night's sleep at the Morton's so that they both would be better able to cope with moving Nathan the next day.

"He's going to have to learn to trust that when we have to leave him we'll always come back," Rance said grimly.

It was a relief to go back to the Mortons' and be fussed over by Kim. They insisted on going down to Wattle Point the next morning to make sure everything was set up for them.

"You don't need any hitch at this stage," David said firmly. He grinned suddenly. "Besides, what a great excuse for a day at the beach, even if it is a bit cool!"

The next morning, Hilda was very quiet and thoughtful on the way to the hospital.

Rance glanced at her a couple times, and then said shortly, "Wishing you hadn't agreed to help me?"

Hilda looked at him steadily. "No, not for a moment, Rance. But I was wondering when I'd have a chance to start looking for my. . . my mother."

"I've already said I'd help you," Rance said impatiently, "but Nathan comes first."

Hilda was silent. This Rance was different from the man she had thought she was getting to know. There was an increasing hardness, a coldness about him that worried her immensely. As they approached the ward, this concern intensified. Rance muttered something angrily under his breath when he saw the old, shabby woman at the nurses' station.

He lengthened his stride as her loud, angry voice reached them. "I demand to see him. He's my only great-grandson. How dare you—"

"They dare because, as next of kin, I insisted they don't let anyone near him. Especially you!" barked Rance.

"You!" spat the small, withered woman as she turned awkwardly around to face the new obstacle. "And where were you all these years, hey? When my poor little girl needed a father for her son, where were you, hey? You religious people are all the same. All talk, talk—"

"That's enough!" Rance said furiously. "Your daughter keeps his existence from me, and you allow my son to be bashed up by that miserable excuse for a man you call a husband, and you dare, you dare—"

"Don't you talk to my gran like that, you big bully!" cried out an angry, trembling voice. "He bashed her more'n he did me!"

The love that transformed the old woman's pale face tore at Hilda's heart. "Oh, my lamb," she cried out in a shaking voice, and dodged past Rance to stumble toward Nathan as he limped down the corridor. "Oh, what did he do to you? What did he do to you?"

Nathan's face crumpled, and then it was hidden as he was wrapped so very gently in the small woman's arms.

Rance took an angry step forward.

"Rance, wait!" Hilda grabbed at his arm. "We're the strangers here. She's all he's had for a long time," she whispered urgently. There had been something else worrying her, too. "And there was something about her that—"

"Gran, are you all right again, now," they heard Nathan's tearful voice say.

"I will be, love, I will be."

But even as the now faint voice tried to reassure him, they saw her stagger. Hilda darted forward. As small as his grandmother was, she was still too heavy for Nathan to hold. As Hilda reached her, the older woman crumpled into a heap on the floor.

"See what you've done now!" screamed a frantic Nathan at Rance. "She's been in hospital!"

The slight figure Hilda was crouched over opened her eyes and tried to sit up. Hilda was frightened by the gray skin and bluish lips. She looked up frantically at the nursing sister as she joined them.

"That's no way to talk to ya Dad," the old lady gasped painfully. "You be a good boy for him, now, ya hear?"

"Don't try and talk," the nurse said sharply.

A hospital trolley arrived swiftly. A white, grim-faced Rance helped the wardsman lift the frail body.

As he went to move back, a withered hand reached out. "So sorry," the whisper of a voice said. "He. . .he took it out on me 'cause I took Nat to hospital the other week. . .after. . .after he hit him."

The nurse tried to hush her again, but her grip on Rance tightened. "He's. . .not bad man. Never touched him before. Just. . .the drink. Upset 'bout Val. So glad ya came back."

The nurse had her fingers on the woman's pulse and nodded urgently to the wardsman. The trolley started moving, and Hilda grabbed for Nathan as he started after it.

"Not now, Nathan," she said tearfully. "Let them look after her first."

The rigid figure stared up at her, tears streaking his cheeks. "But she'll want to see me," he protested, and then turned belligerently to Rance. "And you can't stop me. When you didn't turn up or write, Granddad got upset, and he started drinking. She got punched because of you, and he hurt her bad. I don't want you for a father. Oh, why did you have to come! I hate you, I hate you!"

Chapter 9

As the car pulled into the driveway at Wattle Point and Hilda saw David Morton coming quickly towards them, she gave a silent sigh of immense relief. She never wanted to live through such a tense few hours again.

Opening her door almost before the car cruised to a stop, she stepped out and greeted him loudly. "Hello, David, we're here at last!" As she reached him and held out her hand, she muttered through gritted teeth, "Please do something before I strangle them both!"

David gave her a keen look and moved over to open the back door. Hilda heard him draw in a quick breath as he saw Nathan's poor battered face glaring at him.

"Hello, Nathan. I was beginning to wonder where you all were," David said calmly. "I thought my old friend must have become lost trying to find his way through the city traffic."

Nathan didn't stir. His arms were folded and he merely glared silently back. Rance slammed his door with unnecessary force and marched around to the trunk.

"This is Mr. David Morton who we've told you about, Nathan," Hilda said quietly.

"If my daughter can call your father Uncle, it's only fair for you to call me Uncle David," David said cheerfully. Ignoring the lack of response, he added, "Why don't you take your time going up to the house, while I help with your gear?"

Nathan still didn't stir. David gave a slight, imperceptible shrug at Hilda and moved away.

She knew how bitterly hurt Rance had been by his son's outburst at the hospital. He had been withdrawn and cold ever since. First of all, Nathan had refused point blank to leave the hospital while his gran was so sick. When she had regained consciousness enough to weakly insist he go with his father, she had produced the key to the house for them to go and pack up Nathan's pitifully few personal belongings.

Their arrival at the house with a reluctant, still belligerent boy had precipitated another fight. Rance had taken one look at the few clean-but-worn clothes and coldly dictated there was no need to take any clothes—only school things, toys, and books.

One small boy had one large amount of pride. "What's wrong with my stuff?" he'd shouted back.

Hilda could see how upset Rance was by the state of the house generally, as well as by the ragged, stained clothes. But she could also see the fear Nathan was trying to hide at the thought of not having old familiar things with him in his new life. At last, Hilda had persuaded Rance that Nathan would not be well enough for a few days to take on a massive shopping spree, and should take a basic wardrobe. She pretended not to see the few forbidden items that Nathan threw in the boxes when his father wasn't looking.

Now, as Hilda stared at the angry, rebellious boy, suddenly she'd had enough, both of him and his unreasonable father. "Oh, you poor little darling, can't you manage to undo your seatbelt?" she said in sugary tones. "Here, let me help."

"I'm not a baby," snarled Nathan.

"Then stop acting like one," she snarled right back, "or I'll treat you like one."

His eyes widened slightly, but he didn't move, just eyed her warily. She started to reach for the seat belt button. He pushed her hand away, and in a moment was standing beside her. She returned his glare with good measure. His eyes faltered and he looked away. Then she watched an awed expression transform his sullen features. He had suddenly spotted through the trees the panorama of white sands and blue, tumbling surf.

The peace of the scene was a tremendous contrast to the battle royal that had been taking place between Rance and his son. Hilda joined him and felt her own annoyance and frustration start to drain away.

"God's handiwork is rather wonderful, isn't it?" she murmured as she too drank her fill of the beauty.

Hilda was aware that Nathan turned toward her, but whatever he was going to say was interrupted by a gleeful little shout.

"Unca Wance, Unca Wance, where's you been? We been waiting and waiting to build a sand house."

Jodie came racing along the steep path from the house. She ran toward Nathan and demanded, "Are you Nafin?"

As he stared at her, she suddenly stopped still. Her eyes widened, and her mouth drooped. "Youse poor, poor face." She went right up to him and reached up on tiptoe and tenderly kissed his cheek. "Is better now!" she proclaimed and then whirled toward her father as he hastily approached. "Nafin's hurted his face, Daddy," she said tearfully.

David picked her up and glanced apprehensively at the rock-like figure of the small boy who was staring at the dainty little girl with dazed eyes. One hand had gone up to the spot on his cheek where she had kissed him.

"Yes, he has, princess, and that's why he needs a nice rest here at the beach," Rance's voice said unsteadily.

He had moved next to David and was watching Nathan. Nathan took his eyes off the little girl and looked at his father.

Rance smiled at him gently. "And I think he'll need lots of kisses to help him get better."

Nathan's eyes filled with tears. "I. . .I—"

"It's going to be all right, son." Rance dropped the case he had been carrying and took a few long strides. He crouched down in front of the boy and kissed him on the cheek in the same spot Jodie had. Looking him in the eye he said "I'm sorry. I wasn't angry with you—just angry at myself. I should have accepted my mother's offer to help me clear up things in Queensland, and come down sooner, or taken you back with me. And I did try and ring, but the phone was disconnected."

Father and son searched each other's eyes. Then Nathan's face crumpled. As she saw Nathan suddenly fling his arms around Rance, tears started trickling down Hilda's own face. Her love for this complex man who could apologize to a small boy like that grew by leaps and bounds. Then she stood transfixed as the words started tumbling out of Nathan.

"I waited and waited," the boy sobbed. "I had all my stuff packed up. You didn't come. Then he started drinking again. He. . .he called Mum all kinds of horrible names. I told him to shut up, and he swung at me. Then. . .then he hit Gran real bad. I couldn't wake her up, and. . .and the lady next door rang the ambulance. . .and when he woke up and she wasn't there he went sort of wild, and started hitting and kicking at me. I hid all night. . .and. . .and. . .." The jerky, disjointed words broke off and he suddenly wailed, "Is Gran going to die, too?"

David gestured to Hilda as Rance started to quietly speak again to Nathan. She took the trembling little girl from her father and started back to the house. David grabbed a couple cases and quickly followed them.

"Why was Unca Wance and Nafin cwying?" Jodie said with a big sob of her own, looking back over Hilda's shoulder.

"Because they have both been cross with each other," Hilda managed, as she hurried the little girl away. "They. . .they're both going to need lots and lots of our loving to help them."

Several days later, Hilda remembered those words a little grimly as she watched Rance and Nathan trying to have a game of cricket on the firm, wet sand. She was acting as a reluctant wicket keeper, while Rance bowled gently to Nathan.

She gritted her teeth as a too cheerful, too easygoing Rance called out, "Watch out for this spin ball, mate!"

Nat put up his brand new bat and patted it gently away. "Boy, Dad, that had a great spin on it," he said with a beaming smile.

If only they would stop being so polite to each other! If only Rance would start going easy on trying to give his son everything at once! Rance bowling far too easy balls, and Nat's false appreciation of his expertise was so typical of the last few days.

I never dreamt that one day I'd want to see a father and his son have a good family disagreement, Hilda thought angrily.

But she knew that this state of affairs could not last. They were both too tense from trying too hard to be the perfect father and son. Rance had bought fishing gear and taken Nathan fishing. Nathan had been excited and hugged his father. Rance had bought him this cricket set. Nathan had been excited and hugged his father. She knew from something Nathan had said one day, that he hated cricket, preferring soccer.

The housekeeper, Mrs. Burkett, had turned out to be a pleasant, middle-aged woman who lived in an attached small flat with her husband. She cheerfully bustled around, insisting to Hilda that she didn't need any help at all except after tea each evening, which she left them to clear away. So Hilda had traipsed along after father and son on all their excursions. They had both insisted on her going with them, and she knew they felt more secure with a third person present, so had gone along with it all.

It's time I had a good talk with this perfect father. Hilda listened to Rance's anxious apology for bowling too fast, as Nathan missed a ball.

"Okay, that's it. I've had enough cricket," she called out as she lobbed the ball back. "I'm going back to grab the shower first."

She ignored their protests and started running up the beach. As she reached the path that wound its way up a steep slope through light bush to the house, she glanced back and wasn't surprised to see Rance pulling out the cricket stumps as they prepared to follow her.

Hilda had become more and more annoyed with Rance, too. He knew how anxious she was to drive into Sydney to the address on her birth certificate. She had taken the street directory out of the car and looked up the address in front of him. He had just briefly commented that he had thought it would be in the inner city area. Just over an hour's drive away, he had informed her with a frown.

The main part of the beach house was not large, a basic three bedroom brick veneer, but with excellent kitchen and bathroom facilities. Rance had seemed a little surprised that it was not larger, and had confided that it was much smaller than the other two houses his stepfather owned, one on the Gold Coast, and the other on the Sunshine Coast, north of Brisbane.

Sunday had come and gone with no mention of finding a church to attend. Hilda had shrugged to herself, knowing that Rance was falling over backwards to let Nathan not be upset or put out about his father being a minister. Instead, they had traveled down to Wollongong and gone to the movies. Hilda knew it didn't hurt to miss one Sunday at worship, but it still disturbed her as another indication of Rance's spiritual life not being what it should be. They did not even say grace before their meals.

Hilda had retired early that Sunday night, and read a long passage in the first letter by the apostle John in the Scriptures. It was all about love, and it drove her to spend a long time in prayer.

Now, as far as Hilda was concerned, her holiday had come to an end. Nathan's bruises were still fading in places, but most had already gone. The cuts were healing well, and the swelling on his face had subsided quickly, leaving only a yellowing bruise over his cheek bone and a yellow tinge in one eye. What she knew would take much longer to heal was the bruising on his soul and spirit. And that healing process could take even longer if Rance did not soon come to his senses.

Hilda made straight for the phone.

"Yes, of course you can stay here tonight, Hilda," Jean Drew's crisp voice said. "I've been looking forward to seeing you very much. I'm off duty tomorrow, and was even considering taking a run in the car down there to see you all."

Hilda had showered and was in her room packing when she heard Rance's brisk footsteps and then a knock on her door. She took a deep breath and closed her eyes for a moment before calling out, "Come in, if you're game!"

"That sounds ominous," Rance's amused voice said as he opened the door.

Hilda didn't turn around and continued placing a pair of jeans in the half-filled case on the bed. Rance had come to an abrupt standstill. There was silence, and at last she swung round to face him. He looked from the case to her face and back again.

"You're packing," he said flatly.

"Yes," she said crisply and turned her back on his accusing glare. "I rang up, and there's a train from Helensburg in just over half an hour. If you can't drive me, I'll ask Mr. Burkett next door."

There was another long pause before he said very quietly, "Are you going to stay with Jean?"

Hilda turned around slowly. There was a sick feeling in the pit of her stomach. She wondered for a moment if he had any idea how difficult it was for her to leave. "I've just rung her. I don't think you and Nathan really need me here any longer, and I do have business of my own to attend to."

"Not need you!" Rance burst out. There was a hint of panic in his voice. For a moment, Hilda's heart took a flying leap only to plunge back to earth with a thud when he added urgently, "Nathan can hardly let you out of his sight. For some reason he still can't relax with me unless you're there."

Hilda hesitated for a moment, and then choosing her words carefully she said earnestly, "He's not the only one who can't relax. You're both trying to be someone you're not. Rance, I've tried to tell you, you're trying too hard! You both need a bit of time to yourselves. Let him go and play on the beach by himself if he wants to. You go and read a book if you want to. You don't have to spend every waking moment in each other's hair."

"But we've wasted so much time, Hildie." Pain darkened his eyes. "There are so many years to make up."

"But you can't make them up," Hilda said earnestly. "Can't you see, you've got to learn to accept each other as you are at this point in time. Let the past go, Rance."

Rance raised his eyebrows. "Is that what you're doing, Hildie?"

Hilda looked away and then sank down on the side of the bed. Why did her mother give her away? Who was she? So many unanswered questions!

"What past!" she said at last with a touch of bitterness. "I don't know enough about what happened to be able to say. Perhaps I never will," she added sadly and looked up at him pleadingly. "But I have to try, Rance. I can't let go of what I know so little about."

"But that's what you're asking me to do." He walked away from her, and stood looking out of her window. With his back still turned, he said in a tortured voice, "Nathan is old for his age in so many areas. He's lived with his mother all his life until last year. Her lifestyle was something I ran from so I wouldn't be corrupted, and yet my son has lived it for nine years! What's he seen? What has he done? What's been done to him? Val told me she didn't know for sure where or how she was infected with the HIV virus. She was only actually diagnosed three years ago. Apparently she never told a soul until last year the truth about her bouts of illness. It could have been needle sharing or. . .or. . ." His voice choked, and he hunched his shoulders.

Hilda stood up and went over to him. For a moment she hesitated, and then she said shakily, "Rance, you only did what the Bible says about running from temptation. That's called obedience. If you had stayed, perhaps Nathan wouldn't have a father to love him today."

There was a long silence, then Rance turned toward her. He reached out slowly and caught her by the shoulders. Searching her eyes intently he whispered, "And I would never have met such a beautiful woman. That's twice now you've been God's messenger to me." He took a deep breath and added simply, "Thank you, Hildie."

Hildie wasn't sure who moved, but she felt his arms slip around her as his lips descended to lightly taste her lips. All her love spilled out as she opened to him, and then they were crushed together, and suddenly passion was a white heat that leapt between them. As it had before.

The moment was timeless. It felt so right, so natural to feel his lips move over her face, back to her lips gently as the flames died away. Then they just held each other, savouring their closeness until Hilda moved her head from his shoulder and looked into his face.

"Don't you dare apologize for that kiss," she said with mock sternness.

Rance was very serious. He ran a finger under one of her wayward curls and pushed it back, not taking his eyes from hers. "Hildie, you're so very sweet, but I'm still not sure if either of us is ready for this."

Hilda stiffened, and her arms dropped. He immediately released her, and she backed away a few steps. Ready? She loved him. It was that simple.

"Is. . .is it Maree?" She asked in a stifled voice.

Surprise flashed into his face. He took a step towards her and then stilled at the sound of running steps outside.

"Hey, Dad, Hilda! Mrs. Burkett says tea will be on the table in half an hour. Dad! Where—"

Without thinking, Hilda called out, "We're in here, Nat," and swung away from Rance to fling the bedroom door open.

Nathan stared at her with startled eyes, and then looked at Rance as he appeared behind her. The expression on his face changed as he looked from one to the other. Disillusionment was followed by bitter disappointment. "I thought you two'd be different," he said scornfully.

Hilda didn't understand for a moment, and then her eyes widened in shock. Before she could say anything in their defense, he took off.

"Nathan, wait!" Rance pushed her out of the way and raced after him.

Hilda started to follow, and then stopped. Returning to her room, she made for the mirror, and gasped. Her lipstick was smeared. Her lips were slightly swollen. She was still flushed, and in fact her whole appearance was such that a worldly wise nine-year-old boy could tell she had been well and truly kissed! Besides, that lipstick must have transferred to Rance.

She grabbed a tissue and wiped her lips. A quick comb restored her tousled hair, and then she went to find father and son. They had not gone far.

As Hilda paused at the entrance to the back patio, she heard Rance say firmly, "I don't care what you know happens in bedrooms, Hildie and I were doing nothing wrong. I like her very much. She's my friend, nothing more."

A knife slashed at Hilda's heart.

Nat swung around from staring down the back yard and said with a sneer, "Yeah, yeah, friends have pasho kisses all the time!" He saw Hilda in the doorway, and turned away again.

Rance hesitated. He glanced over at Hilda. Perhaps he saw something in her face that betrayed her pain at his word "like." She didn't want him to merely like her as a friend, she wanted him to love her enough to. . .to. . .

A large, but gentle hand reached out and turned Nathan around. "Nathan, you know I'm a minister, don't you?"

Nathan's lip curled. *I wonder who he's copying,* thought Hilda sadly. It was such an adult expression.

"I think you've been given some very strange ideas about ministers and merely getting up and preaching, and all his talking about God doesn't mean that minister's never make mistakes, Nathan." Rance smiled ruefully. "I know that only too well since I found out about you."

Suddenly he looked over at Hilda again. "Come here, Hildie," he said quietly, "I want you here so Nat can know you agree with what I want to say." When she had joined them, he crouched down to Nathan's level and looked him in the eye. "Hildie and I probably weren't very wise being in her bedroom together, but we would not do anything there, or anywhere else for that matter, that is wrong in God's eyes."

As Rance continued in a very firm, convincing voice, Hilda saw doubt flicker in Nathan's face. "It's not that Hildie and I are different from anybody else. We may want to make love together as married people do, but we would never do that because we both love our Savior, Jesus Christ, too much, and we know it would hurt Him."

Amazement washed over Nathan's face. "You really believe all that stuff?"

Hilda's heart leaped. Rance merely asked, "What stuff do you refer to, Nat?"

" 'Bout God loving the world and Jesus dying on the cross, and. . . and all that."

Hilda held her breath. She heard the slight tremble in Rance's voice as he calmly replied, "I certainly do believe that God loves everyone in the world, and that includes me and Hilda, and you, too. Jesus came and showed us what God's like, and told how God wants us to live. Then He died and rose again, so we could have our sins forgiven and have God as our loving Father to be with us for always."

"Where did you hear about Jesus?" Hilda asked gently.

Nathan looked up at her and scowled. "Mum told me, and then she made me go to a dumb Sunday School last. . .last year. Gran said it was all nonsense, and I didn't have to, but Mum got real angry and upset with her." Suddenly he grinned. "The picnics and Christmas party was beaut though."

"Doesn't anybody want their tea tonight?" a rather cross voice said behind them.

Hilda swung around. "Sorry, Mrs Burkett! I'm starving. I don't know about these two." She glanced at her watch, and looked ruefully at Rance. It was too late to try and catch the train to Sydney.

Rance caught her eye and smiled understandingly. Her heart reached out to him, and his smile broadened. There was a glow about his face she realized she had not seen for many, many months.

He stood up. "We won't be a moment, Mrs Burkett, and thank you very much. You go on home, we'll be okay." As Mrs Burkett disappeared, he looked down at Nathan uncertainly. Then he looked back at Hilda pleadingly.

"Hildie has to attend to some very important private business in Sydney, and she's put it off to stay with us and help us get to know each other better. I went to tell her that the Mortons are coming for the day tomorrow. Would you mind very much if I drove Hildie to Sydney while you stayed and kept Jodie out of mischief?"

Alarm flashed into Nathan's face. "You'll both be back to sleep tomorrow night?"

Rance looked silently at Hilda. She glanced from one anxious face to the other, and her heart melted. "My goodness, you two do look alike!"

Both faces lit up. Their smiles were very similar. The tall fair man and the small boy turned to look at each other. "We do?" There was sheer wonder and delight in Rance's voice.

Hilda laughed gently at them. "Now Nat's face is almost back to normal, you sure do. But it's not just your faces. It's more in your expressions." She shook her head at them, thrilled to see how pleased they both looked. "And the answer is yes. I'll have to ring Jean again, but we'll both sleep back here tomorrow night."

The instant relief that flooded Rance's eyes warmed her through and through. Then a shadow touched her. Would she know more about her mother this time tomorrow night?

She pushed the thought away. "Keeping up with you two trying to be the great Aussie cricket captain and his main spin bowler has made me very hungry," she said firmly. "So let's eat!"

Chapter 10

The Mortons were disappointed when they arrived mid-morning to discover Rance and Hilda were only waiting for them before they left for Sydney.

"But we still hasn't made our sand house, Unca Wance," wailed Jodie.

"I'll help you build a sand castle," Nathan offered gruffly.

Big eyes studied him doubtfully for a moment, and then Jodie beamed. "Now?"

"Whoa, young lady," Kim laughed. "Hat, sun block, and a tee-shirt first. Even if it isn't summer, you'll still get too much sun, knowing how long it takes to build one of your masterpieces."

Rance was still smiling as they drove up the winding road toward the Prince's Highway. "That Jodie!" he chuckled. "She's devastating at three. By the time she's twenty-three she's going to cause havoc in the male population."

Hilda laughed with him, but felt a little wistful. She hoped Jodie never lost her innate sweetness. Looking back over her teenage years and brief stint at university before her mother's illness had brought her home again, she knew she had often been too self-opinionated and abrupt to be very popular with either sex. Perhaps that was one of the penalties of being a spoilt only child. She had always vowed to have more than one child if she ever married.

Hilda glanced wistfully at the man beside her. Then she deliberately turned from those particular hopes and dreams and back to their destination and all it could lead to.

Hilda didn't realize how long she had been silent until Rance asked in a gentle voice, "Worth a penny?"

She looked blankly at him, and then smiled a little sadly. "I haven't heard anyone say that since Mum died." She took a deep breath. "I was just wondering if my. . .if she's had any other children by now."

Rance was silent for awhile, then he said in a troubled voice, "Hildie, sweetheart, have you faced up to the possibility that your natural mother may not want to meet you, let alone allow you to meet any of her family?"

Hilda swallowed. How could she tell him about the sleepless nights, and the times of agonized praying? "I. . .I've told God that I'll leave it in His hands to sort all that out, Rance," she said at last in a low voice.

"Oh, Hildie, I've never known a woman like you!" Rance burst out. Startled, she limut before she could take in what he had said, he added in a quieter voice, "We haven't talked about last night. I meant what I said to Nathan. It was a mistake kissing you like that in your bedroom."

A mistake! The memory of that kiss had sent her to sleep with hope and love and a smile on her lips. And he called it a mistake!

"If you say sorry one more time for kissing me, I'll. . .I'll. . . ," she said through gritted teeth, and then snapped loudly as he started to protest, "I don't want to talk about it. I've got other things on my mind today."

They had reached the intersection with the Southern Freeway. Rance was silent as he speeded up and eased into the traffic. Feeling bitterly hurt at his calling a mistake what she had believed was an earth-shattering experience for both of them, Hilda stared out at the passing traffic through a blur of tears.

As Rance eventually started to speak, she kept her head averted. "I'll go along with you for today, Hilda. But we are going to talk about how we feel about each other very soon." Rance's voice held an unexpected hint of steel. "Just one more thing for you to think about. When David rang me last night, he said that a church in Brisbane had been trying to contact me. Apparently they want to know if I would be interested in entering into discussions with them about a possible ministry there."

Hilda turned to him at that, but as she opened her mouth to say how pleased she was for him, he added quickly, "But we aren't going to talk about that either today. Today is something I've kept you from doing far too long. I am sorry about that, Hildie. It was very selfish of me."

"No, no," she protested with tears in her voice. "I could have said something before this. I. . .I. . .oh, Rance, I've been so scared that for a while I was only too glad to put it off."

Rance's hands clenched, but he did not reach out to comfort her. Instead, he said strongly, "Didn't you just tell me you've put it all in God's hands?"

Hilda's sudden fright subsided. "He loves me and won't let anything happen to me that He and I can't handle together," she murmured at last. "I remember a certain minister saying that in a certain sermon earlier this year."

She threw a smile at him, and he grinned. A slight tinge of red touched his cheeks, and she heard the pleasure in his voice as he said, "Well, wonder of wonders! Someone was actually listening to the preacher!"

"No, no," she laughed, relieved they were getting back on their old footing. "You've got it wrong again, Preacher! I was listening to the Holy Spirit speaking to me through the lips of the preacher."

"Ouch! Putting me in my place!" Rance chuckled and then he sobered and added with awe, "You know that's pretty incredible, isn't it? He uses us so many times to bring a word of comfort to people when we often don't know how they're hurting."

Hilda hesitated, and then said steadily "And He even uses the Vals of this world sometimes when they don't claim Him as Lord. Although I wonder about Nathan's mother. Perhaps something you said years ago did bring her to some faith. She must have been a pretty special person, Rance."

"She was. Especially when we first met, but then. . ." Regret filled his voice. "She never once mentioned sending Nat to Sunday school. Not that we had much time to talk. She was too ill, and every breath was an effort. Last night he told me she insisted he had to go because his father would have wanted him to know all about that 'stuff' as he calls it. It thrills me to think perhaps all my zealous foolishness so many years ago bore some kind of fruit. I always thought my slipping back into my old lifestyle would have invalidated everything I tried to tell my friends about God." Rance snorted with disgust at himself. "Apparently Nathan's been wondering why I haven't mentioned anything about God to him before this."

"So that's why we said grace at breakfast time!"

Rance looked at her a trifle sheepishly. "I've been pretty stupid, haven't I?"

"Well," she drawled, "I'm not so sure about the pretty bit, but I'll give you the stupid part."

He gave a loud laugh. "I'll go along with that. And that's exactly why I need you around!" She stiffened, and he added swiftly, "But, as I said, all that can wait until later."

Hilda forced herself to relax again, but the rest of the way, the thought remained. What did he mean by "all that" in connection with needing her?

When they reached the inner suburb of Paddington, they had to stop a couple times to consult the street directory. At last, after taking a couple wrong turns, they pulled up slowly outside the right address. They got out of the car and stared at the four story building silently, and then looked at each other.

"A hostel," Rance said doubtfully. "Are you sure this was the right street?"

"Well, that sign way down the hill said it was," Hilda replied slowly. She straightened her shoulders. "Only one way to find out."

It was the right address. And no, it had always been a hostel or boarding house, and no, the owner did not have a clue where they could find the people he'd bought it from a couple years earlier.

"And they hadn't owned it that long anyway. I believe the people before them used to put up all types. Sorry can't help youse folks," the unshaven, unwashed superintendent smirked. "The place was a real dump when we bought it a few years ago."

As they reluctantly returned to the car, Hilda muttered, "I hate to

246

have seen it when it was what he calls a dump."

"Me, too," said Rance grimly. "I'd sure call it one now. The smell was dreadful." He looked up and down the narrow street with its rows of old terrace houses, and sighed. "So we start on the neighbors as that lady at the adoption place suggested."

A long, long time later, they closed the gate of the last house in the block and silently started back to the car. Rance sympathetically slipped his arm around the weary, bitterly disappointed Hilda and hugged her. "There's still the electoral roll books, sweetheart."

"With a name like Jones? And we don't even know if it was her real name!" she replied despondently. "I've had enough today. Let's go back and spend some time with the Mortons before they have to go home."

The days were getting shorter, and when they arrived at Wattle Point the sun was very low. It had already slipped behind the hills west of the small village on the coast. There was a strange car parked besides the Mortons' red Camry, but although the house was unlocked there was no one there.

"That's strange, surely they'd be back getting ready for tea by this," frowned Rance. "Not even Mrs. Burkett's here. I wonder—"

"Look," said Hilda urgently. She pointed to a figure racing up the path from the beach. "That's Aunt Jean. Let's meet her, I think something must be wrong."

"Oh, thank God you're back," gasped a pale Jean, as they reached her. "Nathan and Jodie have been missing for over three hours."

Rance's face drained of all color, but he just stared at her silently. Hilda slipped her hand under his arm and clutched him tightly.

After she had regained her breath sufficiently, Jean explained. Nathan and Jodie had raced back to the beach straight after a snack to finish their sand castle. Kim and David had sat in the outdoor furniture where they could watch them.

"When I drove up, they had both dozed off. They said it must have only been, at the most, half an hour," Jean told them rapidly, "At first we weren't too concerned at the two not being in sight. Apparently they'd been scavenging, out of sight at times, for things on the beach to decorate the castle. It wasn't until we strolled down to the beach that we realized they were no where to be seen."

"Did you say three hours ago?" rasped Rance.

"I. . .I arrived about three hours ago," said Jean reluctantly. "A lot of people have been helping us the last hour or more, including the. . . the lifesavers."

Three hours! Hilda looked out at the vastness of the ocean. She couldn't bear the anguish on Rance's face.

"Have. . .have you rung the police?" she asked unsteadily.

Jean was watching Rance. "That's why I was coming back when I saw you arrive."

"Why did you wait so long!" Rance cried out. "They could have been swept out to sea anywhere by now!"

"No!" Jean said sharply. "At first we thought they may have gone for a swim, even if it's been too cold since you arrived here for anyone without wet suits. That's why we alerted the surf club, and it turned out someone from their observation deck had been watching the kids. They saw them running toward the track back through the sand hills. We've been searching the sand hills and the next beach around the headland.

"A while back, a couple of fisherman returned and told us that, when they were parking their car, two kids like them raced past. It was the car park at the other end of the beach. We even thought they might have gone to the little shop near the main road for an ice block or drink, but no one's seen them."

"As far as I know, Nathan never had any money," Rance said with difficulty. "Has anyone been searching the bush the other side of the road?" he asked urgently.

Jean shook her head. "Not to my knowledge."

Hilda drew in a sharp breath. There were only a few houses there, set way back in the bush. The terrain sloped fairly sharply up toward the mountain range. Thick undergrowth underneath towering trees hid many dangers for adults. And they were only children. It would be so easy for them to lose their way.

"But they both loved the beach. Why would they want to go somewhere else?" said Hilda with a puzzled frown.

"Who would know with kids," Rance said briefly and started for the car. "I'll go take a look anyway."

Without a word, Hilda raced to climb in beside him. He glanced at her gratefully, but didn't speak.

Hilda's mind filled with stories she had heard of children lost in the harsh Australian bush. But that was usually in the ranges or the outback. *Surely not here,* she thought with a shudder. *Not so near this little beach resort.*

One single-lane driveway ended at a large brick house set close to a steep cliff. It looked deserted and was guarded by a snarling German shepherd.

"The children would certainly have turned away from here," declared Rance as he turned the car.

"I certainly hope so," Hilda said with a shudder at the thought of the dog terrifying Nathan and Jodie.

The next driveway was much shorter and ended at a small, run-down dwelling of unpainted weatherboard.

"Been here all day," said the elderly man who came out to meet them. "Would have seen them if they came this way."

He followed Rance back to the car and peered in at Hilda. "Sorry, missus," he added gently, "hope your kids'll be okay. It's pretty thick bush around here. I sure wish I could help you look." He thumped his chest. "Old ticker, you know. But I'll sure offer up a prayer or two for your son."

As they drove off, the tears Hilda had been holding at bay spilled over. She realized how much she had grown to love that small boy who so often reminded her of his father. A deep desire to be able to truly call him her son started to burn within her. She wiped the tears away as unobtrusively as she could, but Rance still saw them.

"They'll be all right," he said grimly as they waited for traffic to pass before pulling out onto the main road again. "God hasn't kept Nathan all this time to let something happen to him now." Suddenly he pointed. "That looks like a walking track through the bush. What about we park the car and try along there?"

They walked as quickly as they could along the rough track. Every now and then Rance roared out Nathan's name, and they stopped to listen intently. At times, overhanging foliage almost blocked the path, pulling at their clothes, scratching their arms. It was getting darker. The sun was long gone behind the mountains.

"Do you think they really could have pushed this far through here?" Hilda asked doubtfully.

The track had suddenly became much steeper and rougher as it wound still higher up the mountain.

"I suppose not," Rance said despondently. He yelled out once more, "Nathan! Jodie!"

Hilda froze. Rance looked at her. Then they both heard it again.

"Dad, Dad? Is. . .is that you?" A faint voice sounded in the distance, and then louder, urgent! "Jodie! you get back here! Jodie! The bunyip'll get ya!"

Rance and Hilda were already running as fast as they dared on the rough ground. Then a tiny figure raced around a bend. The little face was streaked with dirt and tears as it hurtled into Rance's arms.

Jodie was too breathless with sobs and fright to speak for a moment. Hilda tore past them.

Then, as Rance hurried after Hilda with his burden, Jodie sobbed breathlessly, "Nafin's hurted. He won't walk, Unca Wance."

When Hilda reached Nathan, he was trying to crawl over a large rock. His clothes were ripped and torn, and as she knelt down, he groaned and fell back. Rance reached them, and put Jodie down. As Nathan stared speechlessly up at his father, his face was white and filled with fear. He actually cringed away from Rance, and a horrified Hilda realized that he expected Rance to hit him.

Hilda was tremendously proud of Rance as he passed Jodie to her and wordlessly scooped up the small boy in his arms. He held him tightly, rocking him ever so gently. After a moment he said in a trembling voice, "Oh, son, son! Don't you ever scare me like this again!"

Hilda was cuddling the quivering Jodie tightly. "What's happened to your legs, Nat?" she asked gently.

"Nafin felled over," Jodie sobbed.

"Shush, darling. He'll be all right now his daddy's here," Hilda murmured and searched for a handkerchief to wipe the little face.

Rance had put Nathan down and was quickly examining him. "I twisted my ankle on a stone and busted my other knee when I fell," Nathan gasped painfully.

Jodie had stopped crying at last and wriggled out of Hilda's arms. She stuck both hands on her hips and glared down at Nathan. "See! I'se told you and told you I had to find our daddies!" She turned to Rance and gave another quivering sniff. "He hunged on to my jeans and wouldn't let me go! And. . .and then he told me 'bout the bunyip," she accused, and then peered uneasily around into the bush.

Hilda's lips twitched. "The bunyip? I thought they were monsters that only lived near billabongs," she said straight-faced. "I don't see any water around here!"

"Of course they are," Nathan said crossly. "And they're only in fairy stories anyway!"

"Oooh, you told a lie!" accused Jodie angrily.

"You'd have got lost or done somethin' stupid like bein' hit by a car crossin' the road like you nearly did before," yelled Nathan furiously. Tears rolled down his cheeks. "Oh, Dad, she wouldn't do what I said!"

"But we'se did see a koangawoo, Nafin! Jus' like I said!"

Hilda began to see light. "You came into the bush to see a kangaroo?"

Rance glanced at Nathan sharply. He looked away guiltily from his father's eyes and down at the large handkerchief Rance had just tied over the bleeding and swollen knee.

Jodie nodded vigourously. "Nafin's never ever seen a koangawoo. But he has now!" she added triumphantly.

"There was a small one just near here, Dad," Nathan burst out with an excited gleam in his eye. He pointed to a small grassy area in through the trees. "He was eating the grass. We were real quiet, but he started to hop away, and. . .and I—"

"He twied to catch him, and he felled over," Jodie chipped in.

"I wasn't trying to catch him—" Nathan started to say angrily, but Rance cut him off firmly.

"Let's talk all about what happened when we get you back to the house. Your Mummy and Daddy are very, very worried about you, Jodie."

Rance hit the horn as they neared the house, and in a few moments Jodie was in her mother's arms. There were more tears from Jodie when Kim started to cry as she clutched her daughter to her. But David was furious.

He rounded on Nathan. "How dare you take a tiny thing like Jodie across that dangerous road and into the bush like that! What on—"

"David, that's enough!" Rance said sharply as he paused from lifting Nathan from the back seat. "I think it may have been the other way round!" He swung around and continued to the house with his precious burden cradled gently in his strong arms. Jean hurried after him.

Hilda paused briefly and said gently to the angry David, "Let's look after them first, and then we'll sort it all out."

The two children were popped straight into hot baths. Mrs. Burkett fussed around, feeding them all after Nathan's ankle and knee had been attended to. Jean declared his injuries appeared to be sprains. Jodie fell asleep and was put down on a bed before they let Nathan tell them what had happened.

Jodie had been horrified when she had found out he had never seen a kangaroo, even at the zoo. Hilda was appalled too, at this further revelation of the restricted life he had led.

Then Jodie had insisted they had to find a kangaroo. He had willingly followed her until he realized she wanted to cross the main road and go into the bush on the other side. When he had refused, she had suddenly taken off, narrowly being missed by a speeding car coming quickly around the nearby bend.

"Boy, she was like greased lightning," Nathan said earnestly, "I yelled and yelled at her, but she just waved at me to follow and ran toward that track."

By the time he had been able to cross safely, she was a fair way into the bush. When he had caught up to her, he admitted that he thought they might as well go a bit farther. Then he had been so excited at actually seeing the small kangaroo, which the adults privately thought might have been a rock wallaby, he had tripped over the rock and gone sprawling. He had managed to crawl a little distance, but that boulder had defeated him.

"I had to hang onto her tight, and threaten her with all kinds of things to stop her tearing off again," he said with a sniffle, fighting back the tears. "She could have got lost or hit by a car, or. . .or anythin'."

Hilda felt a tug of pity for the small boy as he finished, and looked anxiously at David and then his father.

"I'm very sorry Jodie was so naughty, Nathan," David said quietly. "She knows she's not allowed to cross a road by herself. We're just thankful God answered our prayers and kept you both safe from worse harm."

"You're. . .you're not mad at me anymore?" Nathan asked tearfully.

"Far from it!" David said remorsefully. "I'm just so sorry I yelled at you. Afraid it was as much sheer relief you were both okay. Rather, we can't thank you enough for looking after her as you did." He turned to Rance, and now even Nathan could not have mistaken his moist-eyed sincerity, and Rance's pride, as he said, "Congratulations, Rance! That's some boy of yours!"

Nathan stared at the two men in astonishment, and then his pale face blushed crimson. After the Mortons had carefully carried the still sleeping Jodie off home in their car, he asked hesitantly, "Uncle David's a minister like you, isn't he, Dad?"

Rance nodded, looking at him closely and then glancing a little apprehensively across at Hilda and Jean. It was the first time the boy had mentioned his profession.

"Are all parsons like you two?" Nathan asked with a puzzled look on his face. "Sayin' that about prayin' and bein' sorry and all that."

Rance relaxed. "Not only parsons do those things," he said gently and then grinned. "But it's a different matter if you mean are parsons like us because we're charming, full of fun and," he sobered, "love their crazy kids, and get worried sick when they do a disappearing act."

Nathan's face crumpled. "I'm sorry, Dad," he whispered, and then added louder with awe, "You. . .you were really worried about me?"

Rance swallowed, and his voice was choked as he said, "What do you think? I do love you very much." He added in a stronger voice, "And if you ever dare go off without telling me again, I'll be forced to ban all television for. . .for life, probably!"

Nathan's eyes widened and then he grinned back for a moment before suddenly yawning mightily.

"Right! Bed for you." Rance stood up and went over to pick him up.

Hilda hesitated, longing to have the right to go with them as Kim had when David had carried Jodie to bed.

"Night, Hildie," Nathan said sleepily over Rance's shoulder. Then they were gone.

"Well, I suppose I should be going soon," Jean said and started packing up some dirty plates. "Perhaps we should get these out of the way first. I'm sorry I came on an impulse to see you in one way, but glad I was here to help look for those two darling little mischief makers." She paused and looked a little anxiously at Hilda. "The Mortons said they didn't have a clue why you both tore off to Sydney today. Is everything all right, Hilda?"

Before she knew it, Hilda was pouring the whole story of her adoption and search out to the astounded Jean.

"I knew you'd been born at my old training hospital," Jean exclaimed when Hilda had fallen silent, "but your parents never gave a hint you were adopted. And you actually know your natural mother's name?"

Hilda sighed wearily. "Well we aren't even sure if it's her real name or not, not with Jones as a surname. It was Margaret Louise Jones on the certificate."

Jean dropped a pile of cutlery on the floor with a clatter. Hilda looked up to see a very strange look on her face. "Did. . .did you say Margaret Louise?" Jean asked sharply.

"Yes, I did," Hilda said slowly. Jean suddenly hid her face as she picked up the cutlery again. "What's the matter, Jean?"

Jean finished collecting the cutlery, and started for the kitchen. She tossed over her shoulder, "Oh, I'm just tired and clumsy tonight. Thought I'd heard that name before, that's all. But, as you said, I guess it's a pretty common name."

Rance arrived in the dining room just then, and Jean grabbed her bag soon after and left rather abruptly.

Hilda thoughtfully watched the red glow of her car tail lights disappear. Suddenly she felt chilled. As Jean had touched Hilda's arm when she kissed her good-bye, her hand had been noticeably trembling. Suddenly, she didn't believe Jean's casual explanation about dropping the cutlery. Something about the name Margaret Louise Jones had upset her.

Hilda rubbed her arms against the cold wind sweeping off the sea and turned to go back inside. A set of headlights slowed, and turned into their short driveway.

She turned back with a grin. The efficient Sister Jean Drew must have forgotten something. Her heart quickened. Unless Jean had changed her mind about talking about what had upset her.

But the car wasn't Jean's, and a tall, willowy blond climbed out and stood up. Hilda's heart plunged. The woman strolled with a confident swagger over to where she was standing, in a stunned silence, at the foot of the steps.

"Hilda Garrett?" softly drawled Maree Sadler, Rance's ex-fiancée, "Rance's mother told me I'd probably find you here with him and that brat of his. Too bad, sweetie. You lose. He's mine."

Then she swept regally up the steps past the still motionless Hilda, to fly toward the man who had appeared in the open doorway of the house. "Rance, darling! Oh, darling, I just couldn't stay away. I'm so pleased for you."

Then her arms went up around Rance's head and she very enthusiastically kissed him.

Chapter 11

H ilda's heart sank still further the next morning when she arrived at the breakfast table and Rance greeted her with a radiant face.

The night before, she had not been absolutely certain whether Rance had been pleased or not to see Maree. He had certainly let Maree plaster her lips on his, Hilda had thought with a scowl. He had certainly been extremely polite and friendly, until Hilda had pleaded tiredness and left them alone to share the supper she had prepared. Maree's triumphant smirk had kept her awake for hours, long after she heard her car drive off.

She forced an answering smile to his happy one. "How's Nathan this morning?"

"A bit stiff and sorry for himself, but I don't think we need to take him for x-rays," Rance beamed at her. "Hildie, the most marvelous thing has happened."

Hilda thought her heart would break in a million pieces if she actually heard him put into words that he was going to marry Maree after all. She cleared her throat and said swiftly, "Yes. . .yes, I know. I'm very happy for you, Rance."

He looked a little puzzled for a moment, and then he beamed again, "Oh, Maree told you, I suppose. Isn't God good!"

If He was giving Rance what he wanted so much to make him look like this, than yes, God was being very "good" to him, Hilda supposed.

But what about my love for Rance, Lord! her lacerated heart cried out.

Aloud she said rapidly, "I've decided I'll be going home today,

Rance." Dismay filled his face, and she hurried on before he could protest, "I doubt very much if I've much hope of finding my natural parents, and I shouldn't make Jim and Gail wait any longer to tie up things with our solicitors. I'm booked on a flight from Mascot. Can you take me to the airport, or should I get a train to Central and the Mascot bus?"

"You've given up your search," he said slowly. "And that's why you look so unhappy."

"For the present, yes," Hilda said quickly and forced another smile, completely unable to tell him he was wrong. It was the thought of not seeing him and his son everyday for breakfast for the rest of her life that was devastating her.

Nathan scowled savagely when she told him she was leaving, and only brightened up when Rance assured him firmly they would see her again before much longer. He looked warningly at Hilda when she turned sharply toward him. She glared back, but obeyed his unspoken demand not to protest.

"And what about we go and see your gran after we drop Hildie off at the airport?" Rance asked him. He had been very quiet since reluctantly agreeing to take Hilda to the airport. "She's been home from hospital a couple of days now, and you can pick up any of your other belongings you want that we left behind before," he added a little gruffly, to Hilda's delight.

Although Nathan was able to limp painfully without assistance, he agreed to wait in the car while Rance went into the airport terminal with Hilda. "We will see you soon, won't we?" he asked with a trembling lip as she kissed him good-bye.

"Sometime," was all she could manage huskily. She gave him a fierce hug and whispered, "I'll always love you though."

Rance waited with her in the queue while she bought her ticket and had her bag weighed. Hilda risked glancing at him a couple of times. He was grim and remote.

As they at last moved away from the counter, she said quickly, "Don't come up to the departure lounge, Rance. You mustn't leave Nat waiting too long. I'm so pleased you're taking him to see his grandmother."

"Hildie, I. . .I. . ." Rance swept a hand through his hair. "Why are you rushing away like this?" he asked with a hint of desperation in his voice. "You know it's probably going to be weeks, if not months before I can leave here. I didn't tell Nathan, but the police rang this morning and want to talk to him. I haven't a clue how long before the court case comes up and—"

"And you'll manage very well without me here," she said with false cheerfulness. "Nathan already loves you very much. You're probably in for a few more tussles with each other, but you'll work it out." She stopped awkwardly, not at all sure how to say good-bye.

Rance knew. She suddenly found herself wrapped tightly in his arms. His lips desperately devoured hers, and for one blissful moment she kissed him back hungrily. Surely Maree wouldn't begrudge her this last kiss.

Rance showed no signs of releasing her, and at last she wrenched away. Blinded with tears, she spun on her heel and walked swiftly away, forcing herself to ignore his choking protest. The taste and essence of him on her lips had to be savored for the very last time.

Her self-control was very precarious, but she dared a quick glance back from the top of the escalators. He was still standing rigidly where she had left him, a dreadful scowl on his face. When he saw her watching him, he hesitated, then gave a quick salute. As she stepped off the moving stairs and he disappeared from sight, she heard a shout. She thought she heard him say, "Bye, darling," but knew she must have been mistaken and kept walking blindly toward the security check.

———————

Rance was right about the court case taking many weeks to come up. The long, lonely weeks crept by. At first they were only enlivened by a few phone calls from both Rance and Nathan. Rance's letters were friendly, never containing a word about that traumatic good-bye. Hilda rarely answered them. She had decided that last kiss had been one of gratitude, even affection, but she still felt ashamed and guilty for responding so wholeheartedly. After a while, he rarely contacted her, leaving her with very mixed feelings.

When she had first arrived home, she had insisted that Jim let her do some work on the property. He had studied her pale, drawn face and reluctantly agreed. So she drove the tractor occasionally and worked hard in her garden. Then she offered her help with the young people's work at the church and found herself enjoying her involvement at church more than she ever had before.

Hilda missed her father and Polly tremendously, yet as she spent more and more time in reading the Scriptures and applying the promises with faith, the pain continued to lessen. But no matter how busy she managed to be, there was a deep core of human loneliness that only one person could assuage.

She still wondered about her natural parents at times and knew that one day she would have to start the search again. For the moment, she just needed to be in her old, familiar surroundings to sooth her heartache and to try and find out what God wanted her to do in the future. This included wondering about returning to university. The closing date for applying for a place the next year loomed closer, and she knew a decision would soon have to be made.

It was a good season so far, although they could have done with more good falls of rain. The wheat that Jim and his workers had planted grew tall. When the freezing westerly winds swept across the flat paddocks, the waves of green often reminded Hilda of the waves of the ocean as seen from the beaches at Wattle Point and Stanwell Park.

And through it all, Hilda's longing and love for Rance never diminished. Her ever-growing relationship with Christ was the only thing that sustained her through some grim days. Day by day she had to rely on Him to keep going, especially after a letter or a phone call from Rance.

Then one day another letter from Rance arrived. Or rather, Hilda realized, it was a brief note enclosed with a letter from Nathan. Rance wrote "I've agreed to accept the offer of the church in Brisbane. My longing to stay in the ministry has only increased these past weeks. I start early in the new year."

Hilda was thrilled for him, knowing how much he wanted to serve

Christ in that way, and she was relieved that by the comments Nathan made, he, too, was looking forward to the move. They had continued to live at Wattle Point, but Nathan had not enjoyed the small school he had been attending after being used to the large city school. Hilda took a deep breath as she carefully placed the letters with the other small pile in her drawer. Knowing she would have to wait even longer to see them again made the following days seemed lonelier and the nights longer.

Unexpectedly, regular letters from Jean Drew had arrived over the weeks since Hilda had returned. They were always chatty and loving, and Hilda began to find that it was easier and easier to tell Aunt Jean, as she still called her, more and more about her good and bad days. Rance was rarely mentioned, and Maree never.

She was a little surprised that there had not been a whisper about Rance and Maree's engagement being renewed. Then she realized they must be waiting until he could leave Sydney. At the Government Children's Services insistence, Nathan had been going regularly to a counselor. Nathan's grandfather had pleaded not guilty due to diminished responsibility for his actions. Twice the court case had been postponed, much to Rance's disgust.

Winter gave way to an early spring. Then the large old peach trees, that Bob Garrett's mother had planted so long ago, began to spread their carpet of blossoms over the black soil and the green lawns. The heat of the sun increased, and a few scattered storms refreshed crops across the plains.

One particular day, Hilda returned late in the afternoon from a trip with the Stevenses to the annual Carnival of Flowers in Toowoomba, always held in late September. She had not been to watch the huge Carnival's procession for many years and thoroughly enjoyed it. It was a very hot day, and on the way home, Gail and Jim teased her about her sunburned nose and cheeks because she had forgotten to take a hat.

As they pulled up, Jim cocked his head and said, "I think your phone's ringing, Hilda."

Hilda groaned, but as she started to rush from the car, the phone stopped. She shrugged and turned back. "If it's important enough, they'll ring again."

Gail smiled at her sympathetically through the car window. "Have a cool shower and you'll feel better."

"Tanks are getting a bit low," Hilda smiled back. "Thanks a lot you two. It was great fun."

"I'm glad, Hilda," Gail said seriously. "You haven't had a very happy time these last few months."

Hilda forced a smile, but could find nothing to say. The car rolled into motion and soon they were gone. A tremendous feeling of bleakness filled Hilda as she entered the house. Was she always going to feel as empty and lonely for Rance's company as she did now? Today would have been so wonderful to share with him.

O, Lord, I thought I might be starting to get over him by now, she prayed silently as she took Gail's advice and had a shower. *What am I going to do?*

As she dressed, she knew the answer. Keep trusting God, as she had been. Keep letting Him strengthen her day by day, as she had been. Keep serving and loving Him. Keep submitting to His will for her life.

"But some days, it's so much harder than others, Lord," she suddenly pleaded out loud, as she looked in the mirror and wearily brushed out her wet hair. "I get so lonely for even the sound of his voice on the phone."

Then she froze. There was a loud knock on the front door. She still hardly ever thought to lock it, even though friends had warned her she should now that she lived alone. The sound of the shower must have drowned out the noise of a vehicle. She put down the brush on her dressing table and was half way to the door when she heard him.

"Hildie, where are you?"

Her feet suddenly had wings. "Oh, Rance, Rance!"

His face lit up with pleasure as she flew toward him. It was the most natural thing in the world to feel his arms close around her, and feel his lips burning a trail of fire all over her face before settling on her lips.

"Well, really, you two! It's about time!" another familiar voice said with a wealth of satisfaction in her tones.

Hilda lifted a dazed face, and stared. "Aunt Jean, you. . .you. . . ," she managed almost incoherently, from the heaven of Rance's arms. "And Nathan? Is he here, too?"

Jean's face suddenly lost its smile. "No, he's still over with Marian for the moment. We. . .we thought it best. . .that is. . ."

Hilda suddenly realized she was still hanging on to Rance for dear life, and tried to push away. "Oh! I shouldn't have. . ."

"And don't you dare say you're sorry," laughed Rance. His eyes were blazing triumphantly. He gave her another hug, and dropped a quick kiss on her nose before allowing her to slip out of his arms. Then his expression also sobered as she went to greet Jean.

A little breathless still, a thoroughly bewildered Hilda looked from one to the other. "What is it? What's happened? Why didn't you bring Nathan? Is the court case over?"

"Whoa," Rance smiled, but this time, she noticed the smile didn't light up his face. "One thing at a time. First, yes, it's all over, in that the old man was given a suspended sentence because of his deteriorating health and age."

"Because you insisted your barrister bring a plea for clemency," Jean said abruptly.

Rance looked a little embarrassed, and shrugged. "Well, I ended up feeling pretty sorry for him. He's old, and even these weeks in custody were punishment. After all, he had lost a granddaughter he loved in his own fashion."

Hilda took a deep breath, and plonked down on the nearest chair as her legs gave away. "And Nathan?"

"Oh, he's just great. He's changed a lot." Pride and love filled the father's face. Rance moved nearer to Hilda, and suddenly he was so grave, she froze. He sat down beside her and picked up her hands. Then he said very quietly, very earnestly, "Hildie, darling, Jean's got some news for you. It's about your natural mother."

He had called her darling.

Her eyes pleaded with him silently, and then began to glimmer with tears as she read the unmistakable message in his eyes. She was his darling, and he loved her.

"Later, darling," she thought she heard him whisper.

He stood up and beckoned to Jean. Hilda saw her look pleadingly at Rance. He shook his head very slightly, and then Jean suddenly moved and sat where Rance had just been sitting beside Hilda.

Hilda tensed. Margaret Louise Jones? What could Jean. . .?

Jean was very pale. Her hands were clenched tightly in her lap, and she was staring at Hilda with the strangest expression.

"Aunt Jean! You. . ." Hilda looked back at the still figure of Rance, and her eyes grew puzzled, and then widened with excitement. "You've found out about my mother?"

He shook his head slightly, and his voice was choked as he said, "I haven't. Jean has." His sudden look at Jean was very gentle and full of compassion. "You should tell her, but I will if you can't."

Jean was very still, looking down at her hands. "No," she said shakily at last, as Hilda began to wonder if she was going to speak at all, "I have to tell her."

Then an incredible thought struck Hilda. "Are you. . .are you. . .?" she whispered.

Jean looked up quickly. She stared at Hilda, and then she said wistfully, "No, I'm not your mother, but I so easily could have been." She took a deep breath. "Margaret Louise Jones was my only sister."

Hilda stared at her. She swallowed, and opened her mouth, but nothing came out.

"And we're so very sorry, Hildie, sweetheart," Rance said softly as Jean also seemed stuck for words, "but she died very soon after you were born."

There was silence, and then Hilda's eyes filled with tears. "She. . . she died?"

Jean nodded, tears rolling down her cheeks.

"And my father?"

"Roger Jones was a wonderful man." Jean swallowed painfully. "He's the only man I ever loved, but he loved Margaret," she said simply. "I thought Margaret never knew, but now I'm not so sure. It might be why she never told me she was pregnant. When they set their wedding date, I couldn't bear to see them married, so I managed to get a position at a hospital in London to do my midwifery training. Only a few days before the wedding, Roger was killed in a boating accident. I. . .I didn't know that for a long time."

Hilda gave a little moan. How dreadful to lose someone you loved like that. She looked up at Rance, and he crouched down beside her, taking her hands tightly in his.

"I. . .I was very bitter and angry when I was in England, even blaming God for my misery," Jean continued, staring sadly into the distance. "I was very lonely over there at first. My resentment and frustration alienated me from making friends. I cut all ties with old friends here, even Marian. Margaret had written me a couple of letters soon after I left. I couldn't answer them, and when they stopped about the time of the wedding, I wasn't worried. I was so utterly self-centered that I felt only relief not to be reminded of all I had missed out on."

She looked so wretched, that the watching Hilda slipped a hand from Rance and reached out to place hers over the clenched fists of the older woman.

Jean turned sadly to her. "By the time my twelve months training had finished, I had made a few good friends and decided to stay there longer. I wrote to Margaret then, but the letter was never answered. It was almost three years before I returned, and it seemed as though Roger and Margaret had disappeared from the face of the earth. Mutual friends told me about Roger's accident, but Margaret had moved to Sydney soon afterwards and they had lost track of her. I. . . I hadn't heard her name since you told me your mother's name the other night."

A sob shook Jean's body. "I found out a few days ago that you were born eight months after Roger was killed. All this time I thought I had no one, and I can't get over the fact that I never even knew there had been a baby, my niece."

Hilda thought of the brokenhearted young woman finding out she was pregnant. That cheap boarding house in Paddington must have been her only alternative.

"So she must have wanted me after all," Hilda said huskily.

"Oh, yes, she wanted you all right!" Jean said fervently. "You told me you were born at my old training hospital. I always maintained my hospital was the best there was. Margaret must have deliberately moved to be close to it so you could have the best of care. A couple of the nurses who looked after her told me she'd said something about her sister training there."

"You've spoken to nurses who. . .who. . .?"

Jean nodded briefly. "I've kept in touch with a few old friends from those days. Between us, we were able to work out who would have been working in the obstetric unit when you were born." She swallowed, forcing back the tears. "I. . .I had to be certain it was my sister. It's taken me a long time to track anyone down. But staff did remember you because it was all so tragic; one woman losing her baby and never able to have another, and one mother so thrilled to have a baby to remind her of the man she loved, and then dying herself before she could tell them your father's name. Apparently the Garretts fostered you for a long time before they were finally allowed to adopt you when no relatives could be traced."

"Poor Mum and Dad," Hilda whispered. "Perhaps that's why Mum became so paranoid about telling anyone I wasn't their own daughter. She was terrified I'd be taken from them."

Jean nodded again. "More than likely. You see, Margaret told the hospital staff her name was Jones, but it wasn't her legal name, and they had nothing else to go on. She had only been at the boarding house address a couple of weeks and no one knew where she had come from. There weren't any relatives to make inquiries. Even Roger's folk didn't bother to find out how his fiancée was after a couple of months. Probably too painful a reminder."

Jean gave a huge sob. "I don't know if I'll ever be able to forgive myself for letting my envy and resentment cause me to be so heartless and unforgiving toward my sister. Even since I became a Christian a few years ago, I've deliberately kept this part of my life buried deep down. I don't know how God can forgive me!"

"Oh, Aunt Jean—" Hilda stopped, and through her own tears, she suddenly started to smile. "Aunt Jean," she murmured very slowly, and then she said it louder, "Aunt Jean! Oh, all this time you've been my real aunt after all!"

She began to laugh and cry, and suddenly she and Jean were holding each other tightly.

"Oh, don't you see?" Hilda cried, "It's so wonderfully incredible! Of course God's forgiven you! Only He could possibly have arranged for you to have known me since I was a little girl. He gave me parents who loved Him and could teach me about Him. I've even called you Aunt all this time!"

Chapter 12

When Jean and Hilda surfaced from their tears and joy, they realized Rance had disappeared.

"The poor dear," Jean smiled shakily, "he's had a real cot case on his hands for the whole trip. I knew you'd be so disappointed that. . .that your mother and father had died, and. . .and I didn't know how you'd feel about us, and—"

"Oh, Aunt Jean!" Hilda gave her another hug. "I've thought you were absolutely marvelous, for almost as long as I can remember." She gave her a shaky smile. "These last couple years especially." The wonder in her voice was reflected in her shining eyes. "To think it was you who stayed with me when I so desperately needed someone after Dad died!"

"God's ways are perfect," murmured Jean with awe.

"They sure are!" Rance's voice exclaimed behind them.

He was carrying a tray with three steaming mugs. As she thankfully sipped her drink a few moments later, Hilda thrilled that he'd remembered just how she liked her tea. Suddenly a wave of shyness mixed with delight swept over her as she filled her eyes with him. Then her euphoria faded. There was still Maree. She glanced down at the cup in her hands.

"And you, Rance," she murmured with difficulty. "What's been happening with you?"

"You mean, besides trying to keep Jean here in order?" He grinned at Jean.

Hilda was startled. "You mean, you knew?"

"I didn't know what to do," Jean smiled gently back at Rance. "This lovely man was there, and I knew how much he thought of you, so I ended up pouring my suspicions out to him. He's driven me all over the place these last couple months."

"Months!"

Rance's beautiful smile reached deep into Hilda's susceptible heart, and her love for him flared brighter still.

"Yes, it took a long time. A couple of Jean's friends were on an overseas trip. Then we flew to Perth to talk to someone else."

Hilda was beyond words. He had been prepared to go to that time and expense for her.

"The nurse who was with Margaret when you were born has been living there for many years. She's a grandmother herself, now," Jean said quietly. She put down her cup, picked up her discarded handbag and withdrew a long envelope. "She was also with Margaret when she died. That part of the story she wrote down for you. There was no doubt in her mind how desperately you were wanted and loved by your mother."

Hilda looked from one to the other, and then reverently reached out and took the letter. "I don't know if I can take much more just now," she muttered unsteadily. "I'll read this some other time."

"Good," said Rance fervently. Her eyes flew to his, and he gave her a twisted smile. "I mean, there are other things we need. . .I need to talk about."

Before Hilda could begin to wonder what on earth he wanted— no, needed—to talk to her about, Jean stood up and straightened her shoulders. "Yes, of course," she said with some of her old crispness back in her voice. "You have a lot of decisions to make, and I know we promised Nathan we wouldn't be too long before we went back to bring him to see Hilda."

They all heard the sound of a motor, and Rance suddenly scowled. "That sounds like he's already driven the Stevenses around the twist, and they couldn't wait to get rid of him!"

Hilda sprang to her feet with excitement. She was at the driveway before the car had rolled to a stop. It felt so wonderful to see Nathan's radiant face as he tumbled out of the car and into her arms.

Jim's face beamed widely at her over Nathan's head. He gave her the thumbs up sign and then waved as he put the car in motion again. She stared at him in some surprise, and then returned her attention to Nathan as he wriggled out of her hug.

His suddenly scowling face looked so incredibly like his father's a few moments before that she laughed in sheer delight and hugged him again. This time he pushed her away.

"Hildie, I missed you! Why'd you go away for so long!" he accused her.

"Well, just look at you, Nathan Telford! Don't you look great!" Hilda stared at him with delight. She was sure he had shot up. His thin body had filled out. His eyes were clear and sparkling with health and the delight of seeing her again.

"Son, I thought I told you we'd come for you when we were ready," Rance said with so much resigned annoyance that Nathan looked taken back.

"But you've been here for ages, Dad! You've had plenty of time to ask her—"

"Nathan!" roared Rance. "Not another word!"

"But, Dad, I only—"

Jean suddenly grabbed the small boy by the arm. "Nathan, we had other important things to talk about first, and your father hasn't had a chance, so not another word," she said ferociously.

"And if you didn't eavesdrop on other people's conversations, you wouldn't have known anything about it," Rance said through gritted teeth.

"I didn't eavesdrop!" Nathan declared vehemently. "A bloke can't help hearin' you two talkin' right outside his own room, can he? And anyway, it was a brilliant idea, just brilliant!" He turned to Hilda, and stopped abruptly. Surprise and then affront flashed across his face. "What are you laughin' at?"

Hilda had dissolved into delighted giggles. "You're talking at each other just like a perfectly normal father and son!"

Color crept into Rance's cheeks. "Yeah, I guess we are," he said sheepishly, "but I don't know why you find it so funny!"

"Oh, my dears, not funny, just such a relief!" Hilda beamed from one puzzled face to the other.

Nathan's mouth opened, but Jean spoke rapidly first. "Well, whatever Hilda and your dad are talking about, it must be okay, Nathan. Hilda, I do take it we can all stay the night?"

"Oh, can you stay? That would be marvelous!" Hilda was thrilled, and then suddenly she remembered. Her face stilled. "But won't Maree be expecting you?"

Utter astonishment flooded Rance's face, and Nathan asked with surprise, "Maree who?"

"Ah, that explains it!" Jean explained.

Hilda looked from one to the other with bewilderment. Nathan didn't even know who Maree was? Could that possibly mean Rance had not told him yet? She opened her mouth, and then closed it with a snap as she saw the sudden challenge in Rance's eyes, and a flickering fire that looked like. . .looked like anger! Then he spoke, and she knew she was right. He was furious.

"Maree! Why that—" Rance snarled. Nathan jerked around and gaped at him, and he checked himself with an obvious effort. "We're long overdue for a long talk, it seems, Hilda Garrett! I'll get our stuff out of the car," he added in that same controlled voice that was even more frightening to Hilda. He started toward his car. "You come and help me, Nathan," he snapped over his rigid shoulders.

"Aunt Jean, what on earth's the matter with you all?" Hilda gasped as they disappeared.

Jean took her arm, and headed for the house. "Things have been in a muddle, that's for sure, but it's obvious to me there's absolutely nothing the matter," she said with an air of complete satisfaction that only further bewildered Hilda. Then Jean squeezed her arm gently and said tenderly, if a little shakily, "Or there won't be once you and Rance can get a chance to sort things out."

The normally efficient Hilda was all fingers and thumbs as she allocated bedrooms, organized linen, and left them to refresh themselves while she escaped to the kitchen. She grabbed some meat from the freezer to thaw in the microwave.

Then she suddenly sat down on a kitchen chair with trembling legs. It was beginning to all seem like a dream. Jean was her aunt. Rance had kissed her as though he had been as starved for her as she had been for him all these long weeks and months.

A low roll of thunder reverberated in the distance. Hilda wiped a hand across her forehead. It was still very hot, even though it was quite dark now. Suddenly she felt stifled and made for the door.

Rain had been forecast several times the past couple weeks. The farmers in the area had been anxiously watching as heavy clouds had scurried across the sky many times without pausing to water their crops. Hilda had heard of heavy falls in some places, and had prayed that they would not miss out again. A good rain now would fill the heads of the wheat nicely.

Normally this part of the Downs enjoyed a dryer heat than those sweltering on the coast. Tonight, even when Hilda had slipped out of the house by the front door, the air was heavy and very humid.

Funny how hardly anyone ever came to the front door, she mused absently, trying to keep her thoughts off her unexpected guests. Sometimes strangers from the city, like machinery or insurance salesmen, knocked on the front door, but everyone else automatically drove up to the side gate and found their way to the back door. It was always the welcoming farm kitchen they made for.

Hilda had snatched up a torch on the way out, and shone it carefully in front of her as she walked. This burst of hot weather brought the snakes out from their winter inactivity, and she had learned to be very careful.

As she moved slowly away from the house and its surrounding trees, the great pillars of clouds in the east drew her attention. As she watched, distant jagged shafts of light illuminated them. At first they were too far away to hear anything, and then an occasional distant growl of thunder began to rumble.

The air was very still. Not a breath stirred the damp curls on her forehead. Between watching where she placed her feet and being entranced by the distant aerial display, she did not realize she had wandered so far from the house, until she paused and looked back the way she had come. One single beam of light escaped through the branches of the few fruit trees near the house.

Hilda felt tears pricking her eyes. This was her home, not that narrow, unpleasant Paddington street, but these wide open spaces. She had lived here with a pair of the finest people who could have become her parents. But what did the future hold for her now?

"Oh, Lord, I don't know how to thank You for everything You've done in my life," she prayed out loud. She gave a laugh of sudden joy and delight. It was drowned out by a loud crash of thunder that made her jump. "Oh, what can I do for You in return?" she cried loudly, "I need to show You how very much I love You and praise You!"

Another peel of thunder brought her eyes back to the storm. It was much closer now. A bolt of lightning lit up the sky. Thunder rumbled from horizon to horizon. Hilda had always loved storms. While her mother had cowered away inside, she would stand and watch in awe as the thunderbolts hurtled earthward across the flat plains.

Out here there was nothing between her and the angry sky. It was awesome, but it was getting too close. She turned to make her way back to the house. The next flash of light showed a dark shape moving toward her along the track.

"Hildie?"

Rance's voice. Calling out after the roll of thunder had died away.

"Coming, Rance" she called back.

Anytime, Rance. Just call and I'll come.

She stumbled quickly along the track toward him. When she reached him, his hands went out and engulfed hers. They stared at each other for a moment, and then she was being held close to him, and suddenly she knew that this was her home from now on. In the shelter of this wonderful man's arms. Oh, if only he felt the same way!

They stood that way for a long time. Suddenly there was a particularly brilliant flash of light and then another. They both turned instinctively toward the east as thunder rumbled around them.

"Aren't you afraid of storms?" Rance asked softly in the brief silence that followed.

"I love them!"

She found herself almost shouting as noise rose around them

again. Exhilaration was rising in her. She felt herself beginning to tremble as his hand moved to cup her shoulders. He must have felt a tremor, and his fingers tightened their grip as a brilliant flash zig-zagged across the sky and plunged into the earth. They tensed. Waited for the roar and crackle that followed.

"I've never seen anything like this," Rance said with awe.

"We get some truly magnificent storms sweeping across the flat plains." Hilda paused for another roll of thunder. "It's still quite a way off. It could be what we call a dry storm—little or no rain. We get a few of them usually much later every summer. Sometimes they start fires."

Hilda never knew how long they silently stood, as one, absorbed by the awesome display of power. The noise of the thunder kept getting closer. The time between the flashes and the thunder lessened. At last the air around them was filled with a never ending crackle and roar and crash.

"It's absolutely fantastic!" Hilda found herself trying to shout above the noise. A faint breeze sprang up, stirring the air around them. She was vaguely aware that Rance's arms were holding her tightly pressed against the front of him.

"Just a glimpse of God's almighty power!" his voice roared back exultantly.

They stood watching for several more spellbinding minutes. A sheet of lightning ripped into the ground a little too close, even for Hilda. She shrank closer to the security and haven of the strong body behind her as the almost simultaneous thunder roared.

Rance's arms tightened. Hilda felt him tremble. She tensed. They turned and faced each other. One strong finger barely touched her cheek. It moved to her lips, and lingered there. Hilda knew she would not be able to bear it if he didn't hurry up and kiss her again. She moved closer. He stiffened, and then she felt the air expelled slowly from his lungs as he bent his head. This kiss was more tender, more full of love than Hilda had ever dreamed a kiss could be.

"Oh, Hildie, there's never been another woman like you." Rance's voice sounded hoarse, filled with awe and wonder. "I've missed you unbelievably these long weeks."

She only just heard him above the cacophony of noise. A couple of large drops of rain fell on them. He let her go and grabbed her hand.

"We'd better get under shelter as quickly as we can. This is no dry storm," he yelled above the now almost continuous clamor.

Suddenly they were laughing joyously, deliriously at each other. They ran as fast as they could over the rough track.

They were almost at the house when Rance yelled in her ear, "Anywhere we can talk besides the house?"

She nodded silently and led him toward the shed a short distance past the house where the cars were garaged. Just as they arrived, one more ferocious roar of thunder announced the arrival of pelting rain. The impact of the rain was deafening on the corrugated roof, and Hilda gestured silently toward her car. Rance shook his head and pulled her back into his arms against his full length and turned her so they could watch the rain.

She thought she heard him say faintly above the dreadful din, "I love it like this."

As she allowed him to mold his body to hers, her tumult of emotions slowly began to subside, even as the storm outside began to ease. Confusion swamped her, but there was one thing she was sure of now.

The storm died away, and still they held each other silently, until Hilda stirred and put her knowledge into words. "You aren't going to marry Maree." It wasn't a question, but a statement full of delighted wonder.

Rance changed his grip on her and swung her around to face him. He took a deep breath and said wonderingly, "Jean was right. You did think Maree and I had patched things up."

She nodded silently. Suddenly she pulled away from him and went over to a light switch. They both blinked in the sudden bright light, and then looked at each other.

"Did Maree say we had?" Anger flickered in Rance's dark eyes.

Hilda hesitated, thinking back. Suddenly she gave a rueful smile, "Probably she didn't really imply as much as I did to Gail about Jim." She pulled a face. "She was so absolutely confident, I didn't even question it. She said she'd arrived, and I'd lost. Your excitement the next morning seemed a confirmation."

"My excitement. . .?" Rance began with a puzzled frown as he thought back. Then his expression cleared. "Oh, I thought she'd told you that her father told her the church in Toowoomba was sending me a letter of apology and wanted me to resume the ministry there. I was really pleased because a lot of the folk had been very upset, and I knew this would begin the healing process for the church."

Then he scowled as he remembered what else Hilda had said. "As for that win and lose rubbish. . .she didn't have any say in the matter!" Rance said irritably. "I suppose you think she broke off our engagement because of Nathan like everybody else does."

Hilda's obvious astonishment gave him his answer.

"I was a fool," Rance said bluntly. "Last year, I felt pretty lonely. All my old student mates were happily married. I envied David his Kim and Jodie so much. Suddenly Maree was there." He gave an angry shrug. "She was beautiful. Never missed services or the mid-week Bible study I took. We talked at length about spiritual things. She seemed perfect for a minister's wife. Once again I ran ahead of the Lord, and let my heart rule my head."

"But even Dad thought she had broken it off because of Nathan," Hilda said in a dazed voice. Suddenly she wished Rance wasn't so far away. Even the short distance between them was unbearable.

"It all happened almost at the same time unfortunately," Rance said savagely. "It was very convenient for her to act the heartbroken, bewildered little woman. I found out that Maree had discovered I had a very rich stepfather who had no children of his own. She'd worked out in her devious little mind that she could bear to be a minister's wife for a few years, and then she was sure when I inherited all his lovely money and properties, I'd be forced to leave the ministry to carry it all on for him."

Hilda felt a sudden shaft of unexpected sympathy for Maree. "That was a very logical conclusion for someone like Maree who only thought of your work in human terms," she said gently. "Only someone who really walks in the Spirit could understand your love for Jesus and realize your calling by Him to the ministry leaves you no choice."

Rance's eyes came alive again with love. "But you understand, Hildie darling, don't you? You'd always understand the words of the apostle Paul you quoted to me once before." He took a couple paces forward, and placed both of his large hands tenderly on each side of her flushed face. "Woe to me if I don't preach the Gospel," he whispered softly. A light kiss landed on her nose. "You understand, don't you?" he persisted. "I realized at that service center at the freeway that we shared a spiritual oneness I never had with Maree."

She stood helplessly in his hands and simply stared at him.

"You would be there to help the Lord keep that minister on the right track, wouldn't you? You'd be his true right hand, his best friend, the mother of his children, his life's companion, and his wonderful lover," he whispered as his lips touched hers. "Oh, I do love you so much, sweetheart."

And then lips were clinging again, and there was only the taste of him, the feel of him, his strength, their mutual love, and increasing passion.

Hilda didn't know how long they kissed and murmured of their love, saying all the beautiful, foolish things lovers have said since time began, the hows, the whys, when each had recognized that love for the first time.

"It was that madam Jodie that clinched it for me," Rance chuckled softly. "A few seconds after she saw you, she asked me if you were the pretty lady who would be my Mummy!"

Right back then! When she was so worried about him.

He suddenly sighed, and loosened his tight hold on her. "I suppose we'd better get back to the house. It was such a relief when Jean told me she saw you heading off down the track. I was beginning to wonder if I'd ever get you away from Nathan."

He kissed her lightly on the lips, and then he groaned, and gathered her close again. Hilda willingly pressed against his body, giving him all he asked of her sweetness and love.

At last he gave a stifled groan and lifted his head. "I suppose there'll be time later to make plans, but. . ." He hesitated and then said slowly, "You won't mind living in Brisbane for at least a few years will you, sweetheart?"

Hilda was still trying to come down from the heights, and said in a dazed voice, "Brisbane. Why would I be thinking of living in Brisbane?"

Sudden alarm flashed across Rance's face. "You. . .you'd rather I took the offer of the Toowoomba church?" He continued slowly, as he stared at her. "I suppose you don't want to live in a city, do you?"

Hilda gave her head a little shake, as much to clear it as to deny what Rance had just said. "I lived in Brisbane for a couple years when I was at university. It wasn't too bad. But why. . .?" Hilda's eyes opened wide as she suddenly realized what he was talking about. A thrill of delight and love swept through her.

For a moment she was speechless, and then her eyes began to dance mischievously. "Are you asking me to live with you, Reverend Rance Telford!" Her voice held mock alarm and horror.

He frowned. "Of course we'll—" He suddenly recognized the twinkle in her eyes, and her rapidly failing effort to keep from bursting into laughter. And then it dawned on him!

A few moments later, peel after peel of a radiant woman's laughter rang out from that old battered tin shed lit by a naked light bulb.

"For heaven's sake, woman!" grumbled Rance. "I thought this was the most serious question a bloke ever asked a woman. Now, will you be quiet and listen. It's horribly uncomfortable down—"

"Dad!" exclaimed an indignant voice. "Haven't you asked her yet?" Nathan stepped into the light. "What are you doing down there in the dirt?"

Rance glanced with horror over his shoulder and then jumped very self-consciously and quickly from his knees to his feet in one lithe movement. Hilda had just managed to stifle her giggles, but this set her off again. A moment later Rance's hearty roar joined her. They moved together and leaned helplessly against each other.

Nathan looked at them in disgust. He scuffed his heavily mud-coated sneaker, and scowled. "Well! Are ya or aren't ya?" he asked Hilda belligerently.

Rance managed to control his mirth enough to say, "There are better ways to propose, Nathan Telford!"

"And when you find one, you'd better show your father!" laughed Hilda.

Then her laughter faded away, and her face was radiant with love and tenderness as she glanced from the tall, fair man to his smaller replica. "And, it doesn't really matter a bit, after all." She gave a mock frown at Rance, and added quickly, "As long, of course, as there is no misunderstanding. If the question is, 'Will I marry you, and love you both for ever and ever?' the answer just has to be in the affirmative."

Nathan's frown was back. "Does that a. . .affirm business mean yes?" he asked anxiously.

Hilda let go of Rance, and crouched down to Nathan's level. "It sure does mean yes! You'd better believe it!" she said quite firmly.

The boy's face lit up. "Fantastic!" Then he suddenly turned on his heel and raced away. They heard his voice yelling, "Aunt Jean! She said yes! I've got a new Mum!"

Rance moved forward. He stretched out his hands. She reached up and clasped them, and he hauled her to her feet and into his arms again. She went, laughing and filled with love.

"Oh, well," Rance sighed, "I suppose that's just a taste of what it's going to be like down through the years when we try and sneak a few moments to ourselves away from the children."

"The children," Hilda said dreamily, and sighed with contentment at all that conjured up.

"And at least one dog, I suppose," added Rance glumly.

"A dog!"

Rance ran a gentle finger over her open mouth. "Of course. Little boys as well as little girls need a dog. Especially collie dogs called Polly," he said tenderly.

To his surprise, she shook her head wistfully. "No, not another Polly. There could only be one of her. Perhaps a Trixie, instead?"

He kissed her very tenderly. "Anything you say, my darling Hildie. Oh! I forgot!" Rance straightened. He looked down at her lovingly. "By the way, I meant to warn you. Don't let on to your Aunt Jean how much you've always hated 'Hilda' for a name."

The complete change of subject from dreams to such a mundane thing bewildered her. "Why ever not?" she asked sharply.

"I'm sorry, sweetheart," he answered her solemnly. "She told me very proudly once that Hilda has been at least one of the names for the first girl in your family for generations. Hilda was a chief goddess in German mythology. The name means 'battle' in Old German. It's Aunt Jean's second name, too!"

"Truly!" Delight flashed into Hilda's face, and then she scowled fiercely. "I'm sorry, too! Any poor girl we have will never be saddled with the wretched name, especially if it was the name of a goddess! And I've had enough battles to last several lifetimes. It's about time traditions like that from yesterday were well and truly forgotten!"

Much to Jean's disgust and Rance's bemusement, one day in the future, Hilda had her way.

She smiled radiantly down at the squawking little bundle in her arms, and said lovingly, "Hello, Margaret Jean Telford."

A much taller Nathan beamed at them both. "Hiya, Meg!" He held up a firmly held, squirming bundle of brown and white puppy, and added, "Meg, this is our dog, Trixie."

Meg? Hilda looked at him reproachfully, and then up at the proud, beaming Rance. He began to chuckle softly, and spread his hands out helplessly.

Hilda looked lovingly. . .mistily at him. Then her gaze was drawn down at the yawning infant. Her search for yesterday had not been wasted for a moment. God had shown her His overwhelming love and care in the past, and her heart knew beyond a shadow of doubt, there was even more of that never-failing love to be revealed in the days still to come.

SEARCH FOR TODAY

To my brother, Stan Pedler, who has come out of personal trauma and grief to be an effective witness for Christ through the "New Light Ministries" in the Torres Strait islands.

Chapter 1

Because God is faithful. . .
My tomorrows are safe in His hands.
Because I love Him. . .
My yesterdays He'll work out for good.
But today. . .
Ah, today. . .
I must walk with Him hand in hand!

Her silky hair was a mass of golden curls beneath a circlet of red baby roses and frivolous tulle. His heart ached as he watched her slow procession down the aisle toward him. She was more beautiful than he had ever seen her. More beautiful even than on that other wonderful day that now seemed so long ago, the day when she had married him.

Serious, deep blue eyes met his for a long moment. Something flickered in their depths. Something he couldn't read.

Then she was past him, continuing her slow progress to the beat of the wedding march, eventually obscured by the standing congregation as she moved to her place next to Will. Art closed his eyes, swallowing the painful lump in his throat. He clenched his fist on the armrest of his wheelchair and felt like pounding something. . .anything. . . .

Beth was his wife. *His wife!* And despite his useless legs he still loved her. Loved her desperately. What had happened to them? When had it all gone so wrong? Why didn't she—

"Isn't Mummy beautiful!"

He glanced sideways at the small miniature of Beth standing beside him. Jacqueline's wide eyes met his. The admiration and pride in them changed abruptly. The sudden trace of wariness on the dainty little face cut into him.

"Your mother is always beautiful, Jacky."

He forced himself to smile, but his harsh whisper did not change her expression, and she quickly looked away. Robbie peered around her, his eyes wide. Art smiled at him too, and his small son's shy grin pulled at his heart. At least Robbie seemed to have accepted his father's return into their lives much better than Jacky had.

He should never have walked out on them all those months ago. At the time, it had been the only way he had been able to handle the increasing tension, the arguments, the fear. Now he recognized just how much of a coward he had been.

That last bitter row between Beth and himself had really scared him. He had lost control. Had even lashed out at her! Her flushed face and angry accusations had spat fury right back at him.

That's when the realization had hit him, with overwhelming bitterness as never before: he was a wretched sinner. Certainly at least one frustrated, angry schoolteacher had tried to tell him. Certainly his own very religious parents had tried to drum it into him often enough. All of them were right. He was just no good. He should never have married Beth Stevens.

So he had packed up. Gone.

There was a stir behind him, a few murmurs of admiration. Art swung his head toward the church entrance. For a moment he stared. A mist of pride filmed his eyes, and his own pain receded a little. The bride was radiant.

At least this was one thing he had done right, even if the end result for himself had been this wheelchair. If it had not been for him, she would not be here today. Gail Brandon would have been killed in the accident that had wiped out her family. She would never have come to the Darling Downs. But then, if he had not been driving that semi-trailer at that particular place, at that particular moment. . .? As he always did, Art pushed the ghastly memories away.

Gail had paused. Her eyes were fixed steadily toward the front of the church. The light in them made him swallow rapidly. And then the tall figure of his brother-in-law and best friend, Jim Stevens, moved past him to join her. She slipped her hand in his elbow. The organ music swelled to a crescendo and together they started down the aisle.

As they reached Art, Gail gave him a special, warm smile. He grinned up at her, and his smile lingered as they moved slowly past him to at last reach their attendants and the waiting Reverend Rance Telford. For a moment he regretted refusing her request to "give her away" in place of her father.

"There's no way I'd do that from a wheelchair," he'd snarled back at her.

She had scowled right back at him and muttered something about "I don't have anyone else I care enough about."

For a moment he had almost weakened, but he knew just how much he was suffering from the "wheelchair stigma." He wasn't sure whom he disliked the most, people who gave him pitying looks, people who just stared curiously, people who looked briefly and then away, embarrassed, not sure how to talk to a paraplegic in a wheelchair, or people who wanted to know too many details. And there had been some of each when he had arrived at the church. No, he didn't regret his refusal to be part of the wedding party.

Besides, already he was feeling very weary and his back was aching badly. Coming to the wedding had been more of an effort than he had thought it would be. This was his third day of leave from the rehabilitation unit, the second morning without the torturous, daily exercises with the hospital physiotherapists, and his longest time out of the hospital in twelve months.

Beth had been wonderful. His lips curved into a smile. She had certainly helped him as much as she could to recover from the two-hour car trip from Brisbane. It had been his longest since the accident, but he still had not expected the amount of stiffness and pain it had caused.

After the last eighteen months of turmoil and heartbreak, he had been so glad to be back at the Stevens's farm. Feeling part of the family again was wonderful. And yet. . . Art hunched his shoulders.

Even harder than the physical effort of getting into his old, but barely worn suit and tie, getting in and out of the car, the ride to this small church set amidst the grain and cotton farming community of the Darling Downs, had been the memories. Memories that were proving to be strong and heartrending.

With an effort, he forced his mind back to the wedding. Back from memories when he'd been able to walk. When he'd been to his own wedding here, to other special services held in this little building.

Of course, he thought crossly, *this small country church would only have steps and no ramp.*

It had been humiliating as well as scary being fussed around as his chair had been lifted and maneuvered up the steps. Then pews and chairs had been moved around so his chair would fit at the end of a row without being obstructive. But he still felt horribly conspicuous, out of place. . .

As the wedding ceremony ebbed and flowed around him, Art's weariness increased. He could not sing Gail and Jim's choice of hymn, though not because he did not know it. Once he'd known a lot of hymns much too well, for he had felt his father's belt later if he had not sung them. Those days were long gone, but no way he could sing "To God be the glory, great things He has done," when there was precious little God had ever done for him.

But, he had to admit, he saw something almost awesome about the radiance of the bride and groom as they exchanged vows and rings, as they listened to the Bible reading about love being the most important thing. He watched them bow their heads reverently in prayer.

And Art wondered, not for the first time, how Gail could have recovered as well as she had from the deaths of her fiancé and whole family when their car had plunged into his truck. She was by no means a shallow person. In fact, the more he got to know her, the more he admired her. Apparently she had suffered nightmares for months after the accident, and she had had periods of depression.

Never as bad as his though. That first time she had visited him in the hospital. . . He shuddered at the horrible memory of what he had been contemplating, planning. . .what she had by her very visit prevented. . . .

A ripple of laughter swept through the congregation. Art realized that Jim had been given permission to kiss his bride and was doing so very enthusiastically.

"Yuk!"

There was another, louder chorus of laughter. Mrs. Stevens hushed Robbie, and he subsided back on his seat. He looked across and caught his father's eye apprehensively. Art grinned widely at him and winked. A relieved, smile answered him.

Art looked back at the now flushed, even more radiant bridal couple, and then, inevitably, his eyes swung toward the matron of honor. She was looking at him, a smile tilting her beautiful lips. He smiled back, but as she turned her attention away to the continuing service, sharp pain slashed through him.

How long since he and Beth had kissed like that?

He continued to stare at the beautiful woman in the shimmering aqua gown standing beside Gail. He saw her smiling gently across at Will, her tall teenage brother. He watched as she followed Gail and Jim into a back room to sign the marriage's legal papers, and even her straight shoulders and the gleaming back of her head sent a stab of pain through his heart. Jacky was so right. Beth was beautiful.

But her pretty face had not been what had first attracted him to her. There had been plenty of pretty faces only too keen to be seen with the high school football star. Beth had been different. She had a sweetness and innocence about her that had drawn him to her like a magnet. It still did.

"How are you doing, Arthur? Arthur!"

The low insistent voice penetrated through the host of memories of two teenagers not prepared to wait, wanting to take on the world so they could be together forever. He blinked and stared blindly for a moment at the concerned face of Jean Drew, his mother-in-law's friend and the nursing sister who worked in the Sydney hospital where he had been a patient for far too many months before his transfer to Brisbane. She was studying him professionally, her expression guarded.

At last his mouth twisted in an attempt at a smile. "Fine. Just fine," he muttered hoarsely.

Even as he spoke, he knew it was a stupid lie. He had been sitting too long. His back was more than just aching. The pins and needles had been steadily getting worse, and now he was conscious of the fact that his head was starting to throb abominably. At least it should all be over soon. Surely they would not take too long to sign the register and all the other certificates.

"You don't look it," Jean murmured.

He glared at her for a moment, then his shoulders slumped. "Well, what do you think?"

"I think you should let me organize a lift home for you as soon as possible."

The thought of being able to get away from all the curious eyes, of being able to lie down and ease the pressure on his back, sounded like sheer bliss. The doctor had warned him the trip and wedding could be a bit too adventurous at this stage.

He glanced cautiously toward Jacky and felt relieved that she was turned away, whispering to her brother.

"Beth will worry."

Jean shook her head at him. "Not as much as she will if she has to watch your white face during the reception! Got a headache?"

He snorted loudly. Some people across the aisle turned and stared at him. A soloist had not long finished singing about this being "the day the Lord has made." Now soft music was playing against the background of the murmur of voices which had risen while they waited for the bridal party.

Art glared back at some neighbors and friends of the Stevenses and they looked quickly away. For a brief moment he felt a heel. Then he mentally shrugged. Everyone was feeling so sorry for the poor paralyzed bloke in the wheelchair that he did not think he could take much more. "After they leave the church," he muttered at last.

Relief lightened Jean's expression. She nodded abruptly.

Leaving now would mean bed instead of the celebrations at the wedding reception. And he'd had enough of being on a bed the last twelve months. Depression rolled over him in waves. He had always enjoyed parties, and he had been so looking forward to this special day for his old friend Jim and the girl he loved.

When they eventually proceeded down the aisle, Jim and Gail paused beside him. Somehow, he summoned up a smile for them. Jim's handshake was firm and Gail's kiss a little teary. They moved on.

Then Beth was there. Once again Art could not decipher something in his wife's expression. She came closer. Stopped. His heart clenched.

She bent toward him and her delicate perfume invaded his senses. Her lips touched his. For a moment those deep blue eyes stared intently at him, and then she was gone on Will's arm. Art felt as though a flame had briefly touched his mouth.

He sat very still. He only stirred when Marian Stevens leaned over and touched him, gesturing to let her past with her grandchildren. He nodded grimly in response to his mother-in-law's sympathetic smile and moved his chair back slightly. Robbie and Jacky pushed past him excitedly. Then the people filed out after the bridal party, and he carefully avoided the curious eyes once again, only looking around him blindly when the building was almost empty.

His head was feeling more and more as though it would burst, and when Jean at last reappeared and grasped his chair, he could only feel utter relief.

As Jean turned him toward a side door, she said briskly, "I've lined up a couple of guys to help us. That young schoolteacher is getting his car."

"Did you tell Beth. . .?" Then he stopped. There was a rustle of silk and she was there.

"Oh, Art! Are you all right? I thought you looked tired."

"A bit of a headache. Don't fuss."

As soon as the words had exploded from him he was sorry. Her sharp withdrawal from him was more than physical, and quickly he tried to make amends. He managed a weak smile. "Guess the doc was smarter than me after all. Just as well you and Gail organized that Tony bloke to help out in case this happened. Tell the bride and groom I'm sorry. Don't you worry either. All I need is a bed to crash on for a while."

But she was already worried. He knew how valiantly she tried to disguise it from him, but it was there in her clenched fists, the strained smile, the way her eyes avoided his, the way she helped swing his legs so gently into the car.

And he wondered for the thousandth time how long he could bear to have her so burdened by him.

"Please, Beth, enjoy the evening. I'm going to be fine with Tony. At least I've seen Gail and Jim do the deed."

She didn't kiss him again, and he knew she probably wouldn't enjoy the evening.

Beth had been the best thing that had ever happened to him, but how many of her days and evenings had he wrecked forever? And how could he convince her she was only ruining the rest of her life by being tied to a coward of a man with useless legs?

Chapter 2

Beth shivered in the cool night air and pulled her shawl tighter around her shoulders. She glanced over her shoulder into the backseat of the car. Her gaze lingered on her two children snuggled up each side of Will.

"Still asleep?"

Beth looked across at her mother and nodded. "Out like a light. Will is too." She was silent for a moment, watching the headlights cut through the blackness of the flat countryside. "They should have been in bed hours ago," she said at last.

"One late night won't hurt them," Mrs. Stevens said firmly, grasping the steering wheel tightly. After a moment she added softly, "I'm glad they were already asleep when Bob. . ." Her voice faltered.

Beth felt the tears whelm up again. "I still can't believe it," she said in a choked voice. "One moment Uncle Bob was. . .was wishing Jim and Gail all the best, and. . .and by the time their car had driven off he was gone! Poor Hilda."

Mrs. Stevens was silent. Then she said very softly, "I'm glad Jean was there. It would have been so much harder for Hilda if he'd had the heart attack at home when she was by herself. At least she will know that everything was done for her father that could be."

"I don't think she knows anything at the moment," Beth muttered.

They had all been stunned by the collapse of Bob Garrett. Jim and Gail's car with its clanging tin cans and streamers had barely disappeared before the word had swept through the wedding guests that Bob Garrett had suffered a heart attack, and Jean Drew and the minister, Rance Telford, were giving him CPR. With the help of other guests, they had kept it up until the ambulance had arrived. But it had all been to no avail.

After the ambulance had departed with her father's lifeless body, Hilda Garrett had been in deep shock. She moved like a sleep walker as Jean Drew had at last helped her out to the car to take her home.

"Jean's going to stay with her for a few days," Mrs. Stevens said in a choked voice.

"Oh, Mum," Beth burst out, "life's not fair! As though there hasn't been enough grief and pain. First Hilda's mum died, then my dad, then Art's nearly killed. I don't know how Gail copes so well with her family wiped out like that. There's been all those months with me in Sydney with Art. I thought life might be easier for us all with Art well enough to be moved to Brisbane for further rehabilitation. But now. . . now. . ." Her voice choked as the tears slid down her face.

"Now we keep on trusting the Lord to watch over us and work things out for good as He always has," Mrs. Stevens said in a husky voice.

"Do we?" Beth's voice hardened. "I'm not so sure anymore about. . .about anything."

As soon as the words had burst out of her she regretted them; she even knew they weren't really true. Not anymore. She knew how much her own loss of faith over the last few years had hurt and upset her mother. But since Art had disappeared and then ended up in the hospital, she had been coming to grips more and more with spiritual matters. Her faith was gradually being renewed—but still, at times it was all so hard.

"If God was not looking after us, strengthening us, I don't think I would have coped at all since your father was diagnosed with cancer, Beth. Especially after he died." Mrs. Stevens voice was sad, but filled with conviction. "As for Gail, since she accepted Christ into her life and committed herself to Him, her whole outlook on life has been transformed. You saw for yourself today just how at peace she is, and how happy."

A pang shot through Beth. If only Art. . .

She had not spent a lot of time with Gail, but from what everyone had told her, Gail was certainly different now. Finding out that God loved her, and responding to His love personally, had transformed the traumatized woman who had gone to help look after Jacky and Robbie last year while Beth had been at the Sydney hospital with Art.

Beth closed her eyes. Once she had thought her own faith in a loving, caring heavenly Father was unshakable. She had been such a keen Christian, but when she had first met Arthur Canley-Smith she been knocked clean off her conservative, narrow pins by his blond good looks, twinkling hazel eyes, and muscular, rugby-type physique.

She had been so sure God would make Art become a Christian. She had prayed so hard, so many times. She had talked to him often about becoming a Christian. After all, she had loved the tall, rugged young teenager so much, anything else had been unthinkable. But God had never seemed to hear her prayer. Now it all seemed such a long time ago.

She remembered something else her mother had once said to her, and shame filled her again. "You were right, Mum," she said abruptly.

Her mother glanced at her but didn't speak. That was something Beth had always loved about her. She always waited, never rushed in with words, waited until you needed her to speak. If only Beth had tried harder herself to follow that example with Art over the years!

"You told me once, years ago, that we sometimes make it very hard for God to answer our prayers when we disobey His warnings and principles." Beth continued sadly, "Like I did when I married an unbeliever."

Her mother didn't speak for a look moment. Then she said softly, "You've changed a lot since Art left you, Beth, and we're still praying for you both."

"Thanks, Mum. We certainly need every prayer available!"

Neither woman spoke again as they completed the drive home. Will woke up as the car moved slowly over the rough track from the main road into the farmhouse.

Beth turned and smiled at him as he yawned loudly. "Almost home, little brother."

"Hey, Sis! Not so much of the *little*," he protested in his uneven tones. "After all, I was big enough to be Jim's best man today. And your escort."

"Oh, so you were," Beth mocked gently. "But you didn't hang around the matron of honor very much, I noticed."

"You both looked after Jim and Gail very well."

There was pride in their mother's voice, and the two smiled at each other behind her back.

Will yawned again as the car crawled to a stop. "Looks like Art's not asleep yet."

Beth felt the tension start to build up in her as she noticed the bedroom light. "He has trouble sleeping when he gets overtired," she said quietly. *And when his muscles spasm, and when his back aches*, she could have added but didn't.

Several minutes later, compassion swamped her as she studied Art's ravaged face as he looked up at her. His hazel eyes were filled with pain and set deep in his pale face.

"Where's Tony?" she asked, hearing the sharp tone in her voice and regretting it immediately as Art's expression tightened.

"I sent him home," he said abruptly. "I appreciated the fact that he had been recruited to bring me home from the church, help me into bed, and baby-sit me. But—he might be the kid's schoolteacher, but he doesn't have much idea of how to make conversation with a stranger, especially someone in a wheelchair. Besides, I thought you'd be home ages ago."

Beth took a deep breath. "So did I. Unfortunately. . .unfortunately. . ." She couldn't continue. Her voice wobbled, and helpless tears started to run down her cheeks.

"Beth?" Art raised himself painfully on one elbow. "What's wrong? What's happened?"

"Uncle. . .Uncle Bob Garrett had a heart attack."

Art reached up to her. She caught his hand and he pulled her down onto the side of the bed. "Is he okay?"

She shook her head. He gave a sharp exclamation. Briefly she told him what had happened. She felt his arms wrap around her, hug her closer. Then somehow she couldn't stop crying. And she knew her tears were not only for the dear old next door neighbor who had been an honorary uncle all her life.

She had not cried wrapped in the security of this man's loving arms for a long, long time. When her sobs at last died away, she realized she was lying on the bed with Art holding her tightly, her head cradled against his shoulder.

She didn't move for some time. Even if she was only lying on top of his blankets, it was sheer bliss being this close to him after such a long time. Then she felt one of Art's legs spasm and jerk. She started to move, but his arms tightened for a moment before he slowly released her.

"I'm sorry, Beth," he whispered.

As she sat up, she looked at him silently, scrubbing at her wet cheeks. What did he mean? Sorry for what?

He answered the query in her face with a grimace. "I'm sorry I can't get you a handkerchief this time."

She stared at him. And then she remembered. The night her father had died, Art had held her. They had not even been officially engaged then. The second time she had cried buckets was the day their daughter was born, and it had suddenly hit her that her father would never see his first grandchild.

Each time, Art had silently let her weep, offering her the shelter of his arms and his love. And then very, very gently and quietly he would reach for a clean handkerchief and mop up her tears.

"We were so close then, Art," she whispered wistfully as they stared at each other. "What happened to us?"

His face went still. Then he turned his face away and she could only see the tension in his jaw. "Life happened to us. Dirty, rotten, stinking life."

She caught her breath on a stab of pain.

Art closed his eyes. "We should never have married, Beth," he added wearily. "We were too young. Our whole outlook on life was. . . is. . .just too, too different. Our backgrounds were too different. You came from a loving family, and mine. . .well, you caught only a brief glimpse once of what mine was like. I was even glad then that my parents had kicked me out before we met."

Beth froze. What was he saying? That there was no hope for their marriage? Eighteen months ago when he had walked out after that last, dreadful row, she had refused to believe it. Certainly after more than six months of silence from him she had almost lost heart and given up. Then she had found out about the accident. She thought the last few months had drawn them close enough to have a good chance to sort things out. . .to start again. But now?

"We have to talk about that last night, Beth."

Fear swamped her. She stood up. "No," she said fiercely, "not now. Not tonight. We're both exhausted." The tears were ready to spill over again, but she hung onto her self-control grimly. "When you aren't so tired, and—"

Art suddenly exploded. "When I'm not tired! When I'm not in the hospital! When the children aren't around. When I'm not what? There's never been a right time since you walked into my hospital room. When, Beth? Nothing's been resolved between us, and I can't stand it anymore!"

Did that mean. . .? Beth stared at him in horror.

"When I'm not exhausted. When things are more settled," she flared back, "when you're finally discharged from the hospital. When . . .when you. . ." She faltered and stopped.

Art looked at her steadily. "When I walk again? That's not going to happen, Beth, and it's about time you accepted that fact of life."

"But the doctors said—"

He snorted angrily. "They've said a lot of things that just have not happened. And they did say in the very beginning there was only the slightest chance I might one day be able to move on my feet with walking aids. But it's twelve months now. And they are warning me that's more and more unlikely."

"No," Beth denied sharply, "we've got to believe. There's always hope, and. . .and I've been praying awful hard. And so have a lot of other people."

"Don't start all that religious garbage again," Art started to say furiously, then broke off as the door opened.

His mother-in-law strode into the room. She put her hands on her hips and glared at them both. "Don't you think we've had enough drama for one day? We can hear you all over the house."

They both stared at her blankly.

"Is there anything we can get for you, Art?" Mrs. Stevens asked when neither spoke.

After a moment Art shook his head and looked away.

"Then let Beth get to bed." She added abruptly, "If she goes now, she might be able to get up in time to go to church tomorrow. After all, it will be Easter Sunday." She turned and strode out of the room.

Husband and wife stared at each other in silence. Then Art slowly and carefully pushed himself over onto his side facing away from Beth. Without a word, she pulled back the bedclothes and positioned his legs for him.

"Thank you," he said stiffly.

For a moment, she hesitated, and then touched his shoulder fleetingly. "I. . .I wasn't planning on going to church in the morning without you, Art."

He didn't answer, and after a moment, she sighed and left the room.

———

The barking of a dog woke Beth the next morning. She had not slept very well, and she reluctantly opened her eyes to look toward the window where the early morning light cast patterns through the lace curtains. As she turned and surveyed her old room, running footsteps sped past in the hallway outside. Robbie was racing outside to play with Bonnie, the young collie dog Hilda Garrett had given the children.

She tensed, waiting for the familiar bang of the old screen door. When it did not come, she relaxed, remembering that was one of the changes Gail had made here during the last few weeks. A new screen door with a proper spring closing device had replaced the old one that had banged almost as long as Beth could remember.

She looked around her old room. Nothing had been changed in here. It had always been her room. When she had boarded in Dalby so she could go to high school, it had still been her room. Even since her marriage at the end of her final year of school, it had always been here when she had gone home for a visit.

Now things would be different. This house was Gail's home now.

Inevitably she would want to change things around. Already, new bedroom furniture had been put in the master bedroom for the newlyweds, although at Gail's insistence, Will and Mrs. Stevens still had their usual rooms. The plan was to fix up the old play area on the enclosed verandah for Beth and her family when they visited. And that had been where Art had insisted on sleeping. By himself.

"If I need anything during the night, I'll yell out for Jim or Jean," he had insisted belligerently when they had arrived Thursday, just in time for Beth to rush off to the wedding rehearsal. "It'll give Beth a break," he'd added swiftly.

But she knew that was just an excuse. Beth had been careful not to show how hurt she had felt at his rejection of her help once again. He had been allowed home from the rehabilitation hospital in Brisbane for a few weekend leaves, and she had coped reasonably well from the Saturday morning to the Sunday afternoon. But this Easter weekend would be his longest spell out of the hospital since the accident.

Beth raised her head quickly. Had that been something falling?

There was another distant crash, and she was out of bed like a flash and tearing down the hallway. She heard Art's voice, swearing furiously.

When she raced into the room he was sprawled on the floor beside the bed, trying to raise himself up on his elbows. The bedside table was on its side, the paraphernalia on top of it scattered across the floor.

She gave a frightened gasp and rushed forward to crouch beside him. "Art, whatever were you trying to do?"

He glared at her, threw off her hand on his arm, and swore again. She winced but glared right back.

"What does it look like?" he snarled at her.

After months of rebuffs, his sarcasm was suddenly the last straw. Before she could prevent herself, she snarled right back at him, "It looks like you're being a fool trying to get out of bed by yourself!"

A spark of something like surprise lit his eyes for a moment. A faint gleam of satisfaction filled Beth. Perhaps she had been trying too hard to be nice and obliging these last few months.

Art looked away quickly. With a supreme effort he curled over and lifting one leg at a time positioned them. Then he started trying to push himself into a sitting position. It took considerable restraint for Beth to stand back and watch without lifting a hand to help.

With his eyes averted, he growled harshly at last, "I'm not that big a fool. I was only sitting on the side of the bed. Give me a heave."

No please, of course, Beth thought crossly, but she managed not to say it out loud.

Art succeeded in pushing himself to a sitting position with her help and then glared at her again. There was a movement behind Beth, and an expression of relief crossed his face as he stared past her.

"What's going on?" Will's sleepy voice asked.

"I fell off the side of the bed," Art said crossly in a low voice. He gestured with his head toward the wheelchair at the foot of the low bed. "Bring that over behind me."

Beth did so without speaking. Will looked from one to the other and then said quietly, "If we hold you under each arm and haul you up, we should be able to slip it under you."

"Pull that bedside cabinet over in front of me first," Art said curtly. "I can lean on it and take some of my own weight."

He gave them a few more terse instructions, and before long he was in the wheelchair. Will helped Beth pick up the scattered things from the cabinet and then disappeared with a mumbled excuse.

"I knocked the book off the bed when I turned over. When I sat up and tried to reach down for it I lost my balance," Art muttered at last when Beth did not move.

"Did you hurt yourself anywhere?" Beth asked abruptly.

"I don't think so, but perhaps you'd better check my leg. I think I might have bashed it against the cabinet when I fell."

With stiff fingers Beth started to roll up his pajama leg, then caught her breath at a smear of blood. She let out a sigh of relief when she found the source, a fairly small skin tear.

"Nothing some iodine and a couple of plaster strips won't fix," she said cheerfully.

"If only the rest of me was that easy to fix."

Beth looked up at him swiftly. He was staring down at his legs, and when he raised his eyes to look at her they were full of despair and pain.

"I've got blood trickling down my leg where I bashed myself, and I can't even feel it," he whispered harshly.

Pity flooded through Beth, but she bent her head and started wiping away the blood. "Well, that's something to be thankful for, isn't it?" He had shown her many times in the last months how he hated being pitied, so she refused to show him any pity now. "I'll just go and raid Mum's first-aid box."

Still not looking at him, she made for the doorway, but his voice stopped her.

"Do you think she'd be very upset if we went straight home after breakfast?"

Beth swung around. Art was staring down at his leg. He looked up at her and the misery in his face made her say without hesitation, "I'm sure she won't. In fact, it doesn't matter if she does."

Not until she was in the kitchen with the box of plaster strips in her hands did she think about how Jacky and Robbie would take their early return home. "Too bad," she muttered to herself grimly, "It's their father's turn to be put first now."

As she strode purposefully back to Art, she suddenly realized how few times until he had been injured had she really put his welfare before that of the children's, or her own, for that matter. Perhaps that was why he had been surprised at her determination to stay in Sydney and let Jim and her mother look after the children for those long months.

As she sat on the bed to attend to the cut, she was very thoughtful. "Art, how about leaving the kids here with Mum? It wouldn't hurt them to miss a few days school."

"No!"

Surprised at his vehement refusal, she looked swiftly at him. She had really thought he would prefer the peace of the empty house for the rest of the Easter weekend, until his leave from the rehabilitation hospital was finished Monday evening.

"Your mother's going to be busy going to Bob Garret's funeral and knowing her, helping Hilda. I'm real sorry you'll have to miss it.

Besides, the kids have been unsettled enough. I've also missed too much of their growing-up days already." His voice was gruff, and he avoided her eyes. "The kids hardly know me as it is. And Robbie told me this morning that Bonnie is really his and Jacky's dog. Apparently it was one of old Polly's puppies."

Beth took a deep breath. "Yes, I know. About the time Gail came here last year, Jim told me Hilda had promised them one without even asking him or Mum first."

"Well, now that you've been able to rent a house with a decent yard and not just a unit, is there any reason we can't take her home with us?"

Beth stood up. For a moment she wasn't sure what to answer. "Art, I'm not sure about having the dog, at least not yet. If I can get some work, I won't be home much to look after it, or keep it out of mischief."

Art looked up at her, his lips in a firm line. "I was going to tell you after this weekend. This leave has been kind of a trial run. The doctors told me if we cope okay, they think I'll be ready for discharge after another few days back in rehab. I just have to learn more about the exercises I have to do at home. I'll be able to help with the dog, especially after the kids go to school."

Utter delight and relief swept through Beth. "Oh, Art, really?"

He nodded, watching her closely.

She swooped on him, planting a kiss straight on his lips. "I'm absolutely thrilled. Why didn't you tell me before?"

He hesitated. She straightened, and her delight faded. Apprehension filled her as she saw the grimness in his face.

"Beth," he burst out with a trace of anger, "we'd been separated for over six months before the accident, and that happened a year ago now. We haven't talked about the way I left you. As I said last night, nothing's been resolved yet, and I—"

Deeply hurt, Beth drew back. "And you don't know if you want to continue with our marriage," she interrupted harshly.

"No, Beth, I wasn't sure if *you* really wanted me back. After all, it was me who walked out on you." She watched him swallow a couple of times before he continued. "I'm going to be less of a husband to you and a father to our children than I ever was. In fact all I'm going to continue to be is nothing but a burden and a bad tempered nuisance."

Beth drew herself up. "Arthur Canley-Smith, we did have some of this discussion before you agreed to be transferred from Sydney to Brisbane. It's a bit late to be changing your mind now," she flashed at him. "I left the kids all those months with Mum and Jim just to stay with you in Sydney. For goodness sake, they even had to employ Gail to help when Mum became so sick! I've now uprooted the children and myself, rented out our own house in Dalby, rented a house in Brisbane indefinitely to be near the best rehab available. The owner's even let us put in those special rails in the bathroom and bedroom, and that ramp for the wheelchair. What else do I have to do to prove to you that I want you home with us?"

"What else?" He was silent, looking down at his clenched hands. Then he looked up at her intently. After a long moment, he gave a strange little laugh. "I'm afraid I'll have to let you work that out for yourself, Beth, my dear."

Chapter 3

A rt sat perfectly still for a few moments after the flushed, bewildered face of Beth had disappeared.

Not once in all the dreary weeks and months since the accident had she told him she still loved him. Even if she had said the words he wasn't sure if he could believe them. Wasn't that the real reason he had driven off after that last dreadful fight? He had killed her love for him. If she'd ever really loved him. Besides, who could really feel a "death till we part" type of love for a man like him?

Even before they had been married, he had known she wanted him to be different from what he was. And for a while he had tried to be the kind of man she wanted him to be. He had tried his hardest to stop swearing when he realized how much she hated it. After all, with his strict upbringing that had been relatively easy. When she had said she hated him drinking, for years he had even stopped looking in at the pub for a beer on the way home from work.

Drinking! His lip curled. He'd never been much of a one for the beer anyway. It had been mainly the chance to spend a bit of time with his mates and relax after work. But she had never really believed that.

Things had deteriorated even faster between them after Robbie's birth. It had been bad enough before, but then he'd overheard that conversation between Beth and Jim. The murmur of voices from her room had reached him in the hospital corridor, and he'd paused, disappointed that once again someone was with Beth and he'd had so little time with her alone.

Then he'd heard Jim's concerned voice saying, "I know you now feel guilty about marrying an unbeliever, Beth, but Art's a great guy. You've got to hang in there. . ."

Guilty! Beth felt guilty for marrying him! He had gritted his teeth then as he did now at the memory. Everything had been religion's fault. It had denied him his parents, then it threatened his marriage.

Desperately hurt and feeling very insecure, he'd left the hospital without seeing Beth. In the weeks and months that followed he had spent more and more time away from the increasing tension at home, playing pool, playing cards, even playing the poker machines. Eventually, though, when he saw how seemingly levelheaded people put whole pay packets through them, he had steered clear of those.

The one thing he had firmly refused to do after Robbie had arrived was go to church with her again. Being in church, hearing familiar songs and sermons, had been torture. Besides Jim's words, it brought back bitter memories of his mother and father, whom he'd only seen that once since he was seventeen.

Sure, he'd been able to handle going to church occasionally when he and Beth first met, even more often after they were married. But boy! After Robbie had been born, Beth had nagged him more and more! The more she pestered him about religion, the more he had resisted. Nothing would have made him give in. She had treated him as though he was the biggest sinner around, but he could have told her about worse sins than a couple of low-alcohol beers a few times a week and some swear words. In fact, several times he would have loved to shock her religious socks off by telling her a few truths about his so-called very religious parents.

Of course, the final straw had been when he had lost his job as a heavy machinery mechanic because of the rural recession. And his employment dilemma still had not changed. In fact, it was worse now. Not only did he have no job and no income, now he couldn't even walk. Sure, moves were being made for him to be trained in a job that could be done from a wheelchair, but what woman would be prepared to put up with living on the poverty line indefinitely?

If only his parents had not kicked him out before he had finished senior high school. If only he'd been able to fulfill his ambition to go on to university instead of having to settle for a mechanics apprenticeship so he could earn some money to live on. If only. . .

He moved abruptly and started wheeling his chair swiftly from the room. Very rarely did he allow the memories of his early years to rise up. They always made him feel as helplessly angry as he had all those years ago.

A small, miniature tornado tore out of a door and almost collided with him.

"Whoa," he exclaimed, "you shouldn't be running inside like that, Jacky!"

"What would you know? What do you know about anything!"

He gaped at her tear-stained, furious little face. Then his own hardened. "I know that I'm your father, young lady, and you don't speak to me like that," he started sternly.

"Why not?" the rebellious, tense little figure spat at him. "You might be my father, but you're never here, are you? You spoil all our fun! And you make Mum cry!" A sob tore out of the slight figure, and then she whirled away.

Art couldn't move. Anguish gripped him. He knew his little daughter had been very reserved around him, but he had never guessed she. . .

"She hates me. . . ," he whispered.

"Oh, no, she doesn't," the voice of his mother-in-law said softly from behind him. "She's hurt and bewildered, but she doesn't hate you. If you saw how she dwelt on every mention of you these past months, you'd know that."

He stared up at her silently, studying her sympathetic expression. "She's so wary around me. And I don't know how to talk to her anymore."

"You're almost a stranger to her, that's why," Mrs. Stevens said matter-of-factly. "Children grow up fast at her age, and you're just going to have to get to know each other again. Now," she added calmly, "I understand that you'll be leaving this morning, Art."

"Well," he said hesitantly, "that was what I thought best, but I take it Jacky hasn't taken too kindly to the idea." He sighed. "Perhaps Beth was right and we should leave them with you for the rest of the holidays."

"No," Mrs. Stevens said, "you're perfectly right in wanting them to go home with you. It's more than right that you want to spend time together trying to build up your family relationships again." Holding his gaze steadily, she said slowly, "When you're trying to build the bridges again, Art, would you make sure not to disregard the spiritual welfare of your family?"

His expression stiffened, and he looked away. "I leave all the religious stuff to Beth," he said gruffly.

"Mmmm, perhaps that's one of the reasons your marriage has been having such a rough time." Puzzled, he looked back at her. She was staring at him thoughtfully. "My daughter had a lot of head knowledge about. . .about 'religious stuff' as you call it, but I'm not too sure, until recently at least, she had much appreciation of what really living the victorious Christian life is about."

Art stared at her with a frown, not sure at all what she was getting at.

She smiled at him and then turned away. "If Will and I are going to get to church this morning, we'd better all get breakfast out of the way so you can leave," she tossed over her shoulder cheerfully.

By the time the car was packed and good-byes said, Art was immensely relieved to be getting away. He knew they were all disappointed except himself, and even he felt sad at leaving the beautiful, black-soil country. But being with the family again in such a way had brought too many reminders of how it had used to be.

Eons ago. At the beginning.

When Jim had befriended him at school. When he'd brought him home for visits and he'd caught a glimpse of what a loving family could be like. When he and Beth had started going together and taken long walks over the paddocks, talking, falling in love. When they had been married. When he'd been able to help Jim repair the farm machinery. When. . .

At last Beth started the car. She glanced across at him with a cheerful, "I hope we've got everything. You okay?"

He nodded, and managed a smile that he tried to make as reassuring as he could. In fact, since the fall off his bed he'd had several bouts of pain when he moved a certain way. He had even asked his mother-in-law to give him some pain tablets when Beth had been busy somewhere else. Not for worlds would he worry her anymore.

Beth smiled gently back at him, and then they all waved their last good-byes.

"Bye Grandma! Bye Bonnie!"

Art winced at the mournful tones in Robbie's voice, feeling guilty again for being responsible for their leaving a day early.

Beth shot him another quick look and then set the car in motion down the track to the main road.

There was an unusual silence in the backseat. Art thought he heard a quickly muffled sniff and saw Beth glance in the rear vision mirror. She frowned.

Before she could speak, he said quickly, "Well, kids, how did you enjoy your first-ever wedding?"

Silence. Another sniff.

Desperately he tried again. "Did you manage to chuck those boxes of confetti onto Uncle Jim and Aunt Gail?"

"We don't call Gail aunt." Jacky's voice was subdued, but still a little belligerent. "She's just Gail. She said so."

At least it was some response, Art thought with a trace of amusement.

"I like Gail, and I threw my stuff all over her." Robbie said. He sounded cross. "I do hate leavin' Bonnie."

"Threw your stuff," Beth corrected.

"Yes, I know! I threwed my stuff!" Robbie's voice sounded crosser.

Art stifled a chuckle. "As soon as those old doctors tell me I can come home for good, we're going to have to build a kennel for a dog, I suppose," he intervened quickly.

There was a brief silence. Then came a jumble of excited questions and comments from the backseat.

Beth glanced across and smiled at him. For a long time, Art found himself immensely cheered by the gentle approval that had been in her face. However, he was exhausted and in considerable pain by the time Beth at last pulled up in the driveway of the modest weather-board house in the northern suburbs of Brisbane.

Since the accident he'd learned to hate car travel, even the short trip from the hospital to the house on weekends. It seemed to set off the muscle spasms in his legs, and sitting up for so long gave him a bad headache. The trip to the farm had been bad enough, but for some reason, the drive home set off more severe spasms than he could ever remember having, and once again his headache was a shocker. He was certainly paying for the trip to see Jim and Gail married!

He had not even thought of the problem that caused Beth to make a distressed sound when at last he rolled onto his side on the bed.

"Oh, Art, you've got a pressure sore," she wailed.

An expletive slipped past his lips before he could prevent it.

"It is no good swearing about it." Beth sounded exhausted and despondent. "I'm sorry. I should have insisted on rubbing your back more."

"It's not your fault," he growled. "I should know better myself. I'm supposed to change my position often to take the weight off. Let's hope it's improved by the time I go back to rehab."

"Well, there's quite a large red area and it does have a blister on it. Does this mean they might decide we can't manage well enough yet?"

She looked so upset, he forced a smile, "I shouldn't think so. It's not as though I'll be doing all this sitting in a car and a church every week."

To Beth's utter dismay, Art was wrong. The doctors did decide it was too soon for discharge.

By nighttime, Art had still been very pale. Beth had been bitterly disappointed when he looked at her with defeat in his eyes and said quietly, "You'd better ring up and tell them I'm coming back tonight."

Tuesday afternoon, Art told her gruffly that there was even more concern about the increased muscular spasms and bouts of pain than about the pressure area. The couple of bruises and the skin tear had also caused a few frowns.

"So it means they think I need more intensive training here in rehab than I'd get as an outpatient," he explained to Beth in short, clipped words. "They also want me to have a complete rest for a week. And they said to tell you it would be best not even to have visitors. Not even you," he added very firmly.

"Oh, Art!" Dismay and disappointment flooded through Beth. "You didn't do any damage when you fell did you?" she asked anxiously.

For one brief moment, he hesitated, but then he shook his head decisively and looked away. "Definitely not."

She looked at him helplessly. The children would be very disappointed, but a sudden, inexplicable feeling of relief made her feel guilty. Looking after him those few days had been a bigger strain than she'd expected.

She rushed to say as cheerfully as she could, "Oh, well, I suppose that will give the tradesmen more time to finish installing those extra rails in the bedroom."

Art's face tightened, and she knew that somehow he sensed her relief at the delay.

"Before I'm discharged, they want you to come in a few times and have more training in how to help me. Starting next week. In the morning." His voice was abrupt, and for a moment Beth thought he hesitated as though about to say something else. Then his lips tightened and he looked away.

Beth swallowed nervously, wondering how he was going to accept her news. "Art, I hope I won't need to be here Monday morning," she began hesitantly.

His eyes flew back to meet hers. He rapped out, "You don't have to try and help me at all, Beth. I don't know how many times I've told you that."

Beth opened her mouth and then closed it again. The bitterness and resentment that blazed at her from his pale face shocked her. Months had gone by since he had let her see so clearly how he resented her having to help him.

"I've told you before. I can stay in this rehabilitation center until my third party insurance claim is finalized. Then. . ."

He hesitated, looked away, and continued swiftly, "Then there should be enough money to employ a live-in nurse, and I could get a

309

separate unit somewhere."

Despair rocketed through her. Her horrified gaze locked with his in shocked silence.

"Is that. . ." She swallowed on the hard stone in her throat, and tried again. "Would you really prefer that, Art?"

A strange look passed over his face, but he looked down too quickly for her to be quite sure what it had been. Tears blurred her own eyes, and it was her turn to look away. The fear that he still did not want to live with her was never very far from her mind.

"You and the kids would be a lot better off without a paralyzed man to care for, Beth." His voice was low and expressionless.

Beth's mouth went dry. The fear swept in on a relentless tide. Once again she opened her mouth, and then closed it without speaking. *Dear God. Think. Think quickly. Find the right words.*

She had so much she wanted to say. . .needed to say. But she had tried to say them before. Months ago. In Sydney he had not wanted her to arrange for his transfer, had not wanted her to be prepared to have him home. He had been silent then, too, just looked at her doubtfully, but he had not continued his protests about her looking after him, and she had tried to convince herself he had agreed. But now she knew she had only been kidding herself. All along, he. . .he. . .

Art broke the heavy silence, his voice very low, "I need to be absolutely sure you want me home for more reasons than pity, Beth."

Somewhere deep inside her, a fervent, silent prayer went up. What could she say to convince him how much she needed him in her life? Surely he could never doubt that she loved him? Without him, the days were duller, the colors dimmer. . . .

She looked up from her clenched fists in her lap to see him watching her intently. That strange, intense look was on his face again. Suddenly it disappeared, leaving his expression carefully blank. She frowned, trying without success to see what he was thinking.

At last she stood up. Her legs were trembling so much, she held onto the bedside table to steady herself. He looked back at her, and she studied his closed face for a moment, failing, as she had many times before, to read what he was really thinking.

She took a deep breath, and was proud of herself when her voice came out steady and much stronger than her inward shaking indicated. "The children and I have had far too many months already to decide whether we'd be better off without you, Arthur Canley-Smith. All the time you. . .you've been gone we have not, I repeat, *not* been better off. I only asked if another time could be arranged because I have a part-time job interview that morning."

"A job interview!"

She lifted her head proudly. "Yes, with a friend of Reverend Telford. He has a small business near us. He needs help in the office Monday to Friday."

Art looked worried and angry. "But Beth, how are you going to do that as well as look after the kids, and. . .me?"

He stopped abruptly, and after a moment she said softly, "I thought you would be able to help me a bit at home. And you do most things for yourself, Art. It's not as though you don't have the use of your hands like. . . ," she took a deep breath and continued, "like quadriplegics."

"That's right, I'm only a paraplegic, only paralyzed from the thoracic area down. I'm lucky, injury to the neck or lower back is much more common, the doctors keep telling me," he said sarcastically, and then added furiously, "*only* a paraplegic. We musn't forget that. And be thankful for small mercies, and all that garbage."

His explosive outburst made her take a step back. She had known a long time ago from others that he felt like this. But never before had he shown her the depths of his bitterness.

She breathed another silent, fervent prayer for the right words. Her instinct told her that the direction of their relationship depended greatly on the next few moments.

Beth stared back at him steadily, hoping he would see no hint of the dreadful ache that had closed on her heart. "Yes, Art, I am thankful you're not a quadriplegic. I'm also very thankful the doctors here believe you only have that Brown-Sequard Syndrome type of incomplete spinal cord lesion."

Art looked away, and she started to feel angry. While she had been afraid to talk about their marriage, he had refused to discuss his condition with her far too many times. She had been deeply hurt right at the beginning that he would never talk to her about the accident. She had even had to find out how he had really sustained his injuries from the police, Jim, and then much later from Gail.

Apparently Art had not actually been injured beyond a few bruises and cuts when the car smashed into his big interstate semi-trailer. A flying fragment of metal had been flung onto his back when the car's petrol tank had exploded. He had been found next to the unconscious Gail. Her severe injuries had not been consistent with his claim that she had been flung clear. Not until Gail had at long last visited him, and they had talked, had he admitted to dragging her from the car when he had seen the smoke and smelt the petrol. The grass fire that had been started by the explosion had set his clothes alight. If the rescuers had not reached him and Gail when they had. . .

Beth shuddered. As it was, she couldn't bare to think of those dreadful burns that had for so long delayed any therapy and treatment for his back injury. Despite numerous skin grafts, there was still an ugly, deep, twisted scar in the middle of his back.

"One day you're going to be independent again, Arthur Canley-Smith." Beth did not know where the words came from, but even as they burst from her, she knew they were true. His eyes went swiftly to her face.

She glared down at him, and added with burning conviction, "The doctors in Sydney said you should be able to gain some use of your legs again. You may not be able to even walk the length of a football field again in one go, let alone run down one. But that's not going to matter a scrap. And I don't want you ever dare to believe differently. And I'm going to be there to see you do it. Every single, solitary step. . .of. . .the. . .way." She enunciated the last four words clearly and very loudly.

A startled look swept over Art's face. Then she saw utter amazement take its place. Beth felt a sense of satisfaction when it was his turn to open his mouth, and then close it again. His throat convulsed as he rapidly swallowed several times.

She couldn't bear any more. A stifled sob shook her and she

swung away. She had reached the doorway, when his cracked, desperate voice stopped her.

"Beth darling, since when have I become Canley-Smith again? Isn't plain Smith good enough for you anymore?"

She stopped dead. He had called her darling. She couldn't remember the last time he had used any endearment to her.

Slowly she turned around. For a moment they stared at each other. Then an unwilling smile briefly tilted her lips with relief when she saw the teasing glint in his suspiciously bright eyes.

She straightened. "No, it's not good enough," she flung at him, "and at *our* wedding I married a Canley-Smith. Your real name is not plain Smith. You couldn't be plain anything if you tried!"

An expression she couldn't understand flashed across his face. "Oh, Beth. . ." His voice choked and he looked down, fiddling with the rug across his useless legs.

She waited patiently until he slowly raised his head. Then the unconcealed torment and fear in his face put wings on her feet. She was crouched beside him by the time the whispered words escaped him.

"Beth, what if you and those doctors are wrong? The doctors here have had grave doubts about my ever walking again after this long time lapse since the accident. What if I'm never able to be independent, except in a wheelchair, always needing someone, never walking again?"

Her hands crept up around his neck, slowly, fearfully, expecting the usual rejection of her touch. Suddenly he let his head drop against her, and with a tremendous sense of relief she cradled him against her heart.

"Then we will have to let God give us the strength day by day to cope," she whispered tenderly as she stroked his head. "Day by day, Art sweetheart. We only have to cope day by day." She added fiercely after a tense moment, "But we will only be able to do it if we do it together. When I'm weak you'll need to be strong for both of us, and when you're weak, I'll be strong for both of us. But we will see it through together! With God's help, we'll see it through!"

For a moment Art was very still. Then a deep shudder went through him. But, for once, he did not argue or even comment.

313

Chapter 4

Despite her confident words, an icy hand of fear settled deep inside Beth as she reluctantly left the rehabilitation unit and headed for the car park. Her hands were trembling when she unlocked the car and scrambled inside. Helpless tears began trickling down her cheeks. Two clenched fists pounded on the steering wheel. Furious words burst from her. "I won't give up on our marriage, God! I won't, I won't!"

She knew what that scene had been all about. Art had been testing her, perhaps even trying to find an excuse not to come home and be with her, be with his family again. She had a horrible suspicion that he really did not want to see her or the children the next few days, that the medical staff had made no such dictate.

Impatiently she brushed away the tears, gritted her teeth, and started the car. The children had to be collected from school. Groceries had to be bought. She closed her eyes tightly for a moment, and cried out loud, "Oh, God! Oh, God. . .help. . .please help me!"

What if. . .what if she was wrong and Art was right? What if he never walked again? He had always put so much value in physical strength. Even at school, she had been aware of that when he had spent hours in the gym building up muscles, working out so he could be the best, the fittest on his football team.

As she set the car in motion, she muttered fiercely "He *will* walk. It has to be true. It must be true."

Saying the right words to Art had been easy enough. . .*let God give us the strength day by day to cope.*

But how would she cope with each day of uncertainty, with this other deep, inner fear. It was always there in the back of her mind: if there had been no accident, would Art ever have come home? Did he want to be with them now? Did he really want to stay married to her? Did he love her enough to really forgive her?

He had even been angry with the police and hospital authorities for contacting her as next of kin when he had been too ill to prevent them. Still, his bloodless, pain-wracked face had lit up that first day she had walked into his hospital room. But then he had shut her out, refused to talk to her about his condition. Any information about him she had to obtain from the medical staff.

Months after his burns had healed, when his paralysis had showed no real improvement, she knew the staff had been worried about his increasing depression. But with her he had always smiled, pretended everything "was fine, just fine." She had always known that the smile never reached his tormented eyes which he would so quickly hide. Oh, she had tried to talk to him. Tried to get him to talk to her, only to be met by a bland face, a raised eyebrow that all meant he would not let her near him emotionally.

The worst of his depression had lifted after Gail had gone to see him at long last. Beth wondered about that at times. She still wasn't quite sure what had happened that day. Jim had merely told her that Art had been relieved Gail no longer blamed him for the accident. But somehow she knew there was more to it all than that. And never through all the heartbreaking months had he ever let her get really close to him.

Until Saturday night when he had allowed her to cry all over him. Until today. Her heart lifted. For the first time he had briefly let *her* comfort him. Even let her hold him close.

She was late picking up the children, and one look at their scowling faces made her heart sink. "Sorry, kids," she said brightly. "Hope you haven't been waiting too long."

"That's okay, Mum." Jacky's shrug and long-suffering voice made Beth search her face quickly. "I guess Dad held you up at the hospital."

"No, he didn't as a matter of fact." Jacky glanced at her and then away again. "It was very busy at the supermarket," Beth continued

315

evenly. "The car park was full and then there was a long queue at the cash register."

There was silence as she pulled out into the stream of traffic. She frowned slightly. Usually by this time Robbie was chattering away like a magpie.

"And how did your day at school go, Robbie?" she asked gently at last.

There was silence for a moment, and then a very subdued voice said, "Okay, I guess."

Beth opened her mouth, then bit her lip. She could find out what was wrong easier when she wasn't driving.

"Did the doctor tell Dad when he could come home again, Mum?"

Beth hesitated before answering her daughter. "I'm afraid they don't know yet," she said slowly at last. "In fact he needs a lot of rest to get over the trip to the farm. He still needs more training in how to manage at home."

She glanced quickly across at Jacky, but her daughter's head was turned away, hiding her expression. "Now," Beth added quickly, "when we get home, I need help putting my shopping away so we can see what we can do about a kennel for Bonnie."

"Why couldn't we have brought her back with us?" Jacky's voice was belligerent.

" 'Cause when we went to school she'd be lonely durin' the day, stupid!"

"Robbie, don't speak to your sister like that," said Beth sharply.

"Well, she is stupid." There was a sob in the shrill tones. "She said. . .she said Daddy's neva comin' home for good. She said—"

"Robbie! Shut up!" yelled his sister.

"Be quiet this minute," Beth exploded above Jacky's angry voice.

"But Mum—"

"Not another word until we're home!"

To Beth's relief, both children were silent the rest of the trip while she negotiated the heavy traffic. Crisply she demanded their help unloading the car. When the bags of groceries were safely in the kitchen, she rounded on them.

"Right. Let's get one thing very clear. Your father needs more time in hospital right now, but he is very definitely coming home for good once the doctor says he can."

Beth put her hands on her hips and glared from one to the other. Both children searched her face and then looked away. Robbie swallowed and Jacky's head bobbed down.

"Now, what's this all about?"

There was silence.

"Jacqueline. . . ," began Beth sharply.

Jacky raised her head and glared defiantly at her. "It's nothing, Mum. Robbie had a bit of a fight at school today."

"Robbie!"

Robbie glared at Jacky. "Dobber!"

Beth took a deep breath, but before she could speak, Jacky rushed in with, "It's not dobbing to tell your mother you had a bit of trouble at school. Mum told me when you first started school at Cecil Plains to look out for you."

"Jacky, telling tales is not what I meant about looking after your brother," Beth protested.

Two pairs of eyes considered her carefully. Jacky opened her mouth and then thought better of whatever she was going to say. Beth looked from her to Robbie. He was manfully fighting the big tears that had filled his eyes.

Suddenly those sad eyes looked so much like Art's that she couldn't think of a thing to say except a weak, "You kids want something to eat? I bought you some fruit."

Relief flooded Robbie's face as Jacky bounded away to scramble among the various plastic bags on the counter, calling "Great! Some white grapes. I love them."

Beth hesitated a fraction too long trying to decide whether to pursue what had happened at school. Robbie whirled away. He too grabbed a handful of grapes and the next moment both children had raced from the kitchen.

Annoyed with herself, Beth stared after them, and then sank wearily onto a chair. "You're a hopeless mother," she muttered under her breath. "When you were a kid, your mother would have had it out of you in a second!"

She bit a lip. Should she pursue it? Robbie in a fight? That wasn't like her young son at all. Like herself he did have quite a temper, but to her knowledge he had never hit anyone. Then she shrugged. At least his face had not been marked. The fight couldn't have been too bad, and after all, it was only early days at a new school. Some settling in problems were inevitable.

Resolutely she stood up. It was no good wishing her children could have kept going to the smaller country school on the Darling Downs that Jim, Hilda, and herself had attended before going to the senior high school in Dalby. Wearily she started stacking the groceries away.

Worry filled her as she remembered how much they had cost. As usual she had spent too much money, and now there was barely any left until the next week's Social Security check. She dared not accept anymore help from Jim or her mother. Art would have a fit if he knew how much they had already helped out.

She found herself muttering out loud, "Oh, Lord, You know how desperately we need that job," and paused. She smiled slightly at herself.

"Practicing the presence of God" her mother had called it once. Beth had never done it before. But now, in the last few months, she found herself often talking to God spontaneously. Not only at odd moments either. She had spent many minutes on her knees in her bedroom when no one was around. Her one regret was that she had neglected having private devotional times during the years since she had married Art.

A sudden sense of peace came. She stood up and glanced around the small and rather dreary kitchen. For a moment she closed her eyes. "And You are here, aren't You?" she said out loud. "And You will give me strength each day."

"Mum? Who you talkin' to?"

Beth looked up. Robbie was looking around the kitchen with wide eyes. They settled back on her, and then suddenly lit with understanding. "Oh, that's what Grandma does. Can I have some more grapes?"

"If you say please," Beth answered automatically. "Grandma does what too, Robbie?"

"Talks to Jesus, of course."

Beth was still as he trotted off. Then she smiled.

———

When the day of Beth's job appointment came, Rance Telford's friend greeted her with enthusiasm. She took an instant liking to him, but when she hesitantly asked if she could do his office work in the afternoon until her husband was out of the hospital, Bob Lane hesitated for a moment and her heart sank.

Then he shrugged. "Well, I was hoping you could answer the phone and do any reception work. I'm usually out doing jobs in the morning. But if it will only be for a couple of weeks I guess my wife could be here to do that." He beamed suddenly. "Our first baby's due in another few weeks and I—"

"And he wants me at home twiddling my thumbs until then," a cross voice said from behind Beth.

She turned and watched a tired-looking, pregnant woman stride slowly into the office.

"Beth Smith, is it? I'm Janet. I'll be very glad to have your help doing all the correspondence, invoices, and pays, but I can certainly sit and answer the phone and deal with visitors for a few hours each day." She settled on a chair with a sigh of relief, and then looked up and smiled at her husband. "At least, in the short term. Very soon I'll be too busy elsewhere for a while." She turned and surveyed Beth steadily. "Rance said you've just moved here to be near your husband's rehabilitation hospital."

"Actually, Art is expecting to be discharged soon." Beth took a deep breath. She hated putting it into words, but said steadily, "He. . . he's a paraplegic. I would normally have been able to come in at any time during school hours but. . .but they want me at the hospital to have some training in how to help him at home. It's so I can cope better with his daily care, exercises and things. The morning's best because of the showering and. . ." She faltered to a stop and looked away from the sympathetic understanding that had entered Janet's eyes.

"Well, now that you're here this morning," Bob asked a little anxiously, "is there any chance you could work today for a few hours?"

His wife gave a snort of protest, but he said sternly, "Now, Jan, you know that you had a rotten night and should still be in bed. The doctor said your blood pressure's too high and that you've got to rest more."

"Don't. . .don't you need references or anything?" Beth asked unsteadily, relief flooding through her.

"Already have one from Rance," Janet Lane told her. "Oh, and he gave us strict instructions to ask you if you've found a church to worship at yet, and if not to invite you to come along with us to ours."

She grinned at Beth, and slowly, Beth smiled back. "Well, so far I've been too busy on Sunday mornings, either at the hospital or with Art at home. Perhaps later."

"Not too much later," warned Janet with a twinkle, "or the Reverend Rance will be after you."

Beth nodded in agreement, but as she drove to the hospital a few hours later, she wistfully wondered about going to church once Art was home. He had reluctantly gone to church with her from time to time until Robbie had been born. What would his attitude be now to her going regularly again?

Not seeing Art the last few days had been hard. She missed him dreadfully. She was determined that their visit today would be pleasant and cheerful, if nothing else, but when she strode into his room, she paused and exclaimed, "Art, you look dreadful. You're so pale and. . .and. . ."

"Don't fuss, Beth," he scowled, looking away from her. "I'm just back from working hard at physio, that's all." He added rapidly, "Now, tell me what your mother said about Bob Garrett's funeral. You said on the phone that Jim and Gail were coming back for it."

Beth hesitated. She knew this was a ploy to stop her asking questions. He was always so reluctant to talk about himself!

"I shouldn't have let you and the doctors persuade me you needed rest and no visitors," she said crossly. "They've been working you too hard, and I would've told them so!"

"That's why they wanted me to rest after the sessions and not have

320

to entertain visitors," Art snapped back. He glared at her. "Besides, you needed the break as much as me. Now, are you going to tell me about the family or not? How's Hilda?"

Beth sighed inwardly, but went along with him, trying not to let him see how anxious she was.

During the next few days her worry subsided as he gradually seemed less tired and strained. Her own days became increasingly hectic. In the morning she rushed to the hospital then managed usually to swallow a few mouthfuls of lunch before hurrying to work. She was careful never to be late again picking up the children. For a few days she had watched them closely, relieved when they appeared to have no further problems at school.

Art was not allowed home on leave again for several more weeks. He told her they wanted him to be more rested, and have uninterrupted physiotherapy. But something was different about him, and she was still secretly afraid he might have told them he did not want to go home. Jacky and Robbie willingly went with her a couple of times to see their father, but they quickly became bored in the hospital.

She was very tired by the time Art at last was again allowed a weekend leave. At first staying at home over the weekend without having to load the kids into the car and hang around the hospital was actually a relief. But then she found that looking after someone confined to a wheelchair was at times even more difficult than she had expected. Not that Art bossed her around or expected her to be at his beck and call every moment. Perhaps if he had been a bit less polite it would have been more natural? More normal? She just knew that he hated her doing things for him he could not do for himself.

But Beth refused to let him know how much his attitude hurt her. She gritted her teeth, muttered savagely to herself, "Day by day, Lord. Day by day," and kept smiling, although she was still fearful about how they would cope when he came home for good. More and more she found herself "talking to Jesus" and turning to her Bible. And more and more she began to experience the peace and daily strengthening she so desperately needed, especially when Art would be discharged.

Chapter 5

S o, Monday's the big day, Beth?"

Beth looked up and smiled at Bob Lane. "Yes, it certainly is. And you're sure you can manage without me all day?"

"No problem." Bob smiled sympathetically. "Well, only another couple of days to go. We're not busy, why don't you leave a bit early?"

She returned his smile gratefully, grabbed her things, and fled. Janet and Bob Lane had become very good friends even though she still had not managed to take them up on their invitations to visit their church.

———

Beth was filled with trepidation when she picked Art up on Monday. He was tense too and gave one huge sigh as she drove carefully away from the entrance of the hospital. She glanced across at him, but he looked so grim she was silenced.

Neither spoke on the short journey home, and as she at last drove into their driveway and carefully stopped near the front ramp, she was once again battling her hidden fears. She sensed that Art was disturbed about his discharge.

He had been different lately. More abrupt. He had been so angry at her suggestion she have a good talk with his doctor before his discharge, that she had backed off.

Now she wondered if he was scared too. Did he think he would not be able to cope with being with her and the children again week after week? And could he cope with her helping him with the intimate things day by day he could not manage himself?

But at last they were home for good or ill. Turning off the motor, she took a deep breath and smiled determinedly across at Art.

He was staring through the windscreen at the house with such a strange look on his face that her smile faded abruptly. "Wouldn't it be lovely to be back in the country again, even in our own—?" Art's wistful voice cut off.

As nice as this house was, Beth had often thought the same thing after driving through the heavy city traffic. "The tenants in our house in Dalby want to buy it." Beth bit her lip. She hadn't intended to blurt it out like that. She had never found a good time to talk about their own home before. He had never seemed interested, but now Art looked at her swiftly and then away just as fast, but not before she saw the bleakness in his eyes.

She knew how he felt. They had battled so hard to get the deposit to put down on their own home. Now, even with the rent income, it was very hard keeping up the mortgage payments. Having to sell was a distinct possibility.

Without another word, she opened her door and went to unload the wheelchair. By the time she had unfolded it and wheeled it to the passenger side, Art had his door open and was swinging his legs, one by one, out of the car. When he was settled into the chair, she hurried ahead, leaving him to slowly maneuver it up the ramp. Still without a word, she inserted her key in the lock, flung back the door, and waited.

Art paused and for a heart-stopping moment stared up at her. "I'm not sure that I ever really believed this wonderful day would come," he whispered at last. "I can unpack and I won't have to leave again after only one night."

Relief swept through her on a cleansing tide. Before she could speak, a faint grin twisted his lips and he said in a stronger voice with a hint of self-derision, "I feel a bit like the first time we arrived home after our honeymoon."

Her eyes blurred at the sudden vivid memory. They had both been so young, still teenagers, nervous and excited at the same time. And they had both been so much in love.

"For me to carry you over the threshold this time, you'd have to sit on my lap."

She searched his face for a moment, but there was nothing in his expression now except jubilation and amusement. Her heart lightened.

A relieved laugh escaped her. "That might be safer than hauling me over your shoulder in a fireman's lift, then dumping me on the floor as soon as you took two steps inside."

"Let's see shall we?"

Before she could do any more than gasp, he reached up, grabbed her by the arm, and pulled her down across him.

"Art! You. . .you idiot. . ."

She squealed and grabbed for support as his hands left her. The wheelchair bounced forward. One of her legs bumped against the door frame and she was jolted back against him. She squealed again, but they stopped moving. Two strong arms came around Beth again. She tightly clasped Art's neck.

For a moment she revelled in their closeness. Then his arms pushed her away slightly before letting go. Reluctantly she took her hands from his neck and bounced to her feet. She bent over and rubbed at her foot. "Ouch, that hurt. And that was even less graceful than your first attempt, Art Smith!"

She looked up at him, and all laughter fled.

"Not the most sensible thing either," he gasped breathlessly. "You're heavier than I thought."

"Oh, Art, you've hurt yourself!"

He shook his head. "Just winded" he managed.

"Are you sure? Are you in pain? Can I get you anything?"

"Don't. . .fuss. . ."

She stared at him anxiously. His chest was heaving. Those hazel eyes were closed in a face that had lost color, and his hands were clenched in his lap. Nervously she crouched down and put her own hand hesitantly over his and waited.

After a few moments, his breathing eased. He opened his eyes and looked at her. "Worse than the last time, huh?"

Not sure what to say, she stared back at him silently.

Something sparked in his eyes as they looked at each other. "But it was worth it. Like the last time," he murmured.

Art loved the way Beth's smile started in her eyes and then spread all over her face. He could not resist reaching up and tracing her smiling lips. Then it seemed his hand had a mind of its own as he reached around her head and tugged her closer.

"Last time. . ." he felt her lips move against his and then they were still as his silenced them.

Even as he kissed her, Art knew it was a mistake. It would only make it more difficult resisting his burning desire to hold her so close they would never be separated again. But for years he had tried so hard to be the kind of man she needed, and his best had never been good enough. He had an even better reason now not to let her get too close to him: his useless body. And last year he had reached the heights of cowardice. If Gail had not visited him at just the right moment. . . He shuddered.

And now these last few weeks. . .

He took a deep breath, wondering once again at himself. Why hadn't he been able to tell her? Why had he even gone so far as to insist that the doctor and staff not say a word?

Beth straightened and then looked at him with a slightly dazed expression.

He avoided her eyes and said as lightly as he could, "Let's get my gear in from the car and unpack."

You fool, he chastised himself silently. *Why on earth did you go and kiss her like a starving man?*

His lips twisted at the obvious answer. He *was* a starving man, starving for her love, her acceptance. . .her. . .

But as Beth moved away, there was a glow of happiness about her that he could not regret. Having a bit of foolish fun like hauling her onto his lap had felt good. The past years had been so serious, so worrying.

A few moments later Beth returned with his bags and walked toward his bedroom. He wheeled himself slowly after her, his thoughts and emotions still in turmoil, hoping she did not know how much that kiss had affected him. She hesitated in the middle of the room, looking at him expectantly. He glanced around the room casually.

Then he stilled, staring at the huge, slightly lopsided sign taped on the wall above his bed. "Welcome home, Dad," he read out loud. A sudden mist blurred his eyes.

"Jacky insisted on printing the words and then they fought over who colored it in," Beth said softly.

He cleared his throat. "They're good kids."

"Most of the time."

There was a wry note in her voice, and he looked sharply at her. "They been playing up on you?"

Beth was biting on her lip. He knew that habit of old. She had blurted out something she did not want him to know about. He was even more sure of it when she said a little too quickly "No, no, they're fine."

"Beth." He paused then added carefully, "We have to work out ways I can be of use around her. And one of them is sharing the responsibility of the kids. Especially while you have to work." Her head reared back, and he added rapidly, "It's all right, I know the kids have to get to know me a lot better again before I can handle any of the heavy father bits. Your mother has already pointed that out to me."

Beth frowned, but turned away without speaking.

"What's wrong, Beth?"

"They. . .the kids. . ." Beth paused and then swung around. She looked troubled then blurted out "They're really excited about you coming home for good. I had a real battle to get them to go to school this morning, but I think they're also a bit scared about all the changes in their lives lately. You'll have to be very patient with them for a while, Art."

"I'm very much aware of that, Beth."

"I. . .I don't won't you to be hurt by them."

Art felt all his breath leave him in a whoosh. She was worried in case they hurt *him!* And he had been so worried in case he upset them.

Then he remembered the hurt that had clutched him after Jacky had flared at him after the wedding. More recently, he had been aware that Robbie had taken to being very careful around him. And he had discovered that seeing his son scuttle out of the room the moment he realized he was alone with his father had affected him badly.

He forced a smile at Beth's anxious face. "I'll be fine. I promise.

Besides, didn't you say Jim and Gail were bringing the dog this coming weekend?"

Beth's face cleared. She raised her eyes to the ceiling and back. "I'm not sure I've forgiven Jim yet for letting the kids have that puppy of Hilda's," she grumbled.

"Gail assured me she has house-trained it."

"There's no way it's going to be living in the house," Beth stated firmly.

—⁓—

But Robbie and Jacky had different ideas.

Art watched with considerable amusement the next weekend as their insistent faces and voices at last wore Beth down to a feeble "We'll wait and see."

"Okay, kids, outside and play with Bonnie now," Art said firmly, trying hard not to laugh.

As the children raced away, a wildly excited collie dog barking happily after them, Beth looked at him ruefully. "Don't you dare say a word, Arthur Canley-Smith!"

Jim gave a wicked chuckle. She turned and glared at him.

"Don't take any notice of them, Beth," her new sister-in-law said. "Those two little imps twist their uncle around their little finger. . .well, at least they did when it came to having one of Polly's puppies. Oh. . ." Her smile disappeared. "Beth, did your mother tell you about Polly?"

Beth shook her head. "Not a word. Why, what's happened?"

Gail hesitated, and Jim said slowly, "Polly had cancer in the nose and Hilda had to have her put down."

"Oh, no, poor Hilda! She really loved that dog," said Beth sadly. "And so close to losing her father! How is she?"

Jim swept his hand through his hair and frowned. "I'm not really sure. Jean Drew stayed with her as long as possible, and Rance Telford has been keeping an eye on her since. But she's gone off to Sydney with him. We're a bit worried about her, both of them in fact."

Art snorted. "She'll be okay with the Rev. He of all people should be able to stop her making more mischief."

"That's all over, Art." Gail's chin was tilted and her voice firm.

"God's dealt with her about the trouble she caused between me and Jim. We're going to be good friends from now on. In fact, I'm real pleased you've got Bonnie. Perhaps one day she'll have puppies and you can give one to Hilda."

Beth noticed a strange look cross Art's face as he watched Gail. "But then, you'd forgive anybody anything, wouldn't you Gail?" His voice was soft, but filled with admiration.

Beth looked sharply from him to Gail.

Color swept into Gail's face. She tilted her chin and looked Art straight in the eye. "Only because I know that Jesus has already forgiven me. . .forgiven me and made me a new person."

Beth's eyes widened. She looked nervously at Art. He had been so rude to Rance Telford when he visited him during one of his first weekend leaves at home that she expected some kind of explosion.

For a moment there was a very thoughtful expression on Art's face. Then he scowled. Beth opened her mouth, but paused when a twisted grin eased his face.

"How come you've learned to talk so much like Jean Drew, the dragon lady, so quickly?" There was disgust in his voice. "These religious Stevenses and their friends have really got to you, haven't they, Gail?"

"Arthur!"

Gail ignored Beth's exclamation. "It's the Lord Jesus that has 'got' to me, Art Smith. And He could transform your life too if you'd let Him! You need Him in control of your life now more than you ever have."

Beth held her breath. So many times when she had tried to talk to Art like this before their separation, he had bitterly resented it. She looked helplessly at Jim. He was grinning madly at her!

"Don't look so appalled, sister dear. These two carried on like this quite often in Sydney when you were back home with the imps!"

"They did!"

For a brief moment, Beth felt a streak of jealousy. Why did Art tolerate this from Gail and not her?

Jim unconsciously answered her. "He listens to her because she was almost as big a heathen as he still is!"

Art gave a slightly forced laugh, and Beth looked away. She bit her lip. That had been one of the many accusations she had hysterically flung at him over the years.

"Jim Stevens, I was never a heathen," protested Gail with a grin.

Jim stood up. He grinned back at her. "Oh, yes you were, sweetheart. My dictionary says a heathen is an irreligious person, or even more specifically, not a Christian, and you were sure that. The very first time we met you took great pains to tell me you weren't at all interested in finding out about God."

Beth watched Gail's lovely face break into a rueful smile as she too remembered.

"What made you change your mind, Gail?"

Three heads swung toward Art.

He scowled. "Well, something must have happened. I've often wondered. And I don't think I really fit your definition of a heathen either, James!"

"Mmm. . ." Gail's voice was thoughtful. "You've certainly not given me the impression you're uninterested in God. At least. . .," she hesitated, "at least not for a long time. But you've never let me talk about my commitment to Christ before, Art. Are you sure. . .?"

"Wouldn't have asked if I wasn't interested."

Beth again held her breath at the snarled words, but Jim laughed. "I hope you know what you've let yourself in for, Art, my friend. Once you start this wife of mine going on about her conversion, you might find it hard to stop her. I'll go and rescue Bonnie from the imps and leave you to it. Coming, Beth?"

Beth hesitated. Then she said slowly, "No, I'd rather like to hear what Gail has to say myself. I've never really heard what happened either."

She saw the smile exchanged between her brother and his wife before he disappeared, and her own heart ached. She had never known that same depth of intimacy with Art. Never. Not even in those first halcyon days of their marriage.

"Art, before we talk about all that, I haven't said anything about. . . about. . ."

Beth looked sharply at Gail as her voice choked to a stop. She was looking at Art hesitantly. Then she raised her chin decisively and said rapidly, "I'm so glad the coroner's report completely cleared you of any responsibility for the accident. And I'm so sorry I ever thought differently."

Beth gasped. "The report's out! Oh, Art, why didn't you tell me?"

Art avoided her eyes. He had hoped Gail wouldn't mention it until he'd been able to pluck up the courage to show it to Beth. To his utter amazement the coroner had highly commended his efforts to pull Gail from the burning car moments before it had exploded.

"It arrived last week," he growled roughly. "I didn't want to talk about it." He glared at Gail. "Thought I told you a long time ago to shut up about all that sorry business. Now what about this so-called conversion of yours?"

He risked a glance at Beth's face, and winced inwardly. He'd hurt her again, no matter how much she was trying not to let him see. But the report had stirred up all the horror, and he had not been able to bring himself to show it to her.

He deliberately looked back at Gail. She was studying him carefully, and then she smiled at him understandingly.

"You know, I've given a lot of thought to why I first began to take Christianity seriously." Gail propped her chin on her hand. She stared blindly in front of her with a far away look in her eyes. Then she looked up at Art and grinned a little shyly. "You were partly right you know, Art."

He quirked an eyebrow at her with mock indignation. "Of course I'm usually totally right. But which great thing am I. . .er. . .only partly right about?"

He gave Gail a mock scowl, and then glanced suddenly at Beth's uncertain smile and grinned gently at her. He thought her return smile held considerable relief.

Gail laughed and then sobered quickly. "You were right about the Stevens family and their friends. I guess it started with Jean Drew."

Art watched her expression soften as she thought of the nursing sister who had once been her clinical nurse educator at the hospital where Gail had done most of her practical nurse's training.

"I didn't realize until I was in the hospital after the accident how much she had changed from the bitter, sarcastic woman we were all scared of during our training. She was wonderful to me during those weeks when I was confined to bed," Gail added softly.

Art thought of the gray-haired woman who had also visited him often. She had always been there for him, as well as for Beth, during many dreary weeks after the accident.

"Yeah, she's an okay lady," he admitted gruffly.

"It wasn't until Jim mentioned how different she was now she'd become a Christian, that I realized what had changed her so much. Then. . . ," she paused and looked at Beth with a smile, "then I lived round the clock with two very committed Christians like your mother and brother. Gradually it sunk in that their faith and commitment to Jesus Christ touched every aspect of their lives.

"It wasn't that going to church every Sunday and being involved in their church life was just their particular lifestyle, like others I've known. I soon realized it was all far more than that. They weren't perfect, they just enjoyed God. There was a quality of love toward each other and others that I'd never seen so consistently before. There was peace and a joy too, and I desperately needed it all. And what's more they didn't have to do anything in their own strength. They just knew God worked out for good everything that happened in their lives."

Art looked at Beth and caught her eye. He stared at her thoughtfully, remembering what she had said. The color rose in her cheeks and she suddenly looked down at her clenched hands. He scowled. Now what on earth had Gail just said that had upset her so much?

There was a burst of furious yapping outside. Gail paused, and then she shrugged and stood up. "I guess what I'm trying to say is that they never doubted for a moment that God loved them, no matter what. After I asked her, Jean explained about the proof of God's love for all time being that He sent Jesus to die for me. I found I just couldn't turn my back on that kind of loving, and so I asked God to forgive me, and take control of my life and. . ."

The noise of kids and dog drew closer.

331

"And despite all the hassles since then, life's been. . .been great ever since," she finished rapidly.

As the kids rushed into the room with the dog barking at their heels, Art saw a radiance in Gail's face that he had only ever seen there when she mentioned her faith in Christ.

For a moment, depression rolled over him like a dark cloud. A lovely woman like Gail would have no problem getting close to God. She had once urged him to do the same when he had been in the depths of despair at his injuries. He had heard what Beth had said numerous times over the years about Jesus Christ loving him. . .dying for him. He hadn't believed her then, and he just couldn't believe Gail now.

Of course God loved good people like the Stevenses and Gail. But how could God possibly love a man like him? Someone who could never even please his own parents. Someone whose own mother and father hadn't been able to love or forgive. Someone who had deliberately turned away from God time after time.

And now. . .

How could he consider for one moment crawling back to God when he was such a helpless, incapacitated half-man?

"Daddy! Uncle Jim said ta ask you if we can use some old stuff under the house to build a dog's kennel for Bonnie."

"Robbie! I told you Mum said I could use that for a cubby house!"

Art stared at his two children, both racing toward him, jostling each other, trying to get closest to him, pleading eyes and voices trying to get his attention. Just so had they run to him numerous times over the years when they were much smaller.

But not for a long, long time. And certainly not this last week. They had been so careful around him. It had been "yes, Daddy, no, Daddy" until he'd actually wished they had been horrible to him.

Beth stood up. He looked up at her over their heads and their eyes clung. She had been as aware as he of Jacky and Robbie trying to be perfect children.

He knew the lump in his throat would betray him if he tried to speak. Ashamed of his unexpected burst of emotion, he swallowed, and stared at Beth helplessly. She moved swiftly toward him. Then he felt her hands settle gently on his shoulders and his heart swelled with love.

"I said some of that junk under the house might be handy, Jacky." Her voice was very firm. He felt her hands tighten. "Your father can't be expected to make a decision until he knows what you're on about. Let him go and have a look first, and than he can help Uncle Jim sort you terrors out."

He put up a hand and grasped one of Beth's. Immense gratitude flooded through him. She was reestablishing him in his role as father. He glanced up, and her smile was so gentle, so beautiful, his heart ached.

He cleared his throat. "Okay, kids, what about you help me maneuver outside and let me see what you're on about? Sounds like that uncle of yours needs all the help he can get."

Robbie hesitated, but Jacky surged forward. Beth stood back and let her grasp the handles of Art's chair. Gail moved to stand beside Beth and together they watched the trio disappear from the room.

Looking across at Gail, Beth began helplessly, "Oh, Gail. . ."

Gail gave a slight sound and quickly moved to put her arms around Beth. "Beth, dear, it's going to be fine. God hasn't let either of us survive that dreadful accident without many reasons. And Art has changed so much since the first day I met him. Why, just then he actually asked me about my becoming a Christian!"

Beth hugged Gail briefly, and then stepped back and mopped at her eyes. "Gail, I'm so ashamed. While you were talking about what a witness Mum and Jim were to you, I knew that my own Christian witness was far too many times practically nonexistent as far as Art was concerned. Especially after Robbie was born, I was always tired, and I. . .I used to lose my temper at the drop of a hat. I said some awful things to Art. I nagged him so much. . .about going to church with me, even about becoming a Christian."

"A bit like a dripping tap, you might say?"

Beth smiled weakly. "Yeah, guess I was a real example of that verse in Proverbs. My dear Mum's already pointed that one out to me, and also the one about a wife winning her husband by her behavior *without* talking at him." She straightened. Her head went up. "So, no more words from me," she said firmly. "Just prayer. Each day, just prayer, and more even for myself than Art."

"Yes," said Gail slowly, "prayer is vital. But sometimes the right words do have to be said at the right time—God's time. I'm also finding out how much I need fellowship and worship with other Christians. Some days I still miss my family so much." She took a deep breath. "But spending extra time on those days reading and meditating on the scriptures always helps. Especially when I'm prepared to put what I learn into practice," she added with a rueful smile.

Her words pierced through Beth. So few times over the years had she found strength in the Bible like that. She knew so much about what was in it. Her parents had seen to that. But how little during her marriage she'd consistently read, studied, made it a vital part of her life.

She walked across to the window and looked out on the backyard. Jim was standing talking to Art, while Jacky and Robbie were carrying a piece of timber toward them.

"You're right, Gail," she murmured. "Mum always said it contains God's instructions for living. That even includes instructions for praying." Her voice firmed. "I'll do better from now on."

She turned around slowly, and the two women smiled at each other.

Chapter 6

A rt, is there anything else—?"

"No, I'm fine. Just get going, woman!"

Art knew his voice had been too abrupt, and he forced a smile at Beth's worried face.

"Just go, Beth, or the kids will be late for school. I can ring you if anything goes wrong. And you'll be home before the hospital car comes to take me to physio."

Beth frowned. "I still think it's strange that they suddenly decided you needed to go every day. You're so tired after those sessions. And anyway, why couldn't I pick you up in the afternoons after work?"

"Because you'd be too tired running me around every day as well as timing it all with the kids. Because the hydrotherapy takes ages. Because some days they may be able to bring me home earlier than others. Besides," he continued grimly, "the hospital car had to be booked on a daily basis, some stupid red tape, hospital rules or something. And because the doctor said three short sessions were not enough to strengthen my muscles." There was a bite in his voice, and Art once again forced himself to grin at her carefully. "Can't be helped," he added breezily, "the powers that be did dictate, and we obey." He felt immensely relieved when she pulled a wry face, glanced at her watch, and headed for the door.

Art spotted something on the table. He picked it up and hurriedly wheeled after her. "Is this somebody's lunch box?" he called.

Beth gave an exasperated snort and flew back. "Jacky's. Thanks." She grabbed the box, kissed him unexpectedly on the lips, and disappeared out the door.

Art touched his mouth. The kiss had been so natural, so spontaneous. He wheeled himself out the front door so he could wave them off, and his heart glowed when Jacky grinned at him and waved enthusiastically. Robbie, however, only glanced at him quickly and then looked away.

As the car disappeared from sight, a feeling of something like relief swept through Art. He was glad to be alone at last after the weekend. Come to think of it, this was the first whole morning he'd been really alone since the accident last year. This was heady stuff! Now he could choose how to spend the next few hours without being told what to do by some nurse or therapist or doctor.

Silence descended around him for a blissful moment. Then Bonnie gave a short, sharp bark from the backyard where she had been banished. "Well, alone except for one collie dog," he muttered.

The winter day was quiet and sunny. Too soon the cold winds would sweep in, and even subtropical Brisbane would be cold for a few weeks. The breeze that had sprung up was a little cool, but suddenly Art was reluctant to leave the porch. He had spent far too much time indoors these past months.

Bonnie barked again, then whimpered. "Why not?" Art muttered.

He wheeled the chair down the ramp and around to the side gate into the backyard. The lawn was too soft in places for the narrow wheels on his chair, but fortunately there were plenty of sidewalks around the house.

The collie greeted him with delighted yelps. With some difficulty, Art managed to reach up and release the catch on the high gate. Bonnie pushed her way forward, and he just managed to stop her squirming past him and out of the yard.

"Oh, no you don't, you wretch. You're not going to get away from me and give young Robbie something else to be unhappy with his father about." He managed to grab the dog's collar, and hang on until he had moved his chair inside far enough that he could close the gate. "Not real bright, Arthur. You could have lost the dog your first morning alone, and then so much for your assurances that you can cope!"

Art frowned, thinking of the last week. When he had been discharged, it had been arranged that Beth would take him to his physiotherapy sessions at the hospital. The only appointments available for Mondays, Wednesdays, and Fridays had been in the early morning.

Fortunately Beth had been able to continue working for Bob and Janet Lane each afternoon after school that first week home. But it had been with the proviso that his appointments would be switched to the afternoon as soon as possible so she could work the mornings. He knew she had been worried about what would happen if he could still not get afternoon appointments when Janet could no longer work. So, at his session last Friday, he had again asked if there was a vacancy yet in the afternoon appointments. His physiotherapist had looked at him thoughtfully then muttered something about talking to his doctor.

The two professionals turned out to have already had considerable discussion. They had decided that he needed to continue to have daily therapy.

"We probably should readmit you, Art," the doctor said hesitantly. "You insist you can't, or won't do. . .er. . .certain exercises at home, and only three sessions a week is proving not to be enough to ensure the progress we hoped for."

"No! There's no way I want to be readmitted." Art saw the doctor's lips tighten at his vehemence, and added hastily, "Surely there's some other alternative. I don't want to disappoint Beth and the kids. Or me, for that matter," he pleaded wistfully. "I've been in the hospital so long already. What about the hospital transport?" He swallowed, and continued rapidly as he saw the doubtful looks on their faces. "Isn't there any way you could arrange appointments and transport, even if it does mean I have to spend more time here waiting for them to take me home?"

Art suspected that his doctor and the physio had worked hard persuading the powers that be that he needed special consideration. The end result had been that the only way they could fit him in was to call for him late in the morning, and take him home when they could in the afternoon. He knew Beth had been immensely relieved, although she had been worried about his need to go every day and the length of time he would be gone.

But as things turned out, she'd had a phone call over the weekend from a worried Bob Lane. In an attempt to try and control her blood pressure, Janet had been confined to bed by the doctor. They needed someone to work from nine until three. If Beth couldn't do it, they would have to find someone else.

Beth had bit her lip when she told him, then glanced at him apologetically as she hurried on to say how fortunate it was the change in his schedule had already been arranged.

He had really enjoyed his first full week at home, he thought now, as he stroked the dog. Oh, sure, there had been moments of tension between Beth and himself; the hardest thing for Art had been the children's attitude to him.

He had been relieved to have Gail and Jim visit for several hours last Saturday. For far too brief a time, Jacky and Robbie had seemed to accept him while he and Jim had started erecting the wooden shelter that was part cubby house, part large doghouse. But yesterday the two children had been very quiet and avoided being alone with him again, especially Robbie.

Art wheeled over and studied the rough construction they had worked on. Old paving bricks had been put on the ground, and the walls made from old timber found under the house. An old tarpaulin temporarily adorned the roof. Jim had promised faithfully to bring some old pieces of roofing iron and more timber from the farm on his next visit.

"Hope the cold westerlies stay away until he gets back," Art said out loud, "or you'll be cold if that tarpaulin flies off, Bonnie old girl."

Bonnie whimpered, and he felt her long nose nudge under his arm. He chuckled softly and patted her again. "Missing the kids already, are you?"

With a sigh the dog rested her head on his knees, and they enjoyed each other's company for a while, Bonnie lost in some doggie world, and Art thinking about building the shelter. His lips twitched as he remembered the overenthusiastic help from the children. But Jim had dealt with them all calmly and efficiently.

Then he frowned a little. He knew that Jim had been careful to build the shelter next to the wide garden path so it would be accessible to the wheelchair. It still troubled him that the best spot would really have been against the back fence under a spreading poinciana tree.

Then he shrugged. It had been worth it. Jim had also been careful to make sure Art had been included as much as possible in the building, handing him a hammer and a bunch of nails with the laughing comment, "Just because you can't reach the higher bits doesn't mean you get out of all the work."

He had noticed Robbie look at Jim with a wide-eyed stare, and then back at himself. Perhaps one day Robbie too might realize that his father wasn't completely useless.

Jim's attitude had been so typical of his brother-in-law. He was a fine man, and he and Beth had always been very close. Art had accepted years ago that he would never be able to measure up to a man like Jim, especially in Beth's eyes.

Seeing his old mate so happy with his new wife was great, though, and if anyone deserved to find happiness after so much tragedy in her life, it was Gail.

They weren't perfect, just enjoyed God.

Gail's words had crept back into his head constantly since Saturday. He did not know what had got into him. Fancy actually asking her to talk about her religion. No, he corrected himself with a snort, "religion" wasn't apparently the right word. Once before, when they'd first met, she had pointed out to him she wasn't just religious, she was a Christian.

At the time he had mentally placed his ultra-strict parents most definitely in the "religious" category. Their rigid attitude to going to church, keeping the Ten Commandments, and a host of other do's and don'ts had been so different from Gail's—and the Stevenses', come to that.

His frown deepened. Enjoy God? How on earth could anybody "enjoy God"? He doubted if even a saint could enjoy the God of wrath and judgement his parents had believed in!

As always, he deliberately blanked out any thought that included his parents. He swung his wheelchair around so abruptly he bumped into Bonnie. She let out a yelp and ran.

He stopped, held out his hand, and called to her. "Oops, sorry girl. Come on, I won't hurt you again. Someone always gets hurt when I think about my parents." The bitter thought came, *Usually me,* but he pushed it away and called to Bonnie again.

The dog hesitated. Then she seemed to make up her mind he wanted to play. She gave a short bark, put her head down low between her front feet, and then with another playful yap pranced toward him. He gave a low chuckle when she dodged his hand, and took off around the yard. She paused again. With her tail wagging madly, she crept paw by paw closer and closer. Then, with her head down again, she woofed pleadingly at him.

Art found himself laughing at her. He moved his chair abruptly toward her and she took off again, this time racing round and round the rotary clothesline. "You win, Bonnie," he called.

Then he sobered. He'd never be able to chase a dog in a playful mood as he had once. Suddenly his chin went up. But there was no reason he wouldn't be able to chase one somehow, even if it had to be in a wheelchair.

"You wait until I build up my muscles, dog," he said fiercely. "Even if my legs never work properly again, I'll still get about somehow. I'll still chase you, even if it has to be in one of those new motorized expensive wheelchairs!"

Then he stopped. It was the very first time he had verbalized his intention not to allow his useless legs to limit him. A weight suddenly rolled off him.

Okay, so he did not have the legs he'd once had. That didn't mean he could not learn different ways of doing things. His time in rehab had certainly emphasized that. They had assured him he'd even be able to drive a specially adapted car one day. Not one of the huge transport trucks perhaps, but certainly a car.

He looked at the kennel-cubby house again. He had managed to hammer those nails very straight and very effectively. He thought about all the skills for looking after himself that the therapists had been trying to instill in him. Most he was already handling quite well at home.

But the biggest decision still had to be made. What kind of work should he now attempt? What kind of training should he now have? How could he again support his family? Should he seriously consider that suggestion by the occupational therapist about doing some computer course at the Adult Education College? He had never had any chance to learn much about computers, but they had always intrigued him.

Some deep masculine pride inside him had been hurt when Beth had told him about her job, even though it certainly eased their financial difficulties. He had not minded at all her working while he had been also employed—but he felt different now that he and the rest of their family were dependent on her income.

Then Art thought about that for a moment. He took a deep breath. Honesty time. He had to admit it. True, he had never minded her working, but he had minded her earning more money than himself. He had been very relieved when the second baby had arrived and she had stopped work altogether.

Another thought suddenly hit him. After Robbie had been born she had mentioned a few times something about getting a part-time office job. He had been earning plenty himself then and he had dismissed the idea carelessly. Had he been wrong? She had always enjoyed working.

During the months away from Beth, he had finally decided she had become such a pain because of her guilt at marrying him, even more because of her guilt at letting him seduce her so they'd had to marry because she'd been pregnant. He had often wondered if she'd ever have ended up marrying him except for the baby.

But had he been wrong? Had being stuck at home with another baby contributed to her cranky moods? Perhaps that was why she had seemed to always be going out to something at the church, until he'd felt as though he and the kids were being neglected. At the time he had been secretly furious with her, thinking she was becoming too much like his mother, always plenty of time to bake cakes for church suppers and church sick folk but with hardly ever any time left for her family.

Deliberately, he forced his attention away from the past and thought again about the future. He had to do something to earn an income, to support his family. Well, he could never go back to being a specialized mechanic on the big machinery again. Climbing over and under tractors, harvesters, even driving a truck were no longer options.

He shut his eyes tightly for a moment, fighting to get rid of the negative thoughts. A wave of weariness washed over him.

He had not slept very well last night. Perhaps he had been over-tired, but after falling into a brief, deep sleep, he had then lain wide awake for hours worrying about his relationship with Beth, about getting closer to Robbie, about what the doctor had told him, about the future, and then of course, like a nagging toothache, he had not been able to get Gail's words about God out of his head.

A sudden longing for the faith and the peace she so obviously had found swept through him. "Are You as real as she and the Stevenses think, God? Are You really different from what I grew up thinking You must be like? Was everything *they* told me about You lies?" he muttered out loud. "Do You really care about miseries like me?"

He sighed wearily. He really didn't need these thoughts about God creeping in all the time. He had enough day-by-day things to worry about.

One thing he had not expected his first week home was the fact that he would get so very tired still. He knew his tiredness was probably caused by a combination of longer hours out of bed and not having nurses at his beck and call. But above all, the emotional tension between himself and the children, and between himself and Beth exhausted him.

One day at a time, so many people had told him, the doctors, nurses, occupational therapists. One day at a time.

And Beth had brought God into that idea. She sure believed that He was this "day-by-day" thing's very source of strength. His heart softened. Beth was sure some woman.

She always had been of course, but somehow she was different now. Not once had he heard her whine or complain, even when he knew she must be exhausted. He scowled at the thought of the number of times he had felt guilty, his heart wrenched by her pale face and the black circles under her eyes, no matter how hard she tried to use makeup as camouflage.

He had to do something. He had to come up with a way to earn a living, a way to sort out his marriage, a way to tell Beth. . .

There was a firm nudge at his arm again. Determinedly, Art again forced back the dark shadows that could so easily settle on him. "Okay, Bonnie, enough deep thinkin' for my first mornin' alone."

As he made for the gate in the fence again, he smiled slightly at himself. Talking to the dog out loud could quickly become a habit.

The ramp leading to the front door was fairly steep, and when he reached the patio he was a little breathless. He vowed that the ramp they erected to replace the four steps from the back door into the yard would not be as steep, even if longer. He swung open the flyscreen door and then stared with dismay at the front door.

It must have slammed shut when he was in the backyard. No handle, just a lock. For a moment he could not believe what had happened. Then it hit him. He swore violently. "Locked out! You stupid idiot, you've let yourself be locked out!"

For one ghastly moment he had a vision of himself still sitting outside when Beth arrived home, especially if that hospital car never turned up. Even worse, what if Beth rang and he didn't answer the phone? Then all her doubts about leaving him by himself would be justified.

"No way," he said through gritted teeth. "She has enough to worry about."

He thought furiously. *Might be able to find a neighbor home.* Perhaps there would be a window open. Then he grinned. The kids had been playing with Bonnie in the backyard until Beth's exasperated shout had told them to hurry-up-and-get-in-the-car-or-else. Hopefully they had not turned the lock on the back door.

He took a frustrating, exhausting thirty minutes to find somebody at home in the neighborhood, or at least someone who would answer his shouts from the bottom of their front steps. A furious German shepherd had made him beat a very hasty retreat from one yard.

The old man who eventually peered out at him proved, after a brief explanation, to be very friendly, overly helpful, and equally loquacious.

"Lucky it's only a little hilly round here," the old man puffed behind him. He had tucked his walking stick under one arm, grabbed the arms of the wheelchair despite Art's protests, and pushed him back to the house. "Youse woulda found the goin' pretty hard in that contraption. Had to use one for a while after I broke me hip. Now, you wait out here at the front while I try that back door."

Bonnie proved a stumbling block. Art heard her friendly, welcoming barks, and the old man reappeared, rapidly wielding his walking stick. Before he could open his mouth, Art roared, "Bonnie!"

There was silence. Art smiled. "She won't bite. Not much more than a puppy still."

Although still young, Bonnie was a full-sized, gorgeous example of a "Lassie dog," and Art could not really blame his helper for looking doubtful. But, after hesitating momentarily, he disappeared again. Art heard him talking soothing "dog talk" for a brief few moments, and then he relaxed as he heard the back screen door slam shut. A moment later, a triumphant old man was holding the front door open gallantly.

"Thank you, sir, very much," Art said fervently as he wheeled himself inside.

"Oh, me name's Ernie. Everyone calls me Ernie. Been living on this street for over sixty years. Came here when Edith and I married, ya know." He followed Art inside. "She's been gone these last ten years now, has my Edith. Still miss her. Now, what about I make you a nice cup of tea?"

Once again, Art's protests were overruled. But when he was at last sharing a hot cup of tea, he realized how exhausted he felt and was grateful for the drink, even though he wished he could rest quietly by himself.

He soon realized, though, how lonely the old man was. In fact, Ernie proved to have stories of the Second World War that fascinated Art. He told them with such fervor and dry humor that when he at last made moves to leave, Art was genuinely sorry to see him go.

When Art did eventually wave good-bye to his new friend, he felt very weary, and looked longingly at his bed. He had done the transfer from wheelchair to bed plenty of times in the hospital, but he still was not quite game enough to try it with no one about, mainly in case he could not get back on by himself. So he retreated to the lounge and made do by carefully lifting his legs up onto a stool. Then he was only too glad to sit quietly for a while.

The shrill ring of the phone woke him from a light doze. "How are you going, Art?" Beth's anxious voice asked.

His first instinct was not to tell her what had happened. She would only worry. So he said quickly, "I'm going very well, thank you, Mrs. Smith. How about your first morning?"

He could hear the relief in her voice as she replied, "No wonder they need my help in the morning! Just as well I started so early. I would have rung you sooner but the phone has hardly stopped ringing." Her tones softened. "Another customer has just come in. Must go."

Art replaced the phone receiver thoughtfully. Should he have told her? After all, he had coped quite well. He flexed his arms. His muscles would probably be a bit stiff later, and his hands were sore from pushing on the wheels. But he had coped! Jubilation swept through him.

When he unexpectedly heard the car and Beth's light, quick steps run up the ramp, he suddenly knew she had a right to know. She had been with him every step of the way so far. That fact made guilt sweep through him, but he pushed it aside and shrugged. "Just hope she doesn't become any more protective than she is already," he muttered as the front door swung open.

"This is an unexpected pleasure, Mrs. Smith." He forced a smile. "Got the sack already?"

"Nope. Bob came in and agreed to let me scoot home and have morning tea with my husband!"

Art stared at her. A memory of a young man tearing home for a brief morning tea time with his new young bride swept through him. They had been so in love then that they could not see enough of each other. Did she remember too?

Then his leaping pulse quieted. There was not a hint in her smiling face that she had come home on purpose so they could remember.

———

Not coming back to an empty house again was so good, Beth decided, and she found herself beaming at Art as he wheeled himself to meet her.

She studied his face carefully and his smile widened. He knew how concerned she had been having to leave him by himself. She made a rueful face at him. With considerable relief, she saw that he looked a little pale and tired, but otherwise great.

Just great.

A wave of love swept through her. She bent to brush her lips over his, wishing she was brave enough to kiss him properly, wishing he would grab her and kiss her. . .kiss her hard.

But he didn't. Disappointed, she moved away so he could not see her eyes, and said quickly, "We had such an early breakfast that I picked up some fish and chips for a snack."

She heard Art give a sigh of bliss. "You wonderful woman. I haven't had plain old fish and chips for ages and ages, especially wrapped in paper, and straight from take-away."

A pang shot through her. She should have remembered before this how much he loved the thick, salted hot potato chips and the deep fried, fish pieces in crisp batter.

"Well, I'll just get us a couple of plates and—"

"Nope."

She swung around in surprise. For a moment she was mesmerized by his flashing, laughing eyes.

"Don't need plates for a picnic." Before she could catch her breath, he reached for her hand and tugged. "Come on, let's have a picnic. I'm sure your boss won't want you to take too long, but there's a lovely sunny spot right in our own backyard." He hesitated, and his grin slipped a little. "You'd better push this contraption for me though."

346

Surprise flashed through her. He usually guarded his independence fiercely, and she had learned the hard way not to push his chair around.

He was watching her. "I'll tell you why in a moment." Before she could speak, he reached up and grabbed the bundle of food wrapped in several layers of white butcher paper. "Come on, before these get cold, or the car arrives for me."

They relaxed in the sun, Beth on a hastily grabbed blanket; the chips were still hot, and absolutely delicious.

"Hmm, I didn't realize how hungry I was." Beth reached for a piece of fish. "Now, tell me why you wanted me to push your chair out here."

Art hesitated, and then held his hands out. "That's why," he said very quietly.

"Blisters! Art, what on earth. . .?"

"Now, now, don't go into a flat spin."

She relaxed slightly when Art gave a chuckle. He gestured toward the dog. "Blame Bonnie. It was her pitiful, don't-leave-me-kids barking that made me come around here to the backyard in the first place. Straight after you left this morning."

Beth tensed. Once she would have flown in with questions, words. She controlled her tongue with difficulty, and waited.

"The front door slammed shut and locked me out."

A puzzled look crossed Beth's face, and then she gasped in understanding. "Art, whatever did you do?"

"Well, first of all I believe I swore," he said thoughtfully. Then he looked up at her and grinned at her resigned expression. Quickly he told her what had happened, describing his new friend, Ernie, in graphic detail.

When he told her about Bonnie scaring Ernie, she looked down at the now blissfully sleeping dog stretched out on a corner of the rug. Suddenly her lips twitched. "He was scared of this ferocious animal?"

Art looked down at Bonnie. "I'll have you know Ernie was a hero of the armed forces *par excellence!* He was afraid of no enemy soldier or situation with his commanding officer. Especially when they caught him running an illegal gambling ring among his fellow soldiers," he added reflectively. "He took great pains for nearly an hour to make sure I appreciated that major fact."

His voice was indignant, but when he looked up his eyes were dancing. The laugh Beth had been trying to stifle spilled out. And then Art's hearty roar joined her.

When they eventually stopped laughing, Beth scrubbed at the tears running down her face. "I don't know why laughing so much always makes these stupid tears flow. And the last thing I should be doing is laughing, when you were locked out!"

Art was silent. When she looked up at him, his tender smile made her catch her breath.

"I wouldn't have you any other way," he murmured. Their eyes suddenly clung. "It's good to see you shed laugh tears instead of the other kind for a change, Beth."

She was silent for a long moment, the laughter disappearing from her face. "It's good to have someone to laugh and cry with again."

Art looked down. He was silent for a long moment. "When we were first married I used to enjoy doing everything together with you, Beth. Well, that is, all except those times you tried to drag me to church. But then. . . ," he took a deep breath, "then I didn't enjoy anything for a long time."

Beth was silent. Slowly she rolled up the remains of their fish and chips. At last she looked up at him. "I have to take the blame for that, Art. I've been wanting to apologize for the rotten nagging you had to endure, especially after Robbie was born. And I. . .I want you to promise me something."

He looked at her, surprised. Then he scowled.

She continued rapidly, "I want you to promise to put me over your knee and wallop me if I ever start up again."

Art's scowl deepened. Hurt lashed him. He had come so close to hitting her more than once. Then that last dreadful night. . .he had been so frightened that he could sink to such depths; that had been the main reason he had left.

He fought for words. Fought to say how sorry he had immediately been, how bitterly ashamed he still was. But in all these months he had never found the words to tell her how he felt, and he couldn't now.

Then, as he stared at her, awareness hit him. She actually reckoned she had deserved his treatment of her! Sure, her hysterical nagging would have upset a saint, and he sure had been a long way from that, especially that last evening. But he had always believed that no woman ever deserved being hit by any man worth anything, no matter the provocation.

He saw the haunted look of remembrance in her eyes. They also held something else, something he wasn't sure he was really seeing.

They stared at each other silently. Then suddenly, to his utter astonishment, he realized that her deep blue eyes were actually pleading for *his* forgiveness!

Chapter 7

B eth held her breath. She was scared.

Dare she put it any plainer? Would he reject her fumbling attempts to let him know she realized now how much she had provoked him that last night, how much she had been to blame for so much that had gone wrong in their marriage?

He had really frightened her, though, that last dreadful fight the night before he had walked out.

Jacky had been sick, very sick. By the time Art should have been home, her vomiting and diarrhea had left her so listless and pale Beth had known she had to get the small girl to a doctor. Her purse had been practically empty, ruling out a taxi.

The last few months Art had been staying later and later at the pub where he met his mates after work. And that night he had been later than ever before. By the time he had deigned to come home she had been frantic with fear and worry.

As soon as she had heard his key in the door she had flown at him, smelt the alcohol on him, and screamed that he cared more for his mates than her. That his daughter had needed him, but what did he care?

There had been more, much more. He had yelled back at her, even cursed her, and then, "You're nothing but a nagging, useless nuisance."

Then his fist had lashed out at her. She had managed to dodge the blow, but she had tripped and fallen. Her face had hit the kitchen bench and the pain made her cry out. A trickle of blood had run down her cheek. It was only a tiny cut, but the bruise had been there for days.

Dazed and frightened, she had stared up at him from the floor. Never would she forget the look on his face as he stared down at her. He reached out his hand and started to bend down toward her. She had cringed away, scared he would try and hit her again.

Every drop of color had drained from Art's face. Horror had stared from his eyes. He had reeled back as though he'd been struck himself. His expression had changed again. The tears streaming down her face had blurred her vision. Many times she had tried to work out what his expression should have told her. Had it been guilt, hopelessness, anguish, or all three?

Still crouched on the floor, she had tried to stifle the sob that burst from her, wiping at the tears to clear her vision, smearing her face with blood. Then Art had slammed some money down onto the kitchen bench and walked out. His look of fury and disgust had haunted her ever since. How could a man still love someone who disgusted him as much as she had?

Now, as she stared at Art, waiting tensely for his reaction, she wondered if this could be a chance to at last put it all into words. At first, he had been so ill in the hospital that she had been just content to be there with him, sometimes even daring to hold his hand.

When he had recovered from the worst of the burns and been still undergoing tests to find out the extent of his spinal injury, she had tried to find the right time to talk about their marriage. But despite his accusation after Gail and Jim's wedding, that she was the one who refused to talk about it, he had told her in those earlier days that there was no point raking up the past while his future was so uncertain. Since then though, she had been the reluctant one, scared that he wanted to leave them again.

Only once had she made any attempt to talk to him about the night he had left. Such a dreadful look of pain and anguish had entered his eyes before he had turned quickly away that she had been deeply shocked. He had muttered a stifled "Don't, please" and not spoken for the rest of her visit. At the time, the doctors in Sydney had already been worried about his continuing depression. She had been so frightened she would only make things worse, so she had not said another word.

"Art," she began fearfully, "I mean it. I've always been so very sorry for my behavior that night. I didn't know. . ." She swallowed and continued a little steadier, "I'm so sorry that after you lost your job you found it easier to stay at the pub with your friends than come home."

Art was still scowling, and Beth's heart dropped.

"When you didn't come home. . .days after you disappeared that night, one of your mates told me how they'd been trying to cheer you up, offering suggestions of job prospects available despite the rural recession."

She hesitated again, and when he still did not look at her she said slowly, "I went for counselling to Rance Telford, you know."

Art lifted his head and stared up at her with an arrested look in his eyes.

"It. . .it took me a long time to acknowledge my own failures in our marriage. For a long time there was very little reason for you to want to come home to—just a nagging, selfish wife, undisciplined children, and an unkempt house," she said sadly.

Rance Telford had proven to be a wise Christian counselor. As well as helping her sort through specific issues, he had above all pointed her to God's Word and what it had to say about husband and wife relationships, about winning your unbelieving husband by your behavior. She had studied, prayed, and cried many tears of repentance for her initial disobedience and then her part in the breakdown of their marriage.

Beth took a deep breath. "I can't blame you for putting off as long as you could coming home that night to me and the children."

She had also often wondered if he had been afraid to tell her there would be no definite pay packet the next week, if that had been why he had blustered and roared back at her as she had flung all those dreadful accusations at him.

The first couple of days afterward she had been very busy with the ill Jacky, but then she had become more and more frightened when he had not come home. She had phoned a few of his friends, found out about his losing his job. When a week had dragged by with not a word from him, she had been frantic.

By the next weekend she had not been able to stand the uncertainty and the dreadful sense of being alone. She had packed up the kids and visited her mother and Jim, pouring out her heart to them for advice and help. They had been loving and supportive. Jim especially had been very concerned for his friend, but he had sadly reminded her that by marrying someone who wasn't a Christian she had disobeyed God's ways to start with. Her mother was the one who had suggested she needed counselling herself.

When she had returned home, Art had been there and gone. He had taken all his clothes and left a brief note.

She could not believe that the young man she had married with such love could have left her with only a note that simply said "I've been retrenched, but now I've the chance of a job interstate. I'll put money in our joint account when I can, but please don't try to contact me. You and the kids are better off without me. I can't stand any more."

She had felt as though a vital part of her had been ripped out. Never would she have believed she could hurt so much. She had called out desperately to God for help, and she had wondered many times since how she would have survived those dark days without Jesus.

Each fortnight the money had been deposited in their joint account. Sometimes there had only been small amounts, and she had worried about how he was managing himself, if he was on unemployment benefits. Then the weeks had stretched to six months, with no other contact. She'd had to face up to the bitter fact that he never intended coming back to her and the children.

She knew she had changed a lot in those months after his disappearance. Then, one fortnight, no money was put into the bank. Her only contact with Art had ceased.

And she had known. Even before the grave-faced policeman had knocked on her door, she had known something terrible had happened to the only man she would ever love.

"I'm so sorry, Art," she whispered.

As she stared at him pleadingly, to Beth's immense relief, slowly, ever so slowly, his lips smiled. Then her relief dimmed. The smile did not reach Art's hazel eyes. They were filled with sadness.

"You're pretty safe," he drawled. "Ernie would take great exception to his new friend manhandling his pretty wife!"

For a moment she was bewildered. Then she remembered what she had said about giving him permission to wallop her. Her answering smile was a little tremulous. Not even for a moment would she let him see how disappointed she was that he had chosen not to respond to anything else she had said.

She tilted her chin. "I guess I'll be quite safe then."

His eyes darkened even further. The smile was gone in a flash. "You'll always be safe with me, Beth. Always."

The words were a sincere promise. A vow.

She was a little puzzled. Of course she was safe with Art. Except for that one lapse he had always been so protective.

For a moment longer she stared at him, wondering if she should force him to talk about it all. Should she dare to at last put it all into words? She had to try to convince him how sorry she was for her part in the disintegration of their marriage, that she knew now how she had carried on like a spoiled, immature brat instead of a woman who professed faith in a loving and giving God.

Would he understand how afraid she was he would never forgive her, that their relationship could never be completely healed? Did he have any idea how desperately unhappy she was because she feared he no longer loved her enough to really want to come home and be together as a family again?

As it had so many times before, fear of saying the wrong thing, of not being able to convince him how she felt, stopped her. She was terrified if she brought it out into the open anymore, he would be forced to put his feelings into words. Be forced to tell her. . .tell her he didn't love her anymore.

Beth slowly scrambled to her feet. Hating herself for her cowardice, she managed to say brightly "Well, you won't be ready for your physio appointment if we don't break up this picnic, and Bob will think I've got lost."

She stopped, and then in a desperate attempt to cancel out other words she longed to be able to say, she blurted out, "Art, do you think these extra sessions at the hospital will really improve the muscle tone of your legs, stop them getting any thinner?"

She dared to give him a quick, darting look as she moved away. The expression on Art's face made her pause. Then he saw her looking at him, and his expression went blank.

Again.

Beth frowned inwardly. Had she been wrong? Had he been about to talk about their separation, their marriage? For one brief moment she thought she had seen disappointment, even hurt. Then there had been another expression, almost like fear.

But now, as had happened so many times before, Art deliberately chose not to let her know what he was thinking. He grinned a little crookedly. "So the powers that be reckon. Guess we'll just have to wait and see." Averting his face, he started his chair forward, adding quickly, "Come on, can't miss out on the torture session, can we? Especially since they went to so much trouble to work the available transport and appointments out for us."

Beth agreed as calmly as she could, hoping he could not see the way her hands were trembling. Quickly taking her position behind him, she started the wheelchair up the path. Fear kept its clutch on her heart. She knew that one day soon they would have to talk about their marriage and future together.

Oh, Father, I so need Your strength here, she prayed silently, *but I'm just plain scared.*

Terrified might be the correct word, she thought grimly, terrified she would say the wrong thing as she had so many times before, do the wrong thing that would put the last nail in the coffin of their marriage.

When he was still in the hospital, she had been able to convince herself they had plenty of time to sort out their marriage. But now he was home; she knew they would not be able to put the subject off indefinitely.

Despite her apprehension, during the days that followed, Art never once mentioned their relationship again. His leg muscles seemed to be responding to the treatment. At least, she could see they were not still getting thinner as they had been before. If anything, at times she thought they were actually getting more and more back to normal. She knew that could not be with paralyzed legs, that it must be more her own wishful thinking that made her think so. However, he gradually became increasingly independent, managing most things for himself from his chair.

The days began to fly by for Beth. Janet's baby arrived early, and Beth's hours varied considerably, depending on the workload and when Bob could be in the office. The extra money was a relief, but she became very tired. She knew Art fretted about her working hard, so she tried her best not to let him see how exhausted she was some days.

She was thrilled at how much he helped around the house. Sometimes she was astounded at what he managed to accomplish while she was at work. Beds were made, dishes cleared away, and clothes neatly ironed. One day he triumphantly told her he had washed the kitchen and bathroom floors; he looked immensely pleased at her heartfelt thanks.

Before, he had never helped her very much at all, and she had accepted that because he had worked very long hours himself. But she had often thought, especially after the babies had arrived, that he could have helped a bit more.

Some days, Beth even found herself becoming concerned at how much he did do for her. Occasionally his physio sessions really exhausted him. After the first few times, she had given up asking him about them because he had been very terse, not wanting to "rehash the torture" as he put it.

Beth had paid a very rushed visit to see Janet and her baby while they had still been in the hospital. Each day the proud new father regaled her with progress reports, but one quiet Saturday morning she asked Art if he minded keeping an eye on the kids while she paid them a visit.

He smiled approvingly at her. "No problem. I think the plan is to teach Bonnie some new tricks this morning anyway."

An answering smile lit up her face. "I hope I know the first one you'll teach her," she teased him.

"Of course," he said haughtily with a raised eyebrow. "Not to dig up your new pansy plants will be the very first on the list."

Beth laughed ruefully. "Seeing half of them have already been replanted twice, I don't think you'll have much success there.

Actually, I was hoping it might be that she learns she's supposed to sleep in her own kennel outside and not sneak into certain males' bedrooms inside this establishment!"

Art managed to look suitably sheepish for a moment. "Well," he drawled, "apparently she decided the carpet in my room was more comfortable than the one in Robbie's. Besides," he added reasonably, "it was raining outside and pretty cold."

Beth threw up her hands. "All the more reason to keep a wet, smelly dog dripping mud everywhere outside!"

"Well, it wasn't this male who let him in."

Her eyes softened. "But this male was too softhearted to get the other male to chase him out."

Beth thought about the yearning look that flashed into her husband's face all the way to the Lane's house. She knew he was trying so hard to get Robbie to accept him, relax around him, and she had not for one serious moment minded a bit of mud and a few more dog's hairs, if there was any chance father and son could enjoy each other's company as they once had.

Janet and Bob were outside in the front garden when she pulled up. Janet was sitting quietly in a deck chair while Bob was industriously using a digging fork.

"Don't get up," Beth protested as Janet greeted her with a smile and stood up.

Janet stretched. "Almost time for the baby's next feed, and I need a cuppa first."

Bob grinned at them, sweat running down his cheerful face. "You girls go ahead and have your drinks so you can goo-gaa at the baby when he wakes. If I stop now, I'll never get up the energy again to finish this garden bed."

They laughed and left him to it. As Janet bustled around preparing a pot of tea, they chatted about the business and babies. It wasn't until they were both nibbling on some chocolate cookies and sipping their hot drinks that Janet asked how Art was going.

Beth put down her cup carefully. "Very well," she said automatically as she usually did when anyone enquired. Then she stopped and looked up at Janet. "As. . .as far as I know, he's doing well," she added suddenly.

"As far as you know?"

Beth hesitated. "There's just something. . . Oh, I'm just being silly," she burst out suddenly, "but he never has wanted to talk to me about his condition at all. He never has since the accident, but now. . ."

Janet waited silently, and Beth found herself telling her about the times she had thought Art was concealing something from her. "When he was in the hospital I could always ask the nurses as well as his doctor. The other day I even rang his doctor from your office." She shrugged. "He seemed rather surprised that I had rung, but he said Art was doing very well. So I suppose I'm just imagining there's something wrong. It's just a feeling I have, I suppose. But he's so tired some nights after his sessions at the hospital. Sometimes he seems to have quite a lot more pain too, although he usually refuses to take any painkillers stronger than paracetamol. Says he must have been close to being a drug addict in the hospital."

The healthy bellow of a tiny baby sounded from the bedroom. Janet hesitated and then stood up. "Would you like to come and talk to me while I feed him?"

Beth stood up too. "No, no," she said quickly, "I didn't intend to be away too long, but I would love a peep at him."

Janet beamed, and led the way into the small bedroom that had been converted into an attractive nursery. Beth willingly agreed Robert Junior was truly gorgeous. But she had to say a rather hurried farewell as the demand for food became more and more urgent.

Janet carried the squawking infant to the door to see Beth out. Rocking the baby in an effort to soothe him she said quickly, "Before you go, I must ask you. Is there any chance we'll see you at church tomorrow?"

"I'm not sure," Beth said wistfully. "I certainly have been missing fellowship and worship."

On the way home, she thought carefully about how she could broach the subject to Art. There was no way she wanted her church attendance to cause any strife between her and her husband again. She had spent a lot of time in prayer about it all, and she knew she had put off long enough mentioning it to Art. She sent another fervent prayer about it heavenward.

To her utter astonishment, that night after the children were in bed and she had rejoined him in front of the television, he said very casually, "You haven't been to church since we moved to Brisbane, Beth. Haven't you found a church to go to yet?"

She gaped at him, and then looked quickly back at the television when he glanced at her.

"Well, er, yes. As a matter of fact Janet wants me to go with them tomorrow morning," she said rapidly. Then she hesitated before adding softly, "I went to church too many years without you Art, and I. . .I. . .I don't want going to church to be an issue between us ever again." She couldn't continue and fidgeted with her skirt, avoiding his eyes.

"Do they have a Sunday school for the kids?"

His voice was abrupt, and her eyes flew to his face. She could tell nothing from his expression.

She took a deep breath. "Yes, I believe they do. It's called junior church and it's during part of the worship service, after the communion time."

"Good."

She stared at him, but his expression was hidden. "Art. . . you. . .you don't mind if we go to church tomorrow?"

There was genuine astonishment on the face he turned to her. "Mind? Why on earth should I mind?"

"Because. . .because. . ." Beth stopped helplessly.

The expression on Art's face changed. "Because I refused to go with you, never meant I minded you going, Beth!"

"You didn't? But I. . .I thought. . ."

Her voice died away and she stared back at him, remembering all the times they had argued about Christian issues. So many times they had even ended up in furious, shouting arguments about such things as whether there really was a God who cared a scrap about what happened to ordinary people, about whether you had to read your Bible every day and go to church to be a Christian.

"Beth, I wanted you to do whatever you felt you should." His eyes looked away, and she saw him swallow. "It just. . .your going off to church without me made me feel pretty dreadful sometimes. As though you were all good, and I was all bad." The words burst quickly from him.

She gave a startled disclaimer, and he shrugged. Still avoiding her eyes, he added softly, "I know thinking that was pretty stupid. No person is all bad and no person all good, but it *was* the way I felt. That's why I always tried to make sure I arranged to do things on Sundays so I wouldn't be left in an empty house."

Beth felt her eyes fill with tears. There had been numerous Sundays when he must have felt lonely, neglected. If she had been less full of herself, less inflexible and not blind to his own needs, she could have gone with him sometimes. No wonder they had drifted apart those years after Robbie had arrived.

"I'm so sorry, Art, dear. I never realized. . ." Her voice wobbled, but she controlled it with an effort. "It doesn't matter about going to church, Art, I'll. . ."

"Beth, did I ever, even once, ask you not to go to church?"

"No," she said very thoughtfully after a long pause, "no, you never actually asked me not to go, but I knew you resented the fact that I went. And I can't really blame you. My attitude was very bad."

He looked uncomfortable. "I resented those wounded, sometimes angry looks I got because I refused to go with you."

"I did more than look," muttered Beth remorsefully.

"Yeah, you sure did have a good turn of phrase on occasion," he drawled.

Beth sat up straight. "Art, I'm never going to pest you about going to church ever again."

Art returned her anxious look for a long moment. A rather strange expression crossed his own face. "Ever again, huh?"

"I. . .I've already said how sorry I am for the way I behaved about that, Art," Beth said, fighting back a sudden desire to weep.

"So, if I ever have a sudden urge to go to church I have to ask you to take me, do I?"

Beth caught her breath in sudden hope. She bit her tongue and gave a brief nod. Then her hope died when he turned his head away and suddenly swung his wheelchair around and started it rolling toward the door.

"Good," he spat out as though he was angry, "very good. I'm going to bed. You'd better help me up before you leave in the morning. Oh," he stopped and glanced at her briefly, "Robbie and Jacky will want to go to Sunday school or whatever they call it. While you were out they told me they missed going. Apparently they blamed me for that too. Couldn't understand why you hadn't taken them."

He had disappeared from the room before Beth had gathered her scattered wits enough to reply.

Chapter 8

A rt spent a more restless night than he had for a long time. He tried to convince himself it was because he had not had a chance to do the exercises in his room.

He had not done the exercises because Beth had followed him to his room, quietly helped him as she always had to, but then, when he had been at last tucked into bed, bent, kissed him full on his lips, and whispered, "Thank you, Art." He'd felt guilty and an absolute heel.

She'd actually thanked him for telling her he did not mind if she went to church! And then, he'd actually felt disappointed, even angry because she wasn't going to ask him to go with her! There was so much she didn't know, so much to tell her, and he didn't know how to start.

Desperately he tried to push away the memories their conversation had stirred up. He had been haunted for so long by Beth's terrified figure cringing away from him on the floor.

The next time he had seen her had been through a haze of pain-killers. For one weak moment, he had been so pleased to see her again, even though her face had been pale with shock and fear.

Now he was tormented by the fear he had done the wrong thing, letting her stay with him all those months. But her presence had been the only thing he'd had to cling to through the horror. Certainly he had made a few weak attempts to persuade her to go home to the children, especially when they'd had chicken pox, but when she had finally gone for a couple of weeks. . .

He shuddered.

Sometime in the darkest hour of the night, he acknowledged once and for all how much Beth had changed. He wasn't sure he even liked all of that change. Sure, she no longer nagged him and tried to boss him around like she used to. She was also far more tolerant. She was much gentler, more considerate. She handled the children superbly. Come to that, she handled him superbly too!

But she was so subdued, so much quieter than the exuberant, glowing young girl he had married. He could only remember twice in recent months when she had shown in any way that the old spirited Beth was still around. Once had been that day he had "carried" her over the threshold. The other time. . .the other time had been when her indomitable spirit had leapt out at him as she had vehemently declared they would cope.

Then he remembered what else she had said that day. They would cope with God's strength. He still wasn't too sure God would be bothered with himself, but He surely must be helping a lovely woman like Beth.

At last he fell into a restless sleep, but he was feeling decidedly out of sorts when an excited young voice woke him at the same time that a small hand shook his arm.

"Daddy, come on, you've got to wake up 'cause we're goin' to church!"

He groaned, and then opened his eyes. The hand on his arm was snatched away. Robbie was staring at him. An anxious expression suddenly killed the excited, flushed look on his little face. He took a step away from the bed.

"Do your legs hurt, Daddy?" his small voice asked. "Won't you be able to come with us?"

"Robbie!" an exasperated voice exclaimed from the doorway. "Why are you waking your father up so early?"

Robbie looked across at his mother and then back at Art. "You. . . you said we had to hurry up and have breakfast so we could go to church. But Daddy just groaned, so I s'pose he can't come."

His face dropped even further with obvious disappointment, and Art's heart suddenly went out to his small son. He looked across at Beth. She looked distressed and opened her mouth, but to his own surprise he heard himself say, "Oh, that was only a moan because I had to wake up early to get ready for church. I'm certainly not in pain anywhere."

Beth's eyes rounded with astonishment, and then her face lit up as though a light had been turned on deep inside her. Something inside Art splintered into little pieces. She actually wanted him with them that much!

Beth opened her mouth again, and then closed it. He saw her swallow, and he wasn't sure which touched him most, her obvious delight, or the way Robbie's eyes began to dance.

"That's great, Daddy!"

Art's voice sounded rough to his own ears as he growled, "Go on you two. What are you hanging around for? What time do we have to be ready to leave?"

"Mummy said we had exactly one hour to get ready," Jacky's cross voice said from behind Beth. "And I've just fed Bonnie, but nobody's got *my* breakfast yet!"

Beth still seemed to being having difficulty finding her voice, so he growled again, "Because you're old enough to get your own. Go on you two kids, hop to it!"

When they were alone, Art kept his face averted and said shortly, "I'll skip my shower today. If you bring me a dish of water and chuck me some clean clothes, I shouldn't take long."

"Art, are you sure. . .?"

He cut fiercely across Beth's ragged voice with, "It's the first time in a very long while that my son actually looked disappointed at the thought I couldn't go somewhere with him. I don't care where we're going. I'm going because he wants me with him."

He almost added, "And you obviously still do too," but instead he looked up at Beth defiantly. Immediately he wished he had said the words, for a sad look crossed her face before she turned away.

He felt suddenly full of guilt. For the first time he realized just how bitterly disappointed she must have been when he had not wanted to go to church with her. And now he had just stated he did not want to disappoint Robbie, but he hadn't said anything about not wanting to disappoint *her.*

He opened his mouth to say something. . .anything, as long as it took her sadness away, but she was already at the door with a murmur about fetching some water, and the moment was gone.

Beth hurriedly grabbed a basin, held it under the tap, and turned on the water. Suddenly she closed her eyes. Art was actually going to church with her!

"Thank You, Lord!"

She had not realized she had spoken out loud until Robbie's voice said loudly, "Stop talking to Jesus and hurry up, Mum. I don't want to be late for Sunday school."

With a stifled laugh, Beth fled. "Like father, like son," she thought as she raced to be ready in time.

The suburban church was large, and the car park was almost full by the time the Smiths arrived. Several people murmured friendly greetings, but Art heard a relieved note in Beth's voice when she was hailed by a young couple carrying a baby basket.

As always, Art had steeled himself for the curious looks he usually received, but as Beth quickly introduced Bob and Janet Lane, he saw nothing but enthusiasm in their two beaming faces.

"It's good to meet you at last, Art. We've heard so much about you," Bob said with a smile and a firm handshake.

Art threw a glance at Beth. She flushed a little self-consciously but tilted her chin.

Before he could speak, she said hurriedly, "We'd better hurry, it's almost starting time," leaving him to eye her thoughtfully, wondering just what she had said about him to make her blush.

The church service came very close to being a disaster from start to finish. First of all there the church had no ramp and they had difficulty getting the chair up the long steps of the beautiful old building. Fortunately, Bob was there to help, but Beth knew how much Art must be hating the added attention.

Then the church had only old-fashioned pews so that Art had to sit in the aisle, a few rows from the entrance. By his scowl every now and again, Beth knew how conspicuous he was feeling.

To make it worse, the well-meaning minister welcomed him so profusely that Beth squirmed in sympathy for him. Then she was really furious when the insensitive dolt fervently prayed for "our dear brother in the wheelchair." She opened her eyes and looked frantically across at Art just in time to meet his eyes.

Her own widened. He was grinning madly. Then he winked at her, and actually dared to shake his finger at her in admonition for not having her eyes closed during the prayer time. She felt hot color flood her face, and she hurriedly shut her eyes again.

—⁓—

Art's eyes lingered on her for the rest of the prayer. She was more beautiful than ever today. Certainly she looked very different from the last time he'd been in church with her at Jim and Gail's wedding, but she was a delight to behold in her simple, fresh cotton dress.

He had known she would be upset by the minister mentioning him specifically. Glancing up at her in time to catch her worried look had been instinctive. In fact, to his own surprise he had not really minded being mentioned as much as he probably would have. The prayer was so sincere, so earnest. Besides, he needed every prayer available!

Certainly, the way the service had started, Art had expected to feel out of place and uncomfortable. Beth had been pretty embarrassed about having to accept Bob Lane's help, but he had been relieved to be able to "park" near the back of the church where he did not have to endure everyone's eyes.

Even that rather too exuberant welcome had not bothered him too much. At least the guy was not pretending the wheelchair did not exist as so many people did when confronted with it the first time.

He was still staring at Beth when the "amen" was said and she looked up straight at him again. This time she smiled gently with such tenderness in her expression that he turned hurriedly away.

Suddenly he wondered if she prayed for him. And he knew the answer immediately. Of course she did. No doubt she always had. When they had first been married she had tried and tried to get him to read the Bible and pray together with her after the evening meal. If she had but known, he'd inwardly recoiled in horror. Some of his worst memories of his father had been when he had insisted they have "family devotions." It had been anything but "family" and far from "devotion."

A rousing time of song interrupted his thoughts. It was led by an enthusiastic young song leader with an electric guitar. He was helped by an accomplished pianist, a girl playing clarinet, and a gray-haired man on a violin. There was even a drummer behind a small set of drums. An overhead projector threw up the words of each song on a large white screen above the platform.

Art was surprised, and sat up a little straighter. His father's ultra-conservative hair would have stood straight up at this setup!

Art did not know most of the songs, but everyone else seemed to be enjoying singing them with gusto. He glanced at Jacky and Robbie. They were watching everything with wide eyes.

Beth turned her head and caught his eye. He grinned at her again, and she gave him a rather relieved smile back. Then she turned back to sing the words of the current song.

Art found the melody haunting, and a reverent stillness had come over the people as they sang about longing after God as a deer pants for water. Art did not know how a deer felt when it was thirsty, but there had been many times in those days in the hospital burn unit that his tongue and mouth had been very dry, especially after surgery and skin grafts. He didn't think he had ever thirsted for God anything like that, though.

Before he really had time to dwell on it all, they started singing very quietly a song he knew only too well. He had learned it as a boy when he had been forced to go to nearly every meeting at his parents' church. All around him heads were lowered in prayer as they sang softly and reverently. But Art kept his head erect, staring up at the words.

How could the things of earth—like a rotten home life, a broken marriage, a horrible accident, a broken body—possibly become "strangely dim" just by looking into the face of Jesus!

Then they sang the chorus again. Art looked around. Even Robbie knew it and was singing quietly, his feet swinging to and fro. Jacky was sneaking a look at two girls her own age in the seat behind. He saw Beth touch her gently, and she obediently faced the front again.

Then he focused on Beth. As he watched her, she closed her eyes again. Once again, he feasted his eyes on her through the prayer that followed. He saw her nod a couple of times, her lips moving in a silent "amen." Then she gently wiped at her eyes, and he looked quickly away, feeling like an intruder into her deepest feelings about God. To see Beth moved to tears in such a way affected him so deeply he had not a clue what was being said by the song leader as he prayed.

Despite all the problems that her religion had caused in the latter part of their marriage, he had never doubted Beth's belief in God. At times the extent of her commitment to her church had so scared him it had made him angry. At times he had even blamed that commitment for harming their husband-wife relationship, had even, in his most honest moments, acknowledged a tinge of jealousy that she had never seemed as committed to him. And yet he had never had any doubt that she loved him, plain, ordinary Art Smith, at least not until after Robbie was born.

Suddenly, for the first time ever, he wanted to believe like Beth. He wanted so much to believe in a God who really cared. Fear that belief would demand commitment swept over him. He clenched his jaw. This was crazy thinking. Look at how commitment to their church had made his father and mother behave.

But Beth's commitment had not made her like them.

His hands clenched on the hymnbook he had been handed as they entered. Suddenly, for the first time, he saw very clearly the vast difference between his parents' fanatical commitment to their church and Beth's commitment to her God. He realized how stupid he'd been.

His parents' commitment had made them obey every narrow dictate their church imposed on its members. Their commitment to their church had made them rule their only child with a rod of iron.

Beth's commitment was to a loving Heavenly Father, entirely different from the God of anger and retribution he had been taught to fear.

Sure, when they'd first started going out together, he had sneered silently at Beth's attempts to remain pure and holy. "Keeping herself for marriage" had been the way she had put it. The bitter teenager he had been had equated that with the religious rules and regulations his parents had insisted he keep, and against which he had rebelled. At long last he had managed to persuade her differently. But he had always felt a trace of shame that he had only succeeded in seducing her when she had been so upset by her father's death. It had only happened the once. He had seen how stricken with guilt she had been, even more so when they found out she was pregnant.

Over the years, especially as their marriage had deteriorated, one thought had haunted him. Would she ever have married him if that night of loving had never taken place first?

These past months had made him see that her deeper commitment to Christ made her more loving, gave her strength to put up with an unlovable husband. But how *could* God love a man like him? He doubted very much that even the type of God that Beth believed in would accept such a man as he.

———

Beth saw Art's clenched hands and her eyes flew to his face. It was so grim, her heart plunged. She had been thrilled that after so many years, Art was sitting beside her in church again. But if he hated it. . .

"Oh, Lord. . . ," she breathed silently, ". . .please may Your Spirit open his eyes and his heart to Your love. Make Jesus real to him."

Beth had never found out for sure just why Art had become so antagonistic to going to church. She believed it had a lot to do with his parents, but she had never been able to get him to talk much about them. He had really surprised her last night when he had said he had never minded her going, just her insistence that he go also. She still doubted that statement of his. He *had* resented her going, she was sure of it.

When she had wanted to be involved in midweek activities he had been even more resistant, several times informing her sharply not to take for granted that he was her built-in baby-sitter.

She shifted nervously in her seat. Sometimes she had yelled back at him and gone anyway. She tugged at her lower lip with her top teeth.

Rance had pointed her to the scriptures that had told her how displeasing that type of attitude was to God. Through studying the scriptures and prayer, she was still becoming more aware of God's mind on such behavior.

With a start she realized Art had whispered something to her. She looked at him, and he nodded toward Robbie's anxious face.

"Mum," Robbie whispered loudly, "can we go too now?"

Beth glanced around and then felt her face go hot. While she had been deep in memories, some announcement had been made about the children leaving for their junior church.

"They're to go out while we're singing the second verse," Art murmured.

She nodded briefly at Robbie, and avoided his father's amused eyes. Self-consciously she found the number in her own hymnbook as Art pointed to his.

"Mum!"

Beth glanced down at Robbie. He was looking up at her with a scared look on his face. Then he shrank against her and watched the other children moving down the aisle toward the entrance.

She hesitated briefly and then whispered, "You don't have to go out if you don't want to."

She felt Art move suddenly, and she looked down at him. He had a most peculiar look on his face as he watched them.

A small voice whispered loudly, "I want to go, but. . ."

"Would you like me to come with you this first time so you know where to go?"

Jacky was already disappearing with the little girl who had been sitting behind them. A little hand slipped into Beth's. She rolled her eyes at Art and led Robbie out. In a few moments they spotted Bob Lane coming toward them.

"Let me show you where to go, young man," he said softly. He winked at Beth, and with relief she felt Robbie's clinging hand let go and without another look at her he went with Bob.

Art was watching for her return. He gave a relieved smile as she joined him. "Everything okay?" he murmured.

She nodded, joined in singing the last of the hymn, and sat down with considerable relief to enjoy the rest of the service. A large hand reached across and closed on hers. She turned sharply. Art's eyes were soft. Love whelmed up in her for him and she folded her fingers tightly around his. Their eyes clung for a moment, and then Art looked away.

The tenseness had gone from his jaw, and every sense in Beth rose up in thankfulness that he was sitting here beside her, certainly not "all in one piece" but alive and not gone from her forever. And so they sat hand in hand until the end of the service.

Only Jacky chattered excitedly on the way home in the car. Beth glanced several times at Robbie's set expression. She saw that Art had also noticed that something had seriously upset the small boy.

"Well, Robbie, and how did you enjoy your class? Did you make any new friends?" Art caught Beth's concerned eyes as he spoke, and then turned slightly so he could see Robbie's face.

"They were all dumb!" There was a distinct waver in the angry words.

"You're the dumb one," Jacky said haughtily. "My new friend said her brother in your class thought you didn't know nothin'."

Before Art or Beth could speak, Robbie let out a stifled sob, then turned on his sister and shouted, "Well, I'd never heard that dumb old story about that dumb man being let down through that dumb roof before."

"He wasn't dumb, stupid, he was paralyzed like Dad."

Beth and Art looked at each other. Beth opened her mouth in dismay, but Art shook his head slightly at her.

"That's enough, you two." Art's voice was stern. "We've just left church and you shouldn't be speaking to each other like that. Not another word until we get home!"

"That's what Mum always says," grumbled Jacky.

"Jacky, not another word!"

Art had raised his voice, but he managed to control his twitching lips, even when Beth shot a gleam of sheer amusement at him.

She refrained from saying anything until the car was parked in the driveway. "I said exactly the same thing to them their first day back at school after Easter," she murmured for his ears only as she placed his chair next to the car. "In fact," she added thoughtfully, "something had upset Robbie then, and I never did find out what had happened."

"Well, I think that this time we should," Art said quietly.

Both children had bolted for the backyard. Their parents' eyes followed them, and then Beth sighed. "Oh, well, guess I'd better go and see what's upset Robbie. It's a shame. He was so pleased about going."

"Beth. . ." Art paused, searching her face as she turned to him. "I think perhaps I should sort this out."

A shadow touched Beth's eyes. "Art—" she burst out and then bit her lip, her face uncertain.

"I know, love," Art said tenderly, "you don't want him to say anything to hurt me. I think it probably hurts you more now to talk about my being unable to walk than it does me. But if it's about a paralyzed man, I think I'm the expert, don't you?"

Chapter 9

The wheels on the chair made no noise as Art swung down the path to the backyard. He saw no sign of the children but he instinctively knew where they would be.

As he neared the now completed kennel, which Jacky still claimed at times for a cubby house, he heard her shrill voice saying earnestly, "But don't you remember what Uncle Jim said? Jesus can do anything He wants to. If He wants Dad to walk again He'll make him better."

Art froze.

Jacky continued relentlessly. "But, Uncle Jim said we're not to expect God to be like Santa Claus. After all, there must have been lots of cripples like Daddy around that were never made better by Jesus."

Art heard a sudden scuffle. There was a cry from Jacky and then Robbie's furious voice. "Don't you dare call him that. My daddy's not a cripple. He's not. . .he's not. . ."

Jacky burst out of the rough shelter. "He can't walk! He is so too a cripple!" she yelled back over her shoulder, and then froze as she saw her father.

For one horrified moment they stared at each other. She gave a despairing sob and scuttled past him. Before he could do more than open his mouth she was flying toward the house.

He hesitated for a moment, not sure whether to call her back, but the noisy sobs coming from the kennel decided him. He heard Bonnie give a short, soft yelp and knew the dog must be as bewildered as he was.

Beth and Jim had both assured him that the children had apparently accepted what had happened to their father. But now this small replica of himself obviously didn't want a cripple for a father. And who could blame him?

Art remembered only too vividly how he had always hated his own father being so different from his friends' fathers. Too many times his father had ranted and raved at boys he had brought home. Too many times he had shouted at them that they were miserable sinners when they had let a couple of swear words slip out. He would shout Bible verses at them, roaring out that sinners died, that they belonged to the devil and would join him in the fires of hell.

The kids had called his father a weirdo and a religious freak. They had teased Art unmercifully at school, and the older he became the more he had done everything he could to prove to them how irreligious he was himself, that he was nothing like his strange father.

To try and feel accepted, he started swearing more than any of them. As the years progressed he had become more and more rebellious, getting into more and more trouble for fighting, for smoking and drinking.

Then the police had questioned him about some graffiti and vandalism. Fortunately they had never been able to prove anything enough to bring charges. But his parents had not believed his protests of innocence. They had been so shocked that a son of theirs could be in trouble with the police that they had disowned him, kicked him out.

The irony had been that this time he had been completely innocent. But he had been relieved to escape from his parents.

Art took a deep breath. Suddenly he knew what he had to do. He whistled. "Bonnie," he called, "where are you? Come here, girl."

He whistled again, and then the dog bounded out of the shelter and pranced up to him. With relief, Art heard the noisy crying stop.

He patted the dog vigorously and said loudly, "Now, girl, where's that son of mine? I was very interested to hear there was a story at Sunday school about a guy like me who couldn't walk. Do you think he'd tell me about him?"

Bonnie jumped up, putting her paws on his knees. She swiped her wet tongue across his cheek. He tried to dodge her, but she gave a short, sharp bark and gave him another enthusiastic lick on his face.

"Down, ya big slobberer!" Art gave a loud laugh and yelled, "Hey,

Robbie, are you there? Come and rescue me!"

To Art's relief, Robbie slowly appeared. Without any more prompting, Bonnie deserted Art and ran back to Robbie. Then she stopped. Her ears pricked up as a kookaburra chortled nearby, and she suddenly raced away, barking furiously.

Art shook his head. "She's one crazy animal." He grinned at Robbie, carefully pretending not to notice the tearful dirt-stained face. "Mum likes me to keep out of her hair while she gets lunch, so I thought we'd have a few minutes for you to tell me that story you heard today."

Robbie eyed him with a scowl. Then he looked down and kicked his toes against the edge of the cement path.

Art tried again. "Ah, come on mate. I really would like to know what happened to that bloke like me."

Robbie looked up at him with suspicious eyes.

"You see Robbie," Art continued seriously, "I think it might be the story I remember. . ." He took a deep breath and said quickly, "I remember about a cripple. My father told me about it. Only, I haven't ever read it myself, and I'm not sure if I remember properly what happened. Was the man really paralyzed like me?"

Robbie gave one big nod. He took a step closer. "He. . .he'd been paralyzed and couldn't walk for a long, long time and his friends heard about Jesus making. . ." He gulped and continued sadly, "Jesus made lots of people walk again."

A lump lodged in Art's throat at the tears that again whelmed up and spilled over in Robbie's eyes. "Look, Robbie, why don't you climb up here on my knees, let me park this contraption in the shade, and you can tell me all about it."

Robbie looked doubtfully from his father to the chair and back to his face. "Wouldn't that hurt your legs?"

"Well it didn't when your Mum sat on them," Art couldn't resist saying dryly.

Memory flared deep inside him. That day seemed so long ago now. He and Beth had been so close for such a brief time. He winced inwardly. It had been his fault that their intimacy had not continued.

He had withdrawn again, and he knew that had hurt and bewildered Beth. But she had not said another word about it as he'd been sure she would.

"Would. . .wouldn't you like me to push you, Daddy?"

"No thanks, mate. I'm very handy pushing on these wheels now." Art held out his hands. To his utter relief, Robbie came forward and let Art pull him onto his lap. "Hang on tight now."

Art did one of his best wheelie spins and Robbie let out a squeal and grabbed him tighter. Art chuckled, and did it again. Then he had to do it again to head in the right direction. With satisfaction, he noted that Robbie was grinning from ear to ear when they stopped under the poinciana tree.

"I like this spot." Art pulled Robbie into a more comfortable position and hugged him close. "Right, now let's hear this story. I remember something about a paralyzed man whose friends took him to Jesus to see if He would make him walk again. Was that the story?"

Robbie nodded vigorously. "There were lots and lots of people trying to see Jesus, and they couldn't get into the house. So his friends had this great idea about going up on the roof and chopping a hole in it and letting the man down next to Jesus. And they did, and Jesus loved him so much He told him to pick up his bed and walk, and he did."

Robbie paused, and Art waited patiently.

"Well, they thought it was a great idea, but I bet the man who owned the place didn't!" There was disgust in the small voice, and Art controlled his twitching lips with some difficulty.

"Oh, I don't know. The most famous person around was in his house. He was probably enjoying all the fuss," he couldn't resist saying.

Robbie looked up at him doubtfully. "How would you like all that mess in our lounge room?"

Art chuckled, and Robbie grinned back at him.

"Your mum would sure have something to say!" Then, all desire to laugh left Art. "If it meant a man like me could walk again, she wouldn't mind."

"Oh, Daddy, I hate it that you can't walk!"

"It's not exactly fun for me either, mate!"

Robbie sat bolt upright and Art tensed. The words simply flew out of the small boy. "Out at the farm I hated it that you couldn't go down to the sheds again and drive the truck again. And then at the wedding you had to go home and missed all the fun, and I asked and asked Jesus to make you walk again. And at school the kids called you a cripple and I got into trouble for punchin' one on the nose."

Art made a small sound, and alarm flashed across Robbie's face.

"Please don't tell, Mum," he pleaded. "Me an' Jacky decided Mum had enough to worry about without knowing that."

"Mothers have a funny habit of knowing when something like that happens," said Art solemnly, "and sometimes they worry when they think their kids are not telling them things. So, I won't tell her this time, as long as you promise to tell her when you're really upset about something. Okay?"

Robbie studied his father's face. Then he sighed gloomily. "Yeah, I s'pose. And sometimes I hate this big school, and I hate living in a city. I loved being at the farm with Uncle Jim and Grandma and. . . But could I tell you first, Dad? If I get upset again?"

Art's arms tightened, and then he relaxed again. "Yes, of course, Robbie," he said quickly, "but I don't want you to ever wait too long to tell your mother if I'm. . .if I'm not here when you get home from school."

Robbie nodded slowly again.

They were both silent for a moment, and then Art reminded him gently, "You haven't finished telling me why you were so upset today."

Robbie fidgeted with his hands. "When the teacher finished telling the story, I asked her if it was a true one an' really in the Bible," he started slowly. Then he continued very rapidly, the words bursting out of him, "It can't be true, can it Dad? I. . .I told her I didn't believe Jesus did that at all because He didn't make you better at the farm when I asked and asked. . .an'. . .an' a boy laughed. . .and. . ." The rapid words and sad voice died away into a sob.

Art closed his eyes. His arms tightened around the small body nestled so trustingly against him. He had been afraid it had been something like this. All except that bit about. . . His eyes flew open. "Robbie! When did you ask Jesus to make me walk again?"

———

Beth turned away from the kitchen window with a sigh. What on earth was going on under that poinciana tree?

When Jacky had raced past her with tears streaming down her face Beth had nearly gone to help Art then. But she knew Art wanted to be the one to try and sort it out. Then she had seen him successfully coax Robbie out of the rough shelter, so she had decided to leave him to it while she dealt with their daughter instead.

A woebegone Jacky had cried, "Now Daddy will hate me. I called him a. . .a cripple. And he heard!"

Beth had managed to reassure Jacky that her father might be hurt by hearing that, but he would never hate his daughter. When she had returned to her vigil at the window overlooking the backyard, she had been filled with trepidation. Art might never hate his daughter, but she knew how sensitive he was about his disabilities. Then she saw Art had Robbie on his knee and that they seemed engrossed in whatever they were talking about. She breathed a sigh of relief and started preparing a meal.

As her hands flew, preparing a simple salad for lunch, she thought of the church service. Art had actually seemed to enjoy it! Her spirits lifted with hope. It was a start.

She was hesitating about calling them all to lunch when Art wheeled himself into the kitchen. He looked pale and strained. The expression on his face made her go cold.

"Beth. . ."

Robbie bounced in behind Art. "Mum, Dad said we can have half a day off school t'morra!"

He raced through the room, calling to his sister, all animosity forgotten. They heard him start telling Jacky they were to go to the hospital, then the bedroom door slammed behind him.

The small boy's face had been radiant. Beth's eyes went fearfully back to her husband. He had not moved and was watching her intently.

His eyes still held a very intent, considering look, and some other element that for a brief moment she thought was fear.

"Beth," Art said slowly, "I want the three of you to come to the hospital tomorrow afternoon and see some of the. . .er. . .exercises I've been doing at physio."

Instead of feeling the relief she should have, the expression in his face made her begin to tremble. "Why? What does it have to do with what upset Robbie?"

He did not move. Then he said harshly, "He hates thinking I'm a cripple. I need him, you, all of you to see how much mobility I now have."

Very, very carefully, Beth put down the plate in her suddenly nerveless fingers. Then she asked the question that had been troubling her for weeks, the one she had been too anxious, too plain scared of the answer, to ask. "Does this have anything to do with the fact that you were able to be discharged from the hospital without an indwelling catheter, without needing help anymore to go to the bathroom. . .to. . .to. . .?" Her voice faded, and she clutched the side of the table, staring at Art.

"Beth! Don't look like that." Art started toward her, and then stopped abruptly when Robbie raced into the room.

"I'm starving, Mum. Isn't lunch ready yet?"

Beth turned away. Exercising every ounce of self-control she had been learning the past months, she managed to say without a quiver in her voice, "Call Jacky. We'll start as soon as you're all sitting down."

Jacky entered the room slowly and moved reluctantly toward her place at the table, avoiding her father's eyes.

"So, Jacky, are you glad you're going to miss half a day at school tomorrow?"

She looked at her father, and hesitated. "Can I really go, too, Daddy?"

"Well," said Art very seriously, "I really can't imagine this mob going anywhere as a family without the best, most beautiful daughter a bloke like me could ever have, do you?" Then he smiled at her.

Art's smile was full of compassion and tenderness, and sudden love for him burned fiercely in Beth. He always had been a wonderful father.

Jacky gave him a relieved smile, which dimmed a little at his next words.

"However, young lady, because I want you to stay beautiful, I think you should watch what you say in the future, don't you? And the way you say it," he added sternly.

She dropped her head and nodded vigorously. "I'm sorry, Daddy," she whispered.

"Well, that's fine then. Now, whose turn is it to say grace?" Art looked across at Beth. "I think it should be me, don't you?"

Beth's eyes flew wide. She nodded quickly and bowed her head. This was the first time ever that he had voluntarily offered to pray!

There was a pause. Just as she started to look up at him to see if he had changed his mind, Art cleared his throat. His voice was husky but very sincere. "God, we thank You for our family and all Your blessings, especially. . .especially for Mum and this food, amen."

Beth looked up slowly at him. He held her gaze for a brief moment, and then lowered his eyes to his plate.

Robbie had a suppressed air of excitement throughout the short meal. He shared several expressive looks with his father, and Beth could see they shared a secret. Once again, fear clutched its icy hand around her heart.

That night, Beth hardly slept. She spent hours reading her Bible and praying. In the early morning hours she crept silently out to the kitchen for a drink. A crack of light gleamed under Art's bedroom door. She hesitated, but then continued to the kitchen. On her way back to bed a little later, she was relieved to see he had turned his light off.

During the rest of the day he had had plenty of opportunities to tell her what he had meant about "increased mobility," but he had not taken them. In fact he had very obviously managed to avoid being alone with her. He had even refused any help getting ready for bed. Apprehension and that deep-seated fear that she had striven to overcome for weeks had stopped her asking any more questions.

By morning, she was very weary. The spiritual battle had been long and hard before she had at last been able to pray, "I'm so sorry I haven't been trusting You enough. I've been so afraid. Please take that fear away. And. . .and God, I placed Art in your hands long before the accident. Now I again commit him to You. I want what is best for him so that he might come to know You personally and accept that You love him. But, oh loving heavenly Father, I do need him to love me too and to believe that I really do love him."

She was silent for a long moment, and then she gave a low sob of submission. "But I yield our whole relationship and future to Your will for both our lives. Just give me Your strength each day, no matter what!"

In the morning, she and Art hardly spoke to each other before she left the house. He too looked as though he had not slept much, but she had refrained from asking. He had taken one long, hard look at her own face, and turned away without a word.

She had no problem getting a couple of extra hours off work, and Beth picked up two excited children at the arranged time. When they arrived at the physiotherapy department and she saw him, she knew her fears had been justified.

Art would very soon no longer need her, no longer have a reason not to move out again.

He could walk.

Chapter 10

A t first, only Beth saw the tall figure leaning on his walking frame. "I'd forgotten just how tall he is," she thought numbly. "He's even taller than Jim."

Their eyes met across the room. He moved, slowly rolling the walking frame forward on its wheels. Without losing eye contact, he lifted one leg, stiffly, awkwardly, moved it forward. Then he lifted his other leg, took another small step. Then he straightened and stood still.

Across the room their eyes met and clung.

Beth began to tremble. She forced her eyes to break contact and looked down at the children. Then, helplessly, her gaze flew back to Art.

He watched her for a moment longer. He was very pale. Then his eyes drifted to the two children, one each side of her. Even from that distance, she could see how his strong features softened.

The frame moved again, followed by the slow awkward movement of two legs learning to walk again. The movement caught the children's attention.

"Wow, Dad!" Jacky exclaimed out loud.

Robbie looked up at his mother, his eyes dancing. "Did ya see, Mum? Did ya'?" He let go of her hand and raced toward Art. "Dad!" he yelled, and several heads swung towards him. "You *are* walking like ya said. Jesus *is* making ya better!"

A faint tinge of color touched Art's cheeks, but he merely grinned at Robbie. Then his eyes collided with Beth's again and all amusement was gone.

As usual, not to be left behind, Jacky bounded across the room. Beth followed slowly, almost reluctantly.

For weeks now, she had been suspicious. All she had read about paraplegics in the early days in Sydney had made her wonder and wonder many times since Jim and Gail's wedding. And one part of her had been wonderfully glad for Art. The other part, the utterly selfish part she was bitterly ashamed of, had been tinged with a sadness and fear that had stifled the questions she should have asked.

She forced a smile for the sake of the children. Her chin went up. Her eyes challenged him with the question, *Why didn't you tell me?* But the words remained unspoken because she was so afraid she knew the answer.

"Well, aren't you the clever man?" She knew her voice had a touch of shrillness, and she took a deep breath. "I'm very, very glad, Art," she said steadily and finally knew she was.

Art saw the hurt she failed to hide, and he knew that he should have told her. He had hurt her too much in the past as it was.

"I wanted to surprise you," he muttered, not quite truthfully. They both knew the other reason, but he hoped she heard the apology in his voice.

Beth's smile did not reach her eyes. "Well, you've certainly done that."

"Tell her, Dad!"

Art looked down at Robbie's eager little face. Then he glanced around at the other patients nearby and the couple of physios working with them. A few curious glances were coming their way. He knew the staff had speculated about his insistence that nothing be said to his wife.

He looked back at Beth. "I think we should wait until we're home first, Robbie."

Robbie's face dropped, then it brightened. "Go on, Dad, show us how far you can walk."

Art grinned down at him again. "I'll have you know I've been walking for ages already today on this contraption, and if I'm not mistaken, my chief torturer is about to make me do some more."

He nodded toward a tall woman bearing down on them with a determined gleam in her eye.

"Right, Arthur, this your family?" The woman gave him no chance to do more than nod before she said sharply, "No more delay this time. Over to the parallel bars." She bustled away.

Art hesitated. "This is the hardest bit of all." He looked pleadingly at Beth. "I'm not sure if the children should see this. I only started this new trick a couple of days ago."

She looked from him to the two shining faces. "I don't think they will be content to wait outside now." Her voice was very soft. A gleam of sympathy flashed into her eyes and she added slowly, "You're not likely to fall are you?"

"I certainly don't plan to. But it wouldn't be the first time, or the last."

He saw her frown, but he merely pulled a face and started moving slowly to the other side of the therapy room.

They shouldn't have worried. With a few terse instructions, chairs were produced for the two children. They were sternly admonished not to make a sound, and then the "chief torturer" turned her back on them and started bossing Art around.

Beth watched with her heart in her mouth as Art discarded the walking frame and transferred his hands to the parallel bars. He stood erect, and then swung his legs forward one by one, while pushing down on the bars.

Then Beth knew why he had been exercising with hand dumbbells at home. He'd been building up the muscles in his arms and shoulders for this. Even on his first weekend leave after the wedding, he'd insisted on never missing his exercise regime until that last morning.

Now those muscles bunched with the effort. The physio watched him carefully, but Beth could see he had walked up and down between the bars many times before.

Then Beth saw a male assistant approach them with a pair of short crutches that only came to Art's elbows. She sucked in her breath. Then she let it out as a deep shudder swept through her. She couldn't bear to think of those weeks, those months of pain, the training he must have done even before being allowed onto the walker. No wonder he had so often returned home exhausted. And he had not told her any of it.

She saw the jaw muscles tense in Art's jaw. He directed one piercing glance at Beth and then listened to the instructions from the therapists. Obediently he slowly transferred his weight onto the crutches. He took a slow, unsteady step, and then another and another.

"Good. Excellent." The attendants were beaming.

Beth glanced at the children. They looked up at her with serious faces, and then back at their father as he walked toward them. Slowly, so agonizingly slowly, Art at last reached where Beth was standing, riveted to the spot.

Their eyes met and clung. His were triumphant, but begging for understanding, for. . .for forgiveness. Tears rolled unchecked down Beth's face.

For a moment Art was stunned. Beth was crying. Then she smiled radiantly at him. She brushed at her cheeks impatiently and he felt her lips press firmly on his. A fire leapt through him and he almost lost his grip on his crutches.

"You're walking, Art. You're actually walking!"

Art wanted desperately to reach out and wipe away her tears with the back of his fingers. Her skin always felt like soft satin to touch. But if he let go of his crutches to touch her he would fall in a heap at her feet.

Instead he whispered hoarsely, "Yes, Beth, they tell me not to expect ever to run again. I have to wear a spinal brace, but sometime in the future they think I may even be able to manage without crutches."

He saw the questions flash into her eyes, and he shook his head. "I'll tell you more about it when we get home."

The children chattered with excited voices all the way home, but Art sat silently, feeling absolutely drained. So, Beth knew now. Soon he would have no more excuses to impose on her generosity any longer.

His crutches were in the back of the car beside his wheelchair. He would still need the chair for some time when he had a long distance to travel or when he was too tired for the crutches. The staff had insisted he also take the walking frame, but he hated it and hoped he would not need to use it very much.

Each day now, his muscles were getting stronger. Each day he had less pain. Each day he was walking further.

He had no real reason to stay with Beth any longer. With community health care, he could look after himself. Though he knew she would never admit it, Beth would want him to leave again.

When he had walked out on her, he had been absolutely convinced she would be better off without a man like him. Nothing had changed. He was still his father's son. She and the children would still be better off without him in the long run. While he had needed her help in basic ways, he had been able to convince himself he could stay. But now. . .

Neither Beth nor Art spoke directly to each other until they were safely inside and the children had run out to Bonnie to play. Beth busied herself making a cup of tea.

Art watched her swift movements and then said, "Beth, did you know that Robbie had asked. . ." He paused, and then said stiffly, "Did you know Robbie asked Jesus to make me walk again?"

"Yes, of course," Beth said quietly, her face turned away as she searched for a new packet of biscuits. "We've all been praying God would heal you."

Art was silent. He should have known of course. For these Bible-believing Stevenses, praying for him would have been second nature.

He had been confused ever since talking to his son. Could he dare believe that God cared enough about him to answer their prayers, when he'd never even prayed for himself? He shook his head bitterly. Certainly the revengeful, fearful God he'd been brought up to believe in would never do such a thing as heal a sinner like him.

But what if He had? That thought had haunted Art every moment since talking to Robbie.

Beth poured the boiling water into the teapot and carried it across to the table. Still without looking at him, she placed a plate of chocolate biscuits on the table.

Art cleared his throat. "But did you know that the weekend we were at the farm *Robbie* made a very special, very earnest plea to Jesus to make me walk again because he hated having a father that was. . ." His voice cracked. He swallowed, clenching his hands on his lap, avoiding

Beth's eyes. "Robbie hated having a father who was crippled."

"Oh, Art!"

He held up a hand. "That's not all." He was silent for a while. Then at last he shook his head, still trying to come to grips with it himself. "It was no doubt sheer coincidence, but. . ." He paused again, and looked directly at Beth. "Do you remember that Easter Sunday morning at the farm when I fell off the bed?"

Beth frowned, and then nodded.

"I had a lot of pain going home in the car." Beth's eyes widened in distress, and he continued rapidly, "That's one reason I didn't move around and stop that pressure area from getting a blister. It hurt too much."

Beth's eyes flashed, but he said quickly, "I know, I know. Served me right for being so independent. But that's why I insisted on returning to the hospital that night. And at the hospital the nurses ripped into me too about being too independent. The doctor. . ."

Art took a deep breath, "The doctor couldn't at first believe that the paralysis in my legs allowed me to feel as much pain as I told him I had in them. Even. . .even that small tear in my skin was stinging by the time we reached home that day. I think the doc may have been wondering if I was just trying to trick him into giving me more drugs. He thought he had a drug addict on his hands."

"But you'd never take many painkillers because you didn't want to become one," Beth burst out.

"Fortunately, that's what the nursing staff managed to convince him. So, he ended up not only ordering the pain injections but a whole new set of tests as well."

The horrible memory of another reason why he had often refused painkillers made Art swallow. He'd never wanted to risk being tempted again to. . . Before he told her any more of this last incident, should he tell her after all this time about that other episode?

His hesitation was only brief. He had made the decision during the night not to keep anything from Beth ever again, no matter how it made her feel about him. She had a right to know what a miserable, weak coward she was married to before he told her anymore.

"Beth, did Gail ever talk to you about the first time she ever met me?"

Impatience filled Beth's face. "What does that matter now? What kind of tests did the doctor order?"

He ignored her last question. "Unfortunately it matters quite a lot. It explains why I've been so fanatical about tablets."

Beth's clear gaze became puzzled.

"You knew that the staff at the hospital in Sydney had been very worried about my increasing depression?" he asked quickly in an expressionless voice.

Beth nodded. "That's why Jean Drew wrote to Gail asking her to visit you. They thought you were still devastated about the death of her family in the accident, that it was preying on your mind."

Art hesitated again, and then he shrugged. In a clipped voice he said, "They were only partly right. They were right about the depression though. What nobody else knows, except Gail, is that I was so depressed that for a long time I'd only pretended to swallow tablets. I managed to hide enough sedatives and painkillers so I could take them all in one go and end it all. Gail arrived the very day I'd decided I had enough tablets to do it that night. She. . .she saved my life."

For a moment, Beth merely stared at him. He looked grimly back at her and he knew when she suddenly understood.

He had planned to overdose. To kill himself.

Her face went dead white. She stood up, then swayed so that he thought she was about to faint.

"Oh, Beth, I'm so sorry," he groaned, "I just couldn't see any future, any reason to live anymore. Maybe I even went a bit crazy there for a while. I loved you so much, and I couldn't bear what my being a paraplegic would mean to you. The way you refused to stop visiting me in the hospital made me know you would never agree to me living anywhere except with you and the kids. You didn't even go home to them when they were so sick with chicken pox. And I'd already ruined your life enough."

Beth sank back into her chair. Not once did she take her eyes off him. All along she had known there was something. Something to do with Gail. Something more than the fact that he had not admitted his part in pulling her from the wrecked car.

But not this. Never had she dreamed this.

A swift tide of fury surged through her. She felt its heat sweep into her face. "Art, you were so depressed you nearly committed suicide almost ten months ago, and you're just telling me about it now?"

For a moment her anger seemed to confuse him. Before he could speak she jumped up. Hurt and anger swamped her as it never had before, even in the darkest days of their marriage.

"How dare you, Arthur Canley-Smith!" she heard herself shouting at him. "How dare you not tell me something so important! How dare you make decisions for me like that!"

Her voice choked on a sob. Then the sheer amazement in his face spurred her on. "How dare you not tell me you could walk again! How dare you! How dare you not even tell me when you lost your job! How dare you think I'm such a weak wimp I couldn't be told the most important things of all! And how dare you think I believe for one moment that it was love for me that made you not want to live anymore! What kind of love is that? Don't you know your doing such a thing would have destroyed me too?"

Art's face paled. He seemed to shrink back in his wheelchair for a moment. Then he straightened as though recovering from a blow. The resignation and acceptance of her fury showed in his face.

Suddenly she was aware that the two children were standing in the doorway staring at her with frightened faces. Absolute horror swept through Beth. She had lost her temper. She was yelling at Art again, screaming at him as she had vowed to God she never would ever again.

Defeated, she sank back into her chair with a groan and covered her face with her shaking hands. "Oh, God," she groaned out loud, "I'm so sorry."

There was silence for endless moments. No one moved.

Then the loud peal of the front doorbell rang through the house.

Beth jumped. Slowly she raised her head and looked from Art to the children and back again. The children had crept to stand each side of Art. They were close to tears, and clutched at their father. He put an arm around each small body and drew them closer. Suddenly she felt excluded, outside their circle of love.

"I'm sorry. . .I'm sorry I lost my temper. I'm so sorry I yelled," she gasped between quivering lips.

Inwardly her heart was still crying out, "Oh, Lord, forgive me! I've failed You again. Help me!"

The urgent summons of the doorbell rang again. Like an old woman, Beth pushed herself to her feet and made her trembling way toward the front door. She rested her head against the door for a moment, desperately trying to pull herself together.

The verse of scripture she had memorized and repeated to herself over and over the past eighteen months flashed through her mind. The ninth verse of the first chapter of the first letter of John, the apostle of love. If she acknowledged her sin God was faithful and just and would forgive her and cleanse her.

Deep in her soul, Beth clung to the promise, silently pleading for His mercy once again, asking for added strength, for wisdom.

The bell peeled briefly again, and Beth straightened. Very quickly would she get rid of whoever was there. She knew Art had still more to tell her.

What tests had been done? Why could he now walk?

Above all, what did he intend to do now? Had she killed his love? Was he prepared to give their marriage another chance?

Chapter 11

B eth stared blankly at the elderly woman who had given up and was already halfway down the ramp on her way out. "Can I help you?" she called in a husky voice.

The woman clutched at the rail. She turned and stared at Beth, before slowly making her way back. Beth frowned. She did not think she had ever seen this woman before, but there was something familiar about her.

As the woman came closer, Beth saw she was not as elderly as she had first thought. She was dressed all in black. Her clothes were clean and well pressed, but they had been carefully patched and mended in several places. Her hair was golden with only a smattering of gray, but pulled very tightly back and piled into a severe bun on the top of her head. It was her face, however, that concerned Beth the most. It was very pale and strained, deep lines edging each side of her thin-lipped mouth.

She looked at Beth with an arrogant glint in her faded blue eyes. "You took so long to answer the door, I thought nobody was home." The woman's voice was loud and censorious.

Beth was in no mood to be bothered by this strange woman who was probably only peddling goods or her own brand of religion. Before she could say she was not interested, the woman spoke again. "How are you, Mrs. Beth Canley-Smith?"

Beth frowned again. That mocking voice was also familiar. She knew this woman from somewhere. Then she remembered and stood frozen in shock and dismay. She had only met her once before, for a very brief time, at least eight years ago.

"Ah, so you do remember your mother-in-law at last, I see." Art's mother scowled when Beth continued to stare at her blankly. "Well, aren't you going to invite me in?"

Beth stiffened. "After the way you treated your son, and then me, why should I invite you into my home, Mrs. Smith?"

"Canley-Smith!" the woman spat at her. "Canley was my maiden name and don't you forget it!"

Beth's brain was clearing and she was thinking rapidly. She sent up another heartfelt prayer for wisdom. Art's parents had hurt him dreadfully. Since they had kicked him out when he was sixteen and disowned him, as far as she knew he had only seen them the once since.

"You didn't answer my question," Beth said after staring steadily at her for a long moment.

A faint tinge of color touched the woman's cheekbones. "Should I give you a reason for wanting to see my own son, especially as you neglected to tell me that the poor dear is now an invalid in a wheelchair?"

Beth heard the tell-tale squeak of rubber wheels on the tiled entrance behind her. She stood her ground and raised her voice. "Mrs. Canley-Smith, your son would never be a poor anything, no matter what his physical disability."

The tire sounds stopped. She heard a swiftly indrawn breath. She continued to stare coldly at Art's mother. "And yes, you must have a very good reason to come anywhere near us after all the years you've forgotten your son's existence. What do you want, Mrs. Smith? And where's your husband? Is he waiting in the car? Isn't he willing to be contaminated by such sinners as he once told us we were?"

Suddenly all the defiance went out of the older woman. Her shoulders sagged and her eyes dropped. "No," she muttered, "Art's father is not waiting for me." After a long pause she looked back up at Beth with a bleak look in her eyes. "He's gone," she said simply.

Beth stared at her. Did she mean he had deserted her? A movement beside her made her eyes meet Art's. Slowly she moved out of his way.

"Arthur? Oh, Arthur!" The woman started forward then stopped uncertainly.

Beth did not think she had ever seen such a forbidding expression on her husband's face.

He stared at the woman, realizing he had always felt rather sorry for her. She had also suffered at the hands of his father. Once he had blamed her as much as his father for the beatings, the hard work, the more subtle psychological punishments, the hours and hours of being forced to memorize scripture verses, the hypocrisy of their whole lifestyle. He understood now that she had been as much a victim of his father's religious fanaticism as himself.

"Hello, Mother," he said quietly, "what's happened to Father?"

A solitary tear slipped down the lined face. Art was startled. He never remembered seeing her cry before. He went rigid, knowing before she spoke what had brought her here.

"He's gone to be with the Lord, Arthur."

Art closed his eyes. He heard Beth give a soft exclamation. Her hand touched him on the shoulder. He reached up and clasped her hand tightly, drawing her closer, trying to banish the coldness that swept through him.

"I think we'd better go inside, Art," Beth said in a choked voice. "Please come inside, Mrs. Smi—Mrs. Canley-Smith."

Art hesitated briefly, and then spun around and led the way into the lounge room.

Beth saw her mother-in-law look around at the cheap, secondhand furniture. Some had been supplied with the house, others she had carefully chosen after deciding not to move all their own things from the house in Dalby. Mrs. Canley-Smith very carefully sat herself down on the only comfortable lounge chair. Her eyes flew to the two, curious-eyed children staring at her.

"You must be Jacqueline and Robert." There was no softening in the harsh voice. "Hasn't your mother taught you it's rude to stare?"

Beth managed to bite back the hot words that flew to her lips. These were this woman's only grandchildren. She looked gratefully at Art as he moved forward between his mother and the children.

"It's all right, kids," he said gently. "What about leaving us to talk to. . .to this lady. I'm sure you've got plenty of things you could be doing."

He hesitated as the children retreated. Then he looked up at Beth pleadingly before turning to his mother. "Would you like a cup of tea or a cool drink?"

The woman relaxed slightly and to Beth's relief she said graciously, "No thank you, Arthur. I can't stay very long as I have a train to catch."

"When did Father die?"

Beth looked at Art. His voice was expressionless, but his body was tense.

His mother hesitated then said rapidly, "He died from cancer four weeks ago today."

Art didn't move, and anger swelled in Beth toward this woman and her husband who had denied the man she loved all the joy of belonging to a family.

"And you have only just got around to telling us?" she asked ferociously.

The woman looked disdainfully at Beth. "I tried ringing you at your house in Dalby. All they could tell me was that you were living here in Brisbane."

"And of course, you'd conveniently forgotten where my mother and brother lived," Beth condemned.

"It doesn't matter, Beth."

Beth subsided at Art's toneless voice. Then she glanced at him as he added quietly, "Why have you come now, Mother?"

An indignant light sprang into the pale eyes. "To tell you about the money, of course. Why on earth such a godly man as your father would do such a thing, I'll never understand! Such an ungrateful, wicked son as he had!"

They stared at her blankly, and then at each other.

"What money?" Art asked tersely at last, ignoring her contempt as he had learned to many years ago.

"Your father left you one-third of his estate."

Pity stirred in Beth. On her only visit to their property, the poverty that Art's parents lived in had been sadly obvious. Probably his mother needed his inheritance even to help with funeral and hospital expenses.

Art looked stunned. "My father remembered me in his will?"

His mother sniffed. "Your father knew what was fitting and proper. He left equal amounts of all his money to our church, his wife, and his only son. As soon as he found out that nothing more could be done for his cancer, he even sold the farm. Set things up real good for me so I wouldn't have to worry now, he did."

"He sold the farm?"

There was so much pain in Art's voice, Beth moved to stand beside him. She knew that the only thing he had ever regretted leaving was the small farming property that had been in his father's family for generations.

His mother nodded eagerly. "And a nice price he got for it, too. Sold just at the right time."

"So the farm's gone." Beth heard the sadness in Art's voice and face. "My great-grandfather pioneered that country."

Mrs. Canley-Smith pulled back her worn cardigan and glanced at her watch. "My goodness, I'm late. I'm going to have to waste money on a taxi," she said in a vexed voice. "Call me a taxi, Beth," she commanded imperiously as she started to climb to her feet.

Beth hardly noticed. Her eyes were riveted on the watch. In sharp contrast to the poverty-stricken appearance of the clothes surrounding it, the gold and diamonds sparkled and gleamed. Her gaze swung to Art. He too was staring at it.

His eyes narrowed, and then he scowled. "How much money is there?" he asked abruptly.

A look of disgust crossed his mother's face. "That is not a very genteel thing to ask me, Arthur." She fumbled in her worn old handbag and handed him an envelope. "This is a copy of your father's will and the address of his solicitor. He said he'd sort it out with you."

"How much?" he demanded.

His mother drew herself up. "Money! That's all you care about, isn't it? We lived very frugally as good Christians should. Your father made good investments. It's so sad that a third of it will now no doubt be sadly wasted."

"Mother, how much money did Father leave?"

Grudgingly she answered, "Your share comes exactly to five hundred and five."

Beth saw Art relax. In a gentler tone he said, "You'll need that for Dad's medical expenses, Mother."

She stared at him blankly. "Need it for. . .why on earth do I need your thousands when I have my own?"

Beth froze. Art just stared at his mother.

"Why are you looking at me like that?" she said sharply. Then she looked at her ostentatious, diamond-studded watch again. She groaned. "Beth, you haven't rung for that taxi!"

Art suddenly spun his chair around. He dialed, then barked a request for a taxi into the phone, before slamming it down again.

"It'll be here in a couple of minutes. You'd better wait outside," he said in a furious voice. Without looking at his mother again he pushed himself toward the doorway.

His mother frowned and then shrugged as though his behavior completely bewildered her. "I never could understand that boy," she muttered. "He was born rebellious and impossible to control."

"I'm glad about that," Beth was goaded into saying, "or he would have turned out as unloving and hard as his parents."

His mother looked shocked. "How dare you speak to me like that!"

Beth was trembling, worried about Art. "Good-bye, Mrs. Canley-Smith," she said and took the woman firmly by the arm.

The woman pulled her arm away. "Well! After all the trouble I've gone to finding Arthur for those solicitors, that's all the thanks I get?"

"Yes."

Beth was in no mood to be anything but honest. So this woman, who had only ever cared for her religion and her husband, had only come today after all because the solicitors had somehow persuaded her to. Probably threatened to charge her the earth if they had to do it.

The only thing Beth felt was immense relief when Art's mother gave her a look of outrage and stormed her way out of the house. Beth followed her and tensed as the woman paused at the bottom of the ramp.

"You have shown absolutely no reason for me to show you any

consideration," the woman said self-righteously, "but as a good Christian I should tell you that I'm catching the train to Sydney where I'm flying to England to our church's headquarters. I intend to stay in their special guest house for an unlimited period, and I don't know when I'll return, if ever." Then the taxi pulled to a stop and without another word she rushed toward it.

Before it had moved away with its customer, Beth turned and hurried inside. Poor Art. How would he handle this last and hopefully final contact with his mother and father?

As she joined him, he lifted a dazed, pale face from the sheets of paper in his hands.

"It's true. Five hundred and five thousand dollars. My. . .my old man was a millionaire, and they always dressed and lived like paupers."

"I don't care if he was a billionaire, your parents were poverty-stricken in everything that really matters!"

He stared at her and then back to the papers. After a long moment he said in a voice that shook, "Beth, do you realize this means I can now provide for us very adequately? We can pay off the rest of the mortgage on our house. There are all kinds of ways we can use this to produce a regular income."

Hope died in Beth. Now he no longer needed her to look after him. He could set up his own home, employ someone to look after his needs.

"Has that nasty lady gone?"

Beth saw Art force a smile at the two wary faces peering around the doorway. "Yes, she's gone."

Pulling herself together as much as someone could who felt as though a bulldozer had rolled over her for several hours, Beth said tightly, "And gone for good, apparently. She told me she was on her way to Sydney to catch a plane to England. I don't think we'll see her again for a long, long time, if ever."

"To England! She hardly ever left the farm except to go to church!"

"Oh, she's going to church all right," Beth said dryly, "in England."

Art stared at her blankly, then he looked back at the children.

"Are. . . ," Jacky said in a small voice, "are you still mad at Daddy, Mum?"

Beth drew in a deep breath. "I'm very sorry I shouted at your father, but yes, I'm afraid I'm still angry with him."

"Mum! Are ya mad at him for not telling us Jesus made him walk again?" There was horror in Robbie's voice.

"I hadn't finished telling her about all that, Robbie," Art intervened rapidly. "And your mother is angry because there are quite a lot of things I haven't told her that she had a right to know a long time ago. And I'm very sorry about that."

He was looking at Beth as he spoke. His head was up. He was still pale, but his chin was thrust out and a very determined gleam filled his eyes.

"Right," he said, "we're going to settle this once and for all. Out, kids." They didn't move, and his face softened as he looked swiftly at them. "It's going to be okay. Your mother and I apparently love each other enough to become friends again."

Silence filled the room for some time after the children had reluctantly disappeared.

"Do we, Art?" whispered Beth at last. "Do we really love each other enough? Can you really love me after all that's happened?"

Chapter 12

B eth couldn't believe that he still loved her. And who could blame him if he didn't?

Art stared at Beth for a long moment. Then he looked down at the bunch of papers now screwed up in his tight fist. He started smoothing them out automatically, not really thinking about what he was doing. Then he tossed them carelessly onto the table beside him.

"Beth, what did you mean when you said that if I had killed myself I would have destroyed you as well?"

Anguish flashed across her face. The eyes darkened to deep pools of blue filled with pain and. . .and yes, love. Suddenly he realized how incredibly stupid he had been. As stupid as his parents. They'd read the same Bible the Stevenses had, but they had never really lived by its teachings. The Stevens family read the Bible, saw God as Jesus revealed Him, and loved. They loved him. Beth loved him.

Then Beth's chin went up, and she glared right back.

He had always admired Beth's courage. That day he had at last yielded to her pleas and taken her to meet his mother and father, he had admired the way she had faced up to that strange, savage man's fury. She had been so innocent and so shocked at how anyone who read their Bible and went to church could behave the way his parents had that day.

That reaction of hers had always stopped him from telling her the worst of the treatment he had received at their hands. He had doubted then that she would believe him. Now he had doubted how much she cared for him. He had sadly misjudged her. Beth had obviously matured, had grown up.

"I meant exactly what I said, Art," Beth said clearly. "I had never ceased praying for you since that first dreadful week after you disappeared. When you were in the hospital, God was still dealing with me, dealing with my guilt."

Art's lips tightened. "Your guilt? Do you mean your guilt for ever marrying an unbeliever? What on earth are you talking about?"

Beth wrapped her arms around herself and moved away. Her voice became husky. "I blame myself for the fact that you had that dreadful accident. If I had not made your life so intolerable at home, you would never have left the way you did. I could hardly bear the pain and suffering you were going through. If you had died when you said you were planning to, I'm not sure if my faith in God would have been strong enough then for me to have survived." A shudder shook her.

Art was appalled. "Beth, it wasn't your fault that I deserted you!"

She swung around. "Wasn't it?" she said sadly. "There was certainly no love or peace at home for you to want to stay. There wasn't even a clean house and kids that were disciplined properly. And your wife was nothing but a spoiled, nagging brat, who forgot to show you, let alone tell you, how much she loved you." Her lips trembled, and she choked back a sob. "I'm so sorry I killed your love for me, Art."

"Killed my love for—No!" Art stared at her in absolute amazement. "You really think I left because I stopped loving you?"

Beth looked at him from anguish-filled eyes.

"Beth, I left because I hit you! I loved you so much and yet I still hit you!"

She stared back at him in surprise. Then she frowned. "But you never hit me, Art."

He stared at her. Speechless.

Her expression suddenly cleared, "Oh, you mean that last night when I fell and hit my face," she said dismissively. "You'd been drinking. You did give me a fright. It really jolted me into realizing how far we had both sunk. But I realized very quickly how much I had goaded you into losing your temper, especially when you were so worried about losing your job."

Art made a queer sound.

Swift comprehension leaped into Beth's face. "That's why you left? Because you thought you'd hit me?"

Art nodded grimly. "And because I thought I must be like my father after all, no matter how much I'd tried to convince myself otherwise."

"Your father?"

"When my father lost his temper he lashed out at me—physically —and at Mum too, although he stopped that when she threatened to report him to the leaders of their church—or sect, cult, whatever you like to call it. It's certainly not much like your church. But even the leaders drew the line at bashing their wives, although they believed very much if you spared the rod you spoiled the child, even if it meant a few broken bones here and there."

"Broken bones! Art! You never told me your father abused you to that extent!"

"Oh, believe me, Beth," Art said grimly, "I found out there are even worse things than bruised arms, legs, back, and broken ribs from being sent flying over a log. There's distorting the truth and being made to feel from birth that if you don't believe as you should, you're only trash, completely unlovable and of no use to anyone."

Beth stared at him in absolute horror. She had always known that Art had not been able to trust people easily, had always been inclined to downplay any of his own achievements. Never had she dreamed. . . . A groan burst from her lips.

Art didn't even glance at her. Now the words had started they spilled out of him in a torrent. "I had practically no contact with any-one outside our church who didn't believe what they taught. It was forbidden. I only started to realize how cowed and brainwashed the other kids and myself were when I went to a public school for the first time. The best thing my mother ever did for me was insist that she could not teach me at home past primary level, that I had a good brain and I had to go to high school in town. I've often wondered how she convinced my father, as well as the church leaders.

"Then I stayed with your family a couple of times. You were all pretty religious too. I could somehow accept sinners being different. I'd been warned about that. But your love for each other, and your lifestyle, really hit home to me that our way of living was far from being normal. So I rebelled in a big way. By that time I was getting big enough to threaten to hit my father back if he beat me again. Plenty of people, church leaders, teachers, dubbed me uncontrollable. After a couple of years Father and Mother kicked me out. Made quite a ceremony of disowning me."

Beth thought of the first time she had met the scared, defiant teenager. Her face filled with sadness. "That was about the time Jim became friendly with you, wasn't it? He wouldn't tell me much about the trouble you'd been in."

The angry, hazel eyes softened. His face became filled with tender memories. "Yeah. I'd never known anyone like him before. Never had a friend like him before. He's still the most loyal bloke I've ever met. He took me home with him. Your Mum and Dad. . ."

Art's voice choked and he stopped.

After a brief moment, Beth said shakily "Mum told me last year that Dad had told her once the only thing wrong with you was that you needed to be convinced you were lovable."

Art looked at her sadly. "He was a great bloke, your Dad. I was always so thankful Jim didn't mind sharing him with me, letting your parents almost adopt me. I think it probably saved me from serious problems with the police.

"I so envied Jim his family. And then. . .then he had a sister who was boarding in town going to high school. She was the sweetest, most beautiful girl I ever imagined existed. And she actually thought I was wonderful. Actually convinced me for a while that I was worth something. Actually loved me enough for me to dare risk marrying her."

His face became bleak again. "The only thing that worried me more than anything was that she was also very religious."

Beth gave a small exclamation, and he grinned wryly. "Oh, I knew from the start that Jim wasn't real happy about the idea of me as a brother-in-law, even through we were good mates. Remember, he tried to tell us to wait, that we were too young, had too different outlooks on life. But we couldn't wait, could we? After the first few years, though, I realized he was right."

Art swallowed. "Your being so religious and different didn't seem to matter quite so much until after we were married and started having children. But in the back of my mind, I've always known I was like my father, temperament wise. I was scared stiff that if I allowed myself to be sucked into religion again, I'd become even more like my father.

"Not long before Robbie was born I found myself becoming real interested and curious about the God you talked so much about. It scared me and I backed off. Okay, the God you worshipped did seem different from the hellfire and brimstone type of revengeful God I'd been taught about, but I was absolutely terrified if I got involved even with your brand of religion, eventually I'd become as bigoted and narrow, even fanatical about it all as my father was."

He stopped and looked away from Beth's intent gaze. It was a while before he said wearily, "And after. . .after Robbie was born things between us just became worse."

Beth didn't move. The pain swept over her in waves.

He turned back to her at last. The anguish is his eyes was unbearable. A heartfelt prayer for the right words swept through Beth. She moved slowly closer and slipped down onto the chair near him. "After Robbie was born, I let being a mother and being involved at church get all out of balance with being a wife."

"And I was getting more work his first couple of years than I could handle. I was hardly home," Art said sadly. "We just drifted apart."

Beth looked down at her hands. "I. . .I thought you were accepting more hours because you didn't want to be with me and the kids as much," she faltered. "I also knew my faith wasn't what it used to be, and I. . ."

"And you blamed that on me."

Beth looked up. Art had a strange look on his face.

"No," she said sadly, "not entirely. We had been such good friends. We loved each other. We enjoyed doing things together. But all through our marriage, I found that what had been the most important thing in my life until I met you, my commitment to Christ, I couldn't share with you like I wanted to."

Beth hesitated, not sure if she was doing the right thing by putting it into words. "Please try and understand, Art. I. . .I don't want to offend you, or upset you. But no matter what a good friend and person you were, as a Christian, I was disobeying a Biblical principle when I married you. Jim has always loved you, but he was right to be worried. The scriptures make it very plain. The way the old translation of the Bible puts it is that I became 'yoked' together with someone who wasn't a Christian. It. . .it just doesn't work. Then I made it all so much worse by trying to nag you into becoming a Christian *after* we were married. Another Biblical principle blown!"

Art scowled, and she added swiftly, "I only realized after those counselling sessions with Rance Telford, that all through our marriage I'd been trying not to feel guilty because I'd been disobedient. So I blamed myself more than anything."

"I knew that, Beth."

Beth stared at him. "You. . .you knew. . .?"

Art snorted. "Of course I knew you felt guilty about marrying someone who said he didn't believe any of that. . .I think 'that garbage' was the word I used at times."

Brief, ironic amusement lit his eyes briefly. "Why do you think I went to church with you so much in the earlier years? But after I had a son who could become like his father and his grandfather, that was it. I just couldn't risk going anymore. Or that's what I told myself," he added after a slight pause.

"Art! You're nothing like your father!"

"Aren't I? I look like him. I have a temper like him. And Robbie looks just like I did at the same age." Then he stopped. A smile tilted his lips. "Except that I only realized yesterday that in one way Robbie's more like his mother. He actually believes in miracles!"

Speechless, Beth stared at him. Of course she believed that God was a God of miracles. The Creator God could do what He wanted whenever and however. She dismissed that thought matter-of-factly, but was astounded by the rest of his statement. Art was actually afraid of becoming like that hard, cruel man who had been his father.

"Art Canley-Smith, you're nothing like your father! If anything, you even look more like your mother! Not that I'm too sure after today that's much of a compliment!"

Art scowled at her. "Mother was far more rational than him. Besides, everyone used to tell me I was the dead image of my old man."

"That frown is exactly like your mother's was a little while ago!" she said triumphantly. "I bet the people who told you that were only toadying to your father."

Art became thoughtful. "Well, I do remember that it was the people at their church. It used to embarrass me when I was a kid. There were a couple of old ducks who always ooohed and aaahed over my curly blond hair."

"Your hair," Beth said solemnly, suddenly trying hard not to smile. "They told you it was just like your father's? Did you by any chance notice your mother's hair today?"

Dawning comprehension filled Art's face. "They were both blonds," he muttered.

All desire to laugh left Beth. She tugged at her own fair hair. "So are we, Art. Both of us. But I don't think that outward appearances matter very much. Neither do our basic natures."

She hesitated, but then she looked him straight in the eye and said firmly, "Christ can transform people into His own image when they trust Him as their Savior and obey Him as their Lord. I know He's still changing me all the time! I don't believe that anyone has an excuse because of inherited genes, or even their upbringing. Sure, the way we're brought up has a tremendous impact. It can leave us with difficult wounds to be healed. But we have to answer individually to God. Even if you and Robbie are like your father in nature, there's no way either of you need behave anything like your father if you belong to Jesus."

The back screen door slammed. Art was still staring at Beth, an arrested, intent look on his face as Robbie raced into the room. Then he looked sharply at the small boy.

"When's tea, Mum? Aren't ya finished talkin' yet, Dad?"

Beth's heart ached as she watched Art studying Robbie intently for a long moment.

"No, we aren't finished yet," Art said huskily at last, and then added in a much stronger voice, "now scat!"

Robbie looked with disgust from one parent to the other. Then he turned away, but they heard him mutter, "Oh, boy! You guys sure can talk!"

Beth suddenly knew that until now, Robbie had been wrong. They had not really talked like this before in the whole of their marriage. Too many times, all they had wanted to do was score points off each other.

Regret filled her. They had ended up being alienated, both so lonely. When they could have remained best friends, able to comfort and nurture each other, she had sought friendship at church, and he with his mates.

Reluctantly she stood up. "I'd better start tea, I suppose."

Art reached out and grabbed her hand. "Not yet, I still haven't told you about how come I'm walking. And that son of ours will be satisfied with nothing less than a full account."

Beth subsided. "Robbie prayed, and God answered a small boy's prayer in His own way," she said simply. "I just thought it must have been gradually happening."

Art stared at her, a look of disbelief on his face. Then he shook his head in wonder. "It's really that simple for you, isn't it?"

She smiled gently at him, and at last he looked away from her direct gaze.

"Well, I'm not sure whether it was God's direct intervention or not," he muttered at last. Then in a stronger voice he said, "However, my starting to walk did not happen gradually." He paused, and added thoughtfully, "That's the strange thing."

Art ran his free hand through the curly blond hair only slightly darker than his small replica's. "I've been trying to convince myself. . . It *has* to be a coincidence."

"A coincidence?"

"Robbie asked Jesus to make me walk again, and hey presto, the very next day I have feeling in my legs," he said abruptly.

Beth had been walking closer and closer with Jesus the past months. Immediately she knew this was no coincidence. She closed her eyes tightly, her whole being welling up in thanks and praise. When she opened her eyes again, she felt the dampness on her lashes.

Art studied Beth's reaction intently. He saw her lips move silently. Then she opened brilliant, moistened eyes and looked at him. Her face was radiant.

Art swallowed. It couldn't be! Beth and Robbie had to be wrong. The God he knew about was more likely to punish a sinner than do a miracle for one!

"Don't you ever dare doubt again that God loves you, Art," Beth whispered.

His lips were suddenly dry. He moistened them and said hoarsely, "The doctors said they can't be certain, but they think that the fall at the farm must have jolted something in my back that was pressing on the spinal cord."

A slight smile tilted Beth's lips.

He added rapidly, a little desperately, "You know that the scans always showed that there was a fractured disc. I was immobilized all those months while the burns were healing. The fracture did seem to have healed over, but they thought there must be permanent damage of the spinal cord when I still didn't have sensation. Now, they don't seem to know what to think, but whatever was pressing on the spinal cord has been easing off."

"It doesn't really matter the hows and whys," Beth said softly. Her smile was the most beautiful he'd ever seen. "You're walking again."

After a long moment, Art whispered back, "And I'm walking again."

Then Beth was in his arms, holding him tightly. He hugged her to him the way he had so badly wanted to at the hospital. He buried his face against her and inhaled the fragrance that was always Beth. Then he pushed her slightly away, and their lips sought and found each other.

It was sheer heaven.

After an eternity of bliss, Beth stirred. "Oh, Art, I love you so much," she whispered against his lips.

He groaned and plundered her mouth again. When his voice would work again, he managed to say softly, "I sort of gathered that after your outburst just before Mother interrupted us."

She felt his lips shape into a smile against her own. Then he kissed her fiercely again before she could speak the trembling words that were bubbling up in her.

A long time later, he pulled back and gently stroked her flushed cheeks. "All these long months since the accident, I've longed to hear you tell me that, Beth my darling." She felt the deep sigh that shuddered through him before he muttered, "I was so scared I'd killed your love for me, and that it was merely your religious convictions that stopped you telling me you wanted a divorce."

Beth looked startled. "I was so scared I'd killed *your* love for me, and I can honestly say I never once thought of divorcing you. I. . .I was so scared that's what you'd want." A flash of sadness swept through her. "I have to be honest and tell you that I still do wish that we could share a common faith in Christ and love for Him and His church. But I married you because I loved you so desperately, and that hasn't changed. We'll work it out, Art."

She hesitated for a moment, then said distinctly, "This time, I won't nag you, Art. I dare not neglect my own worship and fellowship with other believers or my faith will suffer. If you would come to church with me and the kids occasionally, we'd be so pleased, but I don't want you to feel bad or guilty when you don't want to come," she added firmly.

Art saw the sadness in her eyes before she swiftly veiled them. Suddenly, he remembered his envy of Jim and Gail. Ever since the day they had walked into his hospital room and told him they were engaged, there had been something about them, an intimacy between them that he had longed for himself and Beth. Now a deep inner knowledge was telling him it was their common relationship with Christ that added that extra dimension of oneness.

"Beth," he blurted out, "I don't want us to fight about religion. But I do want us to talk about religious things. No," he corrected himself suddenly, "Gail has always refused to call it religion. I want us to talk about 'Christian' things. After seeing the change in Gail, and listening to her telling us about her conversion, I realized that I was really in the dark about what she was talking about. I want you to—"

The shrill demand of the phone next to them cut him off.

Beth had been staring at him, her eyes gradually widening as his rapid words shot out. Her face had lightened, and suddenly he saw excitement, something like hope fill her face.

Impatience ripped through him as the phone continued its demand for attention. Beth's shared feelings were reflected in her face as she stood up and reached for the phone and said a curt "Hello."

Her expression only changed slightly as she said unenthusiastically, "Oh, hi, Mum. What's up?" Then she raised an eyebrow and a look of surprise flashed into her face. "He is?"

Art hesitated, then he shrugged with resignation at Beth, forced a smile, and started his chair forward. Jacky and Robbie had been banished long enough. A feeling very like relief swept through him as he made his way toward the back door. Perhaps the interruption had been timely after all. If they had started talking then, it might have spoiled their reunion. So many times before, they had just ended up disagreeing violently about religion—no, Christianity, he reminded himself with a self-derogatory grimace.

Chapter 13

Beth hung up the phone with a slight frown on her face. She had heard a ring of excitement in her mother's voice, but Mum had refused to answer Beth's questions.

But, oh, why had she rung just then when Art had actually been saying he wanted to talk about Christ? No, she corrected herself with a tender smile, he'd wanted to talk about "Christianity." To her it was one and the same thing.

"Dad said that was Grandma on the phone, Mum," Jacky's disappointed voice said from behind her. "I did want to talk to her. What did she say about Dad walking?"

Beth looked over her head toward Art as he reentered the room. She frowned again, and said slowly, "She didn't give me a chance to tell her. She was real excited about something and wouldn't let me get a word in. Apparently Rance Telford's going to be preaching at our church here next Sunday. He's accepted an offer to be their new minister. She said some of them will be coming too, and she rang to tell me to be sure and go to church Sunday morning and support him. Then we can have lunch together afterward." Beth paused and added a little anxiously, "She sounded funny, like she was in a big rush. I hope everything's okay."

"Great," Art said cheerfully, "we haven't seen them for far too long. I've wondered what sort of sermon that guy could preach. And I'm glad you didn't tell your mother our news. What say we keep my walking a secret and surprise them next Sunday at church?"

The children chorused their excited agreement as Beth and Art eyed each other. That burgeoning hope in Beth grew stronger. Art was obviously taking for granted he was going to church with them too.

"And *then* they'll all see for themselves how Jesus has made your legs work again, Dad!" Robbie's eyes were dancing, and then he frowned and sighed. "But I do wish we could all go and live back out on the farm with them," he said wistfully. "I'm sure Bonnie liked it more there too. It was real fun running over the paddocks with her."

Beth was still watching Art, and she saw a sudden speculative look cross his face. He looked thoughtfully at Robbie, and then at Jacky who was nodding her head in agreement.

"You really liked the farm, didn't you?" he said very thought- fully. Suddenly he looked up at Beth. "And like me, you've always preferred the farm even to life in a small country town like Dalby, haven't you, Beth?"

Beth hesitated, and then nodded a little reluctantly. "I guess I'll always be a farm girl at heart." Suddenly excitement lit her eyes. "Art! Have you any idea how much longer you'll need physio, now? Is there a chance we'll be able to go home sooner than we thought?"

Art looked from her to his two children. "I believe it shouldn't be too much longer at all. Look, I want you all to realize that they've told me it's not at all likely my back will ever be one hundred percent again. That means I won't be able to go back to driving trucks or heavy machinery. And there are still months, perhaps even years, of hard work ahead to continue to improve my mobility."

Robbie's and Jacky's faces dropped, but Beth said swiftly, "Oh, I took that for granted. After all it's been months already since the wed- ding at Easter when you first started to improve this much."

They smiled a little ruefully at each other, acknowledging that they both knew they had many difficult days still to navigate.

It was Art who said softly, "Day by day?"

Wordless, she beamed back at him as she nodded.

After a brief moment, he broke their eye contact, looked back at the children, and took a deep breath. "There's also something else. I've found that I rather enjoy messing about with computers. So I'm going to do lots of study about them, and see where that leads."

He looked away across the room to where a bundle of crunched up papers still lay. Then he turned back toward Beth. "It looks as though there's no need to worry about money anymore," he said sig- nificantly to her, "so why don't we wait and see what may happen.

Perhaps one day we can live on a farm even. Somewhere not too far from Jim and Gail."

Beth realized with a slight shock that she had momentarily forgotten all about Art's inheritance. They had had far more important things to talk about than the money. Art grinned at her, and she smiled back.

"Your walking's certainly our most important news of all," she said. "Now, what about you tell us all about how it happened."

Art hesitated as if he wanted to talk more about the money, but then he shrugged and turned a little reluctantly as Robbie fired at him, "Just when did they first stand you up and let you try to walk, Dad?"

He made light of it all in front of the children, but in the days that followed, Art bit by bit shared it all with Beth. By the time Sunday morning arrived, Beth knew about the specialists who had examined him those first days after the wedding. They had not been able to understand his expressed wish that his wife not be told, but they had abided by his wishes.

"I was scared stiff, Beth," he had pleaded in answer to her glare. "It was like a dream, something that just couldn't be happening. I didn't dare get your hopes up as well."

"Protecting me still, huh?" she had said with a belligerent glint in her eyes.

"Yeah, I suppose so, but later on, I was scared you'd expect me to stop imposing on you, and. . ."

Beth had snorted ferociously.

Then he had grabbed her, kissed her senseless, but had the grace to apologize humbly. So she forgave him again.

The days when she had been asked to stay away from visiting him had been when he'd undergone vigorous testing and been kept sedated to keep the pain at bay.

During the rest of that week, Beth kept waiting for Art to mention something again about spiritual things. But he never did. Now that his secret was out, he gradually used the crutches more and more. Sometimes too much, Beth felt, but she managed to refrain from saying so, even when he was in pain from obviously trying to do too much too soon.

He was also very tired most days by the time she finished work, and she kept to her promise to herself to allow him to talk in his own good time. But the shadow of not being united in spiritual things never diminished. It saddened her, and she knew it always would, unless Art put his trust in Christ.

Another thing was troubling her. Each day she knew they were becoming closer and closer again. He took every opportunity he could to touch her. They kissed often. His kisses were so tender, so sweet and loving, but she began to ache for the day when they could be husband and wife again in every way. She was only too willing for Art to set the pace of restoring their relationship, but more and more each day she found herself seeking added strength and patience in prayer.

The week ended up being very tiring, both physically and emotionally. She'd had little time to speculate on her mother's phone call, but they all had an air of excitement in the car on the way to church. Jacky and Robbie couldn't wait to surprise everyone, and Beth and Art couldn't suppress their own delight at seeing the family again.

It's only been a week since the last time we were at church, Beth thought with surprise as she drove into the church car park.

Art unconsciously echoed her thought out loud. "Hard to believe it's been a week," he muttered, "so much has happened."

Beth smiled at him, but as she looked away her smile disappeared. If only. . . She deliberately stopped that wistful thought and instead silently gave a prayer of thanks that Art was at least going to be at worship with her again.

Because they had all been so excited, they were in plenty of time, and not a lot of people had yet arrived. Beth had tried hard to persuade Art to let her bring his wheelchair, but he had refused. He did allow her to let him off as close to the front steps as possible, and when she saw the couple of boys Robbie's age watching them alight with wide eyes, she suddenly understood.

Tenderness swamped her, as Art carefully made his way up the steps on his crutches, with Robbie proudly swaggering along beside him. He was a wonderful, loving, and understanding father. She was so grateful he could never be like his own strange father. But what an even more wonderful difference if Art. . .

Once again she pulled up her thoughts, and smiled determinedly as she greeted the boys and the adults with them.

"Park the car, Beth. I'm fine," Art hissed at her a little breathlessly when they reached the top of the steps. "We'll find a seat inside. I don't think the folk from home have arrived yet."

Beth hurried to move the car out of the driveway as another car pulled in. She had just parked the car when Jim's Holden Commodore drew up beside her. Her mother and Will clambered from the backseats to descend on her, and then Gail and Jim were kissing and hugging her in turn.

"All of you!" Beth beamed at them. "How lovely."

"And not only us." Her mother smiled widely and gestured excitedly at another car pulling in beside them.

To Beth's astonishment, a radiant Hilda Garrett bounced from the front seat beside Rance Telford. Then Jean Drew was there also, and a strange boy who looked a little older than Jacky smiled at her shyly.

Beth looked at him, and her eyes widened as she glanced across at Rance and then back at the boy. They looked as much alike as Art and Robbie.

She looked back at Hilda, but before she could speak, Rance Telford said swiftly, "Nice to see you, Beth. I'm sorry, I'll have to go and find the folk waiting to organize me."

Then he bent and gave a blushing Hilda a quick kiss full on her lips and hurried away.

"Hilda! Was that. . .? I mean. . ." Beth's amazed voice tapered off, as there were several chuckles.

"You'd better get used to them," groaned Jim. "They're worse than Gail and me!"

Hilda grinned at her. To Beth's delight she was the carefree, fun-loving friend she had known for so many years, and not the Hilda of recent years who had changed so much since her mother had died.

"Rance and I are engaged to be married," Hilda said with a proud glint in her eyes. She turned to the boy and smiled proudly, "And I'd like you to meet Rance's son, Nathan. Soon to be mine too," she added softly.

Beth shook his small hand politely and said, a little puzzled, "Hello, Nathan. I didn't know Rance had a son."

"Neither did he until last Easter," grinned the boy.

Beth looked at Hilda, who murmured quickly, "A story we'll tell you some other time."

"Well, aren't you a surprise! Congratulations, Hilda," Beth said sincerely to her old friend.

"Oh, there's more surprises than that," Nathan burst out excitedly.

"Nathan!" Jean Drew said with some asperity in her voice. "Didn't we say we'd leave that story until after church?"

"But you don't find out every day you've got an aunt you don't know about," Nathan said blithely.

"Nathan!" several voices chorused in many varying tones of exasperation.

Then Hilda laughed a little shakily at Beth's utterly bewildered face. She glanced hurriedly at her watch, "Oh, dear, I'm so sorry, Beth. There's just no time to go into details now. But very simply, I've found out that Mum and Dad adopted me. My real mother was Aunt Jean's sister so she's my very own, real aunt. As for the rest, Rance and I love each other very much. We're getting married as soon as possible." With a mock scowl she added sternly, "So we can both try and keep this kid in order!"

Art turned a little impatiently to Beth as she slipped into the seat beside him only a couple of moments before the service started. He was about to ask her where on earth she'd been when he saw her shocked, dazed eyes.

"Beth, what's wrong?" he whispered in alarm.

She focused on him, and then reached out and grasped his hand. "Nothing's wrong," she murmured back in a trembling voice. "It seems we're not the only one with a surprise. That family of mine's just full of surprises!"

He saw her open her mouth to add something else, but there was a stir behind them, and then the family filed in. Jim and Gail grinned widely at him, Gail giving him a very cheeky wink as Jim hurried her past to an empty seat. Mrs. Stevens was suddenly there, bending to kiss him before she and Will slipped past them to sit beside an excited pair of children.

As Art turned back to Beth, his jaw dropped. "Isn't that Hilda Garrett and Jean Drew? Who's that boy with them?"

Beth gave a slightly hysterical giggle as she watched the trio find a seat close to the front. "Rance Telford's son, whom he only found he had at Easter. Hilda's engaged to Rance, and Jean Drew's her real aunt!"

She tried to stifle another laugh as Art gaped at her. "You are joking!"

Several heads turned, and Art realized he'd spoken out loud. He glared right back at one couple frowning at them, and then he saw Jim turn around and laugh at him. He gave Art the thumbs-up sign, and Art weakly grinned back in return.

"Beth!"

It was another loud exclamation. Their heads weren't the only ones that swung toward Mrs. Stevens. She was staring at the pair of elbow crutches propped against the wall next to Jacky. Excitement blazed from her face as she looked from them back to Art.

"Is it. . .are they. . .?" Her lips formed the words silently.

Art nodded slowly, and absolute delight and wonder filled her face. Art was vaguely aware that the preservice music had stopped. A hush filled the church as he stared back at his mother-in-law. Then a great tide of love toward her filled him when her eyes filled with tears as she watched him stand up on his own feet to join in singing the first hymn.

The song leader couldn't have picked a more appropriate hymn, he thought, but although he suddenly wanted with all his heart to sing the words, his own voice was choked. "Now thank we all our God, with heart and sound and voices. . ."

The rest of the service was unexpectedly clear and sharp to Art. Some songs he did know and manage to sing, while others he hungrily devoured. The hunger in him that he had stifled so many times before welled up stronger than ever.

And then when at last a radiant Rance Telford spoke, everything seemed to gel, to make sense, and once again he wondered how he could have been so blind, so stupid for so long.

Rance spoke of God as a loving heavenly Father. Oh, he warned them that this Father chastised because He loved, but He only wanted His children to come to Him in full and utter surrender so that He might bless them with all the joy and peace that heaven could hold. He spoke of the Father loving so much He sent His only Son to show once and for all time what the Father was like.

This loving God desired to have fellowship with His people as a loving Father to His children. This God's amazing grace caused Him to pour out blessings that no one could ever deserve, so His children could come to Him without fear, with hope, with love, and obtain strength for each day.

Art felt Beth's hand slip into his. For a timeless moment his own fingers tightened on hers convulsively. He dared not glance at her.

"If you want to know what God is like," Rance urged the congregation, "look at Jesus. He said that whoever had seen Him had seen the Father God. Turn and look fully at Jesus.

"There's no doubt. . .in fact we all know only too well," he said wryly "that we're all sinners. But nobody's sin, no one's," he emphasized passionately, "is so great it cannot be forgiven. But until we surrender it to God, it separates us from our holy, heavenly Father.

"Christ has already paid the price for that sin," he cried out triumphantly. "God loves us! He longs for all sinners, all of us everywhere to repent, to turn to Him for forgiveness, to ask Christ to come and cleanse us, to give us a new life, a new beginning, a new hope, strength for each day, and a joy. . .such great joy!"

Rance's voice rang with conviction and a great joy of his own, and Art's pulses leapt in response. This man had experienced first hand what he was preaching. He knew what it was like to be a sinner. He knew what it was like to find forgiveness, a personal relationship with God.

This was what had transformed Gail. Art felt his whole being yearn for such new life, such joy.

And then Rance was asking, pleading passionately for anyone who had not come to Christ for cleansing, forgiveness, this new life, to make a commitment there where they sat, and then have the courage to move down to the front of the church and make it public.

Art froze. There was a soft rustle of sound as people picked up their hymnbooks. He turned and looked at Beth.

As always, she was conscious of his every move. Without looking at him, she again reached out and took his trembling hand gently between her own. As she felt the tremor in his fingers, her eyes flew in alarm to his face. His face was dead white with strain.

Then she saw the sudden resolve in his face as the congregation stood around them. Still clinging to her hand he pushed himself to his feet, taking her with him. "Hand me my crutches," he croaked softly.

Anxiety filled her eyes, even as a light started burning in them. "Art darling, you don't have to walk down there. Just yield to Jesus right here. We can talk to Rance later. It doesn't matter."

"Oh, yes, it does, Beth. I just know I must."

She stared at him a moment longer. Then she felt her mother nudge her. Art's crutches were thrust into her hands. Silently, with hands that shook, she passed them one by one to him.

All around them, hushed, prayerful voices were singing. Beth could never remember afterward what the song was. All she could remember was the light, the determination, the moisture in Art's eyes as he turned toward her.

"Will you come with me, Beth?" he whispered softly.

All she could do was nod and follow him out into the aisle. She noticed Jim and Gail turn and stare as they moved past them. She heard Jim's loud baritone falter and then suddenly stop singing. Jean Drew saw them. Wonder and thankfulness lit up her face, and her voice rang out triumphantly.

And then together they were standing in front of a radiant, welcoming Rance, who clasped them both by the hand, before they turned toward each other. They smiled in perfect understanding with a sense of oneness as never before. They bowed their heads in prayer.

In praise. In submission and love to the One who had loved them all the way, and would be with them each day of the years still to come.

Epilogue

Once again, the church set in the midst of grain and cotton farms of the Darling Downs was adorned and waiting for a wedding.

On this first day of the New Year, a light breeze had sprung up. Sweeping across the stubble strewn paddocks where the golden grain had been plundered, it brought welcome relief to the heat in the small, weatherboard building.

Art's gaze swept the restless congregation. They were all there. Marian Stevens and Jean Drew were in the very front row where the bride's parents usually sat. Both were gazing around critically at their efforts with the masses of red and white dahlias and roses that wafted their sweet perfume through the whole building.

Across the aisle from them, Nathan Telford was grinning triumphantly at his old friend and partner in mischief, the elf-like Jodie Morton. She was now sitting sedately beside him, having of course won her own way to have "Nafin" sit with her and her mother, Kim.

Jacky and Robbie were sitting beside Will, watching the other two children a little woefully, having been firmly forbidden by their distrusting grandmother to join them. They had been so excited all week at moving permanently back to the Darling Downs to live, although they were weary from the upheaval of moving house again.

Gail was sitting by herself in the front row across the aisle from Art and the bridegroom, waiting for Jim to sit beside her once he had escorted the bride down the aisle and given her away. She was gazing steadily into space, a small, tender smile tilting her lips.

Art scowled slightly. She was rather pale, and he hoped the heat was not too much for her in her condition. This morning he had caught

419

her being sick in the laundry, and to his great delight she had shared their secret, threatening him with all kinds of things if he breathed a word until after the wedding.

Art glanced back at his mother-in-law and her friend. They had turned their attention to Gail. Jean was frowning. Suddenly Marian Stevens leaned over and whispered in Jean's ear. Jean sat bolt upright. "Really?" he heard her exclaim softly. Her friend nodded firmly and then both women beamed at each other.

Art shook with silent laughter. So much for Gail and Jim not wanting to distract any attention away from the bride and groom!

The bride was late. Rance Telford was exchanging nervous smiles with the waiting minister, his old friend, David Morton.

"Where on earth is she?" hissed Rance anxiously.

Art's grin was filled with pure mischief. "Probably decided she couldn't be a parson's wife after all!" he drawled. Then he relented. "Or more likely, probably still trying to find her way through all our stuff at the Garretts's!" He shrugged, "I did try and suggest we wait until after the wedding to move into Hilda's house, but I was howled down."

Trying to distract Rance, he added softly, "We're so thrilled Hilda's going to let us buy those few acres so we can build our own dream home this year." Rance's answering smile was vague, and with a soft laugh, Art gave up on him.

Never had Art dreamed he could be as happy as he'd been these last months. The crutches were still necessary, but the amazed doctors had told him that, at the rate he was improving, he would probably be able one day in the future to throw them away.

The bouts of pain in his back and legs, the endless discussions about moving into Hilda's old home and helping Jim and Hilda with the computerized business side of the two farms, even the occasional mild disagreements still with Beth, nothing had disturbed the deep, abiding joy and peace that was still transforming his life since his commitment to Christ.

The sound of racing motors came at last. A wave of excitement swept through the small church. Rance gave a sigh of relief and tugged at his tie nervously. Art grinned sympathetically. A few moments later

David moved to his place and nodded to them both to take their positions. Confidently, Art leaned on Rance and took the couple of paces forward.

The music peeled out. The people stood. The matron of honor started down the aisle. Art devoured her with his eyes, not even glancing at the radiant Hilda following on Jim's arm.

Then Beth was beside him. Art caught his breath. She was even more beautiful than he had thought possible. Their eyes met and clung. As they linked arms, secret little smiles glowed deep in both eyes. Tomorrow they had an appointment to keep at Art's old football oval. He would walk its length.

But today was even more special. It might be officially Hilda and Rance's big day, but Beth and Art had agreed to privately, silently renew their own marriage vows.

God had given them a new love for each other. God had given them a new marriage. God had kept them each day, and He would continue to do so each day for the rest of their lives!

Now they were truly one flesh in Him.

SEARCH FOR THE STAR

Chapter 1

J ean Drew rolled her stiff shoulders and then moved her head from side to side. It had been a long day's drive from Sydney and she was tired even though she had stopped for a good break in Too-woomba. The rolling hills around that "Garden City of the Darling Downs" were well behind her now and the road ahead across the black soil plains was straight to the horizon.

But it wasn't only her physical condition—and the last rays of the setting sun in her eyes—that made Jean ease her foot on the accelera-tor, she acknowledged with a deep sigh. Ever since saying farewell to the director of nursing, her mind had been in a state of turmoil.

Jean remembered her colleague's parting words with some alarm. Miss Fisher had looked at her sadly and said, almost crossly, "Instead of just long-service leave I suppose soon I'll be saying good-bye per-manently to the best nurse educator this hospital's ever had."

Then, smiling at her confusion, she had added, "The last few weeks you've been so excited about this newly discovered niece of yours. Since she's your only living relative, I just thought you'd be wanting to live closer to her one day."

Jean's immediate reaction had been denial, but the thought had been growing in her mind. Was this God's prompting? Did He want her to move to Queensland to be nearer to Hilda?

Although her nursing colleagues would never believe it, Sister Jean Drew was feeling shy and a trifle nervous at seeing Hilda again. What would be expected from the bride's only relative these next few weeks leading up to Hilda's wedding, not to mention Christmas?

"I shouldn't have let her talk me into coming to stay for so many weeks before her wedding, especially over Christmas," she muttered out loud, and then her lips twisted wryly. There had been no way she could say no, even though she had known she would have to endure the bittersweetness of the Christmas season as well.

Thus, she had delayed making a decision, and only a couple of weeks ago had confronted the director of nursing and requested some of her long-service leave off over the Christmas and New Year summer holidays. Now, remembering the surprised look on Miss Fisher's face, Jean scowled.

"Why, Jean, for years you've always insisted on working Christmas Day," the director said sharply. "I do wish you'd given me more notice. You know these next few weeks leading up to Christmas are the busiest in the hospital year and I've already drafted out the rosters. As usual, the surgeons have also scheduled full theaters to tidy up their waiting lists before the holiday period."

It had been the surprise, and then the disapproval, that made Jean realize just how many Christmases she had spent working to be taken so much for granted. For so many years she had really hated Christmas, happy to stay busy on the wards until all the madness was over.

Even the last few Christmases, when she had been able for the first time to worship as never before and thank God for the birth of Jesus, she still automatically filled the day with work to try and dull the ache of being alone. Despite invitations from her new friends at church, her pride had made her reluctant to take advantage and intrude on their family get-togethers.

So, despite the director's displeasure at the short notice, Jean had stuck to her request for eight weeks' leave. But these last few days, as she had prepared to be away, all her dislike, no, her dread, of the whole Christmas period had welled up inside.

This would be the first time she had seen Hilda, as well as her old friend Marian Stevens and her son Jim and his wife Gail since their brief, wonderful reunion last year. At that time Hilda's fiancé, Reverend Rance Telford, had informed them that the birth mother Hilda had been trying so hard to find was none other than Jean's younger sister who had died several years ago.

Jean had always liked Hilda and felt sorry for her being the only child of older parents. Now, although she hated to admit it, Jean was feeling just the tiniest bit scared at her new status. Hilda had always called her "Aunt Jean," and that was now exactly who she was.

During this long day's drive, Jean had been forced to acknowledge that she was at a crossroads. These last few weeks she had found her job in the large Sydney hospital less satisfying than ever before. She had snapped at a couple of students doing their clinical experience, and then felt ashamed that she had slipped back to her old cranky self, spoiling her Christian witness.

Now Jean was seriously considering the possibility of getting a job closer to Hilda and the Stevenses, but there were few nursing jobs available anywhere at the moment. She certainly didn't think she could live out here in the country, but if there were nothing in Too-woomba, Brisbane was much closer than Sydney.

"Lord, if only You'd speak out loud and clear sometimes and tell a body what You wanted her to do!" she muttered out loud, and then pulled a face at herself.

She knew the answer to that. He did guide, but He also expected her to live by faith, not sight—or hearing!

To try and distract herself, Jean studied the passing countryside more closely. She had traveled this road many times but rarely at this season of the year when most of the golden wheat paddocks lining each side of the road had already been harvested. There was an occasional harvester still working in the distance and several large, grain-filled trucks had rumbled past her on their way to the railway silos.

In the distance she saw a large black car pulled well over to the side of the road. Jean had turned off the main highway some miles back and knew that vehicles along this stretch were not plentiful. But long ago on other visits she had learned that out here, so many miles from anywhere, you always stopped to see if anyone needed help.

Still, even in the country these days, a woman by herself had to be careful. Reluctantly, she slowed down as a male figure opened the driver's door, stood up, and imperiously signaled her to stop. She peered at him as she slowly cruised past and then frowned.

Despite the shining black sedan, she didn't like the look of him one bit. He appeared decidedly scruffy with more than one day's growth of bread. Tall and dark haired, he was wearing jeans and an unbuttoned shirt, which he was at least making some attempt to rectify as she took her time parking the car.

She left the motor running and watched him warily as he approached her. His face was drawn and there were dark circles around his eyes. But there was something familiar about that relieved smile, those thick black eyebrows that almost met, those eyes. . .

She thought she must be dreaming. She closed her eyes tightly for a moment and when she opened them. . .Jonathan. It was Jonathan Howard.

But, she thought suddenly, *he just couldn't be, not after all these years and certainly not right out here on the black soil plains of the Darling Downs in Queensland, at least a thousand kilometers from Sydney.*

The last time she had seen him had been in her office in St. Kilda, a bustling Sydney hospital. He had shaken her hand, formally wished her all the best for her wedding the following week, and then turned and walked out of her life without a word.

The last time she had been able to find out anything about him had been a couple of years ago when she had heard he wasn't even in Australia but was using his surgeon's skills in some little-known locale in Africa.

At closer inspection the years had not been kind to him. His unruly dark hair, which was considerably longer than it used to be, curling down to his shoulders, had even more gray than her own, her silver streaks carefully hidden. His face was more heavily lined than she would have expected.

He leaned down to peer at her through the car window and she caught her breath as his smile widened. It was that same crooked, gleaming smile that had once played havoc with her senses. She only realized she was gaping at him when his smile faltered and a slightly puzzled look crossed his face.

"I'm sorry to stop you, but I wonder if you have a mobile phone or if you could give me a lift," he said rather casually.

His deep, crisp voice stopped abruptly as a frown crossed his face and he looked a little closer at her. She held her breath, waiting for him to recognize her, then a flood of disappointment swept through her when he said, "Look, you're not afraid of me, are you?"

Afraid? Oh yes, she had been afraid once, not of him, but of how he had made her feel, what he had made her confront, what he had. . .

She came to her senses when he took a step back from the car and said impatiently, "For goodness sake, I assure you I'm genuinely stuck out here and only need a lift to the nearest phone."

Jean quickly turned off the motor and scrambled out on slightly shaky legs. "Afraid? Of course I'm not afraid."

Her voice was unnaturally high-pitched and she swallowed convulsively. She was acting like one of her silly first-year nursing students. How stupid could a woman her age get, being thrown into confusion by a doctor she had once worked with all those years ago! *And he's married,* she reminded herself.

She managed to smile at him and say in her usual efficient tone, "I'm sorry, Dr. Howard, of course I'm not afraid. I just couldn't believe my eyes it was you."

Chapter 2

Surprise but not recognition filled his face as he studied her carefully.

Jean was dismayed at the sadness that swept through her because he obviously did not remember her. But then, she had always known that to him, despite being the most senior nurse, she was simply one of the operating theater's staff, even though they had developed a friendly working relationship and even socialized at hospital parties.

She straightened. "You don't remember me, but I was in charge of the theater at—"

"Jean. . .Jean Drew!"

Absolute amazement transformed his features and then he smiled warmly. "Why, Sister Jean Drew, of course I remember you. Or as the new nursing etiquette requires, should it be Miss Drew, RN? Afraid I still call registered nurses 'Sister' even in hospitals! How absolutely amazing to meet you on this lonely country road. Are you going to come to my rescue again after all these years?"

Jean's smile turned into a delighted chuckle. So he did remember her after all. As they stared at each other, she suddenly realized he was still holding her hand between his strong capable ones and she quickly pulled away.

"Oh, I don't think you ever really needed much rescuing, Jonathan."

He chuckled. "Oh, yes, I did, especially that time I slept through my alarm and arrived thirty minutes late for old Fergy's first op on his list. My very first week too!"

She put her hands on her hips in mock indignation. "Now really, Dr. Howard, could I help it if that operating theater autoclave took thirty minutes longer to sterilize Dr. Ferguson's special instruments than anticipated?"

This time he threw back his head and laughed loudly. A lump suddenly lodged in her throat. She realized that the years may have aged him, but his unkempt appearance in no way detracted from that masculine charisma that was part and parcel of such a capable, compassionate man. His mere presence had so often reassured and comforted patients and staff alike.

Jean remembered a little sadly that this was how he had laughed during that first year as Dr. Ferguson's surgical registrar. Later, when he had taken over as chief surgeon, that laugh was heard less and less often and then disappeared altogether. Those last few weeks she had worked with him even his smile had lost its sparkle and had seldom reached those wonderfully expressive eyes that were now filled with delight as he looked at her.

"And what on earth is that old dragon of a theater nurse doing driving by herself so many miles from Sydney?"

"And what is that eminent surgeon doing with a broken-down car, a Mercedes, if I'm not mistaken, parked on the side of a minor country road in the middle of the Darling Downs?" she countered with a tilt of her chin.

"He's going to a wedding."

Something clutched at her heart. "A wedding?" she managed faintly.

"Well, not today, but in a few weeks' time, after Christmas, in fact. A young friend of mine is taking the plunge."

Jean's heart steadied as he continued. "More accurately, I'm escaping for a holiday. I need some R & R in the quiet countryside," he said as he pulled a face. "But it's a little too quiet this evening. I've been stuck here for well over an hour and had almost given up and started walking, only I haven't a clue where I am or how far it is to the nearest farmhouse."

After an uncomfortable pause, she could not wait any longer to find out. "That wedding you're going to wouldn't by any chance be on New Year's Day, would it?"

It was his turn to look surprised as he nodded.

"And it wouldn't just happen to be Reverend Rance Telford and Hilda Garrett's, would it?"

Again he nodded, and then a rather strange expression crossed his face. "And by some weird chance you wouldn't happen to be the 'Aunt Jean' Rance wrote about so fondly?"

It was her turn to nod helplessly and then they simultaneously burst out laughing.

He recovered first, and with his eyes still twinkling said, "Well, Aunt Jean Dr—" He stopped and then added swiftly, "Oh, I'm sorry, that was your maiden name. I don't think I ever did know the name of the man you left the hospital to marry."

Jean froze. Obviously, the hospital grapevine hadn't done its job, but then he probably hadn't given her another thought. And why should he have, she acknowledged fairly. Despite the closeness that had sprung up between them, they had shared only a working relationship, at least from his point of view.

After too long a pause which had him raising those incredibly thick and straight eyebrows, she said, "It's still Drew."

At her quiet tone all trace of amusement disappeared and something besides surprise flashed across his face, but he didn't speak. At last she said reluctantly, "I changed my mind and didn't get married after all."

Now why on earth did she tell him that instead of what nearly everyone else believed was the truth?

He was silent for another moment, and then he said softly, "I'm sorry, Jean, I never did hear that. At. . .at that time I was going through some bad stuff in my own personal life."

Bad stuff? Jean frowned. What did he mean? Could that have been why he had seemed so distracted, so quiet and reserved those last couple of weeks? Embarrassed, she had thought that somehow, despite all her efforts, he had realized how she felt about him, feelings she had only just discovered herself.

Not for the first time did Jean acknowledge she had made a mistake cutting herself off so thoroughly from the staff at St. Kilda. With all that had happened, it had seemed the easiest option at the time. But she had still felt very lonely and had often wondered over the years what she would have done if she had not phoned her old friend Marian Stevens.

She turned and looked toward his car. "Your wife couldn't come with you, Jonathan?"

When she turned back to him she was startled by the change in his face. He had quickly donned that professional mask she had seen so many medical personnel put in place when dealing with distraught patients or relatives.

He opened his mouth, and then apparently changed his mind and merely shook his head. "Perhaps it would be a good idea if we postponed this conversation to some future time," he said abruptly. "Now, I don't suppose you're staying with Hilda Garrett, too?"

She stared at him for a brief moment and then looked away. Inexplicably, she felt hurt at the sudden coldness in his voice. After all, there was absolutely no reason in the world why she should be upset that he so obviously did not want to talk about his wife.

Then she realized what he had said and turned back. "You're staying with Hilda?"

He nodded and said in that same expressionless voice, "Yes, Rance told me she insisted."

He hesitated for a moment and then sighed. "I only arrived back a couple of days ago from a pretty heavy operating schedule overseas to discover my house had not only suffered severe damage in a bad storm but been burgled as well. Apparently when Hilda found out from Rance she insisted I come here while the repairs are being made. He wanted me to stay with him but he's moved out of the Toowoomba manse and is living with his mother and stepfather until he commences at his new church in Brisbane."

Jean studied his face for a moment, noting again the dark circles of weariness under his eyes. Why on earth had he traveled all the way from Sydney when surely he should be nearer to supervise the house repairs? And what about his wife; did she accompany him overseas? Why wasn't she with him now?

It is none of my business, she scolded herself silently.

Jean forced herself to say crisply, "Actually, you nearly made it. The Garretts's farm is not that far from here." She smiled at the face he pulled. "We'd better get moving as it's already much later than I told Hilda to expect me."

When Jonathan's oversized body was at last sitting beside Jean, the inside of her car seemed very small. She straightened, feeling irritated with herself for letting this man affect her so much, and for suddenly wishing fervently they were hours away from the farm.

"Your car is a Mercedes, isn't it?" she asked brightly. "Congratulations, Jonathan, you've obviously done very well."

He snorted and she glanced quickly at him and away again.

"Yes, it is a Mercedes, but it is not my car," he said sharply. "If it had been, it wouldn't have run out of petrol. A friend lent it to me. Mine was in the garage the tree fell on during the storm."

"Oh, dear, your car was damaged too?"

"Yes," he told her just as curtly. "Half the roof of the house was crushed as well. Although my neighbors called the emergency services to put tarpaulins on, the rain had already poured in and now it's unlivable until the builders have finished."

That raised many more questions concerning the whereabouts of his wife, but Jean merely grinned across at him. "Oh, and after escaping that bedlam the borrowed car ran out of petrol, did it?"

There was a long pause and then he drawled, "Yeah."

The word was accompanied by a low chuckle and Jean relaxed at her success in lightening the atmosphere between them. "And the car of eminent surgeon Jonathan Howard wouldn't dare run out of petrol, would it?"

She heard the smile in his voice as he said in a false posh accent, "Most decidedly, Sister Drew." And then he explained in his normal deep tone, "I did know the tank wasn't full, but I think the gauge may not be registering properly. Whatever, I underestimated how many kilometers to the liter it used up."

"But surely you had some idea by the time you'd driven all this way, didn't you? And what about your wife; has she gone to friends also?"

He was silent for a long moment and she glanced swiftly at him in the now rapidly descending dusk to find that he was watching her with a considering look on his face.

"Jean," he said so quietly she found herself tensing in response. "As I never heard about your wedding, obviously you never heard that my wife died not long after you left St. Kilda. I've been based in Brisbane for some years."

Chapter 3

The car swerved slightly as the shock hit Jean.

All those years ago, at the last moment, she had canceled her wedding to a decent man and broken his heart because of Dr. Jonathan Howard. All those years ago, she had hated and despised herself for being stupid enough to fall in love with a happily married man. All those years ago, she had cut herself off from mutual friends and workmates because it hurt too much even hearing his name mentioned.

And all these measures had achieved was to help her become a hard, bitter, lonely woman. It had taken her years to heal, and that healing had only begun when she discovered it was possible to have a personal relationship with Jesus Christ and she yielded her life to Him.

Now, ten years too late, she had just heard Jonathan say he was free after all. If she had only stayed around. . .

Then she realized how horrible and utterly selfish that sounded. To become "free," this man had suffered an incalculable loss.

The old pain and guilt clenched its fist inside her again and she reached out desperately to God. The pain eased and after a moment she breathed a fervent prayer, asking forgiveness for such a petty, selfish thought, and a plea for the right words.

Jonathan was still watching her when she at last turned her head. She hoped he would not notice her tear-filled eyes as she said steadily, "I'm so very sorry, Johnny, I know you loved your wife very much. You're right, I didn't know. I've lost track of most of those we worked with at St. Kilda."

A strange look flashed across his face. "You're the only person who's ever called me that."

Tears threatened to choke her and she looked away. She had forgotten that once, to ease a tense moment in the operating theater, she

435

had flippantly called him Johnny. That had been before she realized her liking for the surgeon was changing to something deeper.

"I. . .I'm sorry."

"Oh, no, don't be sorry," he said quickly. "I like it."

He was silent for a long moment before he said, "Yes, I'm afraid I've got out of touch too. I ended up leaving St. Kilda not that long after you did."

His voice was just a little too casual, but Jean took note that he had not even acknowledged her reference to his wife. "I did hear something about you working in Africa. Is that where you've just come from?" she asked, perhaps too quickly.

He gave a deep sigh and stirred restlessly. "I actually flew into Sydney a couple of days ago, visited the mission headquarters for a debriefing, and then flew to Brisbane to find my house in an incredible mess," he said wearily. "I've been camping there in one relatively undamaged room sorting out what's been stolen for the police and arranging for the repairs to be done.

"Unfortunately, all the reliable builders recommended to me are busy on other jobs and can't start for another couple of weeks or even more. It was good to lock the door behind me and escape at last. I haven't even had electricity in the house."

"No wonder you look so. . .so. . ." She bit her lip, and with considerable relief heard him give a low laugh.

"So disreputable, or should it be old and worn?" he finished for her.

She threw him a grin to find that he had turned and was watching her. "Well, definitely very tired."

Too tired for the man to even bother about his appearance, she suddenly realized.

His steady regard unnerved her and, annoyed with herself, she added crisply, "So, you have been working with a missionary society in Africa. I did wonder about that since I knew you had been a very committed Christian."

He was silent again for a moment but this time she sensed his surprise. She glanced at him with a slight smile to find he was looking at her now with considerable speculation. However, he made no comment, but instead started to tell her where he had been working and some of the primitive operating conditions at the make-shift hospital near a refugee camp.

She found herself fascinated with his quiet narrative, realizing as he talked that he was exhausted and traumatized by what he had seen, and had tried to repair, of the horrors done to human bodies by war. She threw in a few questions that kept him talking in more detail about some of his patients until at last she slowed the car and turned onto the track leading to the Garrett farmhouse.

"Well, almost there," she said with a sigh. "I do hope we'll get a chance to talk some more about your work while we're here. It's fascinating."

"And yours, too, Jean." There was considerable contriteness in his voice. "I haven't even given you a chance to tell me about the surgeons you're keeping in control these days."

She laughed. "I've found that student nurses are much easier any day to terrorize than egotistical doctors in operating theaters."

"Student nurses?"

"After. . .after I left St. Kilda I became a tutor sister." She then added quickly, "When the nurses' training changed from the hospital to the university degree, I became a nurse educator supervising nurses doing clinical experience." She pulled a face. "Like you, after all the years of being called Sister Drew, sometimes it still seems strange to be called 'Miss' on duty. I also organize any hospital in-service training, assess the newest graduates on their practical abilities, and relieve on the wards to keep my hand in."

"It would be interesting to hear what you think about the two training methods," he said in a thoughtful voice.

"Well, that's a real hobbyhorse of mine," she said a shade ruefully. "You'll probably find it hard to stop me once I get going, so it's just as well we've arrived."

"Aunt Jean!"

Jean glowed as she saw the vibrant young woman racing toward the car. Hilda hardly gave her a chance to get out before she was hugging and kissing her.

She had always been fond of this girl but now added love flooded Jean's heart and she tried to stop her eyes from filling with tears.

"There, there, girl, do give me a chance to—"

"Oh, I'm sorry, I didn't realize you weren't alone!" Hilda was staring at the tall figure who had alighted from the car and was watching them both with a rather bemused smile.

Before Jean could introduce him, Hilda gave a delighted laugh. "Aunt Jean, don't tell me you've taken me up on my offer of bringing the man in your life with you and at last introducing me to him!"

Jean felt her face flood with heat. To her utter embarrassment, Jonathan was staring at her with his eyes full of amusement and some other expression she couldn't quite make out under the dim outdoor lights.

Before she could gather her wits, he said easily, "Sorry, Hilda, mistaken identity. I'm Jonathan Howard."

Now it was Hilda's turn to blush. "Dr. Howard! Oh, I'm. . .I'm sorry, Rance had hoped to be here to greet you but he couldn't get away, some urgent hospital visit or something. He was very disappointed."

"I found Dr. Howard stranded on the highway," Jean explained quickly. "He needs someone to take him back to his car with some petrol. What about we phone Jim Stevens and then see about unpacking this car?"

Hilda gave her another quick hug, whispered a fervent "Sorry," and then chanted cheekily, "Yes, Sister Drew, of course, Sister Drew, but no, Sister Drew, I'll soon fill up a can and drive him back myself! Jim's had a hectic day getting the last of the crop in."

Jean smiled at her affectionately and pretended to cuff her ear. Then she felt embarrassed all over again when she encountered the wondering smile on Jonathan's face as they went inside.

"Looks like the old battle-axe has been tamed at last," he whispered, laughing softly in her ear.

Old dragon and now old battle-axe! Jean stared at his back indignantly as he swung past her with her bag he had insisted on carrying. Then she grinned a little wryly. She probably had been all of those things once, but he had a lot to learn about the changes in her life these last few years.

Hilda insisted the car would be quite safe until they had eaten the meal she had prepared. "In fact, I'm sure it would be okay until morning," she said, smiling shyly at Jonathan.

"If it were my car, I wouldn't hesitate, but seeing it's not. . ." He shrugged.

"I'm so sorry about your house, Dr. Howard. Rance told me it was that bad windstorm that hit Brisbane about three weeks ago," Hilda said sympathetically. "But I'm really pleased at the chance to get to know such a good friend of my fiancé."

When Jean saw Jonathan's pleased look, she felt even more proud of her warmhearted niece. After unloading the car and stowing the luggage in their rooms, they rejoined Hilda, and Jean gave in to her curiosity and asked one of the many questions she needed answering.

"How do you happen to know Rance, Jonathan?"

She was immediately rewarded by his brilliant smile. "I met him soon after he started coming to the church in Sydney I was attending. He had not been a Christian for long and still had to sort out some problems from his past. At that time I badly needed his enthusiasm and excitement in his newfound faith in Christ."

He shrugged, and Jean saw that shadow of pain cross his face again. "We just clicked. He's a wonderful young man and sharing with him at that particular time in my own life helped me very much as well. Later he became one of my most reliable prayer supporters when my trips overseas started."

He had answered one question but Jean's thirst for knowledge had barely been quenched.

Although there was no further opportunity that evening for him to satisfy her curiosity, Hilda told her more the next morning while they shared an early cup of coffee.

"Rance was absolutely thrilled that Dr. Howard would be home and able to be at our wedding. Apparently, he helped Rance tremendously to get away from the crowd he had been running around with before he became a Christian."

She pulled a face. "From what he's told me, my Rance was a wild lad then, into drugs and goodness knows what else. He still doesn't like to talk about it much. Dr. Howard took him through basic Bible studies about his new faith, and was always there for him as he sorted out his life.

"He was very supportive, including financially, when Rance was in theological college studying for the ministry. At the time he was having problems with his own son, and I believe he got Rance to talk to him."

"His son?"

Hilda nodded. "I think he's in America at the moment."

Jean toyed with her cup, trying to remember if he had ever mentioned a son. Perhaps all those years ago she had just tuned out painful reminders of his unavailability.

"And what about Rance's son," Jean said to change the subject. "How's young Nathan doing?"

Hilda's face softened. "Getting more and more excited about Christmas and the wedding—in that order too, the poor little scrap. This first Christmas with Rance is showing us again how much he's missed out on."

Jean already knew about the woman Rance had been living with before his commitment to Christ. He had completely cut himself off from her when he was battling the temptation of going back to his old lifestyle. But she had been unable to break her drug addiction and had only this last year, just before she succumbed to AIDS, contacted him to tell him they had a son from those wild days. He had been devastated at the news, but now Nathan was his joy and delight as well as a typical bundle of nine-year-old mischief.

"That old life Rance experienced is one of the reasons why he's had so much success ministering to others caught up in similar lifestyles," Jean said softly. "God has been working all things in his life out 'for good'."

Hilda beamed at her proudly. Her love for Rance glowed from her, and Jean could not help contrasting this contented woman with the distraught girl of the past year.

"Oh, Hildie, I'm so glad you're my very own flesh and blood," Jean burst out in a choked voice. "You're such a great woman. My sister would have been so proud of you."

Hilda was across the room in a flash.

After a couple of hugs and a few tears, Jean pushed her away. "Gracious me, you've turned me into as big a crybaby as yourself!"

Hilda merely kissed her again and smiled mistily. "I don't know what I would have done without you this year. Your own faith and certainty of God's goodness and love has helped me more than you'll ever know."

She looked over Jean's shoulder and said with mild confusion, "Oh, Dr. Howard, I didn't realize you were up yet."

Jean took her time turning around and wishing him good morning, hoping all traces of her tears had gone.

He looked at her keenly as he advanced into the room. "Good morning, Jean." He hesitated and then added softly, "Forgive me for overhearing what Hilda just said, but have you become a Christian since St. Kilda days, Jean?"

"Yes," she said as softly. "Putting my trust in Christ has transformed my life."

She felt the warmth radiate through her at the wonder and the joy she had known these last few years because of the most important decision she had ever made and saw its reflection in the smile that filled his face.

"I'm glad," he said simply.

"You should be," she said, smiling a little shyly at him. "I've longed to tell you for years the impact your own faith in Christ had on my life."

His eyes widened.

"Oh, I always knew that you prayed for and even sometimes with your patients. Some of them told me," she added hastily. "Most who mentioned it were so astonished that you bothered. It's not that you ever said much, but. . ."

She stopped. How could she tell him about the time she had burst into the staff room to find him reading the Bible? After he had gone she had picked up the book he had left on the table and been taken aback to find out what it was.

That particular day had been one of turmoil. It had only dawned on her earlier that morning that her affection for the handsome Dr. Howard was much, much deeper than a woman with a wedding dress already hanging in her cupboard should have.

Desperately seeking answers, after her shift that day she had searched until she found her own old Bible, which had not been opened for years, and started to read.

"Do you pray for your patients now, Aunt Jean?"

Jonathan was delightfully disheveled although his jaw was now revealed in all its square strength. He looked wonderful and Jean turned quickly away, feeling the warmth in her cheeks increase as she focused on Hilda and then nodded.

"Of course, and I even pray for a pesky niece too," she said teasingly, keeping her eyes averted from the tall figure who was pulling out a chair and sitting at the table beside her.

"Knowing you, you've been praying for me ages before we even knew we were related."

"I. . .I hope you'll pray for me too, Jean."

Jean risked turning to face him and caught his piercing glance. There was that touch of pain in his eyes again before he looked away.

"I've been finding hanging onto faith in a loving God very difficult these last few weeks," he admitted candidly.

There was no way Jean could tell him how often and how much she had prayed about and for him these last few years, so she just nodded. "Of course I will, Johnny," she said softly.

Warmth tinged her cheeks as he smiled gently, and she realized she had used her special name for him once again.

Chapter 4

Jonathan was quiet while he ate the breakfast Hilda prepared. As Hilda chattered away about the plans for the wedding and all the things she wanted Jean to help her with, Jean exchanged a couple of little smiles with him in mutual amusement at the excitement of the bride-to-be.

After he had finished he pushed his chair back and stood up, interrupting Hilda in full flight. "I wonder if you'd mind if I commandeered Jean for a little while, Hilda?"

Although he had phrased his request politely, his was the tone of the autocratic surgeon who thought he only had to crook his little finger and susceptible young nurses would rush to do his bidding. *Well,* Jean thought to herself, *I'm neither young nor susceptible any longer.*

Staring up at him indignantly, she saw the slight twitch at the corner of his mouth and knew he was laughing at her. She was sure of it when he added blandly, "We have ten years of catching up to do, and she's going for a walk with me down to the sheds."

As they started across the yard, Jean began to chuckle.

She heard the answering amusement in his voice as he said mockingly, "For a moment there I thought Sister Drew was going to make sure I never got above meself agin!"

She laughed outright. "Was I really that bad?"

"Most definitely! Many times over the years when I've started to fling orders around, I'd remember a certain lady with her hands on her hips reminding me coldly that the nurses took their orders from her, not some cocky young surgeon still wet behind the ears!"

"I never said any such thing."

"Perhaps not, but your flashing blue eyes said it all for you."

"So what brought it on this time? Thought I needed rescuing, did you?"

"Well, your beautiful blue eyes did start to rather glaze over when she started talking about the clothes they are planning for young Nathan to wear. Besides, I wanted to see what you'd do," he added impishly.

Warmth flooded through Jean. She couldn't really remember the last time she had felt so protected and cared for. Her personality was such that she was the one who sorted things out for others.

She laughed with delight. "Well, that did come rather quickly on top of what was happening to get a dress for Beth Smith, her matron of honor."

"Beth Smith?"

"She's the daughter of my friend Marian Stevens and was Hilda's neighbor until her own marriage."

"Oh, is that Arthur Canley-Smith's wife? Rance wrote to me about his accident and the way he's now getting the use of his legs back." His voice deepened. "He was so delighted and encouraged when Arthur committed his life to Christ publicly—and right after he had preached his first sermon in his new church in Brisbane."

Jean beamed. "That was a glorious day. We'd all been praying so much for Beth and Arthur."

Jonathan smiled gently back at her, and then said quietly, "I can't begin to tell you how thrilled I am about your faith in Christ and to hear you talking so naturally about prayer, Jean."

"It's strange, I'm usually much more reserved," Jean heard herself saying thoughtfully, and then added quickly, "but then you were always very easy to talk to, Jonathan."

"Yes, we did enjoy some good talks, didn't we, Jean?" There was a strange note in his voice, but then he said, "Hilda seems a fine Christian as well as a delightful young woman. She seems to be coping with the traumas of this last year very well."

"Yes," Jean agreed, hesitating. "How much has Rance told you about what happened, Jonathan? Did he mention Jim Stevens and Gail?"

"He told me that after her mother had died, Hilda had mistaken her friendship with Jim for the love of her life. She was devastated when she found out he had fallen in love with Gail Brandon."

"Did he tell you about Hilda's father's death?"

He nodded. "It was a tough time for both of them, especially so soon after her mother had died. Rance was trying to come to grips with finding out about Nathan as well as trying to help Hilda through the double grief of losing her father and then finding out about her adoption."

"And it all led back to my sister," Jean said softly.

"Rance has sung your praises almost as much as he's raved about the beautiful woman he's going to marry. I still can't believe that the Aunt Jean he referred to is my very own Jean Drew from years ago."

His very own. . .

A great longing filled Jean. She looked swiftly up at him. There was such a teasing, tender light in his face that Jean's eyes blurred and she stumbled on a deep rut in the black soil.

He reached out and grasped her arm to steady her. "Oops, can't let the bride's aunt break a leg before the big day."

Jean managed to smile back up at him. "Well, she'd be in the hands of the best surgeon she ever worked with if she needed surgery."

He smiled gently back at her but a shadow briefly touched his face before he looked away.

They walked on silently and somehow Jean found her hand remained clasped firmly in his strong one.

They inspected the huge tractor and other pieces of equipment in a large shed. Jim was still using the huge harvester on the Stevens property after finishing the harvest here first.

"The arrangement for Jim to share-farm this place with Hilda should work out very well," Jonathan said thoughtfully. "It is a shame the Garretts didn't have a son to carry on the place."

Then Jean said a little hesitantly, "Jonathan, Hilda said your son's in the USA. I've been trying to remember if you mentioned him years ago."

The hand in hers tensed and he was silent so long she looked up at him inquiringly, wondering whether he resented her wanting to know about him.

"I probably forgot to mention Robert." His tone was tinged with sarcasm and bitterness.

Jean pulled her hand away. "I'm sorry, I shouldn't have—" She took a couple of hasty steps forward away from him but his quiet "Jean" stopped her.

She turned reluctantly toward him. He was standing with his hands tucked into the back pockets of his old well-washed jeans. His shoulders were hunched forward and he suddenly kicked hard at a clump of dirt.

"From several things you've said yesterday, Jean, I gather that you think me some kind of wonderful person. The truth is, ten years ago I may have been a good surgeon, but I was a miserable failure as a father and a husband."

She stared blankly at him, not knowing how to respond to the raw pain and self-condemnation in his face.

"As you know, the study and training it takes to become a doctor is very demanding. Sandra and I met when I was a second-year med student and she was a second-year nurse. We married as soon as she finished her training."

He stopped and Jean's heart ached as she saw him become lost in memories. At last she prompted gently, "You were both so young."

He gave a bitter laugh and started to walk slowly again toward the shade of a couple of old gum trees. Jean caught up with him and boldly slipped her hand around his elbow. His own came to rest on it.

"We were both twenty-one, old enough perhaps in years, but now I know she was a lot more mature than I. During all those years of study at university I drifted away from a close relationship with Christ and became incredibly selfish about my own career. Not long before her death, when I was working with you, in fact, I realized how weak my faith had become."

"Surely she would have understood your dedication to your job?"

"She was wonderful."

Jean wasn't sure if her need to know about him included hearing just how wonderful his wife had been!

But she remained silent, and after a moment he said, "She rarely complained, except when she felt I was neglecting Robert too much.

Even then I would try and not miss out on his special days, but there were few I ever managed to share with them. It took me years to build a relationship with Robert after she died."

"How old was he then?"

"Sixteen, and believe me, he didn't hold back one word of what he thought of his father."

Jean thought of the hurting teenagers over the years she had tried to comfort when someone close to them had died. So many of them had erupted into rage as well as bewildered grief.

"But surely by now he must know—"

"He knows his father spent so much time on his precious patients he wasn't home when his family needed him!" he exploded. "Even when Sandra had been begging me to drive her to visit her mother in Newcastle I didn't have time." His voice choked on the old pain and guilt.

"Jonathan. . ."

It was as though he hadn't heard her as he continued in a low, tortured voice. "Her mother had cancer and had been told she should have another course of chemotherapy which she was refusing. Sandra wanted me to talk to her. I had two full days in theater and booked the next day to drive her to Newcastle, but then just as we were ready to leave there was that inevitable call from the hospital. It was one of the rare times Sandra became really angry with me and said she'd go by herself, as usual. She went for an early morning swim. If I'd been there. . ."

He paused to take a deep breath. "The few times I did go with her we enjoyed that time of the day with the surf to ourselves. No one knows what happened. She disappeared and her body was washed up two days later."

This time it was Jonathan who peeled her suddenly clenched hand from him and strode furiously away.

His face had been filled with such pain, she let him go without protesting. Her heart lifted him up in prayer as she watched him stop and lean against the gnarled trunk of a tree and stare out across the bleached wheat stubble.

She felt stunned. When they had seen each other almost every day she had thought he was one man who had it all together, his career, marriage, and especially his faith and relationship with God coexisting harmoniously.

She longed to follow him but he obviously needed to be alone, perhaps even to pray alone. Reluctantly, she returned to the house.

She was helping Hilda make out lists of things still to be done for Christmas as well as the wedding when she at last heard his steps on the verandah. When he appeared just before lunch it was obvious he had managed to get some sleep.

He still looked bleary-eyed and rumpled as he said, "Sorry if I'm late. Afraid I fell asleep."

His voice was husky with sleep, and Jean busied herself pouring out a cup of tea so she did not have to look at him.

"Please don't ever feel you've got to apologize," Hilda said gently. "Rance warned me you would need lots of sleep and time to recuperate after Africa. I want you to feel free to come and go as you please."

Jean looked up swiftly to find his eyes on her as he sat down at the table. "As far as I'm concerned, there's certainly no need to apologize either," she added. Her eyes were steady on his until she saw a smile creep into them.

"Thank you" was all that he said, but she knew he understood she hadn't meant being late for a meal.

In the following days Jean found that Jonathan Howard crept into her prayers constantly, both during her set-aside morning prayer time as well as throughout the day. To her increasing disappointment, however, she didn't see as much of him alone as she would have liked. She was busy with Hilda and he seemed content to spend most of his time sleeping, reading, or going for long, solitary walks.

She sensed that he was still trying to cope with his experiences in Africa, even before coming home to a damaged house. Almost fearfully, she also hoped his talking about his wife and son had not added too much to the stress he was under.

Rance phoned and expressed his disappointment at not being able to get out to the farm for another couple of days because Nathan had the flu. When he did arrive at last early one morning, it thrilled Jean to see the delight in both men's faces as they shook hands and then hugged each other boisterously.

Then they had wandered off and spent hours in deep conversation. Jonathan reentered the house with a lighter step and his old laugh rang out several times that evening as he joined her in teasing Rance and Hilda. Suddenly Jean remembered Elijah the prophet. He too had needed physical rest and God's ministry to him after a battle with evil.

She was considerably relieved and yet somehow felt rebuffed and saddened that it had been Rance who had been able to help him. It was only as she was standing at her bedroom window staring out across the moonlit paddocks that she acknowledged to herself that her old feelings for Jonathan were returning and could become stronger than before.

"You stupid, stupid woman," she scolded herself out loud. "He still doesn't show in any way that he likes you anymore than he ever did. Besides, you're over forty years old!"

That didn't stop the ache in her heart but it did drive her to her Bible and to prayer.

God had been teaching her many lessons the last few years. That night, when she eventually turned her light off, she immediately fell asleep. Peace had again filled her heart. She still didn't have any direct guidance, but one thing she did know: A loving Heavenly Father was in control and He was still weaving the pattern for her life as she loved and trusted Him. Her pattern may not include Jonathan Howard, but God's grace would be sufficient.

Chapter 5

Jean had mixed feelings that Hilda had waited to buy her dress and veil until her aunt could go with her. While she was thrilled, at the same time it emphasized their relationship and her own new responsibilities to this delightful young woman.

She was relieved to find out that Hilda had done some initial looking, including a trip to some big bridal wear shops in Brisbane. But as she had said with considerable frustration to Jean that first evening, she had ended up with too many ideas and too many choices, "and it wasn't fun at all since Gail and Aunt Marian were too busy with the harvest to come with me."

While Jonathan watched silently, Hilda had then hugged Jean again with that sparkle of excitement that reminded Jean so much of her sister. How she wished her sister could have lived to know her beautiful daughter!

"Oh, I'm just so pleased you're here to come shopping with me before the Christmas rush," Hilda said, her eyes brimming with tears.

The day after Rance's visit they set off for their first shopping excursion. Jonathan had laughed quietly behind Hilda's back as he assured them he would quite enjoy a day by himself.

But despite her initial reluctance, as Hilda tugged her excitedly from one shop to another, Jean began to enjoy herself immensely. For the first time in well over twenty years Jean felt she had someone who belonged just to her, and she felt part of a real family.

When she realized Hilda would soon belong to a husband as well, she felt a momentary tug of self-pity which she dismissed angrily. After all, there was no way she would ever want Hilda to know the loneliness she had experienced.

As Jean discussed animatedly their successful shopping expedition that evening over tea, she saw Jonathan's eyes twinkling understandingly at her. He had been a little distant since he had told her about his wife and she felt a sudden flood of happiness. She grinned happily back at him and then saw the smile in his eyes suddenly disappear.

Hastily she looked away. Hilda was looking at them both and then slowly smiled at Jonathan. Jean looked quickly back at him. His eyes were on his food but she saw the slight smile on his lips.

She took in little of Hilda's excited discourse the rest of the meal. Feeling rebuffed again, she wasn't at all prepared later for his comment when the two of them were clearing the kitchen for Hilda. "And now, what about me?"

Jean looked up and stared at him blankly. A wave of relief swept through her when she saw he was smiling. She smiled back at him and asked crisply, "What about you, Dr. Howard?"

"It's my turn now, don't you think?"

"Your turn for what?"

"For spending some time with you, and for you to help me with my shopping, of course."

His eyes were twinkling and she laughed outright. "Is this that same decisive, extremely competent Jonathan Howard I used to know who kept the whole theater staff on their toes? I doubt if you needed help to buy things even when you were a small boy!"

"But I hate shopping, especially for clothes and especially Christmas presents for people I don't even know."

Christmas presents!

Jean's smile faltered. How could she have forgotten about them! In the past she had sent out a few cards, only buying small gifts for some of the staff she would work with on Christmas Day.

Even since becoming a Christian she'd had to battle these feelings each year, that Christmas was a time to remind her how alone she was in the world. But this year she had Hilda to buy for, and now there was Jonathan. She exhaled slowly.

Jonathan was watching her with a slight frown. "I take it you are going with Rance and Hilda to his mother and stepfather's place for Christmas dinner?"

Jean nodded. "You're going too?"

Somehow she felt immensely relieved. As much as she'd wanted to spend Christmas with Hilda, she had been diffident about intruding on Rance's family.

"With Robert still away, and with my house situation, I couldn't very well say no." He hesitated, and then said slowly, "Besides being the celebration of our Savior's birth, I've discovered Christmas can be the loneliest time of the year and a day I've sometimes wished would disappear from the calendar."

"Oh, you feel like that too?"

He nodded grimly and then his face gradually relaxed into a thoughtful smile. "But somehow, this year seems different."

To her secret astonishment, in the days that followed Jean found he was right. This year was very different. She found herself enjoying writing down a list of all the people she would be spending Christmas and Boxing Day with, staring with tingling delight and amazement at the name of Jonathan Howard at the top of the list.

But their shopping excursion was soon put on hold. Before either had a chance to mention their plans to Hilda, she had started on a massive cleaning of the cupboards. They found her staring with considerable dismay at the contents of a large cupboard in the storeroom attached to the laundry.

She turned and they saw the pain of old memories in her face. "I thought Dad had sorted out all of Mum's things, but it looks as though he just tossed a lot of them in here," she said with a catch in her voice.

Jean looked at Jonathan helplessly and he smiled understandingly at her. There was no way Jean could leave Hilda to do this heartrending task by herself.

Before they knew it, several days slipped by. Not only had the storeroom yielded up treasures and trash that needed dumping, but they found numerous other tasks that had to be done in the sheds. An easy comradeship developed between the three of them that Jean treasured. Jonathan automatically helped and fitted in as though they had known him all their lives.

Then at last Hilda insisted their shopping expedition could wait no longer. At the large shopping center in Toowoomba Jean found herself caught up in the excitement of the atmosphere of the brightly decorated shops and the bustling Christmas crowds.

For a while she and Jonathan wandered around watching an animated display of cartoon characters that enchanted groups of wide-eyed children. Another scene showed a typical snow-covered pine forest with many varieties of animals peeping out at them.

Despite the air conditioning Jean wiped at the perspiration on her face. "Wouldn't mind a bit of real snow right now!"

"I never know why we always have so many displays at Christmas with Northern Hemisphere snow scenes," Jonathan growled. "Look, they've even got pots of red and white poinsettias for sale when ours always flower in July. And I don't see even one wombat, koala, or kangaroo."

Jean tried to hide a smile as she had often thought the same. But she chided him gently, "I once spent Christmas in England and it was a really beautiful white Christmas. It was a lot prettier than a dusty, Aussie outback scene that most people seem to think so typifies us." She gave a chuckle and pointed. "But you're wrong, this time someone else must agree with you."

"You know, I've been realizing more and more since I've been going on these trips overseas, that we Aussies don't really have any specifically Australian traditions at Christmas," Jonathan said thoughtfully, and even a little regretfully. "I am often asked what they are, but when I try to explain I realize I'm describing traditions that are not peculiar to us but the same as found in America and England—ah, that's more like it!"

Another display showed Santa's sleigh being pulled by several large kangaroos across a typical outback scene of red dirt and sparse vegetation.

"Hmm, somehow it looks all wrong," Jean said with her head tilted to one side. "Give me reindeer any day."

They moved on and both stopped before a rough bark and timber construction that sheltered a beautiful, natural nativity scene.

"Now, that's something we all have in common," Jonathan whispered.

Jean couldn't speak. She stared at baby Jesus in His mother's arms. Along with Joseph and Mary, there were animals, and the shepherds and wise men looking to where a single bright beam of light shone from the star down onto the baby Jesus. The brightness of that light cast all except Jesus into shadows.

Jonathan reached out his hand and Jean felt her fingers curl around his. They stood very still for several long moments and then looked at each other. Jonathan's eyes were suspiciously bright and Jean smiled gently at him through her own wet lashes as he squeezed her hand.

There was no need for words. Both had worshiped and paid homage to the real reason for Christmas.

Together they chose gifts for Hilda, Rance, and the entire Stevens clan before tackling the difficult task of buying small gifts for Rance's family neither had ever met. It took them some time to buy just the right gift for Jonathan's son, Robert. Jean was surprised at how hesitant and unsure the usually decisive doctor became and she wondered again about Jonathan's relationship with his twenty-something son.

She found her heart aching for both of them when he said wistfully, "I do wish he could come home for Christmas."

But at last a book about Australian birds and a good dress shirt were purchased. As they left the last shop Jean said triumphantly, "Now there's just Nathan. What do nine-year-old boys like these days, Jonathan?"

He grinned and a look of anticipation spread over his face. "I really don't know, but it's going to be fun finding out!"

And it was. They spent more time in the sprawling toy shop than any other, and Jean was sure they had played with every conceivable variation of truck, car, superhero, and computer game before Jonathan at last made his choices.

She was still laughing as they loaded their purchases into his car. "I hope Rance and Hilda will appreciate the piercing siren on that fire truck."

"From what I've seen of your loving niece, she'll be too thrilled at watching that boy enjoying himself. Rance told me Nathan had a pretty deprived life until he found out about him."

Jean nodded. "It's absolutely incredible the difference in him now, but he's lost a lot of his childhood."

"Well, these should help make up just a little."

"More than just a little," she exclaimed and then laughed. "What if everyone else has the same idea of buying several gifts for him? I know Rance has already bought him heaps of stuff and will probably spoil him rotten this Christmas too."

"Well, kids make Christmas extra special and I haven't had kids in my Christmas for far too long."

Jean silently agreed. She had made it a point of visiting the children's ward each Christmas, but the pale-faced children not even allowed home at that time of the year had only increased her heartache.

"It'll be great fun watching him opening them all and besides, a bit of spoiling won't hurt him his first Christmas with his dad," Jonathan said softly as he looked at his watch. "My goodness, no wonder I'm hungry, it's almost afternoon teatime and we've yet to have lunch. I'm so sorry, Jean, I've been neglecting you."

"Neglecting me? After that huge chocolate muffin and ice cream you insisted I try for morning tea?"

He laughed back at her. "And which I helped you eat, don't forget. Now, where will it be, fast food or plain old fish and chips in the park?" he added teasingly.

She shuddered. "It's far too hot to go to the park." After considering for a moment, she looked at him. "You told me you've never been to Toowoomba before, so I know just the right place."

Jonathan agreed heartily as they ate in the quiet, elegant restaurant perched at the top of the mountain range overlooking the beautiful Lockyer Valley.

"You know, you haven't told me what made you commit your life to Christ, Jean," Jonathan said as they waited for their main course to be served. "I can't get over the difference in you. You're. . .you're so full of the sheer joy of living compared to the woman I remember."

Jean stared out of the window for a moment, wondering how much she should tell him. At last she looked back at him and said softly, "My life was in an absolute mess, and it was actually you who made me turn to the Bible for answers, my friend."

She smiled gently as confusion and then delighted surprise filled his bright eyes. She took a deep breath and continued quickly before her courage failed.

"As I got to know and. . .and like you, I realized there was something about you that was very different from other men. Remember that time one of the theater staff discovered he had an inoperable tumor? You had such compassion for him and spent so much time visiting him in the ward."

He dismissed that with an impatient gesture. "Plenty of other people do those kinds of things, Jean, not only believers."

"Yes, I know, but once I visited him just after you had left. As it turned out, it was only a few days before he died, but at the time I couldn't get over the peace he had despite knowing he was terminally ill. I found myself blurting out something about it and he told me that you had led him to a personal relationship with God. Faith in Jesus Christ had taken away his fear of death and dying.

"One day," she continued quickly before he could comment, "in fact the same day I finished at the hospital, I happened to see the Bible you'd left behind in the staff room. But I was looking for pat answers and I discovered there was so much I didn't understand about what I read that I ended up with even more questions. Then my. . .my situation suddenly became worse and at last, in sheer desperation, I rang Marian Stevens. We'd been friends since our teens, but she had become too religious for me after she got married. We hadn't seen each other for years."

Jean paused, a smile lighting her face. "You know what that woman did after I blurted out to her on the phone some of my questions about God?"

"She wasn't happy to answer them only on the phone but flew down to Sydney to meet you," Jonathan said promptly, a tender look on his face that shook Jean to her depths.

She stared at him speechlessly and he added with a smile, "I asked Hilda if she knew when you became a Christian and she wasn't sure, just that Marian had gone racing off all the way to Sydney and later you had accepted Christ as your personal Lord and Savior."

"Well, er, yes," Jean said weakly, feeling secretly thrilled that he had been interested enough to want to know about her.

There had been more to it than that. She was thankful Marian had kept her secret, and for a moment she wondered if she dared tell him.

Then the waiter brought their meals and the moment was gone.

Jonathan seemed thoughtful but she was glad that he did not return to the subject. Instead, he started chatting away about the upcoming wedding and Christmas celebrations.

"So, are you going to brave Boxing Day with the Stevens clan, Jonathan?" she asked as they lingered over a final cup of coffee. "Every year they go to the river for a bush picnic. We eat leftover Christmas ham, turkey, cake, and lamingtons, and of course watermelon for a hot day."

"Wouldn't miss it for the world," he said cheerfully.

The absolute delight that filled her was disturbing. She was falling deeper and deeper under this man's spell and something inside her warned caution. This man still had the power to hurt her too much. Besides, she had been learning to seek out what God wanted in her life, and so far she didn't know His will on this relationship.

Later that night she escaped to her room with an anxious, wondering heart. "Jean Drew, get a grip on yourself!" she scolded as she stared into the mirror. "The man's already caused you enough grief. Face reality, you're too old now for all this falling-in-love nonsense!"

But she knew that wasn't necessarily true. When she was with Jonathan she felt so much younger than her forty-plus years. And was there any age when a woman was too old to fall deeply in love with an attractive, dynamic man?

Had she ever stopped loving Jonathan Howard?

Chapter 6

I t was a long night for Jean. Part of it she spent in prayer and seeking help from Scripture. Once again she fervently wished that God could tell her directly what He wanted of her in this situation. At last she fell into a restless sleep, and then awakened with little heart or energy for Hilda's task of the day.

"I do hope you don't mind, Jonathan," Hilda was saying when Jean arrived late for breakfast. She turned and greeted Jean quietly and then turned back to the two large boxes on the kitchen table. "Mum and Dad always liked the house to look festive for Christmas and New Years," she added wistfully.

Jean caught Jonathan's eyes and recognized instantly the warning in them. It was unnecessary. She too had seen the moist brightness in her niece's eyes.

"More things to sort through, Hilda?" she asked gently.

"Well, kind of, but I'm not sure I'll be wanting to toss any of these out before the removalist takes my things to the manse in Brisbane." As she spoke, she reached into the box and pulled out a bundle of shining tinsel streamers. "Mum always made a big thing of putting up decorations each year. She said if we did it for our own parties we should do the very best we can to celebrate our Lord's birth."

"It's been quite a few years since I bothered with more than just a wreath on my front door," Jonathan mused and then turned toward Jean. There was a distinct glint in his eyes as he said challengingly, "Well, Sister Drew, are you going to help us put up some Christmas decorations?"

How could she maintain that protective shield around her heart, which she had decided last night was her only defense against this man's impact on her senses, when he looked at her this way?

Jonathan's face was filled with boyish enthusiasm as he climbed the stepladder again to adjust the red, green, and white streamers they had just erected in the lounge room.

"How's that, Hilda?" he called down in his deep voice that always pulled on some inner chord of Jean's being.

"Perfect!"

As he flashed his radiant smile at her niece, Jean knew her resistance to him had once again plummeted to a low ebb. Perfect indeed! Only she didn't mean the hanging bells and the paper and foil decorations!

As she watched him, she realized how different he was from the worn-out, dispirited man who had first arrived at the farm. Perhaps Rance had known how much he would need the peace and quiet here.

Jean's dilemma of the night before slowly faded into the background as the morning progressed. Doing this simple family activity seemed so normal and natural with Jonathan. She could not remember the last time she'd had so much fun, or felt as young as Hilda.

It seemed as if every childish decoration that Hilda had ever made and dragged home from school must have been kept by her parents. What could have been a tearful time full of memories was circumvented by the antics of Jonathan. Jean felt helpless as her admiration for him continued to grow.

Constantly teasing Hilda and herself, he suggested strange places like the bathroom to put some of the more outrageous decorations until everything in the boxes had been used and the house was transformed.

He even held a crude, cut out picture, which they decided was supposed to be mistletoe, over Hilda and gave her a smacking kiss, saying with mock fear, "Seeing as we don't have any of the real thing and as long as you don't tell on me to Rance." Then he had turned toward Jean with a special gleam in his eyes, but she had beaten a hasty retreat. She merely scowled at him a little later as he muttered, "Chicken!" when Hilda's attention was elsewhere.

All morning Jean had found it difficult to drag her eyes away from Jonathan's animated face. Never before had anyone—except this same incredible man—had this impact on her.

Oh, God, I'm already in deep trouble here, she prayed silently several times, and she wondered helplessly what she could do short of packing her bags and removing herself from his vicinity. Hilda needed her, so that was out of the question. But then, she hadn't seen the man for ten years and that had done nothing to stop this quick return of her feelings toward him.

"Well, I think that must be the last of them." There was definite regret in Jonathan's voice as he climbed down from the stepladder and wiped his face with a crumpled linen handkerchief. "Phew, just as well, it's getting very hot. I could certainly do with a drink."

"One coming up." Jean was glad of the excuse to disappear into the kitchen, but as she carried a tray of glasses and ice-cold soft drinks back to the lounge room a few minutes later, she nearly tripped over the unwieldy coil of colored lights Jonathan was trying to unravel.

Hilda was looking doubtfully at him. "I don't think we need to do anything outside this year. After. . .after the wedding there won't be anyone here until Beth and Arthur move in."

She hid her face as she bent over the cable and Jonathan looked swiftly at her and then up at Jean inquiringly.

"Oh, Hilda, but aren't you still planning your yearly barbecue for Christmas Eve this year? Besides, don't stop him now," she managed to say with a teasing laugh, "I'm dying to see Dr. Howard clambering around under the eaves among the spiders and cobwebs. If only old Dr. Ferguson could see you now," she added for good measure as they exchanged smiles of relief and Hilda gave a rather shaky laugh.

Although it was obvious that Hilda loved Rance very much, it was also obvious what an upheaval it was for her to move from her old home. And suddenly Jean was fiercely glad Jonathan was here with her to share that knowledge, and to help make it as easy as possible for this niece she was learning to love more each day.

Not only did they end up stringing the lights around the outside of the house, there was also enough to loop around the lower branches of the old gum tree that gave shade on the hottest day to the back patio where Bob Garrett had built the outdoor barbecue. They had found a couple of long ladders for this task and had almost finished the tree when they heard the phone ring. Hilda dropped her end of the lights and raced to answer it.

Jean hesitated for a moment and then she reluctantly climbed up the ladder to help Jonathan. She had always hated heights and a few moments later thankfully started back down the ladder. She was congratulating herself on not doing anything foolish when her foot slipped.

She gave a startled yelp. The ladder tilted alarmingly and she started to fall. Suddenly strong arms grabbed her and the next thing she knew she went sprawling on top of Jonathan.

Winded, she lay still for a moment and then realized how tightly his arms were holding her. For one delicious moment she wished with all her heart she could stay wrapped and protected by them, then he moved and she quickly started to push herself away.

"Th–thank you," she gasped and tried to scramble to her feet.

At that moment one large hand reached up and settled firmly on the nape of her neck. He tugged gently and she lost her balance and fell against him once more. Long fingers caressed her face as he drew her head down.

With a quickening heartbeat she stared into his dark, passion-filled eyes. The low moan that welled up in her throat was muffled as firm lips possessed hers. Then, suddenly, she was clinging to him and something deep inside her sprang to life.

Jean wasn't sure who pulled away first, but she realized he had moved and her head was being cradled against his shoulder as their breathing gradually returned to normal. Then it hit her what had happened and frantically she pulled away from him and scrambled to her feet.

"Jonathan, Aunt Marian wants to speak to you too!" Hilda called from an open window.

He stood up slowly and they stared at each other. So many times in the days that followed she wished Hilda had not interrupted them just then. Perhaps he would have said something that would have explained the startled, arrested look on his face as he looked at her.

When he had disappeared inside the house, she stood for a moment with her hand touching her quivering lips.

"Aunt Jean, you'll never guess what's happened."

She turned and stared blindly at Hilda for a moment and then realized she was saying something about Beth and her husband.

"What did you say, Hilda?"

Her niece looked at her closely. "Anything wrong, Aunt Jean?"

"No, no, I'm sorry. You were saying something about Beth and Arthur." Even to her own ears her voice sounded strange and she turned away and reached down to pick up the ladder.

"Aunt Marian just rang to say that they've been given a fortnight's notice to get out of the house they were renting in Brisbane."

Jean swung around. Hilda nodded at her and added, "She's absolutely furious. Fancy giving a young family such short notice with Christmas so close! They rang Aunt Marian to ask if they could move in with her until after the wedding, but I told her that's ridiculous. I told her they should move straight here where they were going to anyway at the end of January when Art starts working for Jim."

Hilda took a deep breath and looked worried. "So, Aunt Marian's inviting Jonathan to stay over there for the rest of his stay. I do hope he doesn't mind."

Jean longed to cry out, "No, he can't go! Not when I haven't seen enough of him yet after all these years. Not when I've just realized how much I love him."

The thought almost stunned her as much as his kiss. She swallowed rapidly, trying to think rationally as well as find her voice.

"He won't mind," she managed simply at last, her voice sounding husky. Then before her courage faded she cleared her throat and said, "Hilda, this house only has four bedrooms."

She paused, hoping her niece would not be upset at her suggestion. "Don't you think it would make things much easier for all of you if I moved over to Marian's too? Her house is so much bigger. It's only five minutes away and we could still spend the days here together getting everything organized for Christmas as well as the wedding and the removal of your things to Brisbane."

Hilda's face dropped, and Jean added quickly, "There is no way I'll move until the day they are due to arrive. You won't have to spend another night here alone," she said understandingly and saw the relief on the young woman's face.

Jean could not read Jonathan's expression when he joined them and told them it was all arranged that he was to move to the Stevens home when the other family moved in.

Then her heart leaped when he added casually, "I hope you two don't mind, but I suggested to Mrs. Stevens that it might be a good idea if Jean came too. It will save the brother and sister from having to share a room. From what you've both told me, their two youngsters have had enough unsettled months this last year or so, especially since Art's accident, and the sooner they get settled the better."

It was all said in the crisp, authoritative voice that Jean had heard many times and she relaxed. For years she'd always had to be the strong one, the organizer, the one others relied on and drew strength from. Here was someone who so naturally could shoulder her burdens as well as his own on his broad shoulders.

Then suddenly she knew she was wrong. From things he had said the last few weeks, she knew that he had learned not to shoulder his own burdens. He leaned very heavily on his Lord, handing everything over to Him. Those first two days he had been exhausted and it had been only a passing moment of discouragement.

There was no doubt about Hilda's disappointment but she was very philosophical about it all. "At least with Art being able to walk again we don't have to worry about building those ramps for his wheelchair before they move here." Then her face lit up. "And there will be kids here for Christmas!"

"Mmm, then there's something we haven't finished yet." Jonathan's eyes twinkled at Jean's apparent discomfiture. "We haven't finished with the decorations yet."

She glared at him for a moment and then looked at Hilda who returned her glance with a slightly puzzled look before she turned back to Jonathan. "But we've put up so many already I don't think there's much room left," she said with a slight laugh.

He just smiled at Hilda and cocked one of those incredibly thick eyebrows.

Light dawned on Jean just as Hilda exclaimed, "A Christmas tree! The kids will want a tree!"

"I don't know about kids," Jean said wistfully, "but I haven't even erected an artificial one in years."

"Neither have I," agreed Jonathan.

Hilda looked from one to the other and Jean could see that for the first time she had begun to appreciate how different their Christmases had been from her own family-filled ones.

"Right," Hilda said briskly. "We won't get one until a couple of days before Christmas. With this heat they dry out and drop too much by Christmas despite the bucket of water we stand them in. But the job of getting it is the responsibility of you two while I finish clearing out the rooms. I have a horrible feeling the next few days are going to fly by with all that has to be crammed into them!"

But that wasn't the last of the phone calls that disrupted their program.

"The builder's going to be able to start work before Christmas after all and he wants me to come and finish choosing paint colors and carpets," Jonathan told them that evening after hanging up the phone. "It's a bit earlier than I'd wanted," he muttered as he stretched out in the lounge chair.

Jean stared at him, wondering if she'd heard him correctly. Under his scowl those thick eyebrows actually met in the middle. Then the incredible thought came to her: *He wants to spend even more time with me.*

He looked up so suddenly he caught her staring at him and she hurriedly looked away, something she had been doing a lot of since that kiss.

"Hilda, would you mind terribly if I steal Jean for another day?"

His voice was a little gruff and Jean's eyes swung back to him, her own widening.

Hilda looked from one to the other, something she also seemed to have been doing quite a bit that day. Her eyes started to twinkle.

"Well, as long as it's no more than a day, I think I can spare her. Remember, you promised to get the tree, and Jean was going with me for that last fitting of my dress. I want to have everything ready for the wedding so I can just concentrate on packing most of my things to make room for Beth's," she added with a beaming smile at him.

"Hey, just a moment," Jean protested. "What happened to asking if I wanted to go with you?" She was so confused by the rush of feelings a few minutes ago that she wasn't at all sure it would be wise being with him for a whole day.

Then as he smiled at her and said softly, "I really do need your help, Jean," all her resistance crumbled as she knew it always would with this man.

Later, traveling down the highway to Brisbane, she knew spending more time with him would make it even more heartbreaking if once again they had to say good-bye.

Chapter 7

J ean liked Jonathan's house immediately. It was set on a couple of acres on the southern outskirts of Brisbane, not too far from the glorious beaches of the Gold Coast. Although the remains of the tree had been removed, the tarpaulin still covered the damaged roof.

While they avoided the bedroom where the ceiling had fallen in, several other rooms were also in disarray from the storm. Because the tree had come down in the very center of the house, only the kitchen and laundry had escaped relatively unscathed. However, Jean could tell the rooms had been decorated with a quiet elegance that would be very restful after a day dealing with sick and injured patients.

I could live very happily in this house, she found herself thinking wistfully, and then felt her cheeks burn as she hurried after Jonathan.

The stench of mildew and rotting wool made Jean wrinkle her nose. "Phew, I see what you mean about new carpets."

"And new curtains," Jonathan added grimly. "By the time I got home they had all gone moldy as well. That's what happens in a sub-tropical place like Brisbane. I managed to toss the curtains out but the carpet had to wait. When I eventually got here there were still pools of water on them that had been there for days. I mopped the water off as much as I could. I suspect we'll need more hot days to dry the floor after they are taken out."

While they waited for the builder to keep his appointment, they looked over the carpet, fabric, and wallpaper samples Jonathan had already acquired. Jean knew that Jonathan had made good money over the years but she was impressed that he was not even considering more lavish, expensive replacements. Then again, she mused, from what he had told her about his stints overseas, she was sure his own money had financed the majority of those projects.

The builder arrived on time and was so brisk and competent that when he did leave, Jonathan looked at his watch with satisfaction. "Great, as I hoped we have most of the afternoon to ourselves. After we find some lunch, how would you like to take me to meet Beth and her husband and kids?"

Jean stared at him and then slowly smiled. "You were planning this all along, weren't you?" she accused.

He grinned back. "I just thought if I were in their shoes I'd feel pretty bad about guests having to move out so they can move in. If they meet me I'm sure they'll feel better about it all."

And once again, Jean realized later, this amazing man was proved right. It was obvious as soon as they met Arthur that he was not only annoyed about having to move so soon, but very embarrassed when introduced to Jonathan.

Jonathan cut across Arthur's apologies immediately. "It's I who am imposing on your family, and I'm only too happy to move a few kilometers or so as long as Jean comes with me. We haven't seen each other for ten years and we still have a lot of catching up to do."

Jean felt her cheeks catch fire as Arthur stared at her. She was absolutely speechless as she gaped at Jonathan, who was looking at her blandly, a fact that did not escape Arthur.

Arthur grinned wickedly at her. "I'm very glad to hear that," he said, and then took pity on her and changed the subject by asking Jonathan about his friendship with the "Rev," as he called Rance.

Jean stood up quickly and muttered something about seeing how the kids were and escaped to the backyard where Jacqueline and Robbie were playing with their collie puppy.

As the children bubbled over with excitement about moving back to the farm life they loved, Beth said something about their packing that set Jean thinking.

"No problem," Jean said cheerfully, noticing Jonathan had joined them. "The children have started their summer holidays, haven't they?" When Beth nodded, she asked hurriedly, "Would you like to have us take them back so you could concentrate on packing and moving?"

Jean glanced at Jonathan as she spoke and saw surprise flash into his face. She looked quickly back at Beth who was shaking her head.

"That would be lovely to get them out of our hair, Aunt Jean. But Mum said she was coming down to help us and I don't like leaving them with Jim and Gail when they are still finishing off getting the crop to the railway terminal."

"Oh, I'm sure Jean and I could handle a couple of kids for a few days until you arrive, don't you, Jean?" Jonathan's voice held a smile in it, but his eyes were watching her with a challenging glint. "I happen to know Hilda is all for the idea. I've already asked her."

Jean was lost for words. Then a warm feeling swept over her. They thought alike about so many things and she enjoyed this forceful man taking control.

It was a rush to pack as much as they could cram into the car for the children, have tea, and set off before it became too late. The collie dog, Bonnie, was also established between the two children on the backseat. Although at the start of the trip the children's tongues wagged furiously with excitement, they had traveled not even halfway when all noise and movement ceased in the back of the car.

"All asleep at last?" Jonathan murmured after Jean had twisted around and surveyed the sleeping children.

"Yes, thank goodness," Jean said with heartfelt relief.

He smiled at her and she relaxed in a pleasant haze of weariness. After a comfortable silence she said softly, "You're very good with the children, Jonathan."

"So are you, Jean. It's a shame—"

He stopped abruptly and it took her a moment to realize what he had been going to say. It was a shame she had never had children of her own. Suddenly she longed fiercely for at least one child she could have watched develop and grow. Now her childbearing years were slipping away so very quickly.

It was almost as though he could read her mind when he murmured, "It's wonderful how medical science has made it possible for older women to safely have children."

Emotion clogged her throat for a moment. "I'm not sure if having older parents is really the best for a child."

"It worked okay for Hilda, didn't it? Rance told me her parents were in their forties when they adopted her. Besides, it apparently didn't worry God how old Abraham and Sarah were when He gave Isaac to them, did it?"

"And what about you, Jonathan, would you like another child at your age?"

Jean had blurted out the words before she could stop herself. There was a long silence and the easy atmosphere between them was gone. She was annoyed with herself for not passing his comment off lightly.

"I do know one thing. I'd very much like a chance to make up for the mistakes I made with Robert." He stopped abruptly and then added, "It would entirely depend on who the mother was."

She felt him turn and look at her. Suddenly she could hardly breathe. She didn't dare move.

"If she were committed to doing God's will and that is what His will was," he continued in the same soft murmur, "then the answer would have to be yes."

Somehow she plucked up the courage to turn and look at him then. He darted a quick glance at her before returning his attention to the road.

"How does a person find out what God's will is for something so important, Jonathan?" she whispered desperately.

After a long pause she saw his shoulders move in a shrug. "I believe God shows each of His children His will in ways that are right for that individual. What is right for me may not be right for you. You have to find His way for you, Jean," he added gently.

Nothing more was said that night, but in the busy days that followed his words haunted her. She was sure he had been trying to say more to her than had been on the surface. Was he actually thinking it was possible for them to have a relationship?

Dare she even wonder if he were thinking of marriage, even perhaps of having a child together?

Her prayers and heart-searching intensified. For many years now she had put all thoughts of marriage behind her. Even if Jonathan were growing to love her, could a marriage between them work?

Above all, what was God's will for them, and how and when would she find out?

Chapter 8

S uddenly it was Christmas Eve. To the children's delight, a beautifully decorated pine tree filled a corner of the lounge room. Jonathan and Jean had enlisted their help to choose just the right one and then to decorate it. A tenderness, and a deepening sense of intimacy, had developed between the couple as they had helped the children, and some days Jean had found herself drifting along in an unbelieving haze.

Hilda's wedding dress was safely hanging in her bedroom and all her things had been moved to Brisbane except what she needed for the next week. Jonathan and Jean had moved without any fuss to Marian Stevens's house the day the removalist had arrived with the belongings of the Canley-Smiths.

"Well, the house is still in a mess, but no one seems too worried about it at all," Jonathan had commented with considerable amusement as he drove the short distance back to the Stevens home late that evening after spending all day helping the family to unpack and settle in.

Jean had just smiled wearily at him, closed her eyes, and been almost asleep when he finally stopped the car. There had been more important things to do than unpack everything and keep the place tidy. The Christmas shopping was all done. Food that could be stored in the freezer had been prepared for the barbecue on Christmas Eve and the picnic on Boxing Day.

The women were thankful that Rance and Beth's mothers had been adamant that, with all the upheaval, Christmas Day was their sole responsibility this year.

When she awoke on Christmas Eve morning, the first thing Jean remembered was the tender amusement in Jonathan's voice as he had helped her from the car and led her straight to her room. A tender, gentle wisp of a kiss had brushed her mouth as he left her at her door.

She lay there for a few minutes listening to the warbling of a couple of magpies in the pepperina trees near her bedroom window. Her sleep had been deep and peaceful. The last few days had been too busy to spend much time considering her future, but she knew that the tension and awareness between herself and Jonathan had increased.

She knew that Jonathan felt it too. Sometimes when they had brushed against each other or caught each other's eye, there was an expression of heat in his that caused her to turn away in considerable confusion.

As they had waved them good-bye last night, Beth and Hilda had laughingly told them they were sacked. Both of them were now officially guests again and would be treated as such.

Suddenly Jean remembered Jonathan had said something about driving to Dalby this morning to see the charming country town. Looking her straight in the eye, he had said, "We'll have a chance then for a serious talk."

She had been too tired to realize what he might mean, but suddenly a sense of excited anticipation sent Jean flying from bed and into the shower. She dressed carefully, smoothing on light makeup. As she studied herself in the mirror, she wished for a fleeting moment that she still wore the blush of youth instead of the lines the years had brought.

God can restore the years the locust has eaten.

The thought flashed into her mind and for a moment her hands tightened on the top of the dressing table.

"Oh, God, are You still doing that for us both?" she prayed out loud. The peace that suddenly swept through her was an answer.

There was a knock on her door and she moved slowly to answer it, wishing suddenly she had more time to open the Scriptures and find that passage about the locust and the wasted years. Jonathan was standing with his shoulders hunched and his hands thrust into his pockets.

He was dressed as she had seen him so many times when she had first met him. His dark business suit fitted him perfectly and he looked every inch the successful surgeon.

For a moment they stared at each other, and then her heart took a nose dive at the expression on his face.

"Jean, I'm so sorry, but our trip to Dalby is off."

She was astonished at the depth of her disappointment and couldn't speak.

"I had a phone call a little while ago from my partner's wife. He was supposed to be operating today—a mastectomy for cancer." His words were clipped, expressionless. "He's had an accident, fractured his leg, and is in traction. The operation can't be delayed. There may not be a theater available again for another two weeks. Other surgeons he's tried are either fully booked or already away for the holiday break."

His face suddenly looked so bleak that her hand reached out and closed on his arm. His hand touched hers and then their fingers clung together.

"That's fine, Jonathan, of course you have to go," she said quickly.

"Jean," he stopped and cleared his throat, "you do realize I don't have any choice, don't you?"

She looked at him with surprise, feeling offended. "Goodness, Jonathan, I'm a nurse, aren't I? Surely if anyone could understand about a doctor's interrupted private life, I do," she said teasingly, and was then amazed at the relief that flooded his pale face with color.

His hand tightened on hers and suddenly she was in his arms, his lips plundering hers with something that felt almost like desperation. Then he wrenched himself away and looked at her. His face was transformed, his eyes suspiciously bright.

"Jean."

That one word, her name spoken so tenderly, so full of love. . . And then he was gone.

When she had regained control of herself enough to venture out of her room, Marian met her with the message that Jonathan expected to be home in time for the barbecue.

"He was terribly upset after he got off the phone," her friend teased her. "And I'm sure it wasn't just because his holiday was interrupted. Do I hear wedding bells for you two?"

"Marian!"

Her friend was unperturbed by her shocked face. "I wasn't born yesterday, Jean Drew. It's been obvious to all of us how much you like each other. Why, you can hardly bear to let each other out of sight! Besides, he looks at you in a way there's no mistaking. If you ask me, you're perfect for each other."

Before Jean could recover her senses enough to answer, Marian had whisked herself out of the room. For a long moment Jean stared after her, and then a smile spread across her face and she laughed out loud.

When she next saw Marian she was relieved that she refrained from further comment. The day dragged by, and when it came time to drive over to the barbecue, Jean tried to hide her disappointment that Jonathan had not arrived.

"Never mind, I'm sure he'll get back as soon as he can," Marian said comfortingly, and Jean felt herself blush that her concern was so obvious.

Under the colored lights, which enlivened the outdoor setting, as the smell of cooking meat and frying onions permeated the air, Jean made a real effort to join in the laughter and conversation. When headlights on the track to the house signalled a new arrival, it was Jean who hurried to meet the tall dark figure who alighted from the car.

"You're just in time," she called out. "We've saved a juicy steak just for you."

Then the man moved into the light and a voice with a faint North American accent said, "And that will make me very welcome. I've been starving for a good Aussie steak ever since I left home."

He was in his midtwenties, but it was the familiar slant of his jaw, the dark eyebrows that almost met above his strong nose, and the teasing hazel eyes that made Jean gasp in amazement, and her face light up with delight.

"Robert? Robert Howard? Oh, I'm so thrilled you're here. Jonathan will be absolutely delighted!"

The young man relaxed. "So my father is here. I haven't let him know I was coming. Only made up my mind at the last moment that I was tired of battling the snow and icy winds and only a good dose of a hot Christmas Day could cure it. And. . .and I had this need to see my dad."

As he looked so eagerly around, Jean hated to disappoint him. "I'm sorry, he had an emergency this morning and had to go to Brisbane, but we're expecting him back this evening."

His face fell and he gave a rueful laugh. "Oh, well, it's nice to know some things don't change. Dad always has these emergencies and I suppose I'd better get used to them myself. At my mature age I've decided I'm going to see if I can get into medical school myself."

"I know that will make your father very, very happy," she said quietly. "And I know also how much he was missing you this Christmas."

He looked at her keenly for a moment and then followed her as she proceeded to introduce him to everyone.

To her deep disappointment, Jonathan never showed up by the time they dispersed for the night, but Robert did not seem surprised in the slightest.

"Probably found he had to be on hand for post-op care," Robert said with a resigned shrug that told Jean only too well how many times over the years this must have happened. Despite Jonathan's self-condemnation, Robert realized the necessity for putting another person's life before his family.

And if by any wonderful chance you do become a surgeon's wife, you'll have to accept it as a fact of life too, my girl, she told herself grimly. She already missed him so much that even a few hours spent with him would be worth more than all day with someone else.

At Marian Stevens's insistence, Robert camped on a fold-out bed in the lounge room. When they met in the dining room Christmas morning, he was as disappointed as Jean that his father had still not arrived. Their "Happy Christmas" greetings were a little forced, but fortunately having a hurried breakfast and getting ready for the Christmas service left them little time to dwell on his absence.

All through the service Jean expected Jonathan to slip into the vacant seat beside her. Rance's sermon was as inspiring as always, but Jean still felt a depth of loneliness she had not known. She sadly acknowledged that if Jonathan Howard were to disappear from her life again, her faith in God's sufficiency would be put to the test as never before.

After the service Beth and her family returned with Marian and

Jim and Gail Stevens, while Rance and his son accompanied Jean and Robert back to Hilda's place for quick refreshments—and to exchange presents—before setting out for Christmas dinner with his parents. Apparently, Nathan had already opened some of his gifts from his grandparents before the service, and his eyes glistened with excitement when he saw the pile of gaily wrapped gifts beneath the huge Christmas tree.

"Are. . .are any of them for me?" he faltered as he looked at Hilda.

"Why," teased a wide-eyed Hilda, "didn't Santa Claus find you at your grandparents?"

"Don't tease the young man, Hilda," Jean scolded mockingly. "Of course some are for you, but I was just wondering if we should wait for Dr. Howard."

Robert then cocked his head as if he heard something. "That's probably him now," he said, striding rapidly from the room.

The repeated sound of a car horn sent Jean leading the eager rush outside, but she stopped suddenly and watched as Jonathan saw his son. The wonder and joy in his pale, exhausted face moved her to tears.

"Robert?"

"Happy Christmas, Dad!"

His son gave a choked sound and then the two men were hugging each other. Jonathan pulled back after a moment and then looked around. His searching eyes found Jean and a wary, anxious expression filled his face.

Jean feasted her eyes on him and of their own volition her feet moved her toward him. It seemed the most natural thing in the world for him to pull her into his arms.

She ignored the surprise on the faces of those watching and clasped him tightly.

"I'm so sorry, Jean."

She frowned for a moment and then realized he was apologizing to her for not getting back when he had said. Even more, for having to leave at all when they had not had their "talk."

"There's nothing to be sorry for, my dear," she said simply. "Is your patient all right?"

Relief lit up his tired, black-circled eyes for a moment. "She wasn't for most of the night. The surgery had to be far more extensive then we thought and I had to explain her ongoing care to her when she was completely recovered from the anesthetic, and then later to her husband," he added sadly.

Jean moved closer to him. Without him saying anymore she knew that the woman's future prospects were not good and silently offered him her support and encouragement. Jonathan's eyes softened, acknowledging his appreciation.

Then he turned back to his son who was watching them keenly. "You've met Jean, Robert? Did she explain that we worked together years ago?"

Jean had enjoyed a long talk with Robert at the barbecue. They smiled at each other and she felt the heat flood her face as he said mischievously, "Oh, yes, she explained that and much more. She's one very special lady, Dad."

Someone cleared their throat and they swung around to see Hilda beaming at them. "I hate to break this up, but I'm not sure Rance can hold Nathan back much longer from ripping into all those exciting parcels you two spent so long buying and wrapping."

Jean had already been enjoying her Christmas in a way she never had before, but suddenly with Jonathan by her side she felt as though God could not have blessed her more.

She was wrong.

Nathan had almost finished with his "loot," as Robert laughingly called his presents, when Jonathan rather impatiently handed Jean a beautifully wrapped box. She eagerly ripped the paper off and lifted out a crystal star. Held up carefully to the light, it sparkled and gleamed.

Speechless, she looked at Jonathan.

"It reminded me of that star over the nativity scene at the shopping center," he murmured. "I've thought about that a lot."

So had Jean, but she waited for him to put it into words.

"The. . .the star showed the wise men where God wanted them to go, what He wanted them to do. It led them to Jesus," he finished simply.

There was silence. Even Nathan stilled and looked from one serious adult face to another. Then Jonathan stood up. "If I remember correctly, Hilda, a certain tin shed is still out near your garage?" he asked.

Hilda looked startled and Rance gave a short bark of laughter.

"I told you about that, did I?" His eyes were dancing, but he said solemnly, "Yes, it's still there. I recommend it to you, Jonathan, for what you obviously have in mind. I'm just glad we are not in the middle of a thunderstorm this time! And please, don't worry about being late for dinner. I know Mother will understand. Just one thing—I won't be working again until after my own honeymoon!"

Jean had not taken her eyes from Jonathan, but at that last statement she looked at Rance, wondering what on earth he was talking about. Suddenly she remembered that as a minister Rance performed wedding ceremonies. A tide of warmth swept through her.

When Jonathan looked back at her with his face full of unconcealed love, she knew that Rance had told his old friend about the time he had proposed to Hilda in the old tin shed during a thunderstorm.

She tilted her chin and tried for her best old dragon stare. "Well, what are you waiting for then, Dr. Howard?"

He stared at her, an answering gleam entering his eyes. "Just for this, Sister Drew," he retorted in his most arrogant surgeon voice.

He took a couple of steps closer to where he had flung his suit coat. Impatiently she watched him remove a small gift. Then she felt his hand grasp hers firmly and pull her toward the door.

With dawning hope she realized what a box that size might contain as he raced her past a grinning, startled Robert and across the yard to that old tin shed.

There he stopped and swung her around toward him. "Jean, I've been really seeking God's guidance for what He wants me to do about loving you like I do."

He paused, and she said with a laugh in her voice, "Did He suggest that perhaps you should tell me what you told Him?"

"I didn't want to say anything because I knew you too were still trying to find out His will about a relationship between us."

She reached up and ran a hand lovingly down his cheek where he had not even stopped to shave. "Johnny, you must have been busy this past twenty-four hours to not even take the time to shave," she said irrelevantly.

The hesitancy disappeared entirely from his face and he reached up to take her hand in his. He didn't say anything, just held it tightly in both of his and waited. The blaze of love in his face said it all.

There was so much she wanted to tell him but somehow she knew that he already knew it, or most of it.

Perhaps he didn't know yet that her breaking off her engagement and wedding to Mark had been the hardest thing she had ever done. Perhaps he didn't know that she had found out only the day before the date that had been set for their wedding, that Mark had not canceled it. Instead, he had pleaded with her one more time. He had been very upset at her gentle refusal, and on his way home his car had run off the road and into a tree. She would always wonder if his accident had been deliberate.

Perhaps he did know there would be times when she too might resent the demands his profession would make on him.

Perhaps he knew that she would want to travel with him and share the challenges in Africa as his nurse.

They were both mature in age but also in their faith in Christ. These were all things they could talk about some other time and then leave safely in a loving Father's hands.

But she suspected he already knew about the star.

Otherwise, why would he have given her the crystal one that would hold pride of place in any home they made together in the years to come?

So there was no misunderstanding, she put it into words anyway. "I've asked God constantly about loving you; I've sought His will earnestly and knocked loudly."

The star was still clutched in her hand. Very carefully she put it in a place where a stream of sunlight touched it with a brilliance that made it seem alive.

His hands grasped hers again even tighter and the light in his eyes, the love and understanding, made her swallow before she could continue.

"He opened His Word to me, He answered me, and I found His

will. Like the wise men who followed the star, He led me to Jesus, the Babe of Bethlehem, but also the very Prince of Peace."

His arms wrapped around her and Jean knew that her years of loneliness were gone forever.

"I love you," he whispered at last, and the peace wrapped around them both, holding them safely in His will.

A Letter to Our Readers

Dear Readers:

In order that we might better contribute to your reading enjoyment, we would appreciate your taking a few minutes to respond to the following questions. When completed, please return to the following: Fiction Editor, Barbour Publishing, Inc., P.O. Box 719, Uhrichsville, OH 44683.

1. Did you enjoy reading *Australia?*
   ❑ Very much, I would like to see more books like this.
   ❑ Moderately—I would have enjoyed it more if _____
   _____
   _____

2. What influenced your decision to purchase this book?
   (Check those that apply.)
   ❑ Cover   ❑ Back cover copy   ❑ Title   ❑ Price
   ❑ Friends   ❑ Publicity   ❑ Other _____

3. Which story was your favorite?
   ❑ *Search for Tomorrow*   ❑ *Search for Today*
   ❑ *Search for Yesterday*   ❑ *Search for the Star*

4. Please check your age range:
   ❑ Under 18   ❑ 18–24   ❑ 25–34
   ❑ 35–45   ❑ 46–55   ❑ Over 55 _____

5. How many hours per week do you read?

Name _____

Occupation _____

Address _____

City _____ State _____ Zip _____